THE PALESTINIAN IDEA

In the series *Insubordinate Spaces*,
edited by GEORGE LIPSITZ

ALSO IN THIS SERIES:

Rachel Ida Buff, *Against the Deportation Terror: Organizing for Immigrant Rights in the Twentieth Century*

Greg Burris

THE PALESTINIAN IDEA

Film, Media, and the Radical Imagination

TEMPLE UNIVERSITY PRESS
Philadelphia • *Rome* • *Tokyo*

TEMPLE UNIVERSITY PRESS
Philadelphia, Pennsylvania 19122
tupress.temple.edu

Library of Congress Cataloging-in-Publication Data

Names: Burris, Gregory A. author.
Title: The Palestinian idea : film, media, and the radical imagination /
   Greg Burris.
Description: Philadelphia : Temple University Press, 2019. | Series:
   Insubordinate spaces | Includes bibliographical references and index. |
Identifiers: LCCN 2018030490 (print) | LCCN 2019002176 (ebook) |
   ISBN 9781439916759 (E-Book) | ISBN 9781439916735 (cloth |
   ISBN 9781439916742 (pbk.)
Subjects: LCSH: Palestinan Arabs in mass media. | African Americans in mass
   media. | Radicalism in mass media.
Classification: LCC P94.5.P35 (ebook) | LCC P94.5.P35 B87 2019 (print) |
   DDC 305.89/274—dc23
LC record available at https://lccn.loc.gov/2018030490

For Paula and John

We have been uninvited guests for too long; lingering outside the main march of humanity must not become a habit. Nobody will ask you in; you must march in, believing yourself to be equal to the occasion and suitable for the feast.

—**EDWARD W. SAID,** *The Politics of Dispossession*

Some people envisage revolution chiefly as a matter of blood and guns and the more visible methods of force. But that, after all, is merely the temporary and outward manifestation. Real revolution is within.

—**W. E. B. DU BOIS,** "Where Do We Go from Here? (1933)"

When the horror of reality tends to become total and blocks political action, where else than in the radical imagination, as a refusal of reality, can the rebellion, and its uncompromised goals, be remembered?

—**HERBERT MARCUSE,** *An Essay on Liberation*

Contents

Preface and Acknowledgments

In his eclectic collection of writings and aphorisms entitled *Traces*, Ernst Bloch recounted a strange parable in which a rabbi is asked what the world will look like when the Messiah comes. The rabbi gives a cryptic reply: "To bring about the kingdom of freedom," he says, "it is not necessary that everything be destroyed, and a new world begin; rather, this cup, or that bush, or that stone, and so all things must only be shifted a little."[1] Or, as Bloch's friend Walter Benjamin phrased it in his own version of the tale, "Everything will be the same as here—only a little bit different."[2]

When I first came across this peculiar story, I did not quite know what to make of it. Although I knew Bloch to be a radical thinker—something of a mystical Marxist sage—this notion of everything staying the same seemed a far cry from revolution. What could it possibly mean? It was on a visit to Palestine that one possible interpretation occurred to me.[3] As I strolled down Jaffa's beachside promenade, I encountered a variety of sights and sounds. Within a few short minutes, I spotted an apparently secular couple taking a dog for a walk, some Muslim children flying kites, and an Orthodox Jewish family enjoying a picnic. I heard both Hebrew and Arabic, as well as the sound of bells ringing from a nearby church. All of these sights and sounds demonstrated a present reality that even a century of Zionist colonization, occupation, and ethnic cleansing has not succeeded in eradicating. Despite Israel's best efforts, its policy of *hafrada* (separation) has *not* been achieved. Zionism's supremacist division of peoples must constantly be reinforced, its cracks perpetually papered over. The notion of one state in Palestine is not a future prospect; *it is a present condition.*[4]

In certain circles, such talk immediately triggers alarms. One does not casually wade into anti-Zionist waters without being barraged with reminders about the horrible litany of tragedies that have plagued European Jewish history: the ghettoes, the pogroms, the concentration camps, the gas chambers. In the Zionist imagination, this entity called Israel is all that stands in the way of such barbarities being repeated, and to ponder a world beyond Zionism is tantamount to flirting with the inauguration of the next Holocaust.[5] How, then, are we to proceed? What does Palestinian liberation even mean in a situation that seems forever haunted by the ghosts of Auschwitz?

Contrary to widespread belief, pondering a world beyond Zionism is neither an irresponsible call for wanton destruction nor a recipe for future disaster. De-Zionizing Palestine is, in fact, our only hope of ending *the disaster that is currently ongoing.* Rather than entailing the physical obliteration of Israeli society, the massacre of its citizens, or the bulldozing of its buildings—that is, all of the atrocities that Israel regularly carries out with impunity against Palestinians living in Gaza and elsewhere—moving beyond Zionism involves something quite simple: the uncovering of another world that already inhabits the shadows of the present world, the emergence of a harmonious coexistence from a wretched one, the discovery of equality amidst inequality.[6]

Here I am reminded of that remarkable scene from Michel Khleifi's film *Wedding in Galilee* (1987), in which a uniformed Israeli soldier stands side by side with an elderly Palestinian villager as they work together to retrieve a prized mare that has wandered into a minefield. The contrast between the two characters could not be starker. One is a settler-soldier, the other an occupied native; one is a colonizer, the other colonized. The two men cannot even directly address each other in the same language and must speak through an interpreter. And yet it is only through their joint efforts that the horse is guided to safety. The Israeli supplies a map to the mines, and the Palestinian uses his voice to call his mare. For a fleeting moment, the hierarchies and divisions seem to dissolve, and briefly we see traces of another reality, a reality not of colonization but of cooperation.

Is this not the basic lesson of Bloch's parable? To find paradise, one does not need to look to the mythical heavens or peer into the distant future. The Promised Land is not a clearly demarcated space. It is not a land that exists somewhere *over there*, a territory that is merely waiting to be discovered. Rather, the Promised Land is simultaneously everywhere and nowhere; it is the ground beneath our feet. One must merely recognize this hidden world and seize it. Revolutionary change thus need not entail a violent process of cleaning society's slate. It need not lead us down a destructive path toward new gulags, new killing fields, or new genocides. On the contrary, the parable of the rabbi suggests that a radical transformation of society entails something very small that nevertheless has huge consequences—a very slight shift that nevertheless manages to change *everything*. What is altered is not only the place of objects ("this cup, or that bush, or that stone") but also, crucially, *the relations among them*. "Everything will be the same as here—only a little bit different": no more settlers, but also no more natives.[7] Or, as Edward Said put it some three decades ago, "We say to the Israelis and their U.S. friends, live with us, but not on top of us."[8]

One would therefore be justified in asking, "Who is the more naïve—those realists and political pragmatists who insist on separating the inseparable or those so-called idealists and dreamers who recognize this hidden potential existing all around us, this concealed and suppressed reality of porous borders, interethnic cooperation, and equality?" Contrary to the bleating of the naysayers and cynics, utopia is not located in some unattainable future or on some unreachable soil. *Utopia is already here*, and the actualization of our egalitarian dreams begins simply by locating them in the present—even in Palestine.

It would be impossible to properly acknowledge everyone who played a part in the conception and writing of this book. Although Palestine can be a touchy subject in the U.S. academy, I received nothing but support and encouragement from all of my friends, colleagues, and professors during my time at the University of California, Santa Barbara. In particular, I thank Lauren Alfrey, Kevin B. Anderson, George Blake, Peter Bloom, Anna Brusutti, Alston D'Silva, Rachel Fabian, Cynthia Felando, John Foran, Bishnupriya Ghosh, Hannah Goodwin, Michael Grafals, Summer Gray, Maryam Griffin, Abby Hinsman, Onur Kapdan, Nuha N. N. Khoury, Steve Malcic, Ross Melnick, Steven Osuna, Lisa Parks, Constance Penley, Sarah Rios, William I. Robinson, Adam Sabra, Bhaskar Sarkar, Emily Schneider, Sherene Seikaly, Greg Siegel, John Vanderhoef, Cristina Venegas, Dana Welch, Howard Winant, Chuck Wolfe, Kali Yamboliev, Jasmine Yarish, and Noah Zweig. Others in the Santa Barbara community to whom I owe a debt of gratitude include Rand Clark and Barbara Parmet from the local chapter of Jewish Voice for Peace and Ted Coe and Elizabeth Robinson from KCSB-FM 91.9 for occasionally inviting me on the air. Thanks also go to Stephan Boman and Tess McClernon for all the late-night domino games and to Brian Smith and Elena Sacca Smith for all the forays to Los Angeles.

In early 2011, I enrolled in a Black studies seminar led by Cedric J. Robinson. As we pored over the pages of W. E. B. Du Bois's *Black Reconstruction in America*, C. L. R. James's *The Black Jacobins*, and Cedric's own magisterial

Black Marxism, news about ongoing events from the other side of the globe kept spilling into our classroom conversations.[9] The Arab revolts of 2011 provided a remarkable backdrop to our study of Black radical history—the toppling of the Tunisian strongman Zine El Abidine Ben Ali considered alongside the destruction of the U.S. slave system, the eruption of protests in Cairo's Tahrir Square discussed alongside the saga of Toussaint L'Ouverture and the great Haitian Revolution. From the beginning of my encounter with Cedric's thought, my understanding of what he called the Black Radical Tradition was coupled with a concern for freedom movements in the Arab world, a fusion of interests that is fundamental to the premise of this book. Cedric passed away on June 5, 2016, while I was still working on the manuscript. We lost a giant on that day, but his shadow is still everywhere apparent in my thinking, writing, and teaching.

The Palestinian Idea began its life as a dissertation, and I could not have asked for a more thorough and formidable committee. Michael Curtin provided me with an exemplary model of what it means to be a professor, a mentor, and a scholar; Lisa Hajjar kept me on my political toes; Dick Hebdige kept me on my theoretical toes; Gaye Theresa Johnson's passion for the transformative potential of culture was contagious; George Lipsitz served as my political and moral compass; and Janet Walker never failed to push me in directions that I had not previously considered. I could not have written this book without any one of them.

Once the graduation celebrations in California were over, Lisa Hajjar was instrumental in acclimatizing me to my new social world in Lebanon, and I cannot imagine what my current life would look like had she not been here. I have found a great home at the American University of Beirut (AUB), and I thank my wonderful colleagues in the Media Studies Program: Blake Atwood, George Azar, Noura Boustany, Josh Carney, Nabil Dajani, Hatim el-Hibri, May Farah, Maysaa Kobrosly, Sara Mourad, Toni Oyri, and Zeina Tarraf. Others in the AUB community who deserve acknowledgment include Ira Allen, Doyle Avant, Habib Battah, David Currell, Nada Ghandour-Demiri, Sari Hanafi, Charles Harb, Rania Masri, Patrick McGreevy, Jennifer Nish, Sylvain Perdigon, Nadya Sbaiti, Kirsten Scheid, Michael Vermy, Adam John Waterman, and Livia Wick, as well as my research assistant, Samira Makki; the undergraduate organizers behind AUB's Palestinian Cultural Club; and my students, particularly Ola al-Hajhasan and Maher El Khechen. I also thank Steven Salaita for the many wonderful breakfasts in Beirut. It was a real honor to have him as a colleague, and our conversations always helped me keep my eyes on the prize.

Other friends, comrades, and occasional interlocutors who have left their mark on my work include Marc Albert, Sophia Azeb, Kristian Davis Bailey, Mariam Barghouti, Nick Denes, Kristin Flade, Gene Fojtik, Terri Ginsberg,

Ghassan Hage, Robin D. G. Kelley, Jamil Khader, Joe Lombardo, Alex Lubin, Sunaina Maira, Todd McGowan, Klaudia Rottenschlager, Viviane Saglier, and May Shigenobu. I also owe thanks to the filmmakers, artists, and journalists who have been so generous with their time: Dahna Abourahme, Ala'a Albaba, Jackson Allers, George Azar, Saleh Bakri, Osama Bawardi, Ana Naomi de Sousa, Sabah Haider, Annemarie Jacir, Motaz Malhees, Mai Masri, Nadim Mishlawi, Avi Mograbi, Tamara Qiblawi, Mariam Shahin, David Sheen, and Lia Tarachansky. Special gratitude goes to Mais Darwazah, who allowed me to use a still from her film *My Love Awaits Me by the Sea* (2013) as the cover image for this book. In addition, I must acknowledge the organizers of the Jenin Freedom Theatre and its annual Freedom Bus. They are putting together some remarkable performances and cultural events, and I will always cherish the two transformative weeks I spent with them in March 2015. Without a research grant from the University of California Center for New Racial Studies, my participation in both this visit and a trip to the United Kingdom for the London Palestinian Film Festival in 2014 would not have been possible. I am also grateful to the entire Temple University Press editorial team for their faith in my manuscript and their help and encouragement in transforming it into a book. A section of Chapter 3 was published as a film review of *When I Saw You* in the *Journal of Islamic and Muslim Studies* 2.1 (2017): 92–97, and a previous version of Chapter 6 appeared as "Palestine in Black and White: White Settler-Colonialism and the Specter of Transnational Black Power," in *Global Raciality: Empire, PostColoniality, DeColoniality*, ed. Paola Bacchetta, Sunaina Maira, and Howard Winant (New York: Routledge, 2018). I thank the publishers for allowing me to reprint the material here.

On a personal note, I acknowledge Bryson Newell and Roshni Mahida for their compassion, curiosity, and creativity during the writing of this book and beyond. And finally, I thank my parents, John and Paula Burris. They first set me off on this journey, and while my initial interest in the Middle East came from my father, my love of books was encouraged from an early age by my mother. I dedicate this book to them.

THE PALESTINIAN IDEA

Introduction

I believe that electric light was not invented for the purpose
of illuminating the drawing-rooms of a few snobs, but rather
for the purpose of throwing light on some of the dark
problems of humanity.
—THEODOR HERZL, *The Jewish State*

The language of our darkness [. . .] makes no sense
in the world of their light.
—FAWAZ TURKI, *Soul in Exile*

Somewhere in the skies over Gaza in early 1980, the ruthless General Ariel Sharon—then serving as Israel's minister of agriculture—sat in a helicopter next to a military commander and surveyed the territory below. The commander was worried about defending Netzarim, a Jewish settlement founded in 1972 only a few miles southwest of Gaza City and surrounded by poverty and squalor. Guaranteeing the safety of this colonial outpost in the middle of the overcrowded Gaza Strip had proved to be a logistical nightmare, and the commander wanted to know whether there was any point in maintaining it. Sharon reportedly answered in the affirmative: "I want the Arabs to see Jewish lights every night 500 meters from them."[1]

For Sharon, the settlements served a clear purpose—not just to colonize Palestinian lands but also *to colonize Palestinian minds*. Indeed, some Palestinians had already recognized this insidious aspect of the colonizer's infrastructure, and in 1970 the Israeli military authorities dismissed the mayor of Gaza City for opposing the connection of Gaza to Israel's electricity grid.[2] By brightening the night sky, the Israelis wanted to diminish Palestinian hopes, and by turning on "Jewish lights," Sharon wanted to turn off Palestinian dreams. Electrification would serve as lobotomization; illumination as strangulation. In this context, media were not meant to enlighten; they were meant to blind.[3]

Twenty-five years and two Intifadas later, the military commander's concerns about the high cost of defending Netzarim and other settlements in

Gaza could no longer be ignored, and in his fifth and final year as prime minister, Sharon ordered the evacuation of all settlers from the Strip. In doing so, he effectively turned the occupation of Gaza into a siege and thereby inaugurated what Eyal Weizman calls "an era of colonialism without colonies."[4] The following year, Israeli warplanes attacked Gaza's only electrical power plant, and over the next decade the rolling blackouts and frequent electricity shortages experienced in Gaza would culminate in an all-out electricity crisis, with residents of the Strip receiving fewer than four hours of power per day—a situation exacerbated by intra-Palestinian squabbles.[5] If Gaza was not going to be illuminated by "Jewish lights," it seems that there would not be any lights at all.

While Sharon had been forced to shift gears in Gaza, the project of installing "Jewish lights" in the West Bank only accelerated, and this process continues into the present. Today, the residents of towns and villages such as at-Tuwani, Bil'in, Nabi Saleh, Salfit, and Susya are watching their orchards and pastures gradually turn into a panorama of fluorescent lights, and new vistas of construction sites, high-rise apartments, segregated highways, and fortified security walls are steadily swallowing the agricultural landscapes all around them. For many Palestinians, the night sky has unfortunately become much brighter, and one day there may not be any darkness left.

Is there indeed a link between the colonization of Palestinian lands and the enclosing of Palestinian minds? Such a causal connection is suggested in a memorable scene from the director Elia Suleiman's first full-length feature, *Chronicle of a Disappearance* (1996). An Orthodox priest (Leonid Alexeenko) stands with the Sea of Galilee behind him and addresses the camera directly. Speaking Russian, he describes his surroundings and explains how the gradual dissipation of darkness has led to a crisis of conviction:

> I'm encircled by giant buildings and kibbutzes. [. . .] Not long ago, those hills were deserted. At night when I gazed at the hills from the monastery, I contemplated a particular spot, the darkest one on the hills. Fear would grab me, a fear with a religious feeling—as if that black spot were the source of my faith. Then they settled on those hills and illuminated the whole place. That was the end for me. I began losing my faith. I feared nothing any longer. Now, my world is small. They've expanded their world, and mine has shrunk. There's no longer a spot of darkness out there.

While the priest is still speaking, the audience is shown a series of images— luxury hotels, seaside apartments, and tourists riding jet skis through the waters upon which Jesus had once walked. According to the priest, Israel's settlement of the land has not only altered the physical appearance of Palestine; it has also eroded *the imagination*. The miraculous has been made mundane, and the sublime has been desublimated. For the priest, there is no more darkness, no space that has not been defaced. Everything has been occupied, and for this reason he suggests that there is also no more hope. The gradual loss of shadows has meant the loss of salvation itself.

This psychological dimension of Israel's colonization project, the dimming of Palestinian dreams with the installation of "Jewish lights," can be compared to what the late sociologist Baruch Kimmerling called *politicide*, the endeavor of successive Israeli regimes to *de-Palestinianize* the Palestinians—that is, to deny their existence as a legitimate collective body, to destroy any sense of Palestinian unity, and to erase the possibility of their self-determination.[6] Politicide is meant to succeed where ethnic cleansing has failed. Theodor Herzl's old desire "to spirit the penniless population" of Palestine away has not been fully realized, and the Zionists' organized attempts at expulsion (e.g., the Nakba of 1947–1948 and more recent attempts to gentrify the Arab spaces of Acre and Jaffa and relocate the Bedouin communities of the Negev) or even extermination (e.g., the massacres at Deir Yassin and al-Dawayima in 1948, the massacre at Kafr Qasim in 1956, and the bloodbaths in Gaza in 2008–2009 and 2014) so far have fallen short.[7] Despite such efforts, there are still Palestinians living in Palestine, including some 20 percent of Israel's own citizenry—a demographic reality that struck terror into the heart of Israeli Prime Minister Benjamin Netanyahu on Election Day in March 2015 when he took to Facebook to warn his supporters that "Arab voters are heading to the polling stations in droves."[8] Physical elimination, however, is not the only way to neutralize a population, and politicide therefore represents a different kind of death—not a physical death but a spiritual one. The intention is not to kill a people but *to kill a dream*. In this way, it is hoped that the notion of equality in Palestine—the prospect of the Palestinian Idea—will fade away and become irretrievably lost, hidden somewhere beyond the horizon of the Zionist present.

But before meekly accepting this rather hopeless scenario, it is important for us to ask, "Just how bright are those 'Jewish lights'?" Even if their radiant beams do somehow manage to penetrate the furthest reaches of the Palestinian landscape, does this mean that they can also illuminate the darkest depths of the Palestinian soul? Are there any dark spots left in Palestine, any mysterious shadows from which tomorrow's surprises are still waiting to erupt? Or is politicide complete? Has Palestine become a place where reality can no longer be refused and another world can no longer be imagined? To borrow Cedric Robinson's words, has Palestine become a place where the terms of order are the only terms at all?[9]

It is my wager that there are still dark spots left in Palestine. These cracks and crevices, however, are not to be found buried in some secret soil or discovered on some distant hilltop. Rather, these zones of darkness lie *within,* and the penetrating power of Israel's colonizing lights cannot fully illuminate the inner depths and darkest dimensions of *the radical imagination.* Despite Israel's best efforts, the power of emancipatory thinking has not been completely stamped out. The Palestinians still retain the ability to *dream*—that is, to think beyond those colonizing lights, to transcend the suffocating universe of Zionism, and to challenge the coordinates of reality itself.

Significantly, film and media can act as key sites in which these zones of darkness are detected in the visible world around us. That is, film and media can act as a place in which the ideal can be made material, the impossible possible. We should therefore refrain from reducing media to a simple list of empirical features. Media are more than just the sum of their parts, and we should not think of them only as the finite domain of electric lights, digital signals, and celluloid sheets. While media can sometimes serve as a source of brightness, they can also be *a source of darkness.* Just as media can illuminate, they can also desecrate. On the one hand, film and media can work to perpetuate existing constellations of power (i.e., Zionist settler-colonialism), but on the other hand, they can expose power's hidden fissures and reveal unoccupied spaces.[10] For this reason, Ariel Sharon was only half right. Media do not only shine lights; in the right hands, they can also *cast shadows.* Media possess a radical, emancipatory potential, and they have the capacity to act as a portal into another world—a world that already exists, hidden within the cracks and crevices of the present.

How we view media—a term that I interpret broadly to include film, television, radio, the Internet, social media, staged news spectacles, print media, maps, video games, recorded sound and music, surveillance technologies, and mobile phone applications—is profoundly linked to a deep-seated epistemological division that haunts many of our scholarly paradigms. Like the classic Platonic separation of society into distinct parts, a clean-cut line is imagined to neatly segregate the masculine from the feminine, technology from the humanities, and communications from the arts. The study of media is not immune from this gendered binary, and if certain scholarly works (those dealing with media effects or political economy, for instance) often fall into the former camp, other areas of the field (the literature on, say, fan cultures or psychoanalytic film theory) generally belong to the latter.

A similar epistemological separation also divides the spheres of politics and culture, and traditionally politics has been very narrowly conceived as a field restricted to places like the voting booth and the factory floor or to the activities of lawmakers and various congressional bodies. In recent decades, this masculinist conception of politics has come under increasing scrutiny.

By conceiving of politics as inhabiting a pure space that exists separately from the domain of culture, one effectively fails to appreciate the importance of an array of phenomena—everything from housework, family relations, and domestic space to cultural objects such as film, radio, and television. This objection to the traditional view of politics is perhaps best embodied by that famous feminist slogan "The Personal Is Political."[11] Articulated by members of the U.S. left in the rebellious 1960s and 1970s, this adage was intended not only as an attack on the ruling patriarchal order but also as a subversive barb aimed at the male-chauvinist tendencies within the counter-culture movement itself.

As necessary as this intervention may have been at that precise historical juncture, such a radical opening up of the political sphere does not come without its own set of problems. To say that everything is political is ulti-mately to dilute the meaning of the term. "If everything is political," as Jacques Rancière correctly notes, "then nothing is."[12] Thus, while writers who adhere to a more traditional conception of politics tend to miss the rich po-tential of culture, those who instead subsume politics to culture risk dulling their political teeth. Whereas the former might crudely reduce poetry to an algorithm, the latter can fall into the equally problematic trap of insipidity, glamorizing cultural objects without critically reflecting on the political and economic processes that enable and drive their production.[13]

But recognizing this drawback to the culturalist position does not mean that we should cowardly retreat back into some exclusionary, white boys' country club notion of politics. There is another option. Unsatisfied with both the traditional division of these fields and the complete collapsing of them into each other, Rancière—a thinker whose work will turn out to be quite significant for the rest of this book—offers a potential path forward. In a se-ries of three remarkable interventions—*On the Shores of Politics, Disagree-ment,* and *Hatred of Democracy*—he redefines politics so that it refers not to existing forms of governing and administering but, rather, to their disrup-tion.[14] That is, Rancière identifies politics not according to the field in which it takes place but according to the function that it serves. Nothing is inher-ently political—not even the mere presence of power, as the Foucauldians like to contend. For Rancière, something is political only insofar as it disrupts inegalitarian hierarchies and practices. Something is political only insofar as it challenges the framework within which we experience reality itself. Politics is not an order but an event; it is not a field of knowledge but a hole in that field; it is not a *structure* but a *rupture*.

Consequently, all of those places and practices that are traditionally as-sociated with politics—the ballot box, the opinion poll, the negotiation table—are, for Rancière, rarely political at all. In fact, they are usually the exact opposite of politics; they are *antipolitical* (or, in Rancière's parlance, they conform to the logic of "the police").[15] Whereas politics disturbs the smooth functioning of the existing order, these antipolitical practices and procedures perpetuate it; whereas the former punctures holes in established ways of thinking and being, the latter cover up these holes or deny that they even exist.

Where, then, does one look for politics? For Rancière, politics is always performed; it is always *mediated*. "For political activity to be visible," Rancière argues, "there must be a political stage on which it is able to play out."[16] Politics can therefore not be limited to Election Day votes or stump speeches. Politics can take place *anywhere*. Hence, culture is not a field that exists separately from politics proper; rather, culture is the very field in which politics occasionally erupts. Indeed, emancipatory visions of a different world do not usually arise out of elections or legislation; they arise out of culture, out of art, songs, and poetry.[17] We might therefore suggest a rather provocative thesis and say that culture can sometimes be *more political than politics itself*. Or, to draw an unexpected parallel with Black liberation theology that I develop more fully in Chapter 6, "culture," as the late James Cone put it, "is the medium through which the human person encounters the divine."[18]

Following Rancière, I would like to suggest that we view film and media in this same fashion. Film and media should not be considered always already political objects. Indeed, they rarely are, and we might even say that media usually serve an antipolitical (or "police") function. Like Sharon's colonizing lights, even the most basic of electric media forms, the simple light bulb, can act to perpetuate existing forms of domination, oppression, and exploitation—an argument that we can extend to the various "likes" and memes that circulate through social media.[19]

But while media are not inherently political, they can nevertheless be *made* political. The political nature of media is not their ability to *reflect* reality but to *shatter* it—or, even more precisely, to discover *other realities* hiding in its cracks, to find unoccupied spaces lurking in the darkness in which the rules governing the existing order are negated and alternative ways of thinking and being can be imagined and explored. This is precisely how we should approach film and media in the context of Palestine, and I argue that the political potential of these objects resides neither in their geographic location nor in the identity of their makers but in their capacity to break the Israeli stranglehold on reality and open a window into another world.

This utopian potential is demonstrated in *Ticket to Jerusalem* (dir. Rashid Masharawi, 2002), a fictional feature in which a Palestinian projectionist named Jabir (Ghassan Abbas) encounters numerous difficulties in his quest to take movie reels and cartoons to audiences of children throughout the West Bank. Set against the backdrop of the Second Intifada, *Ticket to Jerusalem* follows Jabir from obstacle to obstacle. His scheduled screenings are constantly interrupted by violence, turmoil, electricity cuts, checkpoints, equipment malfunctions, and terrible road conditions. But ultimately, the most formidable challenge that Jabir faces is not something directly imposed by the Israeli authorities; rather, it is his fellow Palestinians' lack of imagination.[20]

Throughout *Ticket to Jerusalem*, Jabir comes across people who question the wisdom of his chosen profession, sometimes even angrily. When a stranger on the road realizes that Jabir is taking his mobile film unit to the Dheisheh refugee camp, he becomes visibly hostile: "The people at the camp are looking for work, for food, and you want to show them films?" As Jabir drives away, the stranger scoffs, "What an idea! Who cares about movies?" But strangers are not the only ones who try to discourage Jabir. He also encounters strong resistance from friends and family members, including his father and wife. Jabir never directly confronts his inquisitors, perhaps recognizing that any answer he provides will not be accepted. Instead, he just goes about his seemingly Sisyphean task, struggling against both physical and ideological barriers to bring his reels of film to Palestinian children.

It is only at the end of the film that the political dimension of Jabir's labor erupts into plain sight. Jabir becomes friends with a Palestinian schoolteacher who lives alone with her elderly mother in Jerusalem's Old City. A group of Jewish settlers is in the process of occupying their house, taking it over one room at a time. The mother recounts an incident in which a male settler once even removed his clothes and strutted around the courtyard, naked and in full view—a rather vulgar and sexually threatening way to mark his territory. Although the teacher has hired an attorney to try to regain control of her family's property, she harbors serious doubts regarding the fairness of the Israeli legal system.

After intervening in a heated confrontation between the schoolteacher and the settlers, Jabir becomes even more resolute in his obsessive determination to show films to Palestinians, and he decides to smuggle his equipment into Jerusalem to project a film onto the outside wall of his friend's occupied building. After navigating numerous hurdles, the screening turns out to be a tremendous success. When Palestinian neighbors, friends, and relatives gather together in the courtyard to watch the film, the settlers are helpless to prevent the space that they had stolen from momentarily being stolen back. In this way, Jabir's projector—that instrument that so many people had maligned as an unnecessary extravagance—ends up accomplishing something that the politicians and lawyers have consistently failed to achieve: it dissolves the Zionist stranglehold on reality and brings the Palestinian community together in collective unity as they effectively perform a radical act of decolonization, temporarily disrupting the logic of the status quo and reoccupying a Palestinian space located in the heart of the Old City. Once again, culture turns out to be more political than politics itself.

Incidentally, Jabir's fictional quest to project films onto an occupied building has real-life counterparts. Organizers at al-Rowwad Cultural Center in the Aida refugee camp near Bethlehem, for instance, regularly put together outdoor screenings in which they use Israel's Apartheid Wall as a projection screen. Similarly, Gil Hochberg's book *Visual Occupations* opens with the tale of a Palestinian art collective that transformed an Israeli water tower on a deserted military base into an open-air cinema.[21]

With *Ticket to Jerusalem*, Rashid Masharawi, a filmmaker who grew up in Gaza's Shati refugee camp, seems to be communicating a truth that still escapes many observers, and while the corpus of literature on Palestine is immense, a large part of this work nevertheless adheres to that same sullied distinction between politics and culture.[22] Rebecca Stein and Ted Swedenberg tackle this tendency head-on in the introduction to their important anthology on Palestinian culture, and they write that "most radical scholarship on Palestine and Israel has ignored questions of popular culture, or, at best, consigned popular culture forms and processes to the margins of scholarly debate and investigation."[23] While this situation has somewhat improved in recent years with the appearance of several new and important scholarly books, the field of Palestinian cultural studies is still a relatively small one.[24] Like the stranger that Jabir encounters on the road in *Ticket to Jerusalem*, many seem eager to write off culture in advance as being unimportant or somehow secondary to the urgent questions of Israeli oppression, and the possibility that culture might have something significant to say about Palestinian liberation often gets overlooked. As one of the Palestinian women interlocutors tells the director Azza el-Hassan in her documentary *Kings and Extras* (2004), "Now is not the time to be thinking about cinema."

The Palestinian Idea is my attempt to answer this commonplace objection. To put my central contention in the simplest and most succinct terms possible, *film and media have a utopian dimension*, and it is precisely through film and media that hope can occasionally emerge amidst hopelessness, emancipation amidst oppression, freedom amidst apartheid. Indeed, in an inegalitarian world, this utopian dimension is nothing less than equality itself. As I argue, this is even true—or even especially true—in a context as urgent and violent as that of contemporary Palestine.

Chapter 1, "The Palestinian Idea," opens with a demonstration in occupied Hebron in 2013 in which Palestinian activists donned masks of Martin Luther King Jr. and carried portraits of Rosa Parks as they staged a Freedom March and effectively desegregated a segregated street. Examining the media spectacle generated by this protest, I bring together the work of Edward W. Said, Jacques Rancière, and Cedric J. Robinson to locate Palestinian utopia in the heart of the Zionist present. This notion, which I call "the Palestinian Idea," serves as the theoretical linchpin for the remainder of the book.

Chapter 2 begins with a misleadingly simple question: Can a Palestinian cinema even be said to exist? From there, it goes on to investigate the emergence and formation of Palestinian identity. Specifically, I use Catherine Malabou's notion of plasticity to trace out three major ways that Palestinian identity can be conceived: as a response to national trauma (the receiving of form, or Nakba), as a collectively forged spirit of resistance (the giving of form, or Intifada), and as a disruptive negation (the annihilation of form, or disidentity). Here, my goal is to formulate an *anti-identitarian* position without being *anti-identity*. This discussion continues in the following chapter, which turns directly to media and examines Palestinian plasticity in two of Annemarie Jacir's feature films, *Salt of This Sea* (2008) and *When I Saw You* (2012).

Whereas Chapters 2 and 3, "Plastic Palestine: Part One" and "Plastic Palestine: Part Two," concentrate on fiction, Chapter 4, "Hollow Time," turns to documentary. Documentary has long been central to Palestinian filmmaking efforts. The impetus driving the production of such films has often been to contest Zionist narratives at the empirical level by bringing fresh attention to the counterfacts and counterhistories that make up the Palestinian experience—stories and memories that have otherwise been obscured or denied. While such endeavors have their place, they also have their blind spots, and insofar as Palestinian documentary restricts itself to the level of facts, it risks ignoring a perhaps even more important battlefield. This is even true with respect to the dimension of time, and I argue that Zionism has endeavored to colonize not only Palestinian space but also Palestinian time. Drawing from C. L. R. James and Ernst Bloch, I argue that a temporal dimension remains that resists colonization: the future, or Palestine Time. I then turn specifically to Mais Darwazah's documentary *My Love Awaits Me by the Sea* (2013) and argue that documentary can point us to this utopian view of time. The future is already here, Darwazah's film suggests, and traces of this Palestine Time can already be found even in the settler-colonialist present.

Chapter 5, "Equality under Surveillance," takes up the question of Palestinian visibility. Whereas some people have argued that the Palestinians are invisible in the global media landscape, others suggest that they are hypervisible. But whatever position one takes, I argue that visibility itself is not the fundamental issue. Looking at issues of surveillance and spectacle, I claim that our notion of visibility is often tied to cyclical theories of power and resistance—most notably, the work of Michel Foucault. To break out of this cycle, I argue that we must replace the axis of power and resistance with an axis of equality and inequality. I conclude by considering Palestinian visibility and resistance in Hany Abu-Assad's *Paradise Now* (2005).

Chapter 6, "Palestine in Black and White," attempts to make sense of how the Palestinian Idea functions in relation to transnational solidarity. Starting with two social media campaigns that took place in the summer of 2014, I trace the development of two very different "global racial imaginaries"—one linking the white settler-colonialist projects of the United States and Israel; the other bringing together two of the oppressed communities living under those regimes: the Black and Palestinian populations. Examining social media, staged news spectacles, and hip hop music, I argue that we should think of Palestine as a kind of Black Power movement and Black radicalism as a Palestinian struggle. This move, I suggest, will allow us to deepen our critique of oppressive practices in both countries and transform our notion of solidarity itself.

It has been almost four decades since Ariel Sharon crassly remarked that he wanted to install "Jewish lights" in the Gaza Strip to constantly remind the Palestinians of Israel's presence. As I have argued, Sharon intended to colonize not only Palestinian lands but also Palestinian minds. He wanted to create a world in which Zionism has no cracks, a mono-realist world without any shadows. But despite all the blood that has been spilled, all the property that has been stolen, and all the lives that have been lost, Sharon's goal still has not been achieved. Zionism is a failure. As bright as Israel's colonizing lights may appear, they have not managed to penetrate the darkest depths of the Palestinian radical imagination.

1

The Palestinian Idea

With the Palestinians, it's like the end of the world, yet
there's something fresh—you sense things being possible in
the face of so many impossibilities.
—ELIA SULEIMAN, *Film Comment*

We must restore Palestine to its place not simply as a small
piece of territory between the Mediterranean Sea and the
Jordan River but as *an idea*.
—EDWARD W. SAID, *Peace and Its Discontents*

I

Hebron: ground zero of Israeli apartheid. While Jewish settlements are usually constructed on the hills outside Palestinian cities and villages, in Hebron settlers dwell within the heart of the city itself. In 1968, a group of Zionist settlers posing as Swiss tourists rented a room in a Hebron hotel and simply refused to leave. Under orders from Israeli Defense Minister Moshe Dayan, the settlers were later relocated to the city's outskirts, but over the years, more have arrived to take their place, occupying many Palestinian homes, shops, and buildings.[1] In the month of Ramadan 1994, one of these settlers—a Brooklyn-born physician named Baruch Goldstein—walked into central Hebron's Ibrahimi Mosque during Friday morning prayers with a Galil assault rifle and opened fire, killing 29 worshipers and wounding more than 125 others. When Goldstein paused to load a fifth magazine into his weapon, someone in the mosque took advantage of the lull in the killing and managed to hit him with a fire extinguisher, thereby bringing the massacre to an end.[2] Today, Goldstein's grave has become something of a shrine in the nearby Jewish settlement of Kiryat Arba. His tombstone is engraved with an inscription: "He gave his soul for the sake of the people of Israel, the Torah, and the Land. His hands are clean and his heart good."[3]

When I visited Hebron (in Arabic, al-Khalil) in the summer of 2012, I was given a tour of the Ibrahimi Mosque by a local contact. Located on top of the subterranean chambers that are said to hold the remains of Abraham, the site has been partitioned into separate sections for Jewish and Muslim visitors, and to enter one must first go through numerous checkpoints. Once inside the mosque, my guide pointed out a large fire extinguisher sitting on the floor. It is so heavy that it cannot be easily carried and must instead be rolled on wheels. Following Goldstein's rampage, the Israeli authorities apparently replaced the handheld fire extinguisher with this oversize one. In doing so, they took away the object that had stopped Goldstein from killing even more people. Thus, in responding to Jewish terrorism, the Israeli state perversely punished the Palestinians.

The most visible evidence of this cruel Israeli reaction can be found on Shuhada Street. Historically, this was one of Hebron's busiest downtown avenues, but after Goldstein's massacre, it was closed to Palestinian traffic. What was once a busy thoroughfare has since become something of a ghost town, and any Palestinians whose homes or shops happened to be located on it have had their windows barred and their doors welded shut. Today, parts of Shuhada Street are actually segregated for pedestrians with a physical partition: one side for Jews, another side—a much smaller side—for Arabs. In the parlance of Israeli soldiers, the street has been made "sterile."[4]

It may seem farfetched to imagine Shuhada Street becoming a staging ground for utopia. Yet in 2013 that is what happened. In March of that year, a group of Palestinians in Hebron organized a demonstration timed to coincide with Barack Obama's first presidential visit to Israel. Carrying banners and Palestinian flags, they crossed into a forbidden zone, boldly walking into the section of Shuhada Street designated for Jews only. On their faces were masks of Obama and Martin Luther King Jr., in their hands were portraits of Rosa Parks and the former slave Frederick Douglass, and on their shirts were four English words: "I have a dream" (see Figure 1.1).[5]

By resurrecting the imagery and iconography of the U.S. Black Freedom Movement, these Palestinian activists were drawing new constellations of counterhegemonic protest and forging creative links of transnational solidarity across space and time. Using megaphones to fill the air with the music of Civil Rights anthems such as "Woke Up This Morning" and "We Shall Overcome," they violated the soundscape of the occupation and performed an act of what Gaye Theresa Johnson calls "spatial entitlement"—an attempt by oppressed peoples to reclaim usurped spaces with their bodies, voices, and imaginations.[6] Thus, for a few fleeting moments, these demonstrators effectively turned a segregated street into a desegregated stage and transformed a sterilized place into an insubordinate space. They temporarily interrupted the status quo and transgressed the rules and regulations of the Zionist order. As a result, they were swiftly descended on by Jewish settlers and apprehended by uniformed members of the Israel Defense Forces (IDF). As if to reenact a scene from Birmingham or Selma, the settlers ripped the

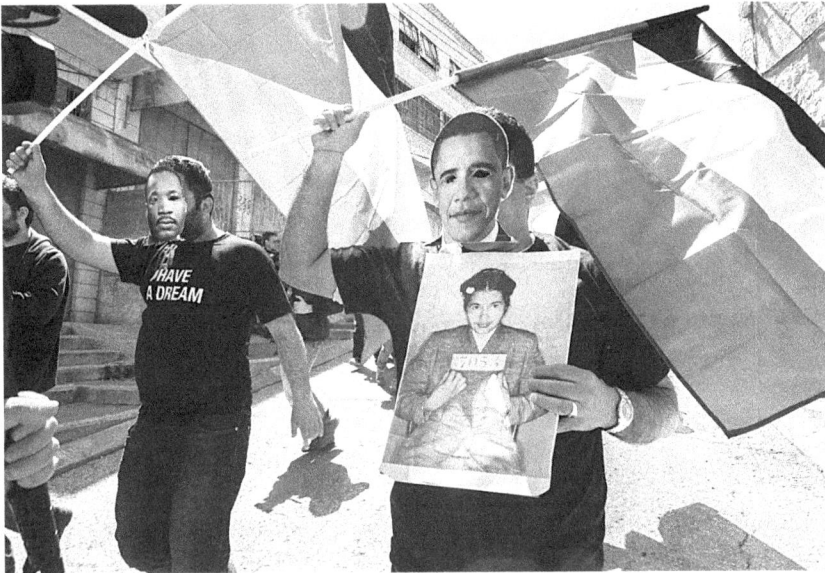

Figure 1.1. Freedom March in Hebron, March 2013. (Yotam Ronen/ActiveStills.)

banners and flags out of the protesters' fingers, and the soldiers placed hand-
cuffs around their wrists. With the masks still on their faces, the demonstrators were loaded onto trucks and quickly taken out of sight. It was as if Martin Luther King had been resurrected only to be arrested yet again.

The protest was thus brought to a halt almost as soon as it had begun. In
this way, an effort was made by the Israeli authorities to contain the disruption, to restore the ruling regime of racial hierarchy, and to sew up the tear
that the demonstrators had ripped in the symbolic universe. In an attempt to
even further paper up apartheid's cracks, some members of Hebron's settler
community took to social media to denounce the march. For instance, the
prominent settler-activist David Wilder—a U.S.-born colonist who regularly
leads Zionist tours of the city with a gun strapped to his hip—went into the
streets to confront the protesters. He later described the scene on his personal
blog, calling it *balagan*, the Hebrew word for a disturbance or a mess.[7] In addition, two leading members of Hebron's settler community penned an official
letter to the IDF in which they likened the demonstration to a "terrorist activity." Singling out the Palestinian activist Issa Amro by name, they urged the
Israeli authorities to "take all actions necessary to put an end to these provocations and incitement."[8] This letter was later cited in an indictment against
Amro when the IDF brought charges against him in September 2016.[9]

But while the protesters themselves could be forcibly removed from the
scene, the images they left behind could not be so easily erased. In open

defiance of a ban by the Palestinian Authority (PA) on the transmission of any images from protests in Hebron for the duration of Obama's visit, photographs of the demonstration were immediately published on the Internet and circulated via social media.[10] Prerecorded videos in which demonstrators such as Badia Dwaik talked about the links between the Palestinian struggle and the Black protests of an earlier era were posted on YouTube. Rather than simply annexing the Civil Rights legacy, the demonstrators were giving it new meaning, using media to interpellate the dead and to let the Black heroes of yesteryear speak beyond the grave. Like apparitions from another dimension, these images demonstrate that another world is possible, a world without divisions determined by ethnicity or religion, a world without apartheid walls, security fences, or segregated streets. They show that the unthinkable can be made thinkable and that the impossible can be made possible.

As even a cursory glance at this episode reveals, media are integral to the Palestinian struggle, and this incident demonstrates the importance of several media forms and objects, including staged news spectacles (the protest march itself), photographic images (the Rosa Parks and Frederick Douglass portraits), social media (the circulation of information via Facebook and Twitter), and recorded sound (the amplification of Civil Rights songs with megaphones). Moreover, this event can also be linked to film and video. In the days before the protest, Issa Amro and other organizers affiliated with the group Youth against Settlements led workshops in which Hebron's youth watched YouTube clips of the Nashville sit-in movement and screened *A Force More Powerful* (dir. Steve York, 1999), a documentary about nonviolent protest campaigns around the globe.[11]

But the significance of this desegregation of downtown Hebron—this invocation of Black Power in the midst of white supremacy and equality in the midst of inequality—should not be reduced to a laundry list of media objects. Even more important, this incident provides us with an opportunity to scrutinize the way in which we make sense of film, media, and culture in the context of Palestine. From this single story of rebellion and repression one could derive a number of different tales. To give a brief foretaste of the debates herein, the media surrounding this prematurely aborted Freedom March could be examined in relation to questions about memory, trauma, and Palestinian identity (Chapters 2 and 3); they could be used to scrutinize the Israeli colonization of time and dueling modes of temporality (Chapter 4); they could be interrogated with the intention of disentangling the complicated web of relations connecting structures of power to acts of resistance and surveillance to countersurveillance (Chapter 5); or they could be investigated in relation to race and transnational activism, particularly as they involve Black-Palestinian solidarity (Chapter 6).

While the images generated by movements of protest may indeed draw our attention to the existence of both oppression and an underlying discontent, this capacity alone should not necessarily be taken as a measure of radicality. Frustration with the way things are is far too common a phenomenon to be confused with emancipation. The point should not be just to dismantle old systems of oppression but to generate alternative, liberatory visions. As Robin D. G. Kelley puts it, the best forms of protest, rebellion, and resistance "do not simply produce statistics and narratives of oppression; rather, the best ones do what great poetry always does: transport us to another place, [. . . and] enable us to imagine a new society."[12] It is therefore my contention that the radicality of a piece of art, a protest image, or a film or media object consists in its ability to create a portal into the impossible and challenge the very coordinates of reality itself; it consists in its ability to magnify the fissures and hidden recesses of the social order around us and open a window into another world.

This, then, is the central question with which this book seeks to grapple: in the context of Palestine, how do we catch a glimpse of this other place, this world that is concealed somewhere within our own world? To put it in philosophical terms, how does utopia erupt from dystopia, the New from the Old, and the future from the present? Or, better yet, *how does equality emerge from inequality?* Using a variety of theoretical lenses and an array of film and media objects, this book seeks to explore this question in relation to Palestine. Each chapter argues that despite appearances, Palestine is not only an unrelenting nightmare of oppression and defeat. There is beauty in the darkness, and contrary to popular belief, equality *does* exist in Palestine, already in the here and now. More precisely, equality is already being *enacted* and *mediated* in Palestine, and it is this scandalous affirmation—this assertion of equality amidst inequality—that I call "the Palestinian Idea."

II

The Palestinian Idea is a term that is peppered throughout the oeuvre of the late Palestinian intellectual Edward W. Said. While today Said is mostly remembered for the academic firestorm he instigated in 1978 with the publication of his landmark book *Orientalism*, I believe his work on Palestine constitutes an even more important legacy.[13] From the beginning of his writing career in the late 1960s until his untimely death in 2003, Said was an indefatigable advocate of the Palestinian cause, and he articulated his arguments in numerous books, essays, interviews, public lectures, television appearances, and even documentary films, including *The Shadow of the West* (dir. Geoff Dunlop, 1986) and *In Search of Palestine* (dir. Charles Bruce, 1998). While some of his views shifted over the course of time—his take on the

Palestine Liberation Organization (PLO), for instance, or his opinion of the
so-called two-state solution—a remarkable continuity remained in his political vision, a consistency encapsulated by his championing of the Palestinian Idea.

For Said, the Palestinian Idea—a concept that he also occasionally referred
to as "the Palestinian answer," "the Palestinian vision," or even "Palestinianism"—was a radically inclusive antidote to the exclusionary discourse of Zionism.[14] As Said articulated it, the Palestinian Idea was "the idea of a secular
democratic state in Palestine for Arabs and Jews," the idea "that men and
women should neither be defined nor confined by race or religion."[15] He conceived the Palestinian Idea as "a vision of the future"—one "based not on ex-
clusivism and rejection, but upon coexistence, mutuality, sharing and vision."[16]
This idea was not to be considered the sole property of any single national,
ethnic, linguistic, or religious body, and as early as 1971, Said argued that it
held an emancipatory promise for *all* of Palestine's peoples, the hope of "a
revolution of Jews and Arabs alike, a revolution that uniquely offers perspectives for radical social change in an area petrified into xenophobia and chauvinism."[17] Against the alarmist charge that the Palestinians want only to drive
the Jews into the sea, Said extended a hand to the Israelis, a peaceful invitation
that could still serve as a basis for cooperation and coexistence.[18] Thus, unlike
the Zionist Idea, which was concerned with advancing only the interests of the
Jewish nation, the Palestinian Idea was entirely ecumenical.[19] It represented a
romantic vision of society not unlike the sentiments reflected in those poetic
lines from the pen of Aimé Césaire that Said was fond of quoting:

> no race possesses the monopoly of beauty,
> of intelligence, of force, and *there*
> *is a place for all at the rendezvous*
> *of victory.*[20]

Although I am deriving the Palestinian Idea from Said's distinct lexicon,
the egalitarian dream it signifies cannot be limited to the corpus of his writings alone, and it goes by many names. In *My Love Awaits Me by the Sea* (dir.
Mais Darwazah, 2013), one of the film's interviewees calls it "the big idea"
(*al-fikra al-kabira*); in *Fix ME* (dir. Raed Andoni, 2010), the director's former
cellmate refers to it as "the big dream" (*al-helem al-kabir*). One can catch a
glimpse of this "big dream" in the activities of Arab and Jewish communists
in the years before the establishment of the State of Israel.[21] One can hear
echoes of it reverberating in the revolutionary rhetoric once deployed by the
PLO in favor of democratic binationalism or in the words of refugee intel-
lectuals such as Elias Sanbar, who proposes building a "democratic state of
Palestine, a state which would tear down the existing walls separating all the

inhabitants, whoever they may be."[22] More recently, fragments of the Palestinian Idea have appeared in the actions of those present-day poets, performers, and protesters who dare to imagine the dissolution of existing divisions and hierarchies—in the scenes of transgression featured in the work of Palestinian filmmakers such as Annemarie Jacir and Elia Suleiman; in the infographics and memes produced by the graphic design team at the website Visualizing Palestine; in the defiant stance of the U.S.-based spoken word artist Suheir Hammad ("Borders are manmade," she writes, "and I refuse to respect them unless I have a say in their formation"); or in the indefatigable spirit of flag wavers such as Ibrahim Abu Thuraya, a double amputee from Gaza's Shati refugee camp who spent his weekdays washing cars and his weekends shouting slogans against the occupation until an Israeli sharpshooter silenced him with a bullet: first Israel took his legs; then it took his life.[23]

But to return to the place from which we started, hints of the Palestinian Idea also emerged in the days before the Freedom March of March 2013, when Hebron's youth prepared themselves by listening to recordings of Martin Luther King's famous "I Have a Dream" speech. Asked whether they, too, had a dream, they responded in the affirmative. "What's our dream?" asked the organizer Issa Amro. The children answered with slogans: "Open Shuhada Street," "Free the prisoners," and "No more settlements."[24] Like the dreams of so many others before them, these Palestinian youths had the courage to dream the impossible. They dreamed of challenging colonialism, overthrowing hierarchy, and ending apartheid. In short, *they dreamed of replacing inequality with equality.*

It is precisely here at these transcendent moments of dewy-eyed optimism, however, that the Saidian conception of the Palestinian Idea begins to falter. When equality is relegated to the future, inequality is given free rein in the present. Conceived as a far-off goal or remote *telos*, the Palestinian Idea is located in the unattainable distance, and it is not clear how we can ever bridge the temporal gap dividing these two incompatible worlds. As long as it remains focused on the future, "a program of equality," as Joan Copjec argues, "is as clearly destined to defeat as is the goal of reaching infinity starting from a finite point."[25]

How, then, do we move from *here* to *there*, from how the way things *are* to how the way things *ought to be*? How do we create equality from a field of inequality—or, to put the question another way, what good is it to spot land on the horizon if we possess no boat to take us to its distant shores? This is the Achilles' heel of utopian thought, and by focusing our attention on dreams of a better tomorrow, we risk ignoring the sheer intransigence of existing institutions and practices. Utopian dreams are intoxicating, but, to recall Fredric Jameson's apt phrase, *history still hurts.*[26] That is, the weight of the past and the burden of the present cannot be overcome by wishful thinking alone, and if we treat emancipation as a completely immaterial mind game, we effectively minimize the enormity of the task that the Palestinians have before them. As Said himself lamented, "One senses that all doors are open to the Palestinian in theory, none in reality."[27] Thus, to the degree that it fails to properly consider the persistence of existing material forces, radical thought risks becoming much less radical, and the empowerment it offers is in danger of becoming as empty as the pie-in-the-sky promises peddled by any common street preacher.

But turning away from the hazards of utopian speculation might take us down a no less treacherous path. Retreating from the uncertain clouds of mysticism and fantasy, one might seek stable footing on the seemingly solid ground of verifiable facts and empirical data. "Be realistic," as the oft-repeated reprimand goes. This injunction amounts to a call for the renunciation of fantasy and the acceptance of the given social reality as the only one. This is the pragmatic world of the realist; it is a world of the possible instead of the impossible, a mono-realist world without transcendence where we can put aside all of our fanciful dreams of future paradise and instead concern ourselves with the cold, hard facts of the existing state of affairs—with policy decisions, acts of legislation, statistics, and sober analysis.[28] Importantly, the realist perspective cuts through traditional political divides, and it has been forcefully articulated by people across the spectrum, by figures ranging from Samuel Huntington to Noam Chomsky.[29] The enforcers of the status quo are thus hardly the only ones who deny the emancipatory potential of fantasy. In Kelley's words, "Dreaming is often suppressed and policed not only by our enemies but by leaders of social movements themselves."[30]

It is when fantasy is relinquished, however, that its necessity becomes most clear. Indeed, *how can one conceive of a different reality without dabbling in fiction?* A world limited to the apparently possible is ultimately a world devoid of possibility.[31] It is a world without the prospect of meaningful change or transformation, a closed world where, to quote the author of Ecclesiastes, "there is nothing new under the sun." In such a situation, the best one can ever expect is the endless rearrangement of the Old. To succumb to realism is to give up on hope. It is, to use Alain Badiou's lingo, to entomb oneself within a suffocating universe of pure Being where there is no rupture of an Event; in Jacques Lacan's psychoanalytic terms, it is to immerse oneself in a purely Symbolic order devoid of its traumatic Real.[32] Conceived in this one-dimensional manner, reality is already fully constituted. Power has no cracks, and there are no emergency exits. Within such an ontologically complete, mono-realist universe, there is no room for the New and no place for the Palestinian Idea. What you see is quite simply what you get.

How, then, does one forge a path that manages to evade both of these perilous pitfalls? How does one walk a tightrope between fantasy, on the one hand, and reality, on the other; between transcendence and immanence; between a crude idealism in which *ideas are everything* and a vulgar materialism in which *ideas are nothing*? If ideas are to exert any significant force on material reality, they must have not only wings but also legs. That is, ideas must somehow be located within the material, the future already within the present. But how?

Here, I would suggest that the problem with realism is that it is not realistic enough. In his or her quest to be pragmatic, the realist—that ever diligent fetishist of facts—mistakes the hegemonic form of reality for *all* of reality and thereby overlooks another important and ever present dimension. Just as a map of the stars is composed of not only bright, twinkling lights but also vast stretches of darkness, reality, too, encompasses much more than just its positive features. *Reality is not simply the sum of its parts.* There are hidden elements all around us, dimensions that lurk unseen and undetected.

This elusive shadow world has been given many names. The ancient Hebrews called it *tohu wa-bohu*, the primeval formlessness and chaos out of which creation emerged; the Sufi mystics referred to it as the *batin*, the secret spiritual realm of hidden meanings behind all existence; Lacan named it the psychoanalytic Real, the constitutive trauma underlying the Symbolic order; Ernst Bloch identified it as "the darkness of the lived moment," the ever present part of our day-to-day reality that exists as a negation, an anticipation, or a hidden potential; Audre Lorde described it as "the Black mother," the ancient and divine darkness that is buried within each and every one of us.[33] But whatever name it is given, this mysterious chasm should not be conceived as something that exists elsewhere, as something alien to our daily lives and located entirely beyond the horizon of the present. This darkness represents another reality in which we are already dwelling, even if we do not always recognize it as such. This darkness, in other words, is already here.[34]

Negativity should therefore not be confused with pure nothingness. *Nothing* can indeed be *something*, and a negation can be positively charged. A focus on the negative should not be mistaken for nihilistic defeat, and we should be careful not to overlook negativity's potential for radical change. Things take shape in the dark, and it is in the mysterious gaps and concealed crevasses that another world comes into being. In Lorde's words, "It is out of Chaos that new worlds are born."[35] Or, to quote Catherine Malabou, "What is rejected, what is excluded, what is denied, is a possibility in waiting, a surprise resource."[36] The existence of this nonexistence—the presence of these gaps, cracks, and ruptures—provides a space for hope. Things can be different; other realities can be found. "Negation," as Malabou writes, "frees up the possibility of another story."[37]

Thus, all utopias cannot be relegated to an unattainable future. The best ones—indeed, the truly revolutionary ones—already exist in the here and now. They are not located on some distant, inaccessible shore; rather, they are already residing among us, inhabiting the darkness of each and every lived moment, a hidden potential whose actualization is neither automatic nor guaranteed. Consequently, fantasy is already in reality; the transcendent is immanent; and the impossible can be made possible.

Fiction, then, cannot always be so easily disentangled from fact, and ideas cannot always be summarily dismissed as illusory, superstructural by-products of existing institutions. Ideas are an intrinsic part of our lived experience. They are a material force precisely insofar as they already inhabit the interstices of the present. While Said managed to avoid much of this theoretical jargon, he nonetheless reached a similar conclusion, and in *The Question of Palestine,* he argued that, rather than arising out of thin air, Zionism developed in dialogue and in tension with existing material forces: "Every idea or system of ideas exists *somewhere,* is mixed in with historical circumstances, is part of what one may very simply call 'reality.'"[38] Said, like many others, recognized that Zionism was not born *ex nihilo* and that it first emerged as a very European response to a very European problem. Specifically, it was conceived as an attempt to counter one form of European barbarity, anti-Semitism, by partaking in another: colonialism, or what the early Zionists proudly referred to as *hityashvut* (settlement).[39]

But if the Zionist Idea developed out of existing historical forces, can the same be said for the Palestinian Idea? That is, should we regard the Palestinian Idea—this transcendent vision of future equality among all of Palestine's peoples—as nothing more than an escapist fantasy? Should we treat it as a naïve delusion or a childish fairy tale that serves only to distract our attention from the more important and serious business of hard political analysis? Or, alternatively, does this utopian dream already exist somewhere *within* the present—as a negation, an anticipation, or a hidden potential? Where, if anywhere, can it be located?

It is my contention that the Palestinian Idea does indeed inhabit the contemporary moment. The arguments advanced in each of the following chapters rest on this fundamental claim: that equality is not an aim but an axiom; that the Palestinian Idea is already being put into practice; and that one does not have to wait patiently for it to be achieved in some far-flung future that will never come. Thus, while I am borrowing the term itself from the writings of Said, I am twisting its meaning and giving it a rather different inflection. Whereas Said presented the Palestinian Idea as a "vision of the future," I am instead locating it firmly within the present. Whereas Said treated equality as the distant end of a long struggle, I am instead identifying it as the point of departure. In this sense, the Palestinian Idea is not won; *it is presupposed.*

III

Admittedly, locating the Palestinian Idea in the heart of the Zionist present is a rather ambitious proposition. To buttress these efforts, I want to turn our attention to two rather different wellsprings of subversive thought: to the work of the French philosopher Jacques Rancière and to the writings of the late Cedric J. Robinson, theorist of the Black Radical Tradition. My decision to put these disparate bodies of discourse together is not meant to suggest that Palestinian thought is inadequate in and of itself to conceive of emancipation. However, I believe that it is in the very nature of radical thought to continuously exceed its own boundaries and limits, and we would be doing Palestinian discourse a great disservice if we treated it a closed field and consigned it to an epistemological Bantustan. As Said once remarked with respect to the Palestinians, "Such a noble and passionate struggle cannot be confined to a lobby, and it must not be allowed to be put into an extreme nationalist, philosophically small-minded ghetto."[40] In line with Said's ecumenical spirit, it is my intention to bring these diverse intellectual traditions into dialogue and let them converse and perhaps even disrupt one another. Exciting things can happen when Palestinian resistance rubs shoulders with continental philosophy, film and media theory with Black Power.

In his writings, Rancière seeks to fundamentally redefine our notion of equality. For him, equality is not something that is handed down from on high. It is not a policy decision, a piece of legislation, or an act by any governing body. Instead, Rancière defines equality as "a supposition to be posited from the outset and endlessly reposited." In his words, "Equality is not given, nor is it claimed; it is practiced, it is *verified*."[41] According to this view, common sense has it all wrong. It is not that there would be no equality without a preceding struggle. For Rancière, the opposite is the case, and there would be no genuine collective struggle against inequality without a preceding supposition of equality. That is, *inequality is opposed because equality is first presupposed*. To study equality, then, we do not need a crystal ball to magically peer into the distant future; rather, we simply need to discover all of the ways in which equality is already being presupposed, practiced, and performed in the present.

To be sure, "equality" is a term that has been used and abused by a host of decidedly inegalitarian power structures and regimes. It is a word that comes all too easily off a neoliberal or even a Zionist tongue. Invoked as an essential human quality or posited as a political goal regarding the distribution of opportunities, equality is not usually understood as a radical concept, and for this reason, some thinkers and activists seem to have expunged it from their political lexicon.[42] However, an equality premised on a preexisting inequality—that is, an equality based on an unequal division of labor; an unequal system of private property; or the privileging of certain ethnic, racial, gender, or sexual groups over others—is hardly worthy of the name. While Israel may appear to display a "visible equality," its entire social and political edifice is based on inequality—a Hebrew Jim Crow experienced by not only those Palestinians who live under occupation in the West Bank and Gaza or in the global diaspora who have suffered expulsion but also those Palestinians who remain in Israel and are subject to both institutional and social discrimination despite holding Israeli citizenship. As the Nazareth-born filmmaker Hany Abu-Assad claims, "Even a dog has more rights."[43] Zionist claims of equality also crumble when one considers the treatment of other groups within Israel: the discrimination faced by Mizrahi and Ethiopian Jews, for instance, or the plight of African asylum seekers (see Chapter 6).

Rancière's understanding of "equality" therefore should not be confused with the more common and flippant use of this term. When Rancière invokes equality, he is conceiving it not as a solution but as a disruption, not as something that *heals* the wounds in the fabric of the social universe but as something that *inflicts* them. To put it in Lacanian terms, when Rancière invokes equality, he is moving from the register of the Symbolic to that of the Real, redefining equality not as a positive part of the existing order but as a rupture within it, as an inherent negation.[44] Such a conception of equality represents a hole in the social order, a present absence that can never be erased or fully stamped out. Indeed, *without equality, inequality cannot exist.*

Fleshing out this argument, Rancière recalls the fable allegedly told by the Roman consul Menenius Agrippa to a group of rebelling plebeians on Rome's Aventine Hill. To quell the uprising, Menenius appealed to the crowd with a metaphor, explaining that society was like a human body. Just as a body has different parts to perform different functions, he argued, society likewise has different groups to serve different roles. Some people are destined to rule; others are destined to be ruled. The Roman consul thus justified the prevailing hierarchy by grounding it in nature. Superiority and inferiority were the simple facts of life, and there was consequently no good reason for the plebs to rebel. But by making such an argument, Menenius performed a subtle act of chicanery. To justify the existing pecking order, he first had to address the revolting plebs as partners, and underlying his apologia was an unstated assumption that they possessed an equal capacity for communication, an intellectual equality that would allow them to fully comprehend his speech. The meaning of Menenius's words was thus contradicted by the form of his argument. To explain inequality, he first had to presuppose equality.[45]

Rancière takes from this tale that every effort to impose hierarchy indicates the presence of its opposite, that *equality must be posited if inequality is to be explained.* This is the soft underbelly of inequality, the chink in the armor that bedevils every attempt to justify hierarchy and order. "The very principle of superiority collapses," Rancière argues, "if it has to be explained to inferiors why they are inferior."[46] If inequality were natural, it would require no explanation; it would go uncontested and just simply *be*. Consequently, equality is not hocus-pocus, and contrary to the claims of the realist naysayers, it cannot be written off as a whimsical triviality and relegated only to the fanciful realm of fairy tales and nursery rhymes. *Equality is real*, and its presence can be detected even at the heart of inequality. As Rancière argues in a memorable passage from his short book *Hatred of Democracy*:

> Equality is not a fiction. All superiors experience this as the most commonplace of realities. There is no master who does not sit back and risk letting his slave run away, no man who is not capable of killing another, no force that is imposed without having to justify itself, and hence without having to recognize the irreducibility of equality needed for inequality to function. From the moment obedience has to refer to a principle of legitimacy, from the moment it is necessary for there to be laws that are enforced qua laws and institutions embodying the common of the community, commanding must presuppose the equality of the one who commands and the one who is commanded.[47]

In an inegalitarian order, equality exists as its repressed negation, and it is because of this hidden presence that inequality can never be as unwaveringly hegemonic as either its celebratory supporters or its scathing critics allege. Exaggerated claims about the stability of existing inegalitarian practices and relations serve to compensate for this fragility. "Existing without reason," Rancière contends, "inequality has an even greater need to rationalize itself at every moment and in every place."[48] The incessant use of propaganda, surveillance, and force and the seemingly endless development of new technologies of coercion and control are not an indication of the existing inegalitarian order's power. Rather, *they are a mark of its impotence*. If inequality were everything, there would be no need to impose it, and the continued need for ever new instruments of discipline and domination reveals existing regimes to be failures, perpetually incapable of fully instituting themselves. Power is never all-powerful, and dominant regimes are never completely dominant.

Lest there be any misunderstanding, Rancière is not suggesting that we callously turn our backs on the myriad oppressive and unjust horrors that plague our present world. Presupposing equality does not mean playing an irresponsible game of make-believe in which we stupidly pretend that the hell of the present-day is actually paradise on earth. No, what Rancière has in mind is something else entirely. He is pointing out a blind spot in our dominant intellectual paradigms, a deficiency that cripples our ability ever to overcome inequality. No method can illuminate everything, and in a significant way, a focus on inequality—however critical it may be—tends to parrot the propaganda peddled by the apologists of existing power formations; inequality is posited as a given, and equality is reduced to a crude caricature of itself, a vague abstraction at best or a foolish pipe dream at worst. Here, Rancière's argument is in line with the thinking of others such as bell hooks and Wendy Brown, who similarly argue that emancipatory politics is subverted as long as it is based on wounds or brokenness.[49] Likewise for Rancière, fire cannot be fought with yet more fire, and if an analysis begins with a supposition of inequality, it will undoubtedly end with more of the same. By presuming inequality, one neglects its opposite; one fails to see the flowers sprouting through the cracks, the submerged reality of equality hidden amidst the hegemonic reality of inequality.

By refusing to privilege inequality in his method, Rancière is setting himself apart from other leftist figures such as Pierre Bourdieu and even his own former mentor Louis Althusser.[50] While Rancière shares these thinkers' critical disposition vis-à-vis the ruling order, he nevertheless disputes the ability of their intellectual projects to effectively undermine existing hierarchies.[51] Rancière's line of reasoning represents a postfoundationalist one. His claim is that *inequality is not everything*. It has no natural foundation, and it is not set in stone. By denying inequality any stable ground in this fashion, Rancière is aiming to pull the rug out from under it and expose its utter contingency. Inequality exists—but only to the degree to which it is performed and practiced.[52]

This lack of any solid roots should not be taken as a reason for despair. On the contrary, it is an opportunity. The social order is always teetering on the edge of an abyss, but it is precisely out of this void, out of this *tohu wa-bohu*, that new and exciting possibilities can sometimes erupt. Inequality is not for certain, and things can be different. This open horizon provides us with a space for hope. The future is not preordained, and there is room for improvisation. *Reality is not yet finished*, and it is in the underlying darkness, in the absence of any firm foundation beneath our feet, that equality can take shape.

While Rancière's approach to equality is not conventional, neither is it a complete anomaly. In treating equality as an axiom, Rancière is modeling his thought after Joseph Jacotot, a nineteenth-century French pedagogue who made intellectual equality the basis of education. Rejecting explication as a method of instruction, Jacotot instead believed that the classroom should be characterized by an egalitarian relationship between the schoolmaster and the pupil, an equality which would allow the latter to discover the intelligence already sleeping within himself or herself.[53] Jacotot's emancipatory model of education can be favorably compared to Paulo Freire's "pedagogy of the oppressed" or to the filmmaking practices of documentarians such as Mohammad Malas, Kamal Aljafari, and Mais Darwazah, who seek to create an egalitarian point of encounter between their films' subjects and viewers.[54] One might also find overlap here with the methods of Myles Horton, the Appalachian teacher whose cadres of students included a young Martin Luther King Jr. and a then unknown Rosa Parks, and with C. L. R. James's radically democratic insistence on the innate ability of every person to fully participate in the management of society—a view summed up in his motto, "Every cook can govern."[55]

These last two examples—Horton and James—lead us toward another body of thought, the discourse of Black radicalism, and although this intellectual wellspring might seem far removed from the subject of Palestine, it has already cast a shadow over this entire discussion—from the use of Martin Luther King masks and Civil Rights anthems by Palestinian protesters in Hebron to Said's penchant for the poetry of Césaire. While the history of Black-Palestinian solidarity stretches back several decades, this imaginative constellation of protest has received growing scholarly attention in recent years, resulting in the proliferation of publications by activists and academics such as Angela Davis, Keith Feldman, Robin Kelley, and Alex Lubin.[56] These works contest hegemonic master narratives at the factual level by subversively shedding light on a counterhistory of transnational activism and resistance that has otherwise been forgotten or erased. But as important as it may be to document new instances of solidarity (e.g., another rap song, another YouTube video, another protest spectacle), we must also delve below the surface of empirical documentation and take our analysis underground; we must ask how these powerful traditions of insurgency speak to one another at the subterranean level—the level of theory, ontology, and epistemology. More specifically, we must ask how the Black Radical Tradition intersects with the Palestinian Idea.

The Black experience in North America has been one of continuous resistance—from slavery to the silver screen and from the insurgencies of Gabriel, Denmark Vesey, and Nat Turner to the fires of Ferguson, Missouri. Indeed, if the protectors of the status quo had once propagated the myth of Black docility, reality has never been so compliant. As James quipped, "The only place where Negroes did not revolt is in the pages of capitalist historians."[57] But whether Black resistance is celebrated or slandered, commended or condemned, it is still often viewed through a very reductive prism and interpreted as an instinctive reaction to injustice. Like Karl Marx and Friedrich Engels's famous contention in *The Communist Manifesto* that capitalism creates its own gravediggers, this logic locates the seeds of Black rebellion within oppressive institutions themselves.[58] To put it in the simplest terms, this is the view that *oppression breeds resistance*. Although quite widespread even among oppression's loudest critics, such a view has the distinct misfortune of divesting the oppressed of any agency. By treating Black resistance in this fashion, even the most sympathetic observers risk inadvertently replicating the conceit of the slave masters. That is, they risk abolishing Black people's most precious resource: the link to their collective past.

This is precisely where Cedric Robinson intervened, and for him Black resistance to slavery emanated not from oppression alone but from a preexisting consciousness—from a Black Radical Tradition that the overseers were simply unable to obliterate. In his view, the slave ships transported not only bodies but also "cultures, critical mixes and admixtures of language and thought, of cosmology and metaphysics, of habits, beliefs, and morality."[59] This surplus cargo served as an inexhaustible resource for Black rebellion; it acted as a constant reminder that the slave master's whip was not the Alpha and the Omega and that alternative ways of thinking, being, and imagining were possible. In the case of slavery, *oppression was not the author of its own resistance*, and "it was the materials constructed from a shared philosophy developed in the African past and transmitted as culture, from which revolutionary consciousness was realized and the ideology of struggle formed."[60]

Accordingly, the U.S. slave system was not a completely dominant enterprise, and it was perpetually plagued by an egalitarian consciousness that preceded it and that it could not eradicate. Thus, the wellspring of inspiration fueling the Africans' rebellion actually predated the institution against which the Africans rebelled. The slave masters' attempts to brainwash the Africans did not generate a rebellious African consciousness; on the contrary, a rebellious African consciousness generated the slave masters' perpetual need to brainwash the Africans. Just as equality inhabits the heart of inequality, one can discover traces of Black freedom even in the direst of situations—even in the bowels of a slave ship.

According to Robinson, this egalitarian consciousness appears as complete anathema to dominant ways of hearing, seeing, and thinking. It is not common sense but *counter*-sense, and it operates as a kind of noise. Robinson thus urged us to pay keen attention to the noise of any age, for it is in the noise that we might begin to discern antidotes to oppressive regimes of power. Indeed, this is a key point at which the Black Radical Tradition and the Palestinian Idea intersect. Like the African slave spirituals that were heard by the North American overseers not as prophetic declarations of the coming day of liberation and the overturning of slavery but as a barbaric, unintelligible noise, those who communicate the Palestinian Idea today are using a language that cannot be comprehended within certain ideological frameworks: words that are not counted as words and speech that is not perceived as speech.[61] Here I am reminded of that moment from Costa-Gavras's film *Hanna K.* (1983) in which a

Palestinian defendant (Mohammad Bakri) explains why he remains silent and refuses to defend himself in court: "Because they would not listen to me. On the contrary, they would not hear me."[62] He knows that to speak of equality within the context of Zionist settler-colonialism is tantamount to making an inchoate noise.

Thus, when Robinson rhetorically asked, "What is the noise of 2013?" at a seminar in September of that year, he might as well have been talking about Palestine; specifically, he might as well have been talking about the noise—the *balagan*—rising up from Hebron's Shuhada Street that March when Palestinian activists wearing Martin Luther King masks desegregated a segregated downtown space.[63] Like the Black Radical Tradition, their message was heard by the soldiers and the settlers, but it was not understood. It was seen but not comprehended. Harmony was taken for disharmony, beauty for *balagan*, equality for terrorism.[64]

Importantly, the notion of blackness put forward by Robinson does not neatly correspond to existing identitarian categories. In his work, blackness is not just a color; it is a consciousness. This means, on the one hand, that blackness is not the exclusive domain of Black people, and on the other hand, that not all Black people partake in the Black Radical Tradition. Robinson thereby refused to essentialize Black people as a homogenously radical group, and, as George Lipsitz observes, he consistently looked to the lower rungs of Black society to discern traces of emancipation.[65] On this point, one may recall Rosemary Sayigh's contention that the revolutionary impulse of the Palestinian Liberation Struggle likewise has its origin in village consciousness.[66]

While Robinson's oeuvre is chiefly concerned with Black resistance to racial capitalism, we would be doing his work a great disservice if we limited its relevance to these historical confines.[67] Indeed, what he had in mind was actually far more ambitious. Robinson aimed not just to critique conventional narratives of Black resistance. Even more, he sought to fundamentally challenge the need of social scientists—including Marxists—to imagine a coherent ordering of the world, "an architecture of reality."[68] Filling his books with the stories of fugitives, maroons, and runaway slaves, Robinson was guided by the conviction that *people refuse to stay in their assigned places.* Indeed, at its heart, the Black Radical Tradition is nothing less than a theory of fugitivity. As Robinson put it in his first book, *The Terms of Order,* "The presumption that differences legitimate or make inevitable hierarchical forms of human organization has been demonstrated to be alien to human nature, that is, unnatural and inhuman. Historically, people have failed to accede to such rankings; by their intransigence they have forced elites to resort to violence, deception, and force to maintain their advantages. Such methods, it seems, have ultimately failed."[69]

The resemblance between Robinson and Rancière here is quite striking, and it is worth pausing to take stock of the many similarities between these two thinkers. Robinson and Rancière were both born in 1940, and they witnessed and participated in the emancipatory movements of the 1960s at roughly the same age—one in California, the other in Paris. In both places, liberation was in the air, and their encounter with the radical thought of their surroundings left a lasting impression that greatly influenced their respective intellectual trajectories. Robinson and Rancière both spent a large part of the 1970s conducting the research that culminated in the publication of their first major works: Robinson's *The Terms of Order* and Rancière's *Proletarian Nights*. These two books appeared just one year apart from each other, in 1980 and 1981, respectively (and, incidentally, only a few years after Said's *Orientalism* in 1978).[70] While the historical subjects of these studies are quite distinct—the Tonga people of Zambia being one of the case studies of the former and the French workers of mid-nineteenth-century Paris being the focus of the latter—both authors threw down a gauntlet and presented a major challenge to some of the same modes of thought and bodies of theory, including orthodox Marxism. Despite their differences, then, Robinson and Rancière come together in a remarkable way. Sharing a distinctly similar theoretical orientation, they are both concerned with upending hierarchical forms of social organization and demonstrating inequality to be an unnatural mode of existence—one that people constantly reject and disrupt.

This similarity also ties their thought back to the intellectual enterprise from which we started: the work of Edward Said. Although slightly older than Robinson and Rancière, Said was also influenced by the events of 1960s, and he later claimed that the process of his conversion from standard academic to polemicist for Palestine began in the aftermath of the Arab-Israeli War of June 1967, a period that saw the flourishing of a renewed Palestinian militancy.[71] For his part, Rancière has occasionally written about Palestine, and in 2012 he canceled a scheduled visit to Tel Aviv University after being urged to do so by the Palestinian Campaign for the Academic and Cultural Boycott of Israel.[72] While Robinson never elaborated on the affinity that exists between his thought and the discourse of Palestinian liberation, he did at least acknowledge it. His book on early film history, *Forgeries of Memory and Meaning*, begins with a quote from Said: "In human history there is always something beyond the reach of dominating systems, no matter how deeply they saturate society."[73] The presence of this epigraph indicates a fascinating possibility, the prospect of these two insurgent traditions coming together and intervening in and perhaps even disrupting each other. Indeed, while both of these bodies of radical thought have developed in very distinct contexts, it is my contention that they share a crucial, defining ingredient: *a passion for equality.*

IV

Armed with the insights of Rancière and Robinson, our view of the Palestinian Idea has come a long way from Said's original formulation of it. Equality in Palestine, I am arguing, is not a utopian fairy tale but *a utopian reality*, and the more empirically driven thinkers among us who would dismiss this notion from the outset do so at their own peril. The Palestinian Idea offers us the ability to discover the New from within the Old, fantasy from within reality, and utopia from within dystopia, and without some form of it, we lack the necessary tools and resources to move beyond the Zionist horizon. In such a stymied scenario, hegemonic constructions of reality are all too easily mistaken for the *only* reality. Hence, to overcome oppression, utopian dreaming is not a distraction; it is an obligation.

This approach to studying Palestine is certainly not the only one, and it differs drastically from the path that many others have suggested. In her call for the development of a Palestinian feminist theory, Nadera Shalhoub-Kevorkian, for instance, argues that our scholarly work must begin from the real-life, day-to-day brokenness and suffering experienced by Palestinian women. "It is impossible," she writes, "to understand Palestinian feminist thought without [. . .] seeing the *nakba* as the analytical point of departure and the moral cornerstone of feminist theorizing."[74] Such a focus on Palestinian brokenness is widespread. However, while Palestinian suffering is certainly real, it is not the only mode of Palestinian existence, and it does not have the final say. Nakba, dispossession, and death are not Palestine's only stories. Liberation is also a lived reality, and I believe that it can serve as a much more radical starting point for analysis than Zionism's victories.[75]

To illustrate this point, let us take an example from *Growing Up in Gaza in the Dark* (dir. Matthew Cassel, 2017), a short documentary that profiles the daily routines of a thirteen-year-old Palestinian boy named Bilal. At the beginning of the film, the audience is assaulted by the relentless sound of Israeli drones flying overhead. The filmmaker turns the camera from the sky to Bilal and asks him to identify this seemingly inescapable sound. Bilal gives an unexpected answer: "It's the sound of birds, maybe a crow." There are indeed birds chirping in the distance, and for Bilal they are apparently the most noteworthy sound he hears. Bilal's attention to the birds is instructive. Just like his love of bike riding and swimming, it shows us that the Zionist domination of Palestinians is not as dominant as we often pretend it is, and there are other modes of existence that defy the oppressive order. Certainly, we cannot forget the drones, but if we focus on only Israel's instruments of oppression, we miss an even bigger picture. Just as Ariel Sharon's "Jewish lights" have been unable to completely colonize Palestinian minds,

the sound of Israeli drones has been unable to completely dominate Palestinian ears. Liberation is also real.[76]

Paradoxically, then, it is even in the midst of Zionist colonization and
hierarchy that one can catch an occasional glimpse of the Palestinian Idea.
Every roadblock, every discriminatory piece of legislation, and every technology of surveillance and control indicates the presence of its opposite, and
the building of new barriers, the erection of new walls, and the continued
institution of ethnic, religious, and racial classification systems all constitute
desperate attempts to suppress Zionism's own inherent negation, the equality residing at the heart of inequality.

Just as equality should not be viewed as a reaction against inequality, and
just as Black radicalism should not be seen simply as a knee-jerk response to
white supremacy, the Palestinian Idea should likewise not be understood
only as a reaction to the brutality of the Zionist occupation. On the contrary,
the brutality of the Zionist occupation is a reaction to the Palestinian Idea. The
imposition of hierarchy and apartheid in Palestine is not a principle but a
consequence, and it is precisely because the Palestinian Idea is constantly
threatening to erupt that the Israeli authorities, along with their comprador
Palestinian partners, must continually act to contain it, ceaselessly working
to paper over power's cracks. Efforts to cover up these gaps extend beyond
the Occupied Territories, and this is also how we should understand the Israeli government's attempts to ideologically police its own citizenry and control the global media narrative—for instance, its employment of a full-time
staff to post Israel-friendly comments on various online forums and its
granting of scholarships to certain university students who defend Israel's
policies on social media.[77]

One method of studying the Palestinian Idea would therefore be to read
Zionist media objects against the grain. Here, one may recall a curious image
sold at many markets and tourist shops throughout Palestine—an artisti-
cally rendered portrait of the Old City of Jerusalem, flanked by a large tree
in the foreground and accompanied by a two-word injunction written in
bold, capital letters: "VISIT PALESTINE." Remarkably, this poster was de-
signed not by a Palestinian Arab but by a Zionist Jew—Franz Kraus, an
Austrian-born artist who immigrated to Tel Aviv in 1934, where he subsequently worked as a graphic designer. Kraus created this particular image in
1936, a full twelve years before the official declaration of Israeli independence, and it was published by a Zionist agency to promote tourism and
immigration from Europe. But even though this poster was originally intended to perpetuate Zionism, it has more recently been reinterpreted in
ways that its creator could have never imagined. The use of the word "Palestine" is seen as contradicting the common slur that Palestine never existed,
the image of the populated city as countering the idea that the early Jewish

settlers colonized an uninhabited wasteland, and the inclusion of a prominent tree in the foreground as a refutation of the Israeli assertion that Palestine had previously been nothing more than an uncultivated desert. Thus,
just as equality resides at the heart of inequality, an oppositional reading of
this media object reveals Zionism to be internally contradicted even by its
own propaganda.[78]

Another example of how a Zionist text can be read against the grain
presents itself in Nurith Gertz's study of the early Israeli documentaries of
the 1940s and 1950s. "Although these documentary films were undisguised
reflections of the official ideology," she writes, "the attempt to suppress other
voices in them was less than fully effective, and from beneath the official
voice, another one [. . .] burst forth."[79] Gertz thus claims that a subversive
kernel can be gleaned even from nationalist Israeli cinema, and while the
overt message of these films was one of collective Jewish unity and patrio-
tism, the sheer excessiveness of their ideological content actually indicates a
far different reality on the ground—a reality of disunity instead of unity and
heterogeneity instead of homogeneity; a reality in which the Zionist project
of creating the Israeli Sabra, the New Jewish Man, was contradicted by the
traumatic memories of thousands of Holocaust survivors; a reality in which
the Jewish community was not a monolith but a highly diverse body of various linguistic, religious, and political persuasions, including anti-Zionist
ones; a reality in which Palestine's populace was not even entirely Jewish but
consisted of numerous ethnic enclaves, national communities, and indigenous peoples.[80]

This practice of compensating for disunity by making exaggerated claims
of unity has survived into the present, and it can be heard today in the frequently voiced demand that Israel be recognized as a Jewish state. The very
fact that anyone deems it necessary to make such a demand in the first place
reveals the bankruptcy of this claim. To recognize Israel as a Jewish state is
not to affirm reality but to deny it. It is both to repress the irreducible alterity that exists within the Jewish community itself and to exclude Israel's
non-Jewish inhabitants from the count of the people.[81]

But as important as it may be to challenge hegemonic assumptions by
subjecting Zionist texts to an oppositional reading, this is not the only way
to study the Palestinian Idea. Indeed, such an approach has the distinct dis-
advantage of continuing to emphasize the voice of the colonizer.[82] Rather
than going down this path, one can instead direct one's attention to the voice
of the colonized—or, in this context, to *the Palestinian radical imagination*.
In the chapters that follow, I therefore turn away from the Freudian slips of
Israel's stalwart apologists and instead seek to discover traces of this radically disruptive equality in the activities of those filmmakers and media
practitioners who are giving voice to the Palestinian Idea. Fragments of this

disruptive equality can be discerned in their actions at the level of both form and content and across the spectrum of media objects and platforms—for instance, in the production practices of the Palestinian filmmaker Annemarie Jacir, who cast Jewish refuseniks as Israeli soldiers in her film *Salt of This Sea* (2008), effectively demonstrating a radical solidarity that cut across the tribalistic divisions and hierarchies manufactured by the existing identitarian order; in the surreal scene from Elia Suleiman's *The Time That Remains* (2009) in which the lead character, played by the director himself, grabs a pole and successfully vaults over the Apartheid Wall, thereby accomplishing the impossible and making literal the Palestinians' refusal to accept Israel's fortified boundaries; or in the "CTRL+ALT+DELETE" graffiti that was painted near the Qalandia checkpoint by an Italian artist acting in solidarity with the Palestinian struggle, a provocative piece of protest art that subversively suggests that we consider Israel's barriers not as permanent features of the Palestinian landscape but as ethereal objects that can be dismantled just as easily as they can be reinforced, as objects that, like any computer program, are sooner or later bound to crash.[83] Or, to return to the instance that inaugurated this discussion, specters of equality can also be discerned in the digital images left by the Palestinian youth who donned masks of Martin Luther King Jr. and carried portraits of Rosa Parks as they courageously desegregated Hebron's downtown streets. Such examples not only indicate that another world is possible; even more, they reveal that this other world is *already here*.

2

Plastic Palestine

Part One

Let me tell you about the Palestinian film industry.
Very simply, we do not have one.
—**Mohammad Bakri,** *The Guardian*

Each Palestinian film that is shot is a miracle to me.
—**Annemarie Jacir,** *Z Magazine*

I

Can a Palestinian cinema even be said to exist? The answer to this seemingly straightforward question is not as obvious as it may seem. In October 2002, Humbert Balsan, the French producer of Elia Suleiman's *Divine Intervention* (2002), approached the Academy of Motion Picture Arts and Sciences (AMPAS) to inquire into the possibility of the film competing in the foreign-language category at the upcoming Oscars. Even though *Divine Intervention* had already received numerous awards and honors at several notable film festivals, including Cannes, Bruce Davis, the executive director of AMPAS, informed Balsan that the film would be considered ineligible because its declared country of origin—Palestine—was not a recognized state. For AMPAS in late 2002, then, it would seem that Palestinian cinema did not actually exist.[1]

When word of this preemptive rejection reached the press, it was received with much consternation. James Longley, the American director of the documentary *Gaza Strip* (2002), for instance, threatened to return a student Academy Award that he had received in 1994 if AMPAS did not rescind its decision and begin accepting Palestinian films.[2] Others reacted to the news by pointing out that the stated grounds for exclusion—the absence of recognized statehood—did not appear in the academy's published guidelines and that the lack of such recognition did not seem to hinder the regular submission of films from other nonstate provinces and territories such as

Hong Kong, Puerto Rico, and Taiwan.³ In response to these mounting criticisms, AMPAS soon relented, and the following year it allowed *Divine Intervention* to be submitted as Palestine's first Oscar contender. Despite this change in AMPAS's position, however, there were still lingering questions, and when Hany Abu-Assad's *Paradise Now* (2005) became Palestine's first Oscar finalist at the seventy-eighth Academy Awards, AMPAS caved to pressure from the Israeli Consulate and credited the film not to Palestine but to the Palestinian Territories.⁴ It was not until eight years later, with the nomination of *Omar* (dir. Hany Abu-Assad, 2013) for a best foreign-language film Oscar that Palestine was finally given a proper acknowledgement at Hollywood's most prestigious awards show.⁵

As the story of Palestine's changing status at the Academy Awards demonstrates, the existence of Palestinian cinema as a cohesive and universally agreed-on body of film cannot be taken for granted. Its status is in constant flux and subject to a variety of competing considerations. However, it is important to note that simply asking whether or not a Palestinian cinema exists does not necessarily imply hostility toward the Palestinian struggle. Indeed, such a question can also serve to draw our attention to the numerous hurdles that have obstructed and impaired this cinema's development. As Hamid Dabashi, the editor of an anthology on Palestinian film, rhetorically asked in an essay in 2014, "In what particular way can we talk about 'Palestinian cinema' when Palestine as a homeland is under occupation [. . .] and Palestinian filmmakers lack the most basic aspects of a cinema industry?"⁶ The contributors to the *Historical Dictionary of Middle Eastern Cinema* likewise claim that, "as an industry, Palestinian cinema still does not exist," and Livia Alexander, another writer with Palestinian sympathies, even made the question of its existence the title of an essay: "Is There a Palestinian Cinema?"⁷

To be sure, Palestinian filmmaking has a long history, and it even predates the establishment of the State of Israel. In their jointly written book *Palestinian Cinema*, Nurith Gertz and George Khleifi divide this history into four distinct phases, the first of which stretches back to 1935, when a man by the name of Ibrahim Hassan Sirhan made a short silent film documenting the visit of a Saudi king to Jaffa and Jerusalem. For the next decade, Sirhan continued his filmmaking activities, and in 1945 he founded the first Palestinian film production studio, Studio Palestine. This early period of Palestinian cinema was brought to a halt with the Nakba, the expulsion of some seven hundred thousand Palestinians from their homes and lands in 1947–1948. Sirhan and his filmmaking partners were driven into exile, and he spent his final years in obscurity, working as a plumber in Lebanon's Shatila refugee camp.⁸

For the next two decades, there was virtually no Palestinian film production. Gertz and Khleifi therefore call this second period "the epoch of silence."⁹ During this time, Palestinian cinema was limited to the activities of those few Palestinians involved in the occasional Jordanian production. After the Arab-Israeli War of June 1967, however, this situation changed, and photographic initiatives to document both the plight of the refugees and the militancy of the resistance gave way to filmmaking activities—first in Jordan, and then, after Black September in 1970, in Lebanon. A new chapter in Palestinian cinema thus began, and this third phase saw the production of more than sixty documentaries and one dramatic feature, *Return to Haifa* (dir. Kassem Hawal, 1981). These films were produced by a number of filmmaking collectives, each of which was supported by a different political faction—most notably, the Palestine Film Unit of Fatah, but also the Art Committee of the Democratic Front for the Liberation of Palestine (DFLP) and al-Ard Production Studio of the Popular Front for the Liberation of Palestine (PFLP).[10] These films were sometimes screened to international audiences, and the first Palestinian film festival took place in Baghdad in March 1973.[11]

During this time, newly emerging Palestinian filmmakers such as Sulafah Jad Allah, Mustafa Abu Ali, and Hani Jawhariya were greatly influenced by Marxist-Leninist ideology and by the revolutionary ideas being developed by anticolonialist artists and activists across the Third World.[12] They were also inspired by the work of European radicals such as Jean-Luc Godard, who paid a personal visit to Amman, where he met with Palestinians and shot footage that eventually appeared in *Here and Elsewhere* (dir. Groupe Dziga Vertov, 1976). This prolific phase of revolutionary Palestinian filmmaking came to an end with the Lebanese Civil War and particularly with Israel's invasion of Beirut in 1982. With the Palestinian leadership forced out of Lebanon, the storage facility holding this archive of material was abandoned, and most of the footage was subsequently lost.[13]

The fourth phase discussed by Gertz and Khleifi began in the 1980s with the pioneering work of Michel Khleifi, a Belgium-based Palestinian director who helped inaugurate a new epoch in Palestinian cinema with his films *Fertile Memory* (1980) and *Wedding in Galilee* (1987).[14] Whereas the previous period had involved the work of film collectives, this new era was marked by independent productions, and whereas the earlier films had come out of an engagement with the anticolonialist politics of the 1960s and 1970s, the new films were deeply connected to the events of their own time—namely, the First Intifada (1987–1993) and Second Intifada (2000–2005). Indeed, Khleifi's feature *Canticle of the Stones* (1989) even mixed documentary footage of the then ongoing revolt with scenes of scripted dialogue, a blending of fact and fiction later replicated in the films of the Second Intifada such as *Ford Transit* (dir. Hany Abu-Assad, 2003) and *Ticket to Jerusalem* (dir. Rashid Masharawi, 2002).[15]

Occasionally referred to as the Palestinian New Wave, this fourth phase has persisted into the present, and it includes the work of a growing number of artists: Hany Abu-Assad, Tawfik Abu Wael, Omar al-Qattan, Kamal Alja-fari, Raed Andoni, Suha Arraf, Mohammad Bakri, Cherian Dabis, Mais Dar-wazah, Azza el-Hassan, Hana Elias, Nasri Hajjaj, Nizar Hassan, Annemarie Jacir, Rashid Masharawi, Mai Masri, Rani Massalha, Rakan Mayasi, Najwa Najjar, Ali Nasser, Arab and Tarzan Nasser, Jackie Salloum, Mariam Shahin, Amer Shomali, Elia Suleiman, Sameh Zoabi, and others. With the critical success of a number of these directors at the Cannes and Dubai film festivals, the Golden Globes, and other major international venues, Palestinian films are now playing to an increasingly global audience, and they are regularly showcased at Palestinian film festivals held (sometimes annually) in cities such as Boston, Chicago, Dubai, Houston, London, Madrid, Melbourne, Paris, Singapore, Sydney, and Toronto. Palestinian cinema thus seems to be charting new territory, and new films by new directors are appearing every year. In the words of Annemarie Jacir, "Palestinian filmmakers are popping up everywhere, like flowers."[16]

Such a quick and condensed retelling of this history, however, may serve to mystify it, and by bracketing Palestinian cinema into four distinct, chron-ological periods, one risks giving it a false sense of linear progression, thereby obscuring its many inconsistencies and contradictions.[17] That is, one risks making Palestinian cinema appear much more cohesive than it actually is. Palestinian filmmakers are still fighting a tremendously uphill battle, and as a stateless and diasporic cinema, Palestinian film defies traditional modes of categorization. Indeed, what makes Palestinian films Palestinian if they are not even shown to audiences in Palestine and if, as Livia Alexander points out, "people in New York are still more likely to watch a Palestinian film than are residents of Nablus"?[18] What makes Palestinian films Palestinian if they are not always shot in Palestine itself, if they are not produced by Palestinian institutions, or if they are not even financed with Palestinian funds?

To say that Palestinian cinema does not exist, then, is not necessarily a hostile declaration, and it can also be taken as an assertion of the Palestinian film industry's nonexistence. The infrastructure for producing, distributing, and exhibiting films is in shambles in the West Bank and almost completely absent in Gaza—Hamas's meager attempts at filmmaking notwithstanding.[19] Indeed, during the First Intifada, Israel shut down all of the cinemas in the Occupied Territories. Since then, very few of these venues have managed to reopen, and even then, they have had great difficulty staying open. Cinema Jenin, for instance, was forced to shut its doors due to lack of financial re-sources in late 2016, a mere six years after being reopened to much fanfare.[20] When two young filmmakers in Gaza, the identical twins Arab and Tarzan Nasser, first received international attention for their short *Colorful Journey* (2010), they had not yet left the Strip and had never even seen a film at an actual cinema. After this information was reported in *The Guardian*, a theater owner in Texas contacted the two brothers and managed to bring them to Austin for their first ever cinema screening in late 2011.[21] Despite the lack of cinemas in Palestine, brilliant efforts to screen films have nevertheless been made. Shashat, a nonprofit organization based in Ramallah, seeks to train and support female filmmakers.[22] In the Aida refugee camp near Bethlehem, for instance, al-Rowwad Cultural Center organizes an annual screening each summer in which films are projected onto Israel's Apartheid Wall. Similar efforts can also be found in Gaza, and in May 2015, organizers put together the first film festival ever held in the besieged Strip. Called the Karama Human Rights Film Festival, the event was held for three days in Shujaiya, a district in Gaza that had seen some of the worst destruction in Israel's bombardment the previous summer. A giant, two hundred-foot-long red carpet leading to a makeshift outdoor screen was rolled out for all of the attendees, and dramatic footage of the carpet set against the backdrop of Shujaiya's ruins and rubble circulated on social media. One of the event's organizers, the Gaza-based filmmaker Khalil al-Mozayen, explained that "the red carpet symbolizes equality—that not only celebrities and high profile personalities or politicians deserve to walk on red carpets but also the people who witnessed the brutal war and experienced the loss of a family member or the imprisonment of another."[23] One of the attendees, a seventy-five-year old Shujaiya resident, told a reporter, "The last time I saw a movie in the cinema was 50 years ago in central Gaza City with my husband. [. . .] Fifty years witnessed two intifadas and three wars. Now I'm watching a movie for the second time in my life and I'm walking on the red carpet for the first time."[24] As a result of the precariousness of the situation, Palestinian filmmakers have had to rely largely on the contributions of private donors and on non-Palestinian financial sources, mostly from Europe. *Wedding in Galilee*, for instance, was financed almost completely by Belgian and French sources, and even though it is commonly viewed as a seminal film in the history of Palestinian cinema, the only Palestinian money used to make it was that which came from the director's own pocket.[25] This situation has continued to hamper Palestinian filmmaking activities. To make *Eyes of a Thief* (2014)—Palestine's official submission to the 2015 Academy Awards—the director Najwa Najjar had to secure financial support from organizations based in Germany, Jordan, Qatar, and even Iceland.[26] Some filmmakers have made a special effort to fund their projects with exclusively Palestinian and Arab resources, but this has proved to be an immensely difficult task. While Jacir's first feature, *Salt of This Sea* (2008), was funded by a hodgepodge of organizations and production companies scattered throughout Europe and the United States, she was determined to rely primarily on Arab funding sources for her second feature, *When I Saw You* (2012).[27] As a result of this self-imposed restriction, Jacir was eventually forced to make the film for only a quarter of its original budget.[28]

While the use of non-Palestinian sources is standard practice, the question of Israeli funding has proven much more divisive—especially since the Boycott, Divestment, and Sanctions (BDS) campaign was officially launched in July 2005. Many Palestinian filmmakers refuse to accept Israeli support as a matter of principle. Omar al-Qattan takes this position; as he puts it, "I would never take money from a state that I believe is racist and discriminatory."[29] One of al-Qattan's fears is that the acceptance of Israeli funds will contaminate the filmmaker's political vision and artistic independence. Elia Suleiman has made this same point. "If you take money from the Israelis," he warns, "you are basically getting into bed with Mephisto. They will ask you to join their festivals. They will try to twist what you say and appropriate your films. There are always strings attached. If you can get away with not doing it, then of course it is better for your health and better for your soul."[30]

Despite these dangers, Suleiman previously used Israeli funds in the production of his own films. As an Israeli citizen, Suleiman is required to pay Israeli taxes, and for this reason he feels that he should have the same access to these government subsidies as any other Israeli filmmaker.[31] Other notable Palestinian directors to have climbed into Mephisto's bed include Tawfik Abu Wael, Ali Nasser, and Hany Abu-Assad, the last of whom worked with an Israeli production company, Lama Films, to make what remains one of the most successful and internationally recognized Palestinian films to date, *Paradise Now*.[32]

There are, of course, benefits attached to using Israeli funds. While on a transatlantic United Airlines flight in December 2017, I was surprised to find a Palestinian film available for passengers to view: *In Between* (2016), Maysaloun Hamoud's captivating directorial debut, which explores the lives of three young Palestinian women sharing an apartment in contemporary Tel Aviv. Of the three hundred films on offer for in-flight entertainment, *In Between* was the only one I found in Arabic. I could not help but wonder how such a small film apparently managed to get such a good distribution deal. The answer came with the film's opening credits, and a production logo for the Israel Film Fund appeared on the screen. Unlike some of the directors already discussed, Hamoud had no qualms about taking Israeli funds. In an interview with the *Jerusalem Post*, she said, "I didn't hesitate to turn to the Israeli film funds for money. Why shouldn't I?"[33] However one chooses to judge Hamoud's decision to use Israeli funding to produce her film, the money did come with certain strings attached. On the festival circuit, *In Between* was identified not as a Palestinian film but as an Israeli-French co-production. For this compliance, it was showered with honors at Israel's prestigious Ophir Awards.

To be sure, directors are not the only ones to face difficult questions regarding their stance toward Israeli-funded projects. Following his appearance in *The Band's Visit* (dir. Eran Kolirin, 2007), the actor Saleh Bakri became a famous face in Israel; he was even voted the sexiest man of the year by an Israeli women's magazine. The son of the filmmaker Mohammad Bakri, whose hard-hitting documentary *Jenin, Jenin* (2003) was initially banned in Israel and later served as the basis for two libel suits, Saleh Bakri became very upset about how his image was circulating in Israeli discourse and has since refrained from appearing in films funded with Israeli capital. As Bakri declared in an interview in 2013, "I was born a Palestinian and will remain a Palestinian."[34] He has become one of the more recognizable faces in Palestinian cinema, appearing in films by Annemarie Jacir, Rashid Masharawi, Rani Massalha, and Elia Suleiman, as well as in shorts and video installations such as Rakan Mayasi's *Bonboné* (2017), Eyas Salman's *Dog Days* (2009), and Sharif Waked's *Chic Point* (2003) and *To Be Continued* (2009).

Importantly, the use of Israeli finances is controversial not only within the Palestinian filmmaking community but also in Zionist circles. In 2014, the director Suha Arraf was ordered to return money she had received from the Israel Film Fund after she registered *Villa Touma* (2014) as a Palestinian film at the Venice Film Festival. Arraf was denounced by several high-ranking Israeli government officials, including the right-wing Economy Minister Naftali Bennett. "You cannot take state money and then spit in its face," Bennett said. "The director, who felt completely Israeli when requesting the grant, suddenly remembered she was 'Palestinian' upon putting it to use."[35] Here it is worth recalling that in 2010, Knesset Member Michael Ben Ari proposed a bill that would have made the public funding of films contingent on every member of the cast and crew swearing a loyalty oath to Israel and recognizing it as a Jewish state.[36] Against such hysterical reactions, one should first of all note that Arraf was not the first Palestinian filmmaker to make use of the Israel Film Fund; Suleiman had used this same resource for *Chronicle of a Disappearance* (1996). Moreover, when Jewish Israeli filmmakers use non-Israeli funds, the Israeliness of their films is never called into question. Indeed, it would justly be considered an outrage if the Australian, Belgian, Finnish, French, German, Romanian, or Swiss co-financers of such award-winning Israeli films as *Bethlehem* (dir. Yuval Adler, 2013), *Gett: The Trial of Viviane Amsalem* (dir. Ronit Elkabetz and Shlomi Elkabetz, 2014), *The Human Resources Manager* (dir. Eran Riklis, 2010), *Sand Storm* (dir. Elite Zexer, 2016), or *Waltz with Bashir* (dir. Ari Folman, 2008) similarly demanded a refund because these films were registered as Israeli productions at various international festivals and competitions.

Ultimately, the notion that the identity of a film can be reduced to the source of its funding is a crudely materialist view. As the case of *Villa Touma* indicates, the question of Palestinian cinema's existence cannot be reduced solely to the absence of infrastructure. It is also tied to questions about the identity of the people behind the camera. As Arraf herself argues, "Films all over the world belong to the artists, not to the funds and not to the countries [in which they are produced]."[37] Thus, before making any grand pronouncements or bold claims about the existence or nonexistence of a Palestinian cinema, we should first ask what it even means to be Palestinian. *Can the Palestinian even be said to exist?* In the pages that follow, I examine this question, navigating a path that takes us through the pronouncements of Zionism, Sigmund Freud's ruminations on Jewishness, the contested terrain of identity politics, and Catherine Malabou's notion of plasticity before finally returning to cinema. Then, in the next chapter, I look specifically at two feature films by Jacir—*Salt of This Sea* and *When I Saw You*—to show how film is not only a key site in which Palestinian identity is produced and reproduced but also a medium that can sometimes disrupt the very framework of identity itself.

II

I will always doubt this collective institution called nation.
—**ELIA SULEIMAN**, *Palestinian Cinema*

Today Palestine does not exist, except as a memory or, more importantly, as an idea, a political and human experience, and an act of sustained popular will.
—**EDWARD W. SAID**, *The Question of Palestine*

Can the Palestinian even be said to exist? For one of Israel's most beloved premiers, the answer to this question seems to have been a resounding no, and in a much quoted interview given near the beginning of her tenure as prime minister, Golda Meir infamously declared:

> There were no such thing as Palestinians. When was there an independent Palestinian people with a Palestinian state? It was either southern Syria before the First World War, and then it was a Palestine including Jordan. It was not as though there was a Palestinian people in Palestine considering itself as a Palestinian people and we came and threw them out and took their country away from them. They did not exist. There is really no such thing as a representative body speaking for so-called Palestinians.[38]

Meir's notorious statement has frequently been recalled by her critics and treated as a stand-in for the entirety of Zionist ideology and Israeli government policy. One Palestinian filmmaker even referred to this slanderous assertion with the title of his short documentary, *They Do Not Exist* (dir. Mustafa Abu Ali, 1974).[39] It is important, however, that we carefully parse the meaning of Meir's words. One might initially be tempted to interpret them as a simple reformulation of one of Zionism's classic arguments, the old notion that Palestine was "a land without a people for a people without a land."[40] Despite occasionally reappearing in contemporary discourse—Assaf Voll's book *A History of the Palestinian People*, which contains nothing but 132 blank pages, for instance, or the strange argument made on the floor of the Knesset by an Israeli politician who claimed that an entity called "Palestine" logically could not have existed because Arabic does not contain the letter "P"—the idea that the land of Palestine had previously been devoid of Palestinians and that the Zionists had colonized an empty territory has been thoroughly discredited and is not taken seriously, even in most pro-Israeli circles.[41] Indeed, the existence of an indigenous population is implied even by Israel's present-day practices and policies. Simply put, if Palestinians did not exist, Israel would have no need to develop and deploy its technologies of surveillance and control against them, no need to separate them with flying checkpoints and concrete barriers. Thus, while Zionist slogans were once formulated to deny the Palestinians' existence, Israel's actions have persistently indicated the opposite. As one Palestinian put it, "When it comes to harassing us, we exist."[42]

But was it really Meir's intent to make such a crude and easily disproven claim? Here, I think it is important to note that, while in this particular interview Meir seemed to suggest that the Palestinians did not exist, at other times she lamented the fact of their existence, reportedly complaining that the number of Palestinian babies being born was making it difficult for her to sleep at night.[43] Thus, if Meir denied the Palestinians' existence at one level, she openly affirmed it at another. Her point was not simply to dispute the empirical presence of non-Jewish, Arabic-speaking bodies in the land of Palestine; rather, her point was to dispute their status as a *nation*. For her, Palestinians existed, but only as benign peasants, as helpful workers, or, most frequently, as hostile savages. As such, they did not constitute a legitimate collective body. Meir saw them as Arabs but not as Palestinians, as people but not as *a* people.

Needless to say, Meir's attitude was remarkably different with respect to the Jews, and her entire worldview seems to have turned on the affirmation of their existence as a united national group. As she asserted in a speech before the Knesset in 1970, "More than anything else in the world, I value one thing, the existence of the Jewish people. This is far more important to me than the existence of the state of Israel or of Zionism, for *without the existence of the Jewish people, the others are neither necessary nor can they exist*."[44] Whereas critical theorists and historians of nationalism such as Ernest Gellner and Eric Hobsbawm would later claim that it was nationalists who created nations and not the other way around, Meir took a different approach. For her, it was the a priori existence of the Jewish nation—the existence of the Jewish people as *a* people—that made Zionism possible.[45]

As these two quotes by Meir indicate, Israel's famed premier attempted to give her assessment of both Jews and Palestinians an ontological grounding. For her, Jewish nationalism flowed naturally from an always already constituted Jewish nation, but because she did not recognize the prior existence of any collective Palestinian body, she consequently deemed Palestinian nationalism to be a gross absurdity. Thus, while the Jews were perceived by Meir to be a legitimate national community, the Palestinians were not, and while the former were history's active subjects, the latter were its passive objects.

Of course, this belief in the primordial existence of the Jews as a collective and unified entity should not be taken as a self-evident truth. Nations are not discovered; *they are forged*, and the formation of any such collective identity necessarily entails both the building of arbitrary borders and the paving over of internal differences. There can be no positive without a negative, no construction without a corresponding destruction, and the acceptance of certain values as a basis for self-identification and affiliation always requires the repudiation of others. "To constitute ourselves," as Joan Copjec puts it, "we must [. . .] throw out, reject our nonselves."[46] Likewise, to conceive of the Jewish community as a cohesive, seamless, and self-contained national unit, one must overlook its inherent antagonisms; one must throw out the irreducible alterity at its core.

One of the ways this is accomplished involves the externalization of these internal fissures onto the fantasized figure of the foreign Other. By conjuring up an ideological scapegoat and treating it as a fantasy screen on which to project this internal strife, an attempt is made to prevent the would-be collective body from tearing itself apart. When this procedure is replicated at the level of the state, it can result in horrific acts of violence—discrimination, segregation, mass incarceration, population transfers, ethnic cleansing, or even genocide. As Slavoj Žižek argues, "The greatest mass murders and holocausts have always been perpetuated in the name of man as harmonious being, of a New Man without antagonistic tension."[47] In Israel, this has meant the denigration of several groups that do not fit the Ashkenazi ethnic ideal—for instance, the Mizrahi Jews who were sprayed with DDT upon arriving in Israel in the 1950s or, more recently, the African asylum seekers whose presence has trigged a wave of hate crimes and racist mob violence (see Chapter 6).[48] It has also meant the demonization of the Palestinians.

A typical example of this phenomenon appeared in the summer of 2014 during Israel's fifty-day assault on Gaza when Stewart Weiss, an American Israeli rabbi and regular contributor to the *Jerusalem Post*, wrote an editorial in which he crudely lumped all Palestinians, Arabs, and Muslims together with Hamas, Hizbullah, al-Qaeda, the Muslim Brotherhood, and ISIS (the Islamic State of Iraq and Syria) and likened them to Morlocks, the subterranean breed of subhuman devils populating H. G. Wells's science-fiction novel *The Time Machine* (1895). In Weiss's ominous words, "Who would have imagined that today, in 2014—long before Wells's tale was meant to take place—we would experience the curse of modern-day Morlocks, savages who dwell underground and periodically surface to disturb the peace and serenity which so many have worked so hard to build?" But Weiss's hate-mongering screed ended on a more optimistic note, and he reassured his readers that there was still one potential redeemer who could rescue the world from this dire threat—the heroic Jew: "All hope is not lost. There is still one savior, one beacon of light that can pierce the darkness—and that is the Jew, in his natural habitat of Israel. [. . .] We are leading the forces of light. [. . . W]e are mankind's best chance to drive the Morlocks back underground—preferably to an early grave—before they plunge all of us into total darkness."[49] Significantly, this simultaneous glorification of the Jew as hero and vilification of the Palestinian as Morlock took place at a time when Israel's claim to act in the name of all Jews was increasingly being called into question, not least by many Jewish civilians and organizations operating both inside and outside Israel, including groups such as Jewish Voice for Peace. By projecting this inner division onto the demonized Palestinian, Weiss was performing an act of ideological disavowal, inventing a monstrous *Other from without* to stifle the subversive *Other from within*. Far from vanquishing its enemies, the figure of the Jew as dreamed up by Weiss actually generates the perpetual need for new external enemies—new whipping boys to blame for his romanticized community's innate antagonisms.[50] On this point, one may be tempted to rephrase Jean-Paul Sartre's old formula about anti-Semitism and the Jew: if the Palestinians did not exist, the Israelis would have had to invent them.[51]

Here we are approaching a key contradiction within Zionism. If, on the one hand, Zionist propaganda declared that the Palestinians did not exist, on the other hand, the forging of a new, muscular identity—the Israeli Sabra—has demanded the creation of an ideological scapegoat. That is, the Jewish nation as conceived by Meir and other Zionists requires both the absence and presence of the indigenous Palestinians—*absence* to facilitate the colonization of the land, *presence* to prevent the eruption of the Jewish community's own potentially volcanic antagonisms. Evidence of this dialectical tension can be glimpsed in early Israeli films that dealt with the Palestinians either by omitting them entirely or, conversely, by portraying them as bloody savages.[52] As Ella Shohat points out, some films such as *Pillar of Fire* (dir. Larry Frisch, 1959) managed to pursue both of these strategies simultaneously, depicting the Palestinians as a vicious threat but relegating them to the darkness offscreen.[53] This same contradiction also manifests itself in the paradoxical Israeli legal category of the "present absentee"—a term used to designate those Palestinians who fled their homes in 1948 but who nevertheless remained within Israel's borders. They are both present and absent, here and not here.[54] Like the Christian mantra that C. L. R. James reformulated to describe the place of Africans in the West, the present absentees and their descendants are *in* Israel but not *of* Israel; they are *in* the world but not *of* the world.[55]

The Jewish nation exalted by Meir and others is therefore not as self-evident as it is made to appear. Its stability cannot be taken for granted, and it is always in the process of being formed and reformed, shaped and re-shaped, constructed and reconstructed. It is in flux, and like any collective identity or national community, its foundations are forever fraught with tensions and perforated with cracks. Thus, while the classic Zionist slogan "a land without a people for a people without a land" has frequently been criticized on the grounds that Palestine was not actually empty, this critique should also be applied to the other end of the equation. The mythic "land without a people" did not exist, *but neither did the fabled "people without a land."*

Was this not one of the great insights of Sigmund Freud? In his final years, Freud turned his attention to the Jews, and in *Moses and Monotheism*, one of his last and most enigmatic texts, he made a rather startling claim—that Judaism's most important prophet was not actually Jewish. In Freud's view, Moses was a renegade Egyptian.[56] The historical accuracy of Freud's sacrilegious thesis—or, for that matter, the historicity of Moses himself—is certainly debatable, but what is important for our purposes is the ethical consequences that stem from this position. Freud was, in effect, making an argument against the notion of ethnic, cultural, or racial purity. For him, something foreign—indeed, something non-Jewish, something Other—inhabited the heart of Jewishness itself. As Judith Butler, drawing directly on this very insight, has more recently asserted, "to 'be' a Jew is to be departing from oneself"; in her words, "Jewishness can and must be understood as an anti-identitarian project insofar as we might even say that being a Jew implies taking up an ethical relation to the non-Jew."[57]

Significantly, *Moses and Monotheism* appeared at a time of heightened anti-Semitism in Europe—a development that forced Freud, as a member of Vienna's Jewish community, to flee Nazi-occupied Austria and seek refuge in London. Placed in this particular context, Freud's thesis may seem counterintuitive or even woefully misguided. At a time when anti-Semitic attacks on European Jews were on the rise, Freud seemed to be committing the unthinkable, turning his critical eye not on the identity of the victimizer but

on that of the victim and casting doubt on the Jewishness of Jewishness itself. Indeed, Freud frankly admitted as much in the opening line of the text,
stating that his goal was "to deny a people the man whom it praises as the
greatest of its sons."[58]

But what if this seemingly suicidal gesture was actually the book's greatest strength? What if Freud's decentering of Jewish identity actually constituted a brilliant subversion of Nazism's terms? Confronting the Nazis' anti-
Semitic claims by enumerating a list of all the Jews' positive features would
have been futile. Such an act might have contested anti-Semitism at the level
of *knowledge*, but it would have been useless at the level of *belief*. In fact, as
Žižek argues, such an endeavor would have served to perpetuate the underlying fantasy structure of Nazism by further reifying the Jew as a solid and
stable figure—one the Nazis depended on to take the blame for the would-be
Aryan nation's internal antagonisms.[59] By instead calling into question the
Jewish credentials of Moses and disrupting Jewish identity from within,
Freud's argument can be seen as an attack on Nazism at the level of belief, as
an attempt to cause their phantom enemy to evaporate and to thereby deprive
the Hitlerian anti-Semites of their obligatory whipping boy. For how could
the Nazis continue to blame the Jew if *the Jew did not even exist*?[60]

Incidentally, while Freud sought to give Jewish identity an anti-identitarian foundation—that is, to ground it in groundlessness itself—Israel's construction of the Jew has required the cancellation of this important insight.
Freud's endeavor was radically subversive in that he sought not merely to
reverse anti-Semitism's terms but to annihilate them. The State of Israel, on
the other hand, has attempted to stabilize Jewish identity as a birthright and
to locate it within fixed and stable boundaries.[61] Israel has therefore desublimated the Jew and flattened out its meaning. Whereas Freud tried to *open*
Jewish identity, Israel has worked to *close* it—a point made by Edward Said,
who argued that "Israeli legislation contravenes, represses, and even cancels
Freud's carefully maintained opening out of Jewish identity towards its non-
Jewish background."[62] In short, *Israel represses Freud*.[63] It is precisely this cancellation—this retreat from the anti-identitarian abyss into the essentialist
realm of fixed, positive identities—that feeds the fires of inegalitarian separation (in Hebrew, *hafrada*), giving retrospective justification to Israel's ethno-
centric practices. Unless those contesting the Israeli colonization and occupation of Palestine wish to replicate the hierarchical discourse and ideological
framework of political Zionism, it is incumbent upon them to heed the lesson
of Freud and to recognize that, like the Jew, *the Palestinian does not exist*.

Such a statement requires immediate clarification, and it should be noted
that the affirmation of Palestinian nonexistence first of all means that there is
no single narrative of Palestinian experience—a point that has already been
amply made by a number of other writers.[64] One can certainly articulate unity

and solidarity, but as long as such declarations are based on the assumption of shared empirical features, they are doomed to collapse. Diversity and difference are always concealed behind claims of similarity and sameness, disharmony behind harmony, heterogeneity behind homogeneity. A Palestinian who was raised in a gated community in the United States, for example, has led a life that is very different life from the life of a Palestinian raised in a refugee camp in Lebanon; a Palestinian born in Jaffa is not the same as a Palestinian born in Ramallah; and the life story of a Palestinian woman from Gaza is very different story from that of a Palestinian man from the same neighborhood or even from the same household. This point is clearly demonstrated in the political, ideological, geographical, and even cultural chasm that separates the Swedish-born Palestinian director Lina Makboul from the controversial plane hijacker profiled in her documentary *Leila Khaled: Hijacker* (2006). Although both call themselves Palestinian, their conversations over the course of the film may lead one to ask whether anything binds them together at all.

Here, one might also consider the wide variety of identities held by those Palestinian artists working behind the camera. Relatively few feature films have been made by filmmakers from the West Bank or Gaza, and people such as Rashid Masharawi remain exceptional. This lack is not due to an absence of desire or creativity but simply an absence of resources. Khalil al-Mozayen, for instance, lost his entire film archive when his office was bombed during Israel's bombardment of the Gaza Strip in 2014. Ironically, he planned to use his destroyed office as the backdrop for his next film project. As he explained to Al Jazeera, "Although Israel's latest war destroyed my office and entire archive of films, I did not lose my determination to continue my film production career. I turned the ruins and rubble of [my office in] al-Basha tower into a real movie scene that highlights the ability of the Palestinian people to rise from the ashes like a phoenix."[65] As a result of these various hardships, filmmakers based in the West Bank and Gaza have more often focused their attention on producing shorts and documentaries.

Many Palestinian features are the work of directors who were born in Israel—people such as Hany Abu-Assad, Tawfik Abu Wael, Kamal Aljafari, Suha Arraf, Mohammad Bakri, Michel Khleifi, and Elia Suleiman. While Maysaloun Hamoud lives in Jaffa, she was born in Budapest. Other Palestinian filmmakers are part of the global diaspora. Mais Darwazah and Mai Masri, for instance, were born in Amman; Omar al-Qattan was born in Beirut; Annemarie Jacir was born in Bethlehem but raised in Saudi Arabia; Amer Shomali was born in Kuwait; Rani Massalha is from France; Jackie Salloum is from Dearborn, Michigan; and Cherien Dabis hails from Omaha, Nebraska. In addition to country of origin, an array of other issues also divide Palestinian filmmakers, including questions of politics, class, religion, and gender—differences that are evident in some of the interviews collected in the documentary *Cinema Palestine* (dir. Tim Schwab, 2013). There is thus no pure Palestinian existence, no single authentic form of Palestinian identity. In fact, the closer one looks, the more one discovers that difference is quite simply all that there is. As James Baldwin once commented in the context of Black America, "It becomes impossible, the moment one thinks about it, to predicate the existence of a *common* experience. The moment one thinks about it, it becomes apparent that there is no such thing."[66]

But to affirm Palestinian nonexistence does not mean only that we should acknowledge a plurality of Palestinian narratives in the place of a single one. Palestinianness is not derived from a single, fixed essence, but neither does it stem from a complex variety of ontological configurations. The diversity of Palestinian experiences emanates not from some preexisting ontological roots but from the utter *lack* of any such roots, not from a presence but from an absence. Simply put, *there is no Palestinian essence*. Like Freud's conception of the Jew, the Palestinian has something non-Palestinian, something Other, at the core—a bone in the throat that can never be swallowed. We might therefore say that Palestinian cinema does not exist because *the Palestinian does not even exist*.[67]

Here we are treading in potentially dangerous waters, and it is imperative that we clearly distinguish the Zionist endeavor to negate Palestinian being à la Golda Meir from the Freudian affirmation of nonexistence. Despite a superficial resemblance between these two positions, they could not be any further apart, and to confuse them would be just as erroneous as, say, mistaking Margaret Thatcher's neoliberal declaration that "there is no such thing as society" for Ernesto Laclau and Chantal Mouffe's post-Marxist assertion that "society does not exist."[68] To fixate on a certain similarity in language would be to overlook an enormous world of difference, and likewise, the gulf separating the Zionist negation of being from the Freudian affirmation of nonexistence is vast. Meir's words amount to a delegitimization of Palestinian claims—there is no ontological foundation to Palestinian identity, and therefore, for the Palestinian, *nothing is possible*. Freud's example, on the other hand, suggests something very different—there is no ontological foundation to Palestinian identity, and therefore, for the Palestinian, *nothing is impossible*. If the Zionist negation of Palestinian being aims to shut down possibilities, the affirmation of Palestinian nonexistence opens them up. If the first serves to denigrate the indigenous cultures, customs, religions, and languages of Palestine, the second seeks not to erase them from the history books but to dispute their ontological fixity. For the former, then, the project of Palestinian identity has no beginning, but for the latter, *it has no end*.

One should therefore be very careful when dealing with those propagandistic film and media portrayals of the Palestinians and other Arab groups that paint them as a bloodthirsty pack of terrorists—a tendency that has been critically documented and explored in the encyclopedic works of Jack Shaheen, as well as in Jackie Salloum's short film *Planet of the Arabs* (2005).[69] Such dehumanizing claims should, of course, be forcefully rejected. However, to insist that the Palestinians are actually a uniformly nice people—that is, to insist that there is a pleasant Palestinian essence—is precisely the wrong way of doing so. Even if we did somehow manage to accomplish the Herculean task of replacing all the negative stereotypes with positive ones, we would still be stuck in the quagmire of essentialized identities. Rather than asking whether the Palestinians are all good or all bad, we should follow Freud and concern ourselves with the task of showing how the essentialist view of the Other is generated by one's understanding of the Self. That is, the Palestinian boogeyman is an ideological trope necessitated by the contradictions woven into the very fabric of Zionism. Indeed, it was for this reason that Said claimed that the Palestinian terrorist was an Israeli invention.[70]

Accordingly, rather than countering the negative portrayals of the Palestinians with yet more reification, one should seek to dissolve the very ground on which these claims rest. Following in the footsteps of Freud, one should affirm the nonexistence of the Palestinian as a solid, stable entity. Palestinian identity is not set in stone, and its destiny has not been divinely preordained. Neither genetics nor political institutions, nor even sheer economic necessity, can ever absolutely determine in advance what it means to be Palestinian. There are no iron laws of history to fix its path, no gods in the heavens to dictate its fate. Palestinian identity has no permanent, determinative roots, and an unbridgeable void—that mysterious *tohu wa-bohu*—undergirds any illusions of solidity. Existing institutions and fields of discourse are certainly involved in the constitution of Palestinian identity, and they attempt to regulate Palestinian bodies by assigning them a particular role and function within the prevailing social order.[71] However, the success of such interpellation is never guaranteed.[72] The potential for negation cannot be fully eradicated, and in the last instance, *change is always possible*.

Far from being nihilistic and disempowering, then, the affirmation of Palestinian nonexistence is radically empowering. It is a gesture that can be favorably compared to a host of other declarations that also aim to distinguish the positive in the negative and discover hope in the darkness: Ernst Bloch's "man is not solid," Jacques Lacan's "Woman does not exist," Laclau and Mouffe's "society does not exist," Stuart Hall's formulation of a Marxism without guarantees, the Black Panther Party's concept of "revolutionary suicide," or even Ghassan Kanafani's enigmatic "man is a cause."[73] In each case, negation should serve not to shut down the conversation but to instigate it, to call into question the coordinates of the given reality and to clear a path for the introduction of new possibilities. What is made can forever be unmade, what is fixed can be unfixed, and what is formed can be unformed. Palestinian identity is entirely contingent—or, to use Catherine Malabou's term, it is *plastic*. It has no solid foundation, but it is precisely because of this lack, this ontological openness, that things can change, that the New can emerge from the Old and equality can emerge from inequality.

Significantly, this also means that there is nothing stable about the relationship between Jews and Palestinians, and the frequently heard claim that peace requires the rigid separation of these two imagined communities—to recall Ehud Barak's campaign slogan in 1999, "Us Here, Them There"—is completely spurious.[74] Like yesteryear's mantra of "separate but equal" proclaimed by the proponents of Jim Crow, the demand for "two states for two peoples"—whether it is issued by an Israeli, a Palestinian, or anyone else—is an attempt to separate the inseparable and ground the ungroundable. Even if two separate states are eventually established, their existence will not be the result of any natural hostility between Jews and Palestinians. Indeed, these two groups cannot even be cleanly separated in the realm of cinema, and films such as *5 Broken Cameras* (dir. Emad Burnat and Guy Davidi, 2011), *Ajami* (dir. Scandar Copti and Yaron Shani, 2009), and *Route 181: Fragments of a Journey in Palestine-Israel* (dir. Michel Khleifi and Eyal Sivan, 2004) are Jewish-Arab co-productions. The Jewish Israeli filmmaker Udi Aloni is even a frequent collaborator with the Palestinian hip hop group DAM. His film *Junction 48* (2016), which stars DAM's leading member, Tamer Nafar, so threatened the authorities in the Israeli municipality of Karmiel that they canceled a screening of it.[75] As these examples demonstrate, conflict in Palestine does not stem from preexisting identitarian differences. *It stems from colonization*, and its perpetuation is therefore not a foregone conclusion. Jewish-Palestinian antagonism is not inevitable, and there are even avenues for transforming this enmity into amity.[76] To recall Frantz Fanon's maxim, "There is nothing ontological about segregation."[77]

To be sure, not all existing forms of Palestinian struggle take this particular route. Reacting against Israeli attempts at erasure, many Palestinians have advocated developing their own brand of militant nationalism. In their view, if the Jews can have their own nation-state, the Palestinians should be able to have theirs, as well. While I accept that all nationalisms are not necessarily the same and that there might even be paths for formulating nonexclusionary forms of nationalism, I also recognize that, as history has shown time and time again, the underdogs who oppose oppression today can all too easily become the enforcers of oppression tomorrow, and as long as the movement against the Israeli occupation is based on a strictly defined and closed understanding of Palestinianness, it risks mirroring the very forms of identitarian hierarchy that it claims to contest.[78]

Thus, rather than canceling Freud's insight and inadvertently reproducing the exclusionary structures and discourse of the existing order, one should seek to ground Palestinian identity in groundlessness. *Either the struggle for Palestinian liberation is open and inclusive or it is not liberatory at all.* Or, to put it another way, the point is not just to critique a particular, historical form of oppression but to dissolve the very foundations on which that oppression rests. This means that the Palestinians' task is not just to fight Zionism in its specificity but also to fight the underlying logic that makes things like Zionism permissible, not just to oppose the Zionist who is colonizing the Palestinians' lands but also to oppose the Zionist who is colonizing their minds. Simply put, to effectively battle the Zionist from without, the Palestinians must also exorcise *the Zionist within themselves.*

III

There is absolutely no political guarantee already inscribed in an identity.
There is no reason on God's earth why the film is good because a Black person
made it. There is absolutely no guarantee that all the politics will be right
because a woman does it.
—**STUART HALL,** "Old and New Identities"

This brings us to the broader topic of identity politics and specifically to the question of how we are to make sense of the relationship between identities and political positions. Here we must not be too quick to draw a direct, causative line connecting one to the other, and even if there appears to be a natural link between them—for instance, between the worker and the proletarian, between the woman and the feminist, or between the Black subject and the Black radical—this bond is far from certain.[79] Every attempt to tie a specific identity to a particular politics is immediately contradicted by the empirical existence of the opposite: the worker who aspires to be a capitalist, the woman who practices patriarchy, or even the proverbial Uncle Tom.[80] Just as there are no natural identities, there are also no natural political positions.[81] Indeed, one does not even have to be a beneficiary of privilege to partake in the perpetuation of discriminatory systems and hierarchies.

But to retreat from the pitfalls of homogeneous identities does not mean that we should seek to uncritically glorify heterogeneity in their stead. Indeed, here we should take note of a development within certain intellectual quarters: the romanticization of hybrid identities—the exilic, the diasporic, or the accented—and the privileging of interstitial spaces and transnational subjects. "If hybridity is heresy," as Homi Bhabha writes, "then to blaspheme is to dream."[82] The only problem with this alluring formulation is that *hybridity is not always heretical.*[83] Although draped in the robes of counterhegemonic subversion, this tendency toward celebration often amounts to little more than an uncritical championing of liberal cosmopolitanism. Hybridity takes many forms, and some of them are downright wretched.[84] I see no particular reason why we should praise the Israeli rebranding of Palestinian food as Israeli, for instance, or applaud the intimate familiarity that many Palestinians have with the sound of Israeli munitions or the bars of Israeli prisons.

Moreover, it should also be stressed that hybridity, diaspora, and exile are not the antidotes to essentialism that they are sometimes claimed to be. "Diaspora, too," as Stuart Hall noted, "has been the site of some of the most closed narratives of identity known to human beings."[85] To be located within the margins of the existing order does not automatically endow one with a radical political agenda or a revolutionary consciousness, and I would instead suggest that we view *all* identities as always already hybrid creations and that all of us are always already decentered subjects inhabiting interstitial spaces. Porosity is not a goal; it is a given, and even the most seemingly insular and homogenous cultural formations are actually bric-a-brac constructions built on completely fragmented foundations. As Said himself recognized, "All cultures are involved in one another; none is single and pure, all are hybrid, heterogeneous, extraordinarily differentiated, and unmonolithic."[86] East is West, and West is East. One cannot look at the Other without looking at oneself.[87]

This lesson also extends to what may be today's diasporic identity *par excellence*—the Palestinian—and unfortunately, a commitment to emancipatory politics cannot be taken for granted even here. Indeed, Palestinian Zionism is not a matter of pure speculation but a real phenomenon. Take, for instance, the case of Mosab Hassan Yousef. Born the son of a Hamas leader, Yousef has gone on to lead a rather different life—spying for Israel, converting to evangelical Christianity, and eventually moving to California, where he wrote *Son of Hamas*, a best-selling book that whitewashes Israel's settler-colonialist practices and demonizes Palestinian resistance; it was subsequently turned into an award-winning documentary, *The Green Prince* (dir. Nadav Schirman, 2014).[88]

While Yousef's story may be extreme, the fact remains that many Palestinians have indeed turned their backs on the Palestinian Idea, albeit usually in less flamboyant ways—for instance, those who do Israel's bidding for the sake of political opportunism, those whose businesses profit from the occupation, those who have chosen the exclusionary path of religious sectarianism, those who are coerced into collaboration, or those who have simply been lulled into passivity. This dog-eat-dog situation within Palestinian society has become a persistent theme in Palestinian cinema—from the scene in Suleiman's *Chronicle of a Disappearance* in which two Palestinians in the same car inexplicably stop at a gas station and begin beating each other with their fists to the short film *Colorful Journey*, in which the directors Arab and Tarzan Nasser, who are identical twins, appear in military fatigues and circle each other with machine guns drawn, Arab versus Arab, Palestinian versus Palestinian. Other films that critically dwell on Palestinian infighting and sectarianism include Hany Abu-Assad's documentary *Nazareth 2000* (2001) and Rashid Masharawi's feature *Laila's Birthday* (2008), the latter of which follows one exhausting day in the life of a Ramallah taxi driver played by Mohammad Bakri. Here one might also be reminded of those Palestinians who contest one form of oppression (Zionist settler-colonialism) only to practice another (e.g., gender inequality). To quote Ella Shohat and Robert Stam, "The 'wretched of the earth' are not unanimously revolutionary."[89]

The popular Palestinian protest slogan "Existence Is Resistance" could thus hardly be more wrong. While this rallying cry may sometimes serve a positive performative function, its meaning is completely false. Existence is most decidedly *not* resistance, and there is no quick and easy correspondence between any identity and a political position.[90] Today's seemingly widespread tendency to pin one's hopes for liberation on existing identity categories—even the apparently hybrid ones—is an exercise in perpetual disappointment.

To be clear, my point is not to deny that identity-based forms of oppression such as racism and sexism stalk our world. They certainly do. But as real as these identitarian injustices are, they cannot be effectively combated by partaking in yet more identitarianism. *Emancipatory politics simply cannot be accounted for unless one looks beyond the plane of identities.* Thus, to be Palestinian does not guarantee fidelity to any specific brand of politics, and it certainly does not imply a natural, instinctive embrace of egalitarian values. The Palestinian Idea is not a birthright, and it cannot be inherited. Equality is not encoded in anyone's DNA—but, for that matter, *neither is inequality.*

How, then, do we bring all of these ideas together—the absence of a Palestinian film industry with the nonexistence of the Palestinian, the minefield of identity politics with the struggle for Palestinian liberation? We should begin by recognizing a formal distinction between these various registers. Ripped from the false certainties and illusionary guarantees of any ontological essence, Palestinian identity is partially shaped by external forces—that is, by the actions of those who do not even self-identify as Palestinian. This often takes the form of trauma—primarily the trauma of the Nakba. While Zionists have often claimed that Palestinian nationalism is nothing more than a belated, jealous response to Israel's victories, a similar position is often held by the Palestinians themselves insofar as they claim that the Nakba constitutes *the* foundational event of contemporary Palestinian identity. Indeed, in many accounts, the Nakba is seen as the glue holding all Palestinians together, the connective tissue that bridges the many religious, socioeconomic, and geographic gaps separating Palestinians from each other. Here, I am tempted to borrow Robin D. G. Kelley's argument about the role of "ghetto-centricity" in Black American identity and claim that the Palestinians are similarly gripped by a certain *Nakba-centricity*. In both cases, the community in question is united by the existence of a perceived underlying trauma.[91]

To be sure, Palestinian trauma is not limited to the events of 1947–1948, and it also includes the perpetuation of smaller injustices in the present, everything from extra airport security measures to the daily humiliations inflicted by Jewish settlers. Palestinian identity is thus sculpted by external parties and imposed on the Palestinians from without. In this sense, Palestinianness can partly be seen as an Israeli creation. For this reason, Rashid Khalidi is only partially correct when he writes that checkpoints and borders serve to remind Palestinians of their identity. Such barriers and bureaucratic obstacles are not only reminders; they are also key sites at which Palestinian identity is itself continually constituted and reconstituted.[92]

Admittedly, I am using the concept of trauma to describe a rather wide range of phenomena—everything from travel inconveniences to the experiences of ethnic cleansing and expulsion. However, I do not think that this broad application of the term necessarily dilutes its meaning. Rather, this is part of the nature of trauma itself. Trauma takes a diverse variety of forms and functions at a number of different levels.[93] In Palestinian cinema, the shift from one form of trauma to another—from a brain wound to a social wound—is plainly visible in Khleifi's feature *Canticle of the Stones*. Mixing documentary footage from the then ongoing First Intifada with scenes of scripted fiction, *Canticle* takes its viewers to a hospital where several Palestinian patients are interviewed about the nature of their injuries. The scene ends with a Palestinian doctor describing how rubber bullets can sometimes fracture skulls and cause brain hemorrhaging, often resulting in death. The camera then fixates on a head X-ray as it is held against a window pane for backlighting. When the doctor removes the radiograph from view, the world behind the glass is suddenly revealed: the Old City of Jerusalem. Significantly, the iconic Dome of the Rock is situated at roughly the same location within the frame that we had previously seen a bullet in the X-ray image. In this way, *Canticle* reveals the interconnected relationship between a brain wound and a social wound. The individual trauma of a head injury thus slides into the collective trauma of the ongoing occupation, the private into the public, the past into the present.

Trauma is therefore intimately involved in the constitution of Palestinian identity. But that is not the whole story, and the Palestinian cannot be completely reduced to some sort of golem or Frankenstein's monster.[94] On this point, let us recall the example of Cedric Robinson and his notion of the Black Radical Tradition. Just as the seeds of Black freedom were located not solely in slavery but in African consciousness, the roots of Palestinian liberation are likewise far deeper than the occupation itself. Indeed, Palestinian identity has a history that predates the arrival of the first Zionist settlers. Local ways of thinking, being, and imagining were already in existence before any Zionist feet had touched Middle Eastern soil, and this indigenous consciousness—in Rosemary Sayigh's terms, this *village consciousness*—has shaped the way that Palestinians respond to the litany of tragedies that have befallen them.[95]

Accordingly, trauma is not a completely one-sided affair, and traumatic events do not fully determine how people respond to them. Oppression cannot completely control the form that resistance to it takes, and there are myriad other factors involved, not least the agency of those being traumatized.[96] This is true even for Palestinian responses to the Nakba, and Constantine Zurayk, the Syrian intellectual and Beirut-based professor who first used the term with respect to the ethnic cleansing of Palestine, had already recognized this indeterminacy as early as 1948, when he wrote a pamphlet specifically addressing the Palestinians' plight: "a blow which will arouse a young man and which will lead to a strong reaction on his part may destroy a crumbling old man. A problem which will awaken an open mind and increase its vitality and efficiency may paralyze a loose, disjointed mind."[97] Not only is Palestinianness thus a response to the Nakba or a byproduct of Israeli state policies. Its constitution also involves the actions and decisions of the Palestinians themselves—in a word, Intifada. Every identification is thus at the same time a potential self-identification. Palestinian identity is not just the hobgoblin of Israeli nightmares; it is also the stuff of Palestinian dreams. The Palestinians not only receive form; they also *give form*.

These two broad processes of identity formation—the receiving of form from without and the giving of form from within—have already been widely recognized in a variety of other contexts. E. P. Thompson, for instance, famously claimed that "the working class made itself as much as it was made," and in her important study on Asian American identity, Lisa Lowe writes that "the boundaries and definitions of Asian American culture are continually shifting and being contested from pressures both 'inside' and 'outside' the Asian-origin community."[98] But however important it may be to distinguish these rival processes, our analysis will ultimately remain limited if it ends there. As we have already seen, not even the practices of self-identification guarantee a disruption of hegemonic narratives. How, then, do we account for the Palestinian Idea?

Emancipatory politics, I am arguing, is not just about the receiving and giving of form. Even more, emancipatory politics *annihilates form*; it disrupts the very framework within which identity is constituted and dissolves the established matrix of relations within which culture is produced. It indicates the power of refusal, the ability to say no and thereby to clear a path for the introduction of new possibilities. In Jacques Rancière's parlance, this annihilation of form is called *disidentification*. It signifies the ability to opt out of existing hierarchies and tear oneself away from inegalitarian regimes. For Rancière, this process is a necessary part of political subjectivization. In his words, "A political subject is [. . .] an agent of disidentification. His name does not express his identity."[99] This is why some of Rancière's key examples of egalitarian politics are those magical moments in which the formation of a collective political subject unexpectedly disrupts existing lines of sociological identification. Such an instance presented itself on the streets of Paris in May 1968 when the chant "we are all German Jews" was suddenly taken up by people who were, for the most part, neither German nor Jewish.[100] But one can think of many other, even more pertinent examples: the claim that "we are all Khaled Said" by those demanding justice after that young Egyptian was murdered by police in Alexandria in 2010 or, better yet, the sentiments that "we are all Palestine" expressed at Palestinian hip hop concerts in the West.[101] At their best moments, those people shouting, tweeting, or sharing such slogans are creating new, nonidentitarian constellations of protest that momentarily overturn existing forms of classification.[102]

This annihilation of form might also be favorably compared to the notion of revolutionary suicide developed by the Black Panther Party's cofounder and leading theoretician Huey P. Newton. Although often misunderstood, revolutionary suicide originally designated not a physical death but a symbolic one. Indeed, Newton even claimed that he had committed revolutionary suicide himself when he refused to cooperate with his prison guards. For him, to do otherwise would have been to commit "reactionary suicide," to give oneself over to the hands of the enemy.[103] Revolutionary suicide thus signifies the power to negate one's own individual identity to become part of the revolutionary collective. It means that the person who wants to effectively attack the oppressor from without must also kill the oppressor from within.[104] In the words of another Black radical of that era, Assata Shakur, "Revolution is about change, and the first place the change begins is in yourself."[105]

To be clear, the concepts of disidentification and revolutionary suicide do not amount to forms of masochistic self-hatred. They aim to annihilate not the content of culture but its form, calling for us to rethink the exclusionary, segregated framework in which identity is constructed. That is, these radical ideas are *anti-identitarian,* but they are not *anti-identity.* The same goes for the Palestinian Idea, and just as revolutionary suicide did not mean that the Black Panther Party was anti-Black, the Palestinian Idea is not anti-

Palestinian. Indeed, it is not even anti-Jewish.[106] Instead, the Palestinian Idea is *anti-inequality*, and it can therefore disrupt Palestinian institutions and practices just as much as Israeli ones.

It was precisely this potential—the prospect of challenging indigenous forms of chauvinism—that had so excited a young Leila Khaled about the idea of revolution. As she put it in her autobiography, "How could we liberate Palestine and the Arab homeland, if we ourselves were not liberated? How could we advocate equality and keep over half—the female half—of the human race in bondage?" For Khaled, Zionism provided the Palestinians an opportunity to practice this kind of self-criticism; in her words, "It forced some of us to re-examine the foundation of our society on our own. We discovered that our society was rotten, traditional, unprogressive. Our defeat was indeed our salvation, our means of regeneration and renewal."[107] On this point, it is worth noting that while both the First and Second Intifadas initially seemed to offer Palestinian women new opportunities to organize and mobilize, the advances they made were eventually annulled by a patriarchal backlash.[108] Feminist organizing in the face of Zionist colonization continues to be a tremendously difficult task. Indeed, upon screening Maysaloun Hamoud's *In Between*, some conservative Palestinians declared it *haram* (forbidden), and a fatwa was reportedly issued against its director.[109] Clearly, if the Palestinian struggle is to be truly emancipatory, it must operate on multiple fronts.

Accordingly, what the Palestinian Idea offers it not just the stale repackaging of identity politics but something altogether different. Like Rancière's notion of disidentification and Newton's concept of revolutionary suicide, the Palestinian Idea functions not to expand the plane of identities but to punch a hole through it, and if the dueling forces of Nakba and Intifada serve to continually construct and reconstruct Palestinian identity, the Palestinian Idea is anti-identitarian dynamite. It is an explosive negation, a call to disorder that blasts an opening in the established universe.

These three registers—the receiving of form, the giving of form, and the annihilation of form—coincide precisely with the modalities of what Catherine Malabou calls *plasticity*. Developing this notion through her innovative readings of G. W. F. Hegel, her interventions into the discourse of neuroscience, and her work on trauma, Malabou sees plasticity not only as the ability to bounce back or adapt but also, much more radically, as *the ability to explode*.[110] If plasticity has more traditionally been conceived solely as a positive process, Malabou endeavors to discover its radically negative dimension, and her notion of plasticity should therefore not be confused with simple flexibility or elasticity. Rather, for her, plasticity

> has three principle significations. On one hand, it designates the capacity of certain materials, such as clay or plaster, to receive form. On

the other hand, it designates the power to give form—the power of a sculptor or a plastic surgeon. But, finally, it also refers to the possibility of the deflagration or explosion of every form—as when one speaks of "plastique," "plastic explosive," or, in French, *plastiquage* (which simply means "bombing"). The notion of plasticity is thus situated at both extremes of the creation and destruction of form.[111]

The relevance of Malabou's trifold definition of plasticity for Palestine should be immediately obvious. The first mode—the receiving of form—coincides with the traumatic imposition of identity from without; to use Palestinian parlance, this is what I am calling the forces of Nakba. The second mode of plasticity—the giving of form—corresponds to the practices of self-identification, or the forces of Intifada. Malabou's third mode of plasticity—the annihilation of form—is the one that is most often overlooked, but it is also the most radical. Destructive plasticity coincides with disidentification or revolutionary suicide. This is where we should locate the Palestinian Idea, the scandalous supposition of equality amidst inequality. For Malabou, this third mode of plasticity signifies the power to create an opening where previously there was no opening. In her words, it is "the constitution of an exit [. . .] where no such exit is possible."[112] Like a plastic explosive, it blasts a hole in the given order and thereby opens a door into another world—a world that is already here, hidden in the shadows of this world. Through destructive plasticity, the Palestinians possess the power to refuse, the ability to ignite an *ontological explosion*.

IV

It's difficult to make independent cinema, but it's also a privilege.
—**Annemarie Jacir**, *Le Mur a des Oreilles*

There is nothing, so you are free—and terrified.
—**Huey P. Newton**, *Revolutionary Suicide*

If the question that began this chapter—the question of Palestinian cinema's existence—initially appeared simple and straightforward, the various twists and turns of the subsequent discussion have proved rather complicated. Unlike other artists working in relation to a number of other national cinemas and media capitals, Palestinian filmmakers continue to lack the basic infrastructure for film production, and there is no proper Palestinian film industry. As we have seen in our exploration of Palestinian identity, however, there is a way to turn this unfortunate situation on its head, and the lack of a well-established and smoothly functioning film industry is also an opportunity.

This absence is also a freedom—a freedom to develop in ways other than the established ones. The discriminatory practices and hierarchies of other film and media industries do not have to determine the shape of Palestinian cinema, and despite their hardships, Palestinian filmmakers have a chance to create a new kind of cinema. Glimpses of this potential can already be seen with regard to gender hierarchies, and a significant number of women have emerged as major Palestinian filmmakers—Dahna Abourahme, Suha Arraf, Cherien Dabis, Mais Darwazah, Azza el-Hassan, Annemarie Jacir, Mai Masri, Najwa Najjar, Jackie Salloum, and others, including Alia Arasoughly and all of the filmmakers associated with Shashat, the women's cinema organization in Ramallah. The absence of an established film industry also provides room for experimentation, including political experimentation, and if other national film industries often shy away from producing films that arose controversy by disrupting the status quo, Palestinian cinema still retains this ability, this explosive plasticity. There are an endless number of directions Palestinian cinema can take. Like the Palestinian itself, Palestinian cinema is a radically open enterprise.

Cinema is thus one of the sites in which Palestinian plasticity is rendered visible. Film does not just present Palestinian identity as a preconstituted and fully formed category; it takes part in its very creation. Moreover, at its best, film is also one of the places where the terms of Palestinian identity can be annihilated and new emancipatory possibilities can be brought into being. In the next chapter, I turn specifically to the cinema of Annemarie Jacir, one of the most gifted Palestinian filmmakers operating today. Focusing on her first two features, *Salt of This Sea* and *When I Saw You,* I examine how these two films engage with the plasticity of Palestine and deal with memories of the Nakba, specters of the Intifada, and the explosive politics of disidentity. Both films certainly have their merits. However, I argue that while the former only points toward the contingency of existing identity categories, the latter goes a step further and delves into the emancipatory potential of destruction.

3

Plastic Palestine

Part Two

Palestinians [. . .] have not often realized, I think, that the
Palestinian for which they have struggled and continue to
struggle is yet to be made, is still in the making.
—EDWARD W. SAID, "Arabs and Jews"

Plasticity, far from producing a mirror image of the world,
is the form of another possible world.
—CATHERINE MALABOU, *What Should We Do with Our Brain?*

I

Salt of This Sea (dir. Annemarie Jacir, 2008) has an appetite for transgression. Like its central protagonist—a young, working-class Palestinian woman from Brooklyn who is returning to the land of her grandparents to reclaim an unpaid debt—the film transgresses physical borders, taking viewers to both sides of Israel's Apartheid Wall, from Ramallah to Jerusalem and from the green forests of the Hebron foothills to the blue waters of the Mediterranean Sea. But spatial boundaries are not the only lines that this film crosses. It also violates the frontier of time. While *Salt* is set in the present, every scene is haunted by traces of the past. Thus, whereas the film has sometimes been called a romance, a road movie, or even a heist film, I prefer to think of it as a ghost story. In *Salt*, Israel is not a desert that has miraculously been made to bloom but a graveyard. It is a land filled with the phantoms of the Nakba, a historical trauma that keeps exceeding the confines of the past and spilling over into the present.

Before the opening credits even begin to roll, *Salt* transports us to another time, and we see grainy, black-and-white newsreel footage from 1948: tanks, warplanes, and the destruction of buildings, houses, and homes. This short montage ends with a tragic image—a crowd of Palestinians, mostly women and children, desperately wading into the sea and climbing aboard a ship, probably never to lay eyes on Jaffa again. The entire sequence—culled from footage gathered by Rachel Leah Jones for her film *500 Dunam on the*

Moon (2002)—lasts a mere thirty seconds, and it is the only segment of the film that does not take place in the present. Situated at the beginning of an otherwise fictional film, this brief foray into history gives the audience a glimpse into the underlying disaster that anticipates and animates the story that follows.

Concise as this opening sequence might be, its significance should not be underestimated. Even though the Nakba is largely regarded as the seminal event in the constitution of modern Palestinian identity, it has rarely been so directly depicted on the screen. Some claim that the Nakba, as a collective trauma, simply eludes representation. This is an argument made by Joseph Massad, and he writes that "the absence of any thorough cinematic treatment of *al-Nakba*, the foundational trauma of the Palestinian struggle, seems related to its unrepresentability."[1] For Massad, the Nakba functions in Palestinian film as a structural absence. Although it is too painful to be shown directly, it nevertheless continues to have an effect on cinematic narratives. That is, the Nakba is present even in its absence. In Massad's words, "The very unrepresentability of the *Nakba* is what has structured Palestinian cinema all along, which is why this cinema fails to say what it must but cannot say."[2]

The notion of structural absence and the question of trauma's unrepresentability have been discussed in a number of other contexts. Bhaskar Sarkar, for instance, makes related claims with respect to post-partition cinema in India, and similar arguments have been formulated vis-à-vis Korean film.[3] However, the paramount example remains the Holocaust, and an entire field of academic inquiry—trauma studies—has developed largely as an attempt to deal with the physical and mental anguish that this event continues to inflict.[4] Some have argued that the horrors of Nazism can never be properly represented in fiction. This is the position advanced by the late Claude Lanzmann, the director of *Shoah* (1985), and in his critique of *Schindler's List* (dir. Steven Spielberg, 1993), he maintains that the Holocaust is "unique in that it erects a ring of fire around itself, a borderline that cannot be crossed because there is a certain ultimate degree of horror that cannot be transmitted. To claim it is possible to do so is to be guilty of the most serious transgression."[5] According to Lanzmann, any attempt to re-create the Nazi atrocities cinematically will always fall short. It will inevitably diminish and desublimate the Holocaust, turning the Horror into just another horror and thereby doing a disservice to Nazism's many victims. In Theodor Adorno's oft-quoted words, "To write poetry after Auschwitz is barbaric."[6]

Such a view amounts to a prohibition. It reduces the question of representation to a strict and misleadingly simple binary in which something is either depicted on-screen or it is not. Cinematic representation, however, has never been so clear-cut, and even if we accept the general claim that the

Holocaust cannot be properly depicted in realist terms, this does not mean that it cannot be portrayed in other ways—in fragments and distortions, with metaphor, or even through its very absence. Indeed, is this not precisely the function of art: to communicate what cannot otherwise be communicated and to represent what cannot otherwise be represented?[7] Recognizing this potential, Adorno himself later clarified his own statement, writing that "perennial suffering has as much right to expression as a tortured man has to scream."[8] We therefore should not strictly prohibit artistic representations of the Holocaust. Art is not impossible after Auschwitz; on the contrary. "[In order] to show Auschwitz," as Jacques Rancière argues, "art is the only thing possible."[9]

As the foundational trauma of contemporary Palestinian identity, the Nakba has similarly left its trace on Palestinian cinema, and it would therefore be incorrect to say that it has *never* been represented in film. Indeed, portrayals of the Nakba even appear in two films that are sometimes cited as being the first Palestinian fictional features: *The Dupes* (dir. Tawfik Saleh, 1972) and *Return to Haifa* (dir. Kassem Hawal, 1981). Although neither of these films was helmed by a Palestinian director, both were based on stories by the late Palestinian writer Ghassan Kanafani, and *Return to Haifa* was even financed by the Popular Front for the Liberation of Palestine (PFLP), the political organization to which Kanafani belonged before he was assassinated in 1972 by Israeli agents.[10] In *The Dupes*, scenes of the Nakba come in the form of brief flashbacks, and one of the main characters has fragmented recollections of past battles fought with Zionist militias. *The Dupes* is also noteworthy for weaving into its fictional narrative segments of documentary footage from Palestinian refugee camps—austere images of impoverished faces staring out from behind barbed-wire fences.[11]

Return to Haifa's treatment of the Nakba is even more sustained. The film's Iraqi director, Kassem Hawal, reportedly cast more than three thousand Palestinian refugees as extras. They came to the set dressed in the same clothes they had been wearing when they were forced into exile some thirty years earlier. With their help, the film's production crew temporarily transformed Lebanon's northern port city of Tripoli, 1981, into the port of Haifa, 1948. These staged re-creations of the Palestinians' expulsion appear in the film's opening scenes, and several flashbacks of the Nakba take place throughout the subsequent narrative. Significantly, *Return to Haifa*, like the original short story on which it is based, also includes recollections from the point of view of its main Israeli character, in which Nazi soldiers storm her home in Poland and murder a young, Jewish boy in cold blood. One of the very first Palestinian fictional features therefore not only refused to demonize the Jews; it went so far as to criticize European anti-Semitism and acknowledge the trauma of the Holocaust. *Return to Haifa* thereby advanced a point that I consider fundamental: the claim that the struggle against Zionism and the struggle against anti-Semitism go hand in hand.[12]

Depictions of the Nakba have also appeared in more recent examples of cinematic fiction.[13] Ali Nasser's *The Milky Way* (1997), for instance, concerns the inhabitants of a small Palestinian village, two of whom are clearly traumatized subjects: Mabruq (Suhel Haddad) and Jamilah (Mihaela Mitraki). One is the archetypical "village idiot"; the other, a disturbed mute. As the film progresses, the source of their symptoms is revealed through flashbacks. As children, Mabruq and Jamilah both witnessed the slaughter of their families by Israeli soldiers—the former in 1948, and the latter in 1956. These subjective flashbacks are formally set apart from the rest of the film. In the case of Mabruq, we see a close-up of a boy's face. The camera slowly pulls back, revealing devastation all around him—burning fires, trails of blood, and dead bodies lying in the grass. This eerie sequence appears twice in the film: first when Mabruq dreams of having a future family; and then when he attempts suicide by hanging himself from a tree. Jamilah experiences similar visions, and her epileptic-like fits lead her father to complain that she behaves as though she is possessed. The atrocities that these two troubled characters witnessed as children thus continue to haunt them in the present, and fragments of these "demon memories" come back to them in moments of distress and duress.[14] Notably, while *The Milky Way*'s presentation of the Nakba is particularly striking, it is not the only recent film to depict this foundational trauma, and re-created scenes from 1948 also appear in Elia Suleiman's epic *The Time That Remains* (2009). Early in that film, several young Palestinian men are rounded up by Israeli forces and taken to the grounds of a mosque. After being identified by a hooded informant, they are bound, blindfolded, and beaten, and some are executed.[15]

Thus, the Nakba does appear in Palestinian cinema, but as these various examples indicate, it usually appears through distortions, fragments, or flashbacks. While documentary cinema has sometimes dealt with memories of the Nakba—most notably, Michel Khleifi's *Ma'loul Celebrates Its Destruction* (1985) and Mohammad Bakri's *1948* (1998)—it is usually through fiction that the truth of the Nakba emerges. We might therefore surmise that, as a traumatic event, the Nakba cannot be adequately represented in realist terms. On this point, *Salt of This Sea* is no exception, and while Jacir's film is very direct in its presentation of Nakba footage, the sequence lasts for only a few fleeting moments before the film dramatically changes course, both visually and aurally. The grainy, black-and-white footage abruptly cuts to the shining, blue waters of the Mediterranean, and the somber sound of a few dark notes being plucked on a solo oud suddenly transforms into an upbeat, multi-instrumental Arab pop melody.

This distinct cut between the pre-titles sequence and the rest of the film

Figure 3.1. An impossible shot of Jaffa in *Salt of This Sea*.

initially appears to function as a clear, *Wizard of Oz*–like barrier separating fact from fiction and segregating the harsh, black-and-white world of reality from the colorful, creative realm of fantasy and the imagination. Upon closer inspection, however, this stark dichotomy falls apart. The last shot of the archival footage, a final view of Jaffa from the point of view of the departing refugees (Figure 3.1), is an unusual shot indeed. In fact, it is an *impossible* shot—impossible because there were no cameras aboard those ships and no documentary film crews to record the final glimpses that the refugees caught of their stolen city on the sea. This last shot would therefore appear to be fabricated. Though filmed in the present, it has been altered and drained of its color to graphically match the images from the past.

What do we make of this fugitive footage? I believe that the historical impossibility of this shot is significant because it indicates yet another impossibility—an ideological impossibility. The practices of conventional historical research privilege certain sources over others—the written word over oral testimony, the official published record over personal memoirs, and so on. As a result of this methodological discrimination, what is commonly presented as nonpartisan research is often based on a thoroughly partisan hierarchy of sources—a hidden bias that can sometimes cover up or even erase the existence of real, historical crimes. In re-creating the events that led up to the establishment of the State of Israel, some scholars have used the assumptions of positivist historiography to justify the silencing of Palestinian voices. Most notoriously, Benny Morris openly admits his distrust of Palestinian sources. As he puts it, "There is simply no Arab *documentation* of the sort historians must rely on," and he writes off the historical archive contained in Palestinian memory and oral testimony as being "slight, unreliable, tendentious, imaginative, and occasionally fantastical."[16] From this perspective, Palestinian recollections of the Nakba do not constitute a legitimate source for historical research and investigation. They are something else, something less than history—a kind of fantasy or fiction.

Of course, a major reason why Palestinian sources of historical data seem so scarce is that they have been destroyed. It is simply not the case that such primary sources never existed; rather, they have been *made* not to exist. From the beginning, the Zionists recognized the subversive potential of memory, and they worked hard to contain this threat, perpetrating a cultural genocide that involved such acts as the planting of forests to conceal depopulated Palestinian villages; the switching of Arabic place names for Hebrew ones; and the theft and destruction of Palestinian property, including books and even entire libraries, a crime explored in the documentary *The Great Book Robbery* (dir. Benny Brunner, 2012). In the first year after Israel's establishment, some thirty thousand Palestinian books were confiscated by the new government in West Jerusalem alone.[17] As a consequence of this intentional erasure, Palestinian history must be recovered by other means.

If history is indeed written by the conqueror, as the old adage goes, we must therefore do more than simply add new information and data to existing research paradigms. We must go a step further and challenge the authority of those very paradigms. In the case of Palestine, this means that we must work to overthrow the hierarchy of sources that perversely ends up privileging the perspective of the ethnic cleanser over that of the ethnically cleansed and the perspective of the colonizer over that of the colonized. One should therefore not blindly accept the conventional framework in which culture, oral testimony, and memory are consigned to a place of diminished importance. Historical truth does not lie in empirical facts and data alone, and if we want to take Palestinian views of the Nakba seriously, we must also delve into those sources that the official historiographers frequently dismiss as bits of unreliable and inconsequential fiction—memory, oral testimony, and the historical archive contained in art, literature, and film.[18] This is the realm of what George Lipsitz calls "counter-memory," a concept he develops in relation to the novels of Toni Morrison and Zora Neale Hurston. "Counter-memory," as he puts it, "is not a denial of history, only a rejection of its false priorities and hierarchical divisions."[19]

Thus, by slyly smuggling an impossible shot of Jaffa into the opening moments of *Salt of This Sea*—that is, by camouflaging a piece of fiction with the black-and-white appearance of nonfiction—Jacir seems to be making a very profound point. Instead of accepting the epistemological dictates of those officially sanctioned paradigms that would have us privilege Zionist documents over Palestinian voices and thereby reproduce inequality ad infinitum,

Jacir signals the importance of counter-memory by providing an otherwise impossible perspective. Fiction is not a diversion from truth; rather, *truth is located in fiction itself.*

This approach contrasts sharply with the tactics deployed by another film released the same year, the highly celebrated *Waltz with Bashir* (dir. Ari Folman, 2008). In *Waltz*, the Israeli director Ari Folman uses animation to document his autobiographical search for his lost memories of the time he spent as a soldier in Lebanon. In particular, Folman is concerned with piercing the wall of amnesia obscuring his memory of the Sabra and Shatila massacre of 1982. The film dramatically concludes with Folman's sudden recovery of these repressed memories, and in the final scene the animation suddenly switches to actual footage from the aftermath of those bloody events: heartbreaking images of dead children and the sound of screaming mothers. While Folman's film uses both animation and newsreel footage, truth is clearly on the side of the latter. The contrast between *Salt* and *Waltz* is striking. Whereas *Salt* opens with archival footage and subtly moves into fiction, *Waltz* opens with animated fiction and eventually closes with archival footage. This structural divergence indicates a very different understanding of the relationship between reality and fantasy. While *Salt*, on one hand, hints that the road to truth is necessarily paved with fiction, *Waltz*, on the other hand, practices old-fashioned ideology critique by suggesting that fantasy stands opposed to raw reality and that fiction is something that obscures or distorts truth. Thus, if for *Salt* the facts are just a beginning, for *Waltz*, they are an end in themselves.[20]

Apart from its opening montage, *Salt* takes place entirely in the present. The film begins and ends at Ben Gurion International Airport in Tel Aviv. Soraya (Suheir Hammad), *Salt*'s central protagonist, arrives there with a smile, excited to see the land of her ancestors for the very first time. She is immediately singled out for interrogation. Beneath a framed portrait of David Ben-Gurion, Israeli security personnel repeatedly ask her the same condescending questions as they make jokes to each other in Hebrew, examine the contents of her luggage, and eventually subject her to a humiliating strip search.[21] At the film's conclusion, Soraya is back at this same location. Having overstayed her visa, she awaits deportation. In the weeks separating these two moments, Soraya goes on a journey of discovery. She takes up residence in the West Bank where she gets a job waiting tables at an upscale Ramallah restaurant and makes friends with Emad (Saleh Bakri) and Marwan (Riyad Ideis). One is a fellow waiter whose attempts to obtain a permit to study at a Canadian university keep getting denied by the Israeli authorities; the other is a Palestinian artist who harbors dreams of becoming a filmmaker.

After Soraya's efforts to retrieve her grandfather's money from a Palestinian bank are repeatedly thwarted, Soraya and her two friends decide to take matters into their own hands. Together, they rob the bank and sneak into

Israel to see life on the other side. First, they go to Jaffa and visit the former house of Soraya's late grandfather, now occupied by a liberal Jewish Israeli woman. After Soraya heatedly confronts the house's new inhabitant, she and Emad leave Marwan behind and proceed to find the remains of Emad's village, al-Dawayima. The two spend several nights living in the ruins, and a romance begins to develop between them. They even flirt with the utopian idea of starting over and building a new life for themselves in this abandoned place, creating a new Palestine rooted in the ruins of the old. These dreams are dashed when the pair encounter an Israeli professor (Juliano Mer-Khamis) who is visiting the site with his students. No longer able to conceal their presence, Soraya and Emad go back on the road, driving with no clear destination. They are soon discovered by the Israeli police and apprehended. Their adventure exploring the criminality of freedom is over. The film ends back at the airport. Emad has been arrested, and Soraya awaits her imminent deportation. Like her grandparents before her, she is being expelled from Palestine.

As this quick synopsis indicates, *Salt*'s narrative takes place in the contemporary moment. What, then, is the relationship between the pre-titles sequence and the rest of the film, between 1948 and present-day Palestine? Importantly, Jacir herself sees *Salt* as dealing with the Nakba, and in an interview about the film, she specifically mentioned the Nakba no fewer than ten times. In her words, "*Salt of This Sea* is about a woman who carries the trauma of the *Nakba* three generations later"; "I wanted to make a film about the *Nakba*"; "This film is about the *Nakba*. It's about our trauma of the *Nakba* and what it means for Palestinians today"; "I had never seen a fiction film about the *Nakba*, and I needed that. I wanted that story to be told."[22]

How do we reconcile Jacir's concern for history with her decision to set *Salt* in the contemporary era? How does Jacir imagine that a film that takes place in the present might be capable of telling a tale about the trauma of the past? While one might initially be tempted to point out how trauma continues to haunt new generations through memory, or even "post-memory," long after its initial cause has come to an end, this answer (though true) is not completely satisfying.[23] Indeed, while the term "Nakba" refers to a precise historical event—the destruction of more than four hundred Palestinian villages and the expulsion of some seven hundred thousand Palestinians from the land of Palestine in 1947–1948 —it has a much broader meaning. The Nakba also signifies the more general oppression that the Palestinians continue to experience. The book is not closed on the Nakba, and the dispossession of the Palestinian people persists into the present with every house demolition and every illegal settlement. Such incidents should not be understood as isolated, unrelated occurrences but as an interconnected web of ongoing oppression stretching back to the very beginning of the Zionist project of settler-colonialism. As Eyal Weizman observed in the aftermath of Operation

Cast Lead, Israel's bombardment of Gaza in 2008–2009, "The destroyed village of 1948 and the destroyed camp of 2009 stand [. . .] on a historical continuum of ongoing destruction and denial."[24] Paradoxically, this ongoing nature of the Nakba is even implicitly recognized by some of its most flagrant perpetrators. This is the mirror-image world of Zionist settler-colonialism, a topsy-turvy realm in which a figure such as Ariel Sharon can perversely declare that "the War of Independence has not ended. No, 1948 was just one chapter."[25] Just as fact bleeds into fiction, the past boils over into the present, and to historicize the Nakba—to limit it to only the distant past—is to blind oneself to the ways in which it is still with us. The Nakba is very much a part of the present and as such cannot be consigned to the history books or relegated to the field of memory. In Palestine, the trauma is not yet over. To quote Jacir, "It's not of the past. It's now."[26]

In *Salt*, the Nakba appears in all of these forms: as a historical event, as a traumatic memory, and as an ongoing catastrophe. As soon as Soraya enters Israel, she sees evidence of the historical Nakba. On the bus ride out of Tel Aviv, her eye is drawn to stones on the side of the road. These are not just ordinary rocks but relics from the past, the remains of depopulated villages. Toward the end of the film, these phantoms take center stage when Soraya and Emad make camp in the remains of al-Dawayima, the site of one of the worst Nakba massacres in which more than a hundred Palestinians were murdered. Survivors and soldiers alike later reported acts of rape, the burning of houses with people locked inside, and the smashing open of babies' skulls.[27] Significantly, when the Israeli history professor arrives there with his students, he claims that the ruins are relics of the ancient Jewish past. As this scene suggests, memory, too, is a perpetual battleground, and counter-memory is forever in danger of being appropriated and turned into its opposite.

Importantly, *Salt* draws connections between the past and the present, and all of the contemporary injustices that the film depicts are part of the same historical Nakba narrative: the invasive interrogations, the checkpoints, the television headlines that Soraya reads about new land confiscations, or even the grotesque scene in which Israeli security forces arbitrarily make Emad strip naked after randomly pulling him over in the night. This continuity is most poetically portrayed in the scene in which Soraya goes for a swim. Alone against the powerful waves of the sea, she turns her body around and beholds Jaffa. Significantly, this is the same view witnessed by those refugees who, like her grandparents, were forced to flee their homes in 1948. In fact, it is the same perspective as the impossible shot smuggled into the film's black-and-white opening montage—only this time in bright color. A connection between these two scenes is even made aurally: on the film's soundtrack we hear the same, ominous oud notes that had earlier played during the pre-titles montage. Continuity is thereby established between the past and the present, between the refugees of 1948 and their modern-day descendants, including those Palestinians in the global diaspora such as Soraya.

In *Salt*, all of these manifestations of the Nakba play a fundamental role in the formation of Palestinian identity, and this relationship with trauma is most clearly evident with respect to Soraya. She does not emerge from her encounter with Zionism unscathed, and if she had initially arrived in Tel Aviv filled with naïve and idealistic dreams about exploring a mythic land of sunshine and oranges, her experiences in Palestine shape and mold her in ways that she did not anticipate. By the time her journey is aborted, she is a changed woman. This is signified by the radically different posture she adopts toward the Israeli security personnel at the airport. Previously, she had smiled at them and identified herself as an American; by the end of the film, she refuses to call herself anything other than Palestinian. To the confusion of her Israeli inquisitor, she claims that she was born in Jaffa and insists that her U.S. passport is actually a Palestinian one.[28]

Soraya's dramatic transformation is the result of both external and internal processes. Just as Palestinians receive form, they also give form, and while the Nakba may force itself upon the Palestinians, they nonetheless exercise agency in determining how they respond to it. Nakba is continually countered by Intifada, and in *Salt*, this second mode of plasticity appears most explicitly in the bank robbery scene.[29] While Marwan waits in the getaway car, Soraya and Emad transform themselves into something of a Palestinian Bonnie and Clyde. Like some outrageous Orientalist nightmare, they enter the bank brandishing weapons and donning the stereotypical garb of Islamic terrorists. Fleeing the scene of the crime with cash in hand, the trio then dispense with their costumes only to put on another disguise, and they quickly adopt the look of Jewish visitors. Seeing their yarmulkes and U.S.-Israeli solidarity T-shirts, the Israeli border guards wave them across the checkpoint without hesitation.[30]

Within a matter of minutes, *Salt*'s protagonists thus swing from one extreme to another, from Muslim boogeymen to Zionist tourists. In this exaggerated way, the film reveals the contingency of identity formations and categories. Identity is always a performance, and by continually shaping and reshaping, molding and remolding their identities, Palestinians do not merely read lines from a script; they also have a hand in writing them. Each articulation of what it means to be Palestinian is not just a flat description of the ways things are; it is also an assertion. In *Salt*, this plasticity is evident even at the level of film production, and Jacir made a number of ironic casting decisions. While the character of Emad is stuck in the West Bank, the actor who plays him, Saleh Bakri, holds Israeli citizenship, and while the film's Israeli professor is a hardened Jewish nationalist, he is played by the late Juliano Mer-Khamis, the mixed Jewish-Palestinian actor, activist, and filmmaker who co-founded the Jenin Freedom Theatre.[31]

But while *Salt* clearly demonstrates Malabou's first two modes of plasticity, its engagement with the third is more ambiguous. To be sure, traces of destructive plasticity appear throughout the film, and Soraya's rebellion against Israel's imposed borders is also a rebellion against the ways that these divisions have been internalized and reproduced by certain Palestinian individuals and institutions—from Ramallah's business elites to the pitiful Palestinian bureaucrats whose many agreements with Israel have rendered them powerless, unable even to perform the simple task of issuing Soraya a passport. Through her actions, Soraya is effectively saying no to these hierarchies. She is rejecting her assigned place in the prevailing social order and thereby exploding the frame within which Palestinian identity is conceived and formulated.

Thus, *Salt* does indeed present fragments of the Palestinian Idea, and by presupposing equality, Soraya cuts through the various ethnic, class, and gender-based hierarchies that pollute the Palestinian landscape. However, the film has contradictory tendencies, and it is in danger of healing the very wounds in the social order that it inflicts. In *Salt,* there is simply no place to go. Soraya's house in Jaffa has another tenant, and even the ruins of al-Dawayima offer no refuge. There is no space—neither physical nor metaphysical—that Israel has not already colonized. Zionism cannot be escaped; politicide appears complete; and in a certain sense, return is impossible.

There is a comparison to be drawn here with one of Kanafani's best-known stories, "Returning to Haifa," in which a Palestinian couple goes home to Haifa after nearly two decades in exile, only to discover that their old house is occupied by a Holocaust survivor and that their long-lost infant son has been raised to be a Jewish Zionist now serving in the Israeli military.[32] Like *Salt*, Kanafani's tragic story suggests that a simple return to the way things were is impossible. Things have changed in irreversible ways, and salvation does not lie in the re-creation of the past.

Despite the glimmers of hope scattered throughout the film, then, the narrative of *Salt* turns out to be rather hopeless. At the end of the film, Soraya's adventure is over, and she is back at the airport, awaiting deportation. Just as a portrait of Ben-Gurion watched over her initial interrogation, *Salt* ends with another symbol of Israel's continued authority and power, and the film's final frames are dominated by a sculpture of the assassinated Israeli Prime Minister Yitzhak Rabin, a figure celebrated in the West as a man of peace but remembered by Palestinians as one of the military commanders responsible for the ethnic cleansing of Lydd and Ramla during the Nakba.[33] The bleakness of *Salt*'s ending thus cancels out some of its previous achievements, and as the end credits begin to roll, very little has changed. The Nakba continues with new expulsions, and Israel's hegemony seems complete.

To be clear, the problem with this ending is not defeat in and of itself. In cinema, a defeat can contain within it the seeds of future redemption.[34] However, with Jacir's film, this is simply not the case, and the problem with its concluding depiction of defeat is its apparent finality. There seems to be no path forward, and while *Salt*'s remarkable opening had announced that reality is open to the play of the imagination, the ending returns us to more practical, less plastic ground. In a strange way, *Salt* risks mirroring the propaganda of Israel's apologists. Despite its openly aggressive tone toward the ongoing project of Zionist settler-colonialism, the film nevertheless perpetuates the ideological view of Israel as an all-powerful entity. Palestinians can certainly resist, the film seems to be saying, and they can play an infinite number of identity games. Soraya can change herself, but this personal liberation fails to effect any broader transformation at the level of the social order. Consequently, *Salt* stops short of fully delving into plasticity's explosive potential, and despite hints to the contrary, the film fails to escape the plane of identity. Israel has no cracks. Zionism wins. The Palestinian Idea begins to dissolve and fade away.

II

Shortly after completing *Salt of This Sea*, Jacir received an unwelcome surprise. When she attempted to return home to Ramallah from travels abroad in November 2007, the Israeli Border Police barred her entry into Palestine. An Israeli government official later told Jacir's attorney that she had been deemed a "security problem," and she was subsequently turned away from the border seven more times, even for her own wedding.[35] Even though Jacir had been traveling in and out of the West Bank her entire life, this door was suddenly closed to her. Like Soraya, Jacir found herself in exile, and she consequently relocated to Amman. Describing these developments in 2011, Jacir explained:

> I live in Jordan because it's as close as I can get to Palestine right now.
> [. . .] Being so close, in Amman, has not made it easier, only more difficult, more painful. A short drive and I can see Palestine from here.
> Over the valley, I see the hills, even recognize the cities. My friends, my family, my apartment in Ramallah are there, but I can no longer reach them. Palestine is becoming a memory, and I struggle to hold the visuals, the reality of my life there, as close to me as I can.[36]

It was out of these particular circumstances that Jacir conceived of her next feature film, *When I Saw You*. Like *Salt*, *When I Saw You* is a very personal film, and it is deeply linked to Palestinian experiences of exile. However, there are a number of major differences between the two films. While *Salt* takes place in present-day Palestine, *When I Saw You* is set in the late 1960s in neighboring Jordan. The most important distinction, however, is to be found not at the level of plot and setting but in the two films' varying conceptions of return. If the earlier film suggested that return is necessary but impossible, *When I Saw You* insists on turning this impossibility into a possibility. That is, while *Salt* remains trapped in the plane of identities, *When I Saw You* goes a step further, plunging into the emancipatory potential of explosive plasticity.

When I Saw You follows the story of Tarek (Mahmoud Asfa), an eleven-year-old Palestinian boy who has been forced into exile in Jordan with his mother Ghaydaa (Ruba Blal) in the wake of Israel's conquest of East Jerusalem and the West Bank in June 1967. In the confusion and chaos of war, the pair is separated from Tarek's father, and the young boy spends his days watching for new arrivals to the refugee camp, hoping to spot his missing parent among them. Tarek does not adjust well to his new surroundings; he complains about the food, gets kicked out of school despite his obvious mathematical abilities, and has trouble making friends. Fed up with refugee life, Tarek decides to simply go home. One day, in defiance of all of those in the camp (including his own mother) instructing him to wait—in Arabic, *stanna*—he sneaks away, determined to wait no more. Taking charge of his own fate, he begins walking back to Palestine.

After spending a night alone in the Jordanian desert, Tarek is discovered by Layth (Saleh Bakri), a Palestinian man who is training with a group of commandoes, the fedayeen. Initially, Tarek tries to continue his journey, but he soon becomes a temporary member of Layth's group. He trains with them, paints political posters with them, and sings songs with them around the campfire. One of the fedayeen even gives Tarek music lessons on the oud. Whereas the people in the camp had treated Tarek as just another mouth to feed, the fedayeen view him as a friend and a comrade, and they see value in him that previously went unrecognized. Desperate to find her missing son, Ghaydaa eventually discovers Tarek at the fedayeen camp, but before she can take him back to Harir, a radio broadcast announces that it has been destroyed by Israeli warplanes. They have nowhere to go.

Tarek's old feelings of suffocation gradually begin to return, and when a group of the fedayeen are dispatched on a night raid to Palestine, Tarek tries to go with them. He is sternly reprimanded by the commanding officer, Abu Akram (Ali Elayan), and ordered to stay behind. Thus, Tarek is told to wait at the fedayeen camp just as he had been told to wait at the refugee camp. Determined not to give up on his dream, Tarek leaves the company of his new friends and secretly takes off for Palestine during the night. The next day, his mother and a group of fedayeen go searching for Tarek, and they find him just as he is about to cross the border. After an Israeli patrol vehicle makes its pass, Tarek sees an opportunity, and he begins running across the frontier. Disobeying Layth's plea to wait, Ghaydaa rushes to Tarek and takes him by the hand. Instead of holding him back, however, she joins him. Together, they run toward the border, leaving Jordan and its camps of refugees and fedayeen behind. The film thus ends with a hopeful image: mother and son throwing caution to the wind and returning to Palestine hand in hand.

As this brief summary of the film indicates, *When I Saw You* is spatially divided into two camps: a camp of refugees (the fictitious Harir refugee camp) and a camp of commandoes (the fedayeen). In addition, throughout the film, another place is present but mostly through its absence: Palestine itself. The characters no longer inhabit this territory, and apart from a few distant glimpses, they are no longer even able to see it. Instead, they *imagine* it, and just as the film is spatially divided between the Harir refugee camp and the fedayeen camp, it is also temporally divided between those whose notions of return remain stuck in the past and Tarek, whose eyes are set firmly on the future.

These various elements all correspond to Malabou's three modes of plasticity. The Harir refugee camp is the traumatic place where the Palestinians receive form; it is the film's stand-in for the Nakba. The fedayeen camp, however, is the place where the Palestinians can create their own form and mold themselves; it is the site of self-identification, a space inhabited by what I am calling the forces of Intifada. Although these two spaces are different and even contradictory, they nevertheless operate on the same horizontal field, and it is Tarek who represents the ability to pierce this plane, to disrupt and disidentify with existing modes of thinking, being, and imagining. That is, Tarek does not merely receive and give form; he also annihilates it, and it is precisely through his character that *When I Saw You* moves beyond *Salt*, presenting us with the Palestinian Idea.

Salt was concerned with the ongoing catastrophe of the Nakba, and *When I Saw You* is haunted by the same traumatic specter. Indeed, it is significant that Jacir chose for the film to make its Israeli debut at the first Nakba Film Festival.[37] Organized by Zochrot, the Israeli organization dedicated to promoting awareness of the 1948 catastrophe, the festival coincidentally took place in late 2013 at a time when protests were erupting against what was then threatening to become the next manifestation of the Nakba, the Israeli government's so-called Prawer Plan, which would have displaced thousands of Bedouins from their homes in the Negev Desert. As the journalist Alex Shams noted at the time, "The culmination of the festival at a moment of national, and global, protest was a potent reminder that the threat of dispossession and exile stalks Palestinians well into the 21st century."[38]

In *When I Saw You*, the main avatar of the Nakba is the fictional Harir refugee camp. This is a place of death, a kind of Palestinian purgatory where refugees wait indefinitely for a solution that will never come. Here, old refugees from the 1948 Nakba intermingle with new refugees from the 1967 Naksa (the setback), and in their misery they become virtually indistinguishable from one another—an observation that horrifies the young Tarek. In the camp, all the good values of communal living seem to have been reversed. The children fight over their toys instead of sharing them. The teacher does not teach, and when he suspects that Tarek is illiterate, he expels him. Harir is thus a perverted place, a place where the Palestinians turn on one another and victim becomes victimizer. The camp's inhabitants seem to have suffered a symbolic death and turned into a kind of Living Dead.[39] They have accepted a helpless, passive existence for themselves—forever in limbo and waiting for the conflict to be settled by other people. Having renounced their own political power and agency, they have become an antipolitical community whose only byword is *stanna* (wait). Later in the film, the connection between the Harir camp and the Nakba is further solidified when we learn that the camp has been leveled by Israeli jets. Massacre thus follows massacre, and tragedy comes on the heels of tragedy. Within the physical and ideological boundaries of Harir, the cycle of violence and trauma appears inescapable.

Importantly, Israel alone cannot be completely blamed for the problems of the camp. At Harir, there is one single moment of levity, a wedding party filled with joyful clapping and singing. But even this scene of laughter and merriment cannot completely mask the underlying hierarchy, and the gender divisions within the crowd are conspicuous. The inhabitants of the camp are trapped, and even in their celebrations, they reproduce the problems of the past. It is therefore not only the ethno-supremacist hierarchies of Zionism that have caused Harir's perversity but also the stale divisions within Palestinian society itself, and if the camp dwellers are to ever break out of their Living Dead status, they must also rethink indigenous forms of oppression that are practiced within their own community. To use Huey Newton's terms, they must turn their reactionary suicide into a revolutionary one and attack not only the oppressor from without but also the oppressor from within.

While the Harir refugee camp represents the forces of Nakba, the group of fedayeen signifies the forces of Intifada. Their activities indicate the ability not only to passively receive form but also to actively give themselves form, and for the duration of Tarek's time amongst them, the fedayeen exhibit a willingness not only to oppose Zionism but also to challenge indigenous practices of oppression, including hierarchical divisions of class, race, gender, and age.[40] In *When I Saw You,* this is most clearly expressed through culture. The artwork that Tarek helps the fedayeen paint, for instance, includes images of liberation. This potential is also communicated through music, and—in stark contrast to the social divisions on display during the Harir wedding party—the multiracial, multigenerational, and mixed-gender group of fedayeen join together to sing "Min Sijn 'Akka" (From Acre Prison), a moving

Palestinian resistance ballad that was originally written as a funeral dirge to commemorate the public execution of three Palestinian fighters in 1930 by the British colonial authorities.[41] Rather than passively accepting their fate, the fedayeen are thus actively involved in the constitution of their own identity, and they draw imaginative constellations of protest, looking to the rebellions of the past as inspiration for the rebellions of the present.[42]

Yet however preferable the community of fedayeen is to the refugee camp, this group does not necessarily possess all of the answers. There are a number of indications that the liberation they represent is already slipping through their fingers. Indeed, when Tarek attempts to leave the fedayeen camp on the second morning, Layth issues that same injunction that Tarek had so often heard in the refugee camp: *stanna*. Here we should also recall that Tarek's training regimen with the fedayeen frequently involves a rather peculiar exercise: perpetually running in circles. Despite their optimism and bravado, the fedayeen are ultimately going nowhere, and this subtle critique is missed by the film's negative reviewers who accuse Jacir of romanticizing history.[43] In exploring the fedayeen's limits, *When I Saw You* seems to be addressing the problems of stagnation and institutionalization, and while Palestinian identity may occasionally intersect with the Palestinian Idea, they are hardly synonymous terms. If the forces of Intifada can sometimes be emancipatory, this possibility cannot be taken for granted. Indeed, just as the formulators of Zionism inadvertently replicated the ethno-essentialist, nation-state logic underlying European anti-Semitism, Palestinian practices of self-identification and resistance can likewise mirror the very forms of oppression that they claim to contest.[44]

This tendency toward slippage and decay is evident in the iconic image of the late Palestine Liberation Organization leader Yasir Arafat, and even though his likeness appears in both of these films, it is presented in radically different ways. In *Salt*, a large, framed portrait of Arafat decorates a wall in the office of the Palestinian functionary who denies Soraya's request for a passport. The film thereby associates Arafat with corruption and collusion, and by presenting his image in the form of a framed picture, it also suggests a symbolic link with another figure of oppression, David Ben-Gurion, whose portrait similarly hangs on the wall behind Soraya in the airport interrogation room. *When I Saw You*, by contrast, presents Arafat through the medium of television, and Jacir incorporates actual interview footage of Arafat explaining the goals of the Palestinian struggle. As he states in his stunted English, "We creates a new people. Instead of being refugees, to be fighters. [. . .] We were refugees, homeless. We became now fighters, freedom fighters."[45] Thus, while *Salt* presents Arafat in all of his institutionalized decay, Jacir's second film gives us an earlier version of the famous leader from a time when he was at the height of his revolutionary potential.[46]

The difference between these two, opposed views of Arafat should not be seen as a self-refuting contradiction on the part of Jacir but, rather, as a testament to the slippery, unstable relationship between identity categories and political positions. Just because a person, a people, or a place may at one time embody the values of emancipation, there are no guarantees that this gateway will remain open for long. Things easily change, and the path to emancipation can disappear just as suddenly as it had appeared. Indeed, *Salt* performs this slippage itself, and as we have already seen, the film ends up papering over the very holes in reality that it had previously opened. It is in this light that we can perhaps make sense of Jean Genet's seemingly harsh declaration regarding his support for the Palestinian cause. "The day the Palestinians become institutionalized," he said, "I will no longer be on their side. The day the Palestinians become a nation like other nations, I will no longer be there."[47]

Importantly, *When I Saw You* already hints at Arafat's downward slide, and while his televised image and assertive words appear extremely empowering in the terrible context of the Harir refugee camp, they also carry with them a certain danger. As noble as Arafat's declared intention of turning homeless refugees into a new Palestinian nation might seem, it risks falling into an unfortunately familiar trap. To be more precise, this aspiration is threatened by the same hazard that was encountered by the Jewish community with the advent of political Zionism and the establishment of the State of Israel. The Zionist project of creating the Israeli Sabra—the New Jewish Man—required the negation of exile. That is, Zionism entailed the complete abdication of the Jewish experience of *galut* (exile or diaspora). Gabriel Piterberg argues that this dismissive and even openly hostile stance toward the Jewish condition of exile has been articulated by an array of Zionist luminaries ranging from historic icons such as Theodor Herzl to more recent figures such as the novelist A. B. Yehoshua.[48] As Ben-Gurion himself once declared in a public debate, "The exile in which the Jews lived and still live—is to my mind a miserable, poor, wretched, dubious experience, and it shouldn't be a source of pride, on the contrary—it should be comprehensively negated."[49] Or, as Benjamin Netanyahu more recently bellowed in his belligerent response to a United Nations resolution condemning the continued construction of settlements in December 2016, "Enough of this exile mentality."[50]

In so forcefully rejecting *galut*, Zionism's various proponents and practitioners have effectively worked to desublimate Jewish identity. This has meant turning Jewishness into a birthright and thereby abandoning Freud's lesson about the nonexistence of the Jew. Or, to put it another way, it has meant eradicating plasticity's potential for explosion and confining Jewishness to the straitjacket of essentialist, ontologically grounded categories. As a result, the victim-victimizer relationship historically experienced between

Jews and anti-Semitism has been mistaken for a permanent, ahistorical condition, and the ever changing, unstable nature of social roles has consequently been lost.

If instead of negating *galut* we embrace it—that is, if we understand Jewishness not only as an identity but also as a way of relating to otherness and displacement—it becomes something else, a social position that can potentially be inhabited by *anybody,* even by the Palestinian.[51] This lesson has great resonance for our conception of Palestinianness and the Palestinian cause. To interpret Arafat's words in a strict, literal fashion by renouncing the Palestinian condition of exile and engaging in the project of creating a New Palestinian Man is to fall into the same quagmire as Zionism. Like the fedayeen in Jacir's film, Arafat did not possess a monopoly on revolution, and equality was not an inherent part of his identity. To capture the Palestinian struggle's emancipatory potential, one must therefore look beyond the suffocating plane of fixed identities. Instead of negating Palestinian *galut* (in Arabic, *shatat*) and installing a new, harmonious Palestinian identity in its place, one must look for a way to explode form and annihilate existing modes of thinking and being.[52]

In *When I Saw You*, this anti-identitarian dynamite is embodied by the character of Tarek. Unlike the refugees and fedayeen, Tarek is not defined by the particular coordinates of any positive, localized space, and he is not limited to either camp. Instead, he represents a disruptive, destructive force that can potentially cut through *any* space, a force that is everywhere possible but nowhere guaranteed. To the constant pleas and commands of those around him to patiently wait, Tarek's reply is uncompromising: "You're suffocating me." While Tarek is undoubtedly shaped by his circumstances, the Nakba does not have the final say, and Tarek rejects the identitarian framework that he inherits. He does not let the past determine his future, and he refuses to be confined within any predetermined limits. To recall C. L. R. James's aforementioned formula, Tarek is *in* the two camps, but he is not *of* them.[53]

While Tarek cannot be relegated and defined by any particular physical space, there is nevertheless a certain spatial dimension to his revolt. This is manifested in his insatiable will to return to Palestine. Here it is worth pausing to ask, What does return even mean? To where and to what are the Palestinians supposed to return? Does return mean going back to the past, to a place that no longer exists except as a memory? What does one do after returning? What does return mean for the land's current inhabitants? Is there a way to conceive of return so that it points not to the past but to the future?

In pondering these questions, one would do well to consider Robert Warrior's cautionary take on the Exodus story. He suggests that we look at the myth of the Promised Land with new eyes, reading it not from the perspective of the conqueror but from that of the conquered. His oppositional reading of the biblical narrative privileges the point of view of the land's indigenous inhabitants, the Canaanites, and as a Native American himself—a member of the Osage Nation—Warrior recognizes that one people's utopian dreams can all too easily turn into another people's dystopian nightmares and that one group's salvation can mean another group's ruin.[54] Warrior's reading of Exodus clearly has relevance for the contemporary era, and it calls into question the mythological justifications underlying the Zionist project of settler-colonialism.[55] But it would be a mistake to pretend that the Palestinians' current position in the social order is a permanent one, and we must be careful in how we treat the Palestinian Right of Return. Just as Zionism has proved that the Jew can slide from victim to victimizer, so, too, can today's Canaanites become tomorrow's conquerors.

It is therefore crucial to recognize that return is not as simple and straightforward as it might initially appear. Return can take many forms, and some of these can be monstrous. Indeed, there would be nothing liberating about return if it entailed the establishment of new hierarchies or the instigation of new ethnic cleansings. In *When I Saw You*, this is signified by the fact that return does not represent the same thing for all of the film's characters. Everyone in the film wants to return—the old refugees from 1948, the new refugees from 1967, and, of course, the fedayeen. But while the dream of return appears to be a universally shared aspiration, none of these characters is able to accomplish it. Return remains an elusive impossibility, forever out of reach, and while the inhabitants of the refugee camp are waiting for official channels to arrange their return, the fedayeen are waiting for a signal from their commanders to tell them that they are finally capable of matching Israel in military might. Even those fedayeen who are dispatched on a night raid to Palestine quickly return to their camp. Despite their differences, then, the refugees and the commandoes have this trait in common; both groups are stuck in Jordan, and these spatial confines correspond to ideological ones. *They cannot return because they have secretly internalized Zionism's hierarchies.* That is, Israel is not the only entity preventing their return, and by ceaselessly telling themselves and each other to wait, they are also preventing their return themselves.

Tarek, however, is unique. Along with his mother, Ghaydaa, he is the only character who is able to transform his dream of return into an actual act. While the others continually locate Palestine in the past, Tarek accomplishes the impossible. He does not forget the past, but he nevertheless locates Palestine in the here and now. Importantly, Tarek is able to do this because of the disruptive power of equality. Properly conceived, the Right of Return should flow from the Palestinian Idea and not the other way around. Any return worth pursuing must stem from a presupposition of equality—a presupposition, in fact, that the film's other characters lack. Thus, Tarek's liberation does

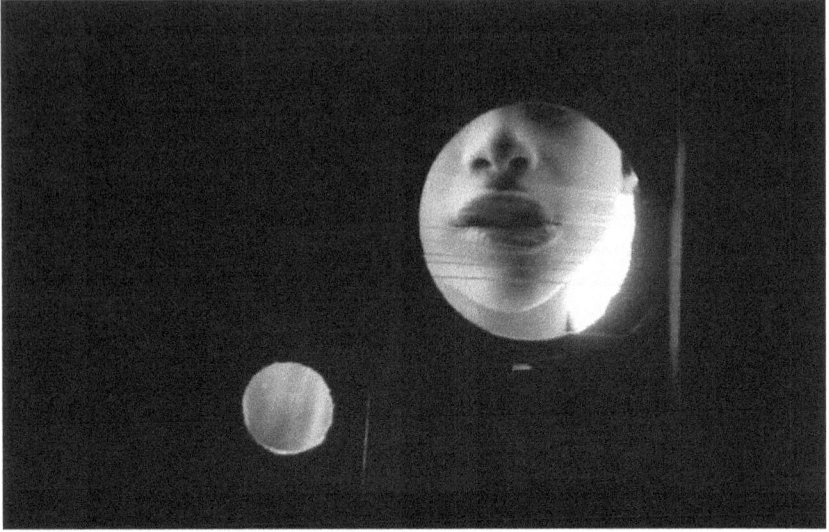

Figure 3.2. Tarek examining the hidden spaces of an oud in *When I Saw You.*

not begin with his flight toward the Israeli border at the end of the film. Rather, it begins much earlier, with his radical presupposition of equality in a social order of inequality and with his adamant refusal to accept the physical and ideological parameters governing the world around him. For Tarek, *liberation is now.*

Hence, while Tarek's revolt does indeed involve a physical, spatial return to Palestine, this is hardly the only consequence stemming from his scandalous supposition of equality amidst inequality. The Palestinian Idea is not only about reclaiming lost lands *over there*; it is also about reclaiming spaces and dimensions that already exist *over here*, the gaps and absences that are already present all around us, concealed and out of sight. In *When I Saw You*, this is signified by Tarek's penchant for discovering hitherto hidden spaces. When one of the fedayeen, Jawad (played by Jacir's real-life spouse and filmmaking partner, Ossama Bawardi), gives Tarek an impromptu musical lesson, Tarek puts his face against the opening in the body of the oud. As if to explore the otherworldly dimension of music, he curiously investigates the unseen space hidden within the wooden instrument—a space right in front of us that usually goes unnoticed (see Figure 3.2). A similar instance takes place over the campfire, and in the foreground, two of Tarek's handmade toy soldiers curiously shift from one side of the frame to the other and back. This repeated cut does not make sense until another camera angle reveals that the shots of the toys are from the perspective of Tarek, who is playfully closing one eye and opening the other. The displacement of the objects is thus a parallax, a visual illusion achieved simply by shifting one's perspective. As in Ernst Bloch's fable of the rabbi recounted in this book's preface, this parallax represents a very slight shift that nevertheless manages to change *everything*. Through Tarek's eyes, things are different.[56]

Significantly, the production of *When I Saw You* also involved the uncovering of mysterious, hidden spaces in Jordan's Dibeen Forest, and when Jacir's crew was scouting for shooting locations, they located an entire subterranean network of forgotten caves and tunnels that had previously been used by Palestinian fighters. As Jacir writes, "We discovered the most intricate tunnels connecting to each other, a whole underground world. We even found the tunnel where they built a hospital. Deep in the mountains, you enter a small hole to discover seven or eight large rooms, and inside [are] the remnants of the former hospital including medicine, bottles, IV bags, and other supplies." For Jacir, making this discovery was like stumbling on a "lost world."[57] Like equality itself, these various forgotten spaces lie hidden in plain sight, present even in their absence.

Of course, equality is not the only thing hiding in the cracks and crevices of the present. There are also monsters in the dark, and revolutionary transformation is not inevitable. In Kanafani's words, "The danger in a time of defeat is that it contains within itself the simultaneous potential for both construction and demolition."[58] On this point, it would again be useful to draw a comparison between Jacir's cinema and Kanafani's fiction, and if *Salt* bore a resemblance to "Returning to Haifa," *When I Saw You* shares features with Kanafani's novella *Men in the Sun*.[59] In Kanafani's tragic tale, three Palestinian refugees—an adolescent, a grown man, and an elder—are living in exilic destitution in Iraq. Each of them has come to Basra in search of work. Lured by the prospect of finding employment in Kuwait, they are each trying to smuggle themselves across the Iraqi frontier. For a fee, a Palestinian lorry driver agrees to conceal them in his vehicle's cavernous water tank as he crosses the checkpoints into neighboring Kuwait. In the film version of the story, *The Dupes*, the space in which these three men hide is depicted as a dark and menacing chasm. The hatch leading into this space appears on-screen as a gateway into a terrifying unknown, an opening into a mysterious, black void that encompasses almost the entire film frame.

While Tarek's discovery of hidden spaces indicates the transformative potential of explosive plasticity, the three protagonists of *Men in the Sun* are not so fortunate. Whereas Tarek is determined to go west, Kanafani's characters are heading east—that is, they are going in the wrong direction, not toward Palestine but away from it. This movement on the map corresponds to a symbolic loss, and before climbing into the truck's empty cavity, the men first remove several layers of their clothing to withstand the suffocating heat. It is as if they are stripping off layers of their very identity.[60] This loss signifies not emancipation but death and decay, and they are committing not revolutionary suicide but reactionary suicide. Accordingly, when the driver takes longer than he had anticipated at one of the desert checkpoints, he returns to his vehicle, only to discover that all three of his passengers are dead, killed by the scorching heat. His truck has become their coffin, and he tosses their corpses into a garbage heap.[61]

If these three refugees entered the void only to perish, Tarek emerges to see the light of day. The experiences of exile and diaspora and the condition of Palestinian *galut/shatat* have not destroyed him. Instead, they have revealed the presence of something within him that is indestructible—the explosive, plastic potential of equality.[62] As a disruptive negation, equality is something that can never be fully stamped out, and if *Men in the Sun* presents us with a warning about the dangers of the abyss, *When I Saw You* looks into the darkness and finds neither nihilism nor death but salvation itself. Return may currently be impossible, the film seems to be saying, but that is no reason to give up hope. Like Tarek, one should dare to *demand the impossible* and work to transform reality. One should challenge the very coordinates of the present so that what is impossible today can become possible tomorrow.

Importantly, Tarek's liberation is quite different from that of Soraya. The protagonist of *Salt* remained trapped within the horizontal plane of identity, and her personal, subjective liberation had no counterpart in the objective situation. By the end of the film, Soraya might have attained more confidence with respect to her own identity, but the hegemony of Israel remains intact. Zionism has no cracks. The ending of *When I Saw You*, on the other hand, is noticeably different. Throughout the film, Tarek's mathematical skills are frequently demonstrated, and when he approaches the Israeli-controlled border, he uses this flair for numbers to count the time intervals separating the Israeli patrol vehicles' periodic sweeps. That is, he uses math to locate the holes and gaps in the Israeli security forces. In *Salt*, Zionist hegemony appears complete, but this picture is not so certain in *When I Saw You*. Israel's power may be formidable, but it is not invincible. Like any other structure, it is fraught with fissures and perforated by cracks, and while *Salt*'s ending is closed, *When I Saw You*'s is radically open.

To be clear, even though Jacir's second feature is set in the 1960s in the crucial years immediately preceding Black September, it is not just a story about the past. It is a story about the present, and each of the film's communities has its contemporary representatives. Just like the refugees at the Harir camp, there are people today who have consigned themselves to a fate of passivity and handed their agency over to others. They are the Living Dead of the contemporary moment. There are also those who, like the fedayeen, have chosen to fight back, only to inadvertently replicate the identitarian logic that they claim to contest. But we would be remiss to stop here, and Tarek has his descendants, as well. While Tarek may be the film's major representative of the Palestinian Idea, he would hardly be alone in the landscape of the present. To take just one example, let us return to March 2013, when a group of Palestinian youth decorated themselves in the iconography of the Black Freedom Movement and desegregated Hebron's downtown streets. Like Tarek, these dreamers were piercing a hole through existing modes of thinking, being, and imagining. For them, equality was not a demand but a starting point, and if anyone else in the Hebron community had counseled them to wait, these youths refused. Like Tarek, they were determined to wait no more. For a few fleeting moments, they were not merely communicating a utopian dream for the future; they were demonstrating the existence of that utopian dream in the present. Like Tarek, they were exploring hitherto hidden spaces, casting shadows on the lights of colonialism, and exploding the coordinates of their inherited framework. Not content with their assigned ideological, cultural, and spatial place in the prevailing social order, they disrupted it by moving from a politics of identity to a politics of disidentity. It is through such figures that we continue to get a glimpse of the Palestinian Idea.

4

Hollow Time

Time is on the side of the oppressed.
—**MALCOLM X,** *Malcolm X Speaks*

Natives do not adhere to settler timelines.
—**STEVEN SALAITA,** *Inter/Nationalism*

Tomorrow is now.
—**AMAL AMIREH,** "Activists, Lobbyists, and Suicide Bombers"

I

Midway through Mais Darwazah's poetic 2013 documentary *My Love Awaits Me by the Sea,* one of the film's Palestinian interlocutors puts forward a rather startling thesis and declares that Israel's days are already at an end: "The Zionist project is over. It's a bankrupt vision. It has no future." Sitting casually in a garden and rocking a crying baby on her lap, Darwazah's interviewee speaks her mind quite frankly, and her opinion comes across not as a militant battle cry but rather as a matter-of-fact description of reality. "I know very soon people aren't going to want to be Zionist anymore," she continues. "It's an outdated mode of thinking."

When *My Love Awaits Me by the Sea* played at the London Palestine Film Festival in 2014, it was greeted by a mostly sympathetic audience. However, in a discussion with the director that followed, one spectator in the crowd voiced frustration with this scene in particular, claiming that such a bold pronouncement regarding Israel's future was entirely premature and unrealistic. He wanted to know how anyone could honestly agree with such an assertion, especially when the memory of Israel's latest round of atrocities in Gaza was still so fresh and when Israel's displays of power and brute force appeared as strong as ever. Bristling against these remarks, Darwazah took the side of her film's interviewee. Even if Israel continues to occupy Palestine for many years to come, she argued, it nevertheless still lacks a future. In her view, Zionism is an entirely closed ideology, an ideology bereft of any path out of the present. Accordingly, whereas Ernst Bloch might have once declared that "the tomorrow in today is alive," Darwazah asserted the opposite. For her—at least with regard to Zionism—the tomorrow in today is not alive but dead.[1]

From these comments, it was clear to me that the audience member and the film's Palestinian director were speaking past each other. Although they were using the same language and uttering the same words, their intended meaning was quite different. While the former conceptualized time in a Newtonian fashion as an objective, linear process, the latter treated it in a subjective way—as a task, a project, or even a vision. We might say, then, that this exchange was an example of disagreement in the Rancierian sense of the term: not a conflict between two people who say two different things but a conflict between two people who say the same thing ("the future") but understand something entirely different by it.[2] This brief altercation between a skeptical audience member, on the one hand, and an adamant filmmaker, on the other, was therefore not just an encounter between two competing opinions. Even more, it was an encounter between two temporal modalities—a clash between two incompatible constructions of time.

Critical discussions on Zionism often focus on the Israeli colonization of space. Under successive Israeli regimes, the Palestinian landscape has undergone continuous spatial change—from the annexation of lands and the bulldozing of homes to the erection of checkpoints and the construction of walls. Importantly, the sheer breadth of this "spacio-cide" cannot be fully represented by lines on a two-dimensional map.[3] On this point, one may recall the case of downtown Hebron, where Jewish settlers have taken over the floors of Palestinian buildings—apartments from which they frequently throw trash, acid, and human excrement onto the Palestinian marketplace below them. In Palestine, colonization is not only horizontal; it is vertical, and Israeli and Palestinian jurisdictions are often separated level by level, layer by layer. These overlapping geographies even correspond to overlapping mediaspheres, and in the West Bank, one can connect to several competing Israeli mobile networks just as easily as one can pick up a signal from the two Palestinian mobile companies, Jawwal and Wataniya.[4] Zionist colonization has thus transformed Palestine into what Eyal Weizman calls a "hollow land"—an elastic, ever shifting geography in which multiple territories inhabit the same territory and multiple spaces inhabit the same space.[5]

But space is not the only thing that can be colonized. Just as the land of Palestine is composed of multiple, overlapping geographies, the time of Palestine likewise consists of contradicting yet coexisting clocks. Time is not only an objective, linear process that continues marching on regardless of any changes in the human world around it. It is also subjective; it is something we continuously construct and experience—for ourselves and for others. Time can be slowed down, sped up, or even made to stand still. It can be focused on the past, stuck in the present, or pointed toward the future. Like space, time is curved. Or, to put it another way, in Palestine time is hollow.

Just as the Palestinian Idea serves to annihilate our notion of identity, this scandalous presupposition of equality amidst inequality has the capacity to explode our understanding of time, and while Israel has colonized Palestinian time in multiple ways, it has been unable to completely stamp out all of the traces of tomorrow inhabiting the interstices of today. Time is hollow, and it can therefore also be bent in directions that run against the grain of Zionism. Like space, time can be insubordinate, and if some modes of time are susceptible to colonization, there are other modes that resist it. Drawing on the work of thinkers such as C. L. R. James and Ernst Bloch, I argue that reality has a utopian edge and that the Palestinian future is already here, buried within the suffocating universe of the Zionist present. Whereas the previous two chapters concentrated on fiction, I now turn to documentary and argue that documentary cinema can play a role in constructing this quasi-mystical aspect of time. Indeed, a fidelity to this subjective, future-oriented notion of time—a Palestine Time that the Zionist clocks simply cannot capture—is precisely what separated Mais Darwazah from her inquisitor that November night in London. Moreover, it is this temporal aspect of the Palestinian Idea, this ghost from the Palestinian future, that also haunts her film *My Love Awaits Me by the Sea*.

II

This Palestinian moment [. . .] feels like an eternity.
—**Elias Khoury**, "Remembering Ghassan Kanafani"

From its inception, Zionist discourse has been thoroughly enmeshed in colonialist conceptions of time. For the early Zionists, the Jews were not only a people without a land; they were also *a people without a time*. Or, more precisely, they were a people *outside* of time. As a scattered diaspora, the Jews were imagined to be standing outside the triumphant continuum of history, and by establishing a Jewish nation-state, the Zionists believed that they would once again take their rightful place on the world stage. That is, with the founding of Israel, *the Jews would return to time itself*. Gabriel Piterberg argues that this belief in the return to history (in Hebrew, *ha-shiva la-historia*) constitutes one of the foundational myths of Zionism. "So long as they were exiles," he writes, "the Jews remained a community outside history, within which all European nations dwelt. [. . .] The return of the Jewish nation to the land of Israel, overcoming its docile passivity in exile, could alone allow it to rejoin the history of civilized peoples."[6]

For Zionists, this historical homecoming meant becoming modern, progressive, and civilized. Early Zionist literature is littered with such language. Indeed, in *The Jewish State* Theodor Herzl declared his intention for the Jewish nation to become "the most modern in the world."[7] Here we come to yet another example of how the Zionist uplifting of the Jews necessitated the beating down of Palestine's indigenous people. Just as the Jews' possession of the land required the Palestinians' dispossession, and just as the affirmation of the former's national identity entailed the denigration of the latter's, the celebration of Israel's modernity involved a denunciation of Palestine's backwardness. If the Zionists would not share space or status with the Palestinians, neither would they share time; while Israel was to be part of the vibrant present, the Palestinians were to remain stuck in the parochial past.[8]

Zionist discourse thus projects the Palestinians into static antiquity. Conceived as such, the Palestinians come to resemble not people but ancient objects. As Chaim Weizmann, Israel's first president, said vis-à-vis the Palestinians, they were "the rocks of Judea," "obstacles that had to be cleared on a difficult path."[9] This way of treating the Palestinians has not been limited to the rhetoric of political leaders. It has also appeared in some key Israeli anthropological works, a trait identified and critiqued by Talal Asad, among others.[10] Such discourse constitutes the first of three ways that Palestinian time is colonized. Of course, such a partisan parceling out of time is not unique to Zionism. Johannes Fabian argues that this allochronic approach to temporality is common to European colonialism. Colonialist discourse denies a temporal coexistence between the European Self and the non-European Other. This imagined distance in time is established through language, and colonized subjects are denigrated with derogatory adjectives—"traditional," "tribal," and "primitive." While these terms are treated as objective, scientific categories, they are actually dripping with prejudice.[11]

But the Zionist colonization of Palestinian time is not limited to discourse. It also entails real, concrete actions by the Israeli state. That is, the colonization of Palestinian time is not only imagined; it is also rigorously enforced. To put it simply, *Israel slows down Palestinian time*—or, as Julie Peteet argues, Israel *steals* it.[12] This is the second form that Zionism's temporal colonization takes, and as a direct result of the numerous barriers, walls, checkpoints, and various other security measures imposed by Israel, Palestinians experience time differently. Theirs is an existence defined by long queues, segregated roads, and greatly impeded movement. It is an existence defined by *waiting*, and any visitor to the West Bank will immediately notice how much the slowness and frustration experienced there contrasts with the speed and efficiency of Tel Aviv, a difference that reinforces imagined allochronic distinctions between Israeli forwardness and Palestinian backwardness.

But if these first two forms of temporal colonization refer to Zionist discourse and Israeli actions, there is a third form that involves the minds of the Palestinians themselves—a feeling of being trapped in time, unable to progress beyond the ravages of the Nakba. Notably, even though the Nakba will forever be associated with 1948, it neither began nor ended during that calendar year. Indeed, some observers such as Joseph Massad see the Nakba as beginning in the nineteenth century with the arrival of the first Zionist settlers in Palestine and continuing into the present with every new act of dispossession and occupation. "Much as the world would like to present Palestinians as living in a post-Nakba period," Massad claims, "I insist that we live thoroughly in Nakba times."[13]

Under such a conception, the Nakba is not so much an event as it is *an ongoing catastrophe*—a perpetual purgatory or perhaps an eternal hell. To the degree that the Palestinians experience the Nakba in this fashion, it represents a modality of time, a disaster without end. As Elias Sanbar suggests, it was as if the clock stopped with the onset of the Nakba, and since that moment, the Palestinians have been unable to move forward, stuck in a seemingly infinite loop of tragedy and despair. "By departing from space," he writes, "the Palestinians [. . .] also departed from time. Their history and their past were denied. Their aspirations and their future were forbidden."[14] For the Palestinians, then, it is as if *time has stopped,* and the Nakba appears as a present and permanent condition. This is what I am calling Nakba Time.

Significantly, Nakba Time corresponds to similar psychic conditions experienced by other aggrieved communities that have undergone trauma.[15] Frank Wilderson, for instance, sees such a temporal dynamic at work with respect to Black Americans. He argues that for the African slaves and their descendants, time froze in the Middle Passage.[16] Moreover, as we have already seen, Zionist discourse likewise presents *galut*—the Jewish experience of exile—as an existence outside the continuum of time. Thus, while for the Zionists 1948 represented the moment when the Jews returned to history, for the Palestinians, the opposite was true: it represented not a return but an expulsion, not only from the land, but also from time itself.

All three of these forms of temporal colonization have their cinematic counterparts. Ella Shohat has identified certain early Israeli films such as *Hill 24 Doesn't Answer* (dir. Thorold Dickinson, 1955) as belonging to a heroic-Zionist genre that glorified the image of the Israeli Sabra by juxtaposing it against the backwardness and savagery of the Arabs.[17] Many Palestinian films, however, have focused their attention on the second mode of temporal colonization: the Israeli theft of Palestinian time. They include fictional features such as *Ticket to Jerusalem* (dir. Rashid Masharawi, 2002) and *Rana's Wedding* (dir. Hany Abu-Assad, 2002), as well as documentaries such as *Crossing Kalandia* (dir. Sobi al-Zobaidi, 2003).[18]

But the third form of temporal colonization, Nakba Time, has also found its way onto cinema screens, and many Palestinian filmmakers have constructed characters and communities that seem to exist in a sort of static timelessness. Michel Khleifi's landmark *Wedding in Galilee* (1987), for instance, provides contradicting details regarding the time in which the film is set. While the Israeli uniforms and vehicles appear to be from the 1980s, the legal framework of the film refers to the 1950s and 1960s, a period in which the Palestinians of the Galilee were living under Israeli martial law. Further adding to the film's sense of timelessness is the mukhtar's senile father who repeatedly talks about Palestine's previous oppressors, the Ottomans and the British. In *Wedding in Galilee*, it seems that the past is not yet past.[19]

This distorted temporality is even more explicit in *Villa Touma* (2014), Suha Arraf's film about four Palestinian women living an isolated, aristocratic existence in Ramallah, cut off from the world around them. For the first half of the film, we are led to believe that they are living in the 1960s, but as the film progresses, we learn that it is actually set in the early 2000s, around the time of the Second Intifada.[20] Other examples of timelessness include the documentary films of Raed Andoni—*Fix ME* (2010) and *Ghost Hunting* (2017)—in which the filmmaker obsessively focuses on his inability to move beyond his own trauma. This is especially true for *Ghost Hunting*, which shows Andoni enlisting the help of several other Palestinian former prisoners to re-create the conditions in which they were tortured. For them, it is as if time has stopped, and while their bodies may have left the Israeli prison, their souls and spirits are still languishing there.

But the Palestinian director who has perhaps most famously dealt with Nakba Time is Elia Suleiman, and his films, with their long, awkward silences and their constant scenes of repetition, represent what Kamran Rastegar, following Jean-Luc Godard and Dante, calls *purgatorio*.[21] As Rastegar point out, this temporal distortion can be glimpsed throughout *The Time That Remains* (2009)—for instance, in the multiple shots of the protagonist's mother sipping coffee on her balcony with a view of Nazareth in the background. As the decades pass, her character ages, but the setting remains unchanged. In Suleiman's cinema, the Palestinians are stuck in *purgatorio*. The calendar no longer says 1948, but it might as well.[22]

While the Zionist colonization of time can appear all-encompassing, it would be a mistake to give it more power than it actually has. Indeed, if we limit our conception of time to just these three forms, we would be blinding ourselves to a temporal mode that resists colonization: *the future*. To be sure, not all forms of future-gazing should be weighed equally. A better tomorrow cannot be conjured into existence through magical thinking, and it is for this reason that utopian dreaming has often been derided and dismissed as a flight from reality. "Pure wishful thinking," as Bloch put it, "has discredited utopias for centuries."[23] But perhaps there is another way to conceive of the utopian future—not as a far-flung prospect that will never come but as something that is actually grounded in reality all around us, as something that already exists in the here and now.[24]

Such a utopian conception of the future is common to a variety of thinkers associated with the Black Radical Tradition. Just as we initially drew from this wellspring of insurgent thought in developing our notion of the Palestinian Idea, we can also use this resource in our interrogation of time. Indeed, "the future in the present" is a phrase found in the oeuvre of C. L. R. James.[25] Unlike many other radicals of his time, James was convinced of the power of the everyday. He conceived of utopia not as something that must be created out of thin air but as something that already exists, even if in submerged form. For him, the time of the future was *now*. In *Facing Reality*, a short book he wrote with Grace Lee Boggs (then Grace Lee) and Cornelius Castoriadis in 1958, James argued that forms of socialism could already be found in the daily interactions taking place on the factory floor. Accordingly, the point of political action and revolutionary struggle was not to create something out of nothing but to bring these submerged tendencies out into the open: "Social upheavals bring out what already exists in society, even though only in embryonic form, or as aspiration. But they exist."[26] Unlike many other Marxists and radical agitators, James insisted that socialism was not just a future prospect but a present reality that merely had to be discovered. In his audacious words, "Socialist society exists."[27]

While James was undoubtedly a materialist thinker, his particular brand of materialism nevertheless contained a utopian core. For him, socialism already existed within the heart of capitalism, racial harmony within disharmony, the future within the present. James's position thus contained a quasi-mystical aspect, and he urged his readers to see two realities within the same reality and two times within the same time. Indeed, Fred Moten has gone as far as to liken James's position to that of the prophet—that is, "the one who tells the brutal truth, who has the capacity to see the absolute brutality of the already-existing and to point it out and to tell that truth, but also *to see the other way, to see what it could be*."[28]

Significantly, traces of James's utopian materialism can be detected in Cedric Robinson's thought. While Robinson's writings on the Black Radical Tradition seem preoccupied with history, I would argue that his vision was animated by a passion for the future. By shedding light on the fugitive moments of the past, Robinson endeavored to outline traces of tomorrow. This dimension of his work is most apparent at those moments when he dips into mysticism, identifying those men and women throughout history who fought and died for freedom as "divine agents" and even arguing that Black churches might eventually give birth to a "social movement [that] will obtain that distant land, perhaps even transporting America with it."[29] For Robinson, the Black radical past was not just a stale history lesson; it was a window into another world, a hidden world that already exists, a world in which alternative ways of thinking, being, and imagining are already taking shape. In Robinson's hands, the Black radical past was thus transformed into a window into the Black radical future.[30]

Black radicalism, however, is not the only domain in which the future is located within the present. Such a utopian materialism also characterizes the work of Bloch and Walter Benjamin.[31] Indeed, for Bloch—a philosopher whom Theodor Adorno once credited with "restoring honor to the word 'utopia'"—history was filled with traces of tomorrow.[32] Bloch built his entire philosophical enterprise around this basic assumption. In his view, fragments of the future could be discerned all around us as anticipations of that which is still "Not-Yet-Conscious." Bloch had little patience for those forms of thought that remained focused on the past as past, and he even attacked psychoanalysis on these grounds, arguing that *there is nothing new in the Freudian unconscious.*"[33] Thus, while other thinkers have concerned themselves with discovering how the past shapes the future, Bloch started from the presupposition that the future is already embedded in the past. Like James, Bloch claimed that "the Now itself still contains *unopened* future" and that it was therefore our duty to try to uncover it.[34] For Bloch, such a view of utopia was not just wishful thinking. On the contrary, he warned that if our assessment of reality did not take the future into account, it would, in fact, be incomplete. In his words, "Reality without real possibility is not complete, [and] the world without future-laden properties does not deserve a glance."[35] Accordingly, for Bloch, the future was actually commonplace. Every mundane moment was a potentially magical one, and the ordinary was potentially extraordinary. Or, as Benjamin famously put it in the last line of his "Theses on the Philosophy of History": "Every second of time was the strait gate through which the Messiah might enter."[36]

Such an open future, I argue, is also alive in Palestine. Indeed, it is precisely this Messianic Time—or, better yet, this *Palestine Time*—that manages to resist Zionist colonization. While Israel's apologists and politicians may project the Palestinians into the past through both word and deed, and while the ongoing trauma of the Nakba may seem to propel the Palestinians into the psychological limbo of Nakba Time, there nevertheless remains a temporal dimension beyond Zionism's reach, a future within the present that continues to animate the Palestinian struggle. In short, *colonialist constructions of time are not the only constructions of time*, and each moment that Zionism fails, each instance in which the specter of Palestinian liberation manages to seep through the governing order's cracks, we see traces of this Palestine Time already in the here and now.

III

Such a notion of time complicates our understanding of the place and purpose of Palestinian cinema. To be sure, in the hyperpolitical and violent context of Palestine, filmmakers carry an enormous burden. How does one represent Palestine faithfully, responsibly, and authentically in a global media
environment that has so long neglected and excluded Palestinian voices? How
does one account for the future in an environment that seems to be completely overwhelmed by the exhausting confines of the present? For many
observers, then, Palestinian filmmakers have a duty, first and foremost, to use
cinema as a medium to communicate and explicate the nature of the Palestinians' oppression, including the colonization of Palestinian time. Palestinian
films are thus often praised (or condemned) with regard to how accurately (or
inaccurately) they are perceived as capturing the reality of the occupation. As
a Palestinian refugee in Lebanon plainly put it to the Syrian documentarian
Mohammad Malas, "We want your film to show and talk about how oppressed we are."[37] Indeed, on a number of occasions, I have attended screenings in which audience members expressed frustration with films for not
satisfactorily demonstrating the direness and severity of the Palestinians'
situation.

For these critics, it would seem that Palestinian films are sufficiently political only insofar as they are filled with images of falling bombs and dying
bodies. While there is obviously a need to refute the propaganda that would
otherwise deny Palestinian suffering, the belief that cinema should serve
only—or, at least, primarily—to document pain and oppression seems to
imply that Palestinian speech is worthy of our attention only insofar as it
takes the form of a bloodcurdling scream. Hamid Dabashi actually praises
this aspect of Palestinian cinema, labeling it "traumatic realism"—a term that
we might also extend to other media beyond film.[38] Indeed, even Palestinian
video games often restage real-life episodes from the history of the conflict,
and while these games may allow players to fight against Israeli soldiers, they
nevertheless remain fixated on the occupation in such a way as to foreclose
the possibility of thinking beyond it.[39] They remain "preoccupied by the occupation," to borrow Ghassan Hage's turn of phrase.[40]

Palestinian fiction thus often plays a documentary role and concerns itself
first and foremost with the painful parameters of the Zionist present. Here
one might be reminded of the realistic mode of fictional-film making that
became popular among politically conscious European directors in the 1960s
and 1970s. Joan Mellen gave a name to this genre, calling it the "fictional
documentary," and it encompassed such films as *The Battle of Algiers* (dir.
Gillo Pontecorvo, 1966), *Vladimir et Rosa* (dir. Groupe Dziga Vertov, 1971),
and *Z* (dir. Costa-Gavras, 1979). In her words, those making such films as-

sumed that there was truth in fiction and that "through fictionalizing history, we reexperience it more authentically."⁴¹ Many Palestinian features seem to embody this ethic, and insofar as they serve to communicate and explicate the nature of Israel's oppressive occupation, these films resemble yet another wave of the fictional documentary genre.

If Palestinian fictional film derives its strength from its "traumatic realism"—that is, from its ability to illuminate the colonialist horrors of the Zionist present, including the colonization of time—what, then, is the role of Palestinian documentary? To be sure, documentary has long been the dominant form of Palestinian filmmaking, from the early documentaries of the pre-1948 period to the largely lost newsreels of the militant 1970s. Like fiction, Palestinian documentary seems to have an obsession with oppression, and today, there is no shortage of documentaries seeking to educate audiences about Israel's ongoing colonialist crimes. According to this didactic view of documentary, film is a medium with the power to fill the empirical gaps in global narratives about Palestine. That is, if Zionist discourse has prevented people from seeing the present reality of Palestinian pain and suffering, documentary can act to remedy this cruel omission, and it is hoped that, by countering Zionism at the level of fact, such films can persuade antagonistic audience members to rethink their political position and perhaps even to join the Palestinian cause. As implied by the title of the film *Occupation 101* (dir. Abdallah Omeish and Sufyan Omeish, 2006), documentary is meant to provide audiences with a basic crash course regarding the names and dates and facts and figures of the occupation.

Take, for example, those activist documentaries dealing with the West Bank's growing population of Jewish settlers. This violent rabble regularly engages in such deeds as the occupation of Palestinian land, the theft of Palestinian drinking water, the poisoning of Palestinian livestock, and the so-called price tag attacks that involve vandalism and the painting of anti-Arab graffiti on Palestinian homes and places of worship—all often under the protection of the Israel Defense Forces. The documentarian with an eye for social justice may feel compelled to expose these acts and thereby penetrate the shroud of secrecy that shields the settlers' actions from greater public scrutiny. Indeed, this aspiration seems to be the main impetus driving the production of films such as *Encounter Point* (dir. Ronit Avni and Julia Bacha, 2006), *5 Broken Cameras* (dir. Emad Burnat and Guy Davidi, 2011), and *Thank God It's Friday* (dir. Jan Beddegenoodts, 2013), and these documentaries fight Zionist narratives through a process of demystification, exposing audiences to new empirical information.

Merely becoming aware of the facts, however, does not inevitably bring about any particular political change. Awareness does not dictate interpretation, and merely learning more information about the settlers' actions does not necessarily entail a rejection of them. Indeed, who could possibly know more about the settlers' violent activities than the settlers themselves? Yet in their case, knowledge of these actions does not usually result in an ideological about-face whereby the settlers come to question their own behavior and adopt a critical stance toward their own colonialist practices.[42] Instead of decrying these deeds as clear-cut instances of criminality, they justify them as holy and righteous acts.[43]

In recent years, this indeterminacy of the facts has become especially important to grasp as Zionist discourse seems to be entering something of a post-factual era. While Zionists were once content to contest Palestinian claims at the level of facts ("The Nakba did not happen!"), today their discourse is growing ever more slippery, operating less at the level of knowledge than at the level of belief ("Yes, the Nakba happened, and we might have to carry it out again!"). That is to say, when it comes to empirical facts, the gulf between pro-Palestinian and pro-Israeli narratives is becoming easier to bridge, and it is even possible to imagine a scenario in the not-too-distant future in which there is no division between them at all. This strange factual alignment between the two warring camps functions like a perverse mirror. The work of Palestinian historians to document the Nakba is strangely echoed in the writings of neo-Zionists such as Benny Morris and Ari Shavit, who admit the historicity of the Nakba but justify it as a necessary act; the attempts by the Israeli nonprofit organization Zochrot to bring the names of Palestine's depopulated villages to greater public consciousness are reflected in the rhetoric of far-right Jewish settlers who demand that liberal Zionists stop denying the massacres that brought about the establishment of the State of Israel; and efforts by a new generation of social media activists to expose the occupation's crimes meet their match in an Israeli public that is increasingly greeting the revelation via social media of new compromising photos of soldiers engaging in torture and brutality not as a scandal to keep secret but as something to shamelessly celebrate.[44] Clearly, the facts do not speak for themselves, and even the most seemingly subversive bits of information can be appropriated, their counterhegemonic force tamed and brought to heel. To recall the words of Herbert Marcuse, facts can be "quickly digested by the status quo as part of its healthy diet."[45] The Israeli occupation is not made of snow; exposing it to the light will not necessarily melt it away.

What does this mean for documentary cinema? Has this medium for truth telling lost its political edge in this brave, new, and increasingly post-factual universe? Empirical revelation, to be sure, is not the only arrow in the documentarian's quiver, and as important as it may be to uncover Israel's concealed crimes, at a certain point, one must stop squabbling over statistics and take the fight underground. The facts do not constitute the only battlefield upon which the Palestinian struggle is being waged. There are other realities and other times, and documentary cinema can also be used as a medium to explore these other worlds. Documentary need not be caged by hegemonic (i.e., Zionist) constructions of reality, including hegemonic constructions of time. In contrast to those who praise Palestinian cinema for its "traumatic realism," I would instead insist on celebrating its "utopian realism"—that is, its capacity not for elucidating the facts of the existing order but, rather, for exploring all of the holes and gaps, its ability to take us into the abyss, into the darkness of the lived moment, or the *tohu wa-bohu*, that we are otherwise trained not to see. In Palestine, documentary has the power to investigate not only the Zionist present but also the Palestinian future.

IV

The ocean of possibility is much greater than our customary land of reality.
—**ERNST BLOCH,** *The Utopian Function of Art and Literature*

The sea will take its revenge.
—**JACQUES RANCIÈRE,** *On the Shores of Politics*

We're even greedy in our dreams.
—**PALESTINIAN RESIDENT OF JERUSALEM,** *My Love Awaits Me by the Sea*

An example of such cinematic future gazing presents itself in the documentary *My Love Awaits Me by the Sea*. The second full-length film by Jordan-based Palestinian documentarian Mais Darwazah, *My Love* is inspired by the real-life tale of Hassan Hourani, a Palestinian artist and children's storybook author from Hebron who spent years dreaming about the sea, only to visit it and drown.[46] Hourani's presence in Darwazah's film is faint; he appears only through his drawings, a few excerpts from his writings, and a single photograph. Rather than being some sort of biographic documentary about his life, however, *My Love* turns Hourani's longing for the sea into a metaphor—a metaphor for hope. Just as Hourani traveled from the West Bank to Jaffa in search of the sea, Darwazah journeys from the Jordanian desert to the Mediterranean in search of Palestinian dreams, and just as Hourani achieved his fantasy only long enough to succumb to the waves and drown, Palestinian dreams are also laden with danger.

Notably, Darwazah is not the first filmmaker to focus on such an elusive subject as Palestinian dreams. In 1980–1981, the Syrian documentarian Mohammad Malas interviewed refugees dwelling in the Palestinian camps of war-torn Lebanon and asked them to recount the dreams that came to them in their sleep. During this time, he met 230 people and heard more than 300 dreams. Malas finished shooting footage for this film, which was eventually released as *The Dream* (1987), one year before the Sabra and Shatila massacre of 1982, and many of his interviewees were presumably killed, if not by the Phalange's butchery, then in the brutal War of the Camps that soon ensued. Without even realizing it, Malas was filming ghosts. The dreams they recount can be divided roughly into two categories: those about the past and those about the future. While the former are invariably nightmares about the Nakba, the latter involve fantasies about returning to Palestine. Notably, these dreams also include occasional appearances by famous Arab leaders—people such as Yasir Arafat, Camille Chamoun, and Gamal Abdel Nasser. Sometimes these luminaries appear in the dreams dressed in the same clothes worn by the dreamers, and they interact with the people of the camps as if there were no differences between them. The refugees' dreams are thus sometimes infused with equality itself.[47]

But while Malas's film is concerned with those dreams that haunt Palestinians at night, Darwazah is interested in those dreams that linger throughout the day.[48] *My Love* thus jettisons the types of questions that are usually associated with documentaries about Palestine. Darwazah does not seem interested in investigating the nature of Israel's settler-colonialist regime, and her film makes no attempt to provide viewers with any sort of "Occupation 101." Instead, it asks, what is the nature of Palestinian dreams, and how do Palestinians continue to dream while they are still inhabiting the living nightmare of the Zionist present? Thus, even if it begins with a ghost from the past—the ghost of Hassan Hourani—*My Love* is even more strongly haunted by the presence of an altogether different kind of phantom: the ghost of the Palestinian future.[49]

Of course, the sea is not universally regarded as a symbol of hope. Just as the sea can be romanticized as a place of emancipation and liberation, it can just as easily be understood as a site of suffering and death. The same waters that freed the Israelites drowned the pharaoh's army, after all, and as Christina Sharpe and other writers contemplating the Atlantic slave trade have argued, the ocean is a site of genocide, a tomb.[50] This grim historical reality continues into the present with the harrowing journey of those contemporary refugees and asylum seekers attempting to cross the Mediterranean. In Palestine, too, the sea is not free from oppression. Israel's occupation extends even there, a reality experienced daily by Gaza's constrained fishermen. Palestinian cinema has also tapped into this darker image of the sea. *Return to Haifa* (dir. Kassem Hawal, 1981) begins with a re-creation of Palestinians from that city being pushed into the sea, and Annemarie Jacir's *Salt of This Sea* (2008) similarly presents the sea as a place of death. Like Hourani, *Salt's*

leading protagonist almost succumbs to the waves. For Jacir, the sea symbolizes oppression and exile, and it is utterly bereft of hope.

Despite the cruel realities of the sea, there are other people who have
nevertheless chosen to treat it in a much more positive fashion. Under this
conception, the sea serves a clear purpose: it is a mental placeholder for liberation at a time when liberation seems so impossibly distant. For these
dreamers, the sea represents a fluid, ever changing space where new possibilities lie just beneath the surface, barely concealed and ready to emerge into
plain sight at any moment. Such an example of how the sea can be mobilized
as a metaphor for hope presents itself in the work of Ala'a Albaba, a Palestinian artist from Ramallah's al-Am'ari refugee camp. I spent ten days on the
Jenin Freedom Bus with Albaba in March 2015, and in each Palestinian city
and village that we visited—from Jericho to Bil'in and from Nabi Saleh to
Umm al-Khair—Albaba painted large, colorful murals featuring his proposed new icon for the Palestinian refugee: the fish. For Albaba, the fish is a
symbol ripe with potential. Having been denied access to their sea, the Palestinians in the West Bank are like fish out of water. Moreover, the fish is a
creature that moves freely throughout its aquatic environment, and for Albaba, the sea thus represents a place without the borders, barriers, and checkpoints that strangle everyday life for Palestinians.[51]

It is this more optimistic, even romantic view of the sea that is put forward in *My Love Awaits Me by the Sea*. In this film, the sea exists as a metaphor for nothing less than utopia—the dream of a Palestinian future free
from the clutches of Zionist colonialism. Crucially, Darwazah is not content
to relegate this utopian vision to the literal, chronological future, and
throughout the film she strives to locate traces and fragments of this Palestinian future—this Palestine Time—hidden within the interstices of the Zionist
present. Water thus permeates the film from beginning to end. In fact, the
very first thing the film presents its audience is not an image but a sound. As
the opening credits appear on-screen against a black background, we hear the
waves of the sea. From this moment forward, water is omnipresent—from the
scenic watercolors that Darwazah paints to the Palestinian baby playing in a
swimming pool, from the audio of Darwazah's mother recounting her childhood memories of the sea to the West Bank refugee spending his days on top
of his roof with his feet in a small basin of water.

Thus, for Darwazah the sea is not just a distant dream or childish fai-
rytale. It is an everyday reality—a counterhegemonic reality hidden in the
shadows of the Zionist present. This point is humorously made toward the
end of the film when Darwazah interviews an elderly widow. When Darwazah tells her the name of the film, *My Love Awaits Me by the Sea*, the widow
takes it literally and responds with coarse words: "Keep the motherfucker

sitting by the sea." She then goes on, however, to urge Darwazah to embrace her love: "How long will he wait? Will you go to him? [. . .] What are you waiting for? To turn forty!? Just go!" The film then cuts to Acre, where several Palestinian youths are fearlessly jumping into the sea from the heights of the city's ancient stone walls, an image that appears on the cover of this book.[52] Embracing one's dreams is frightening and dangerous, and—as the case of Hassan Hourani demonstrates—it can even be deadly, but one must clasp them and not let them slip between one's fingers. The sea—that hope for a Palestinian future—is not just a lofty, unattainable prospect. It is already all around us, even in the midst of oppression and occupation. Darwazah finds evidence of this with every Palestinian she encounters. Like James's notion of socialist society, it already exists and needs merely to be recognized. In short, *the sea must be seized.*

Two of the methods by which Darwazah manages to attain this utopian realism are her use of framing and her interviews. At certain points in the film, the framing is quite limited and even suffocating. For instance, the film begins with a hand-held camera pointed down at Darwazah's feet as she takes off her shoes, walks in the sand, and wades into the water. It is a framing technique that is repeated throughout the film, and it feels very restricted and controlled. However, Darwazah uses this constraining camera movement only to burst out of it at key moments—particularly when she finally arrives at the sea itself. In this regard, the watercolors that she paints are instructive. They always begin with a frame within the frame, but as she adds more elements to the picture—trees, pathways, and, most important, bodies of water—the frame is overwhelmed. Her watercolors start with a frame only to transgress it, just like the film's overall arc.

Through her careful and deliberate film framing, Darwazah frequently draws her viewers' attention to sounds and images that are not normally highlighted in documentaries about Palestine. While the occupation and its crimes are not absent from *My Love*, they are certainly not the focus and are instead relegated to the background. While other Palestinian filmmakers bombard audiences with images of oppression, Darwazah is attracted to other things, even mundane things—a refugee making fattoush, a wandering cat, a flock of birds, a crying baby, some burning falafel. Moreover, while many other filmmakers focus on the Apartheid Wall, Darwazah instead focuses on its cracks, the spaces that literally separate the wall's segments.[53] She even has one of her interviewees, a Palestinian accordionist, play his instrument through these cracks. Darwazah's decision to frame Palestine in such a way as to emphasize the everyday and the ordinary—the holes in oppression rather than the instruments of oppression—is actually far more political than those images of falling bombs and dead bodies found in more didactic docu-

mentaries. Whereas the latter remain trapped within a hegemonic construction of the present, Darwazah transcends it. She refuses to allow the Israeli
occupation and its colonization of Palestinian bodies, land, and time to take
center stage. For Darwazah, Palestinian revolution is not something that will
naturally occur at some particular time in the future. Instead, revolution exists now as a potential already inhabiting every single moment, even the mundane ones.

The political stakes of Darwazah's framing methods can be demonstrated
by briefly comparing the film to *Salt of This Sea*. Both films contain a key
scene on Jaffa's beachfront promenade, but even though they were filmed in
the same location just a few years apart from each other, there is a significant
difference between them. When the protagonists of Jacir's film reach Jaffa, the
camera shows an Israeli flag flying atop a rock in the sea—a reminder of Israeli settler-colonialism that any visitor to Jaffa will surely recognize. Such
symbols of Israeli oppression are ubiquitous in *Salt*, and there seems to be no
place out of their reach. Conversely, when Darwazah finally reaches Jaffa toward the end of the film, she carefully frames the picture to show as much of
the sea as possible without polluting her cinematic landscape with the Israeli
flag. Her sea is apparently a sea free of Zionism. One might say that by choosing to omit the Israeli flag in this way, Darwazah was neglecting an important
and very real piece of reality. But one could also argue the opposite and say
that by focusing solely on the flag, others (including Jacir) are missing an even
greater picture. The sea is a lot bigger than one Israeli flag, and if others are
unable to take their eyes off the flag, Darwazah remains steadfastly focused
on a much broader and more beautiful landscape. Likewise, those filmmakers—even those fictional-film makers—whose representations of Palestine
remain focused entirely on oppression end up subverting their own cause,
inadvertently giving Zionism much more power than it actually has. They
remain trapped in hegemonic constructions of reality, including hegemonic
constructions of time. As oppressive as the occupation is, it is not the Alpha
and the Omega of Palestinian existence, and there are other realities, other
worlds—indeed, other *times*—that Zionism has been unable to touch.[54]

One of the most notable features of *My Love* is its interviews. Rather than
interviewing celebrated heroes and famous leaders, Darwazah turns her camera to the unknown and the anonymous: a shy old woman in a bakery whose
heart bleeds for her son living in Germany, a young refugee in a Syrian camp
getting ready for his wedding, an old man walking down a street in Jaffa
whose eyes light up with childlike enthusiasm when he begins talking about
the city as it used to be. Very little information is given about the interviewees, not even their names, and it is left up to the viewer to infer as much as he
or she can about their identity and background. Rather than asking these
anonymous Palestinians typical questions about daily life under occupation

or about their views regarding different Palestinian political factions, Darwazah asks them abstract questions about hope, love, and the sea. Their answers show how the mundane can become magical and how emancipation already exists in the here and now.

A particularly memorable interview occurs at night outside of the walls of Jerusalem's Old City. Sitting on the ground smoking cigarettes are three young Palestinian men. While other filmmakers or passersby might be tempted to see them as ordinary, as just part of the typical flora and fauna of Jerusalem, their answers to Darwazah's questions about hopes and dreams reveal something extraordinary. When Darwazah asks how they can realize their dreams for a liberated Palestine, one of them offers a very profound answer. "The dream we speak of," he says, "doesn't vanish when you wake up. It exists when you're sleeping, awake or dead. It is living with you. Its lifetime is longer than yours. The dream doesn't depend on its fulfillment, but on how you can live it." Here, this anonymous Jerusalemite's words approach something akin to prophecy, and he speaks of Palestinian dreams as something sublime, as something that already exists despite the presence of Zionist colonization. His words recall the message of other revolutionaries, people such as the Black martyr Fred Hampton, who famously declared, "You can jail a revolutionary, but you can't jail the revolution."[55] What Darwazah's interviewee is talking about is, in fact, Palestine Time, and his utopian notion of the future is something that clearly already exists in the present.

There are two other instances during this interview that are worth noting. At one point, an organized tour of Zionist settlers arrives in the nearby distance. Another member of this Palestinian trio explains that "this is the other life. In Jerusalem, there are two lives. We're the original. No one knows what the other is, but both are moving in opposite directions." What he is describing corresponds exactly to the argument I am making here. These are indeed two different lives. They are two different, coexisting universes—two worlds in one world and two realities in one reality. One is a world of equality; the other, of inequality. Even more, they are two different temporal modalities. As Darwazah's interview comes to an end, one of the Palestinians concludes by playfully recalling what it often feels like to be in Jerusalem in the late hours of the night. "How often have you felt you're the King of Jerusalem, going home at night when Jerusalem's deserted? Remember? Not a single soul in the entire city. Four A.M. and the Old City lights are off, streets are empty." This observation should not be taken either as a fairy tale or a childish game. Just as James described socialism as something that already exists, even on the factory floor, and just as Benjamin declared that "every second of time is the strait gate through which the Messiah might enter," this Palestinian in Jerusalem is pointing out another reality and another time hidden within the recesses of the hegemonic order. He is locating the seeds of a utopian future in the interstices of the already existing present. His humorous declaration that "we're the Kings of Jerusalem" should thus not be taken as a joke; it is description of the hidden reality we are trained not to see. And it is precisely this conception of time, this Palestinian future that is already here, that *My Love Awaits Me by the Sea* dares to document.

5

Equality under Surveillance

I can't explain how the resistance arose. But it's clear a few
hundred years aren't enough to crush a people out of
existence. The source of the revolt may be hidden as dark and
as deep as that of the Amazon. Where is it? What geographer
will go in search of it? But the water that flows from it is new,
and may be fruitful.

—JEAN GENET, *Prisoner of Love*

There is a Palestinian mode of existence that remains free
and autonomous from the occupation.

—GHASSAN HAGE, *Alter-Politics*

I

After a brief opening sequence set in the present, Elia Suleiman's third
feature film, *The Time That Remains* (2009), returns us to the past and
specifically to July 16, 1948, the day that Nazareth's Palestinian leaders
surrendered to Israeli forces. In the film, we see that city's Arab mayor
(George Khleifi) as he races to a hilltop church to meet with a delegation of
local Palestinian notables and Israeli military commanders. He finds the two
camps silently positioned on opposite sides of a small room, staring at each
other in silence: the Arabs against one wall, the Israelis against the other.
After the grim-faced mayor signs a treaty forfeiting control of Nazareth, he
is invited to join the victorious soldiers for a photograph commemorating
this historic occasion. A photographer suddenly appears and walks to the
center of the room. As the Israelis encircle the mayor and proudly pose for
the picture, the photographer bends over to peer into his camera. In the
process, he inadvertently points his backside toward the Arabs behind him.
The Palestinians are thereby left out of the frame. With the click of the camera, their presence is effectively erased and made invisible—out of sight, out
of mind. Just as they are getting the ass of history, they also get the ass of the
photographer (see Figures 5.1 and 5.2).

In staging this scene, the director Elia Suleiman resists showing the audience the point of view of the photographer; instead, he focuses his lens on
the people on the opposite side of the room. That is, while the photographer

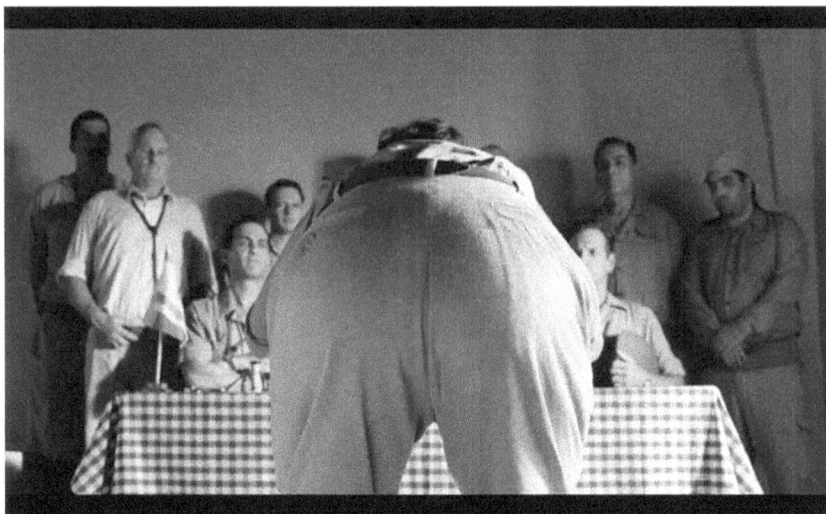

Figures 5.1 and **5.2.** Shot and reverse shot. The Palestinians get the ass of history in *The Time That Remains*.

takes a picture of the Israelis in front of him, Suleiman shows us the Palestinians behind him. In this way, Suleiman boldly announces his intentions for the film. While media have often been used to render the Palestinians nonexistent, *The Time That Remains* will bring them back into the picture, putting them in front of the camera rather than behind it. In short, Suleiman intends to give the Palestinians *visibility*.

Edward Said once wrote that "the whole history of the Palestinian struggle has to do with the desire to be visible."[1] This struggle over visibility is not confined to only the moving image; it also extends into other media fields, including cartography. While more than four hundred Arab villages were depopulated and destroyed during the 1947–1948 Nakba, many other Palestinian population centers have since been erased in a different way—by simply omitting them from the map. Israeli planning councils were formed in 1965 to identify all existing villages and towns within the country's borders, but in performing this task, they excluded most rural Palestinian communities. Palestinian places thus became blank spaces, and their invisibility on official Israeli maps was subsequently used by the government to deny them basic infrastructure. To this day, many of these "unrecognized villages" within Israel's 1948 borders still lack proper electricity, running water, paved roads, and easily accessible schools.[2] In response to such forms of cartographic erasure, many Palestinians have engaged in the creation of virtual maps, using the Internet to restore the names and places of villages that have been lost, neglected, or destroyed.[3]

The struggle over visibility, then, cannot be written off as an entirely superstructural matter. In some cases, visibility—or the lack of it—corresponds to real, material conditions. For this reason, making the Palestinians visible has often been posited as a radical act of resistance in and of itself. But is it really so simple? While some people assert that the Palestinians have been rendered *invisible*, others maintain that they have actually become *hypervisible*. This view has been advanced by friend and foe alike. Already in 1978, for instance, Paul Virilio saw the Palestinians as a hypervisible model for future political struggle. Recognizing their ability to use media across nation-states' borders, Virilio referred to the Palestinians as "the masters of an audio-visual empire, of a State founded on roads, airways and images."[4] On the other end of the political spectrum, the U.S. journalist Leon Wieseltier, speaking at a debate between Edward Said and Bernard Lewis in 1986, argued that Said's claims about Palestinian invisibility lacked any substance. As Wieseltier put it, "The notion that the Palestinian people [. . .] have been erased or made invisible seems to me perfectly ridiculous. Which intelligent leader of the American media does not know that the Palestinians are a stateless people?" For him, the situation of the Palestinians not only was well known but had, in his words, "reached the status of cliché."[5]

Whether the Palestinians are deemed invisible or hypervisible, the assumption that Palestinian visibility automatically works against Zionism should not go unquestioned. Quite often, being visible is not empowering; it is oppressive. Visibility, too, can be used as a settler-colonialist weapon, and there is hardly anything radical about the visibility of Palestinian bodies when they are viewed through the lens of Israeli security technologies. Neither is there anything radical about the dissemination of Palestinian images when they are used with the intention of perpetuating the settler-colonialist status quo. Here, I am thinking specifically about the images of "good Arabs" that are used to prove Israeli tolerance toward its non-Jewish minorities and the images of "bad Arabs" that are used to paint Israel as a perennial victim of terrorism, as a democratic country that is forever fighting a just struggle for survival against the evil barbarians at its gates.[6]

There is thus more to visibility than what meets the eye, and in this chapter, I briefly survey two forms of Palestinian visibility: the visibility of Palestinian bodies through Israeli security technologies and their visibility through protests. I therefore touch on two distinct bodies of media studies literature: surveillance studies and the discourse on tactical media and spectacle. Initially, these two fields appear quite distinct from each other. While one tends to treat the viewed body as a passive object, the other considers it an active participant in the crafting of its own image, and while the former emphasizes the agency of those who are watching, the latter emphasizes the agency of those who are being watched. Despite this difference, I believe that these two positions share a focus on power and resistance, particularly as conceived by Michel Foucault. While this view of power relations has its merits, I claim that it is ultimately inattentive to the question of emancipation. That is, Foucauldian-inspired analyses of power tend not to allow a place for negation—for destructive plasticity—and they thereby risk eradicating the possibility of the Palestinian Idea. I therefore argue in favor of shifting our view from visibility to *visuality*, and rather than approaching surveillance and spectacle from an axis of power-resistance, I instead approach it from *an axis of equality-inequality*. I conclude by discussing a film that deals with all of these conceptual issues, Hany Abu-Assad's *Paradise Now* (2005).

II

Common to the study of surveillance are several images and figures—from George Orwell's Big Brother to Foucault's famous deployment of Jeremy Bentham's Panopticon.[7] One could potentially add many other metaphors to this list: novels such as Franz Kafka's *The Castle*, the paranoiac works of Philip Dick, dystopian films such as *Minority Report* (dir. Steven Spielberg, 2002), or even the term recently used by industry insiders to discuss the surveillance capabilities of unmanned aerial drones: the Gorgon Stare.[8] All of these images and figures point toward both the use of high-tech gadgets and devices for surveillance and the ability of surveillance not just to record our activities but to transform our consciousness—that is, to make us believe we are being watched even when we are not. It has therefore been argued that technologies of surveillance can serve to modify our behavior. We act as if Big Brother is watching, so the argument goes, even if Big Brother does not really exist. Surveillance, then, is not just repressive; it is also productive. This is precisely what Foucault famously called "biopower."[9]

But translating the insights and concepts of surveillance studies into a context like that of occupied Palestine is not a straightforward endeavor. As a field, surveillance studies has tended to focus on the modern state. However, our understanding of surveillance is impoverished if we delink it from the study of race and empire and from the history of transatlantic slavery and European colonialism.[10] Indeed, as Simone Browne has argued, even Foucault's basic model for surveillance, the Panopticon, has a racial history, and Bentham first conceived of it while traveling on a ship that was transporting African slaves. One can only wonder how much the conditions of his ship's imprisoned cargo influenced his designs.[11] Moreover, many of the most standard methods of surveillance used today such as fingerprinting have their origins in the governing of European colonies in places such as India and North Africa.[12]

It is imperative that we keep this view of surveillance in mind when studying contemporary Palestine, and there are at least three major ways that Israel's surveillance regime operates differently from the models usually presented in surveillance studies discourse. First, although Israel is a global leader in the development of surveillance technologies, it also relies heavily on a low-tech gaze. Here one might think both of Israel's use of Palestinian collaborators and its complicated color-coded ID system, a system that was initially introduced in 1949 to the 165,000 Palestinians who remained within Israel's borders as a method of keeping the 750,000 Palestinians who had been expelled from returning.[13] Second, whereas many scholars understand the practices of surveillance as having replaced earlier and more vulgar methods of discipline and control, in Israel public spectacles of punishment still have an important place in the daily maintenance of order in the West Bank, particularly at checkpoints.[14] Third, whereas surveillance is usually understood to be directed at the controlling of bodies, in Palestine Israeli instruments of surveillance are also intended to control territory and resources. Furthermore, with respect to all three of these characteristics, it is worth noting that in many cases Israel has outsourced its surveillance operations to the Palestinian Authority (PA), particularly in the years following the signing of the Oslo Accords in 1993 and 1995. Indeed, in 2017 a draconian new cybercrimes law made criticism of the PA on social media a punishable offense, and it was quickly used against people such as Issa Amro, one of the activists who took part in the Freedom March in Hebron in March 2013.[15]

Some of these aspects of Israeli surveillance can be seen in a new device that suddenly appeared on top of the Apartheid Wall near Bethlehem in April 2014. In that month, participants in the second annual Palestine Marathon reported that a device on top of the wall had turned on its axis and followed them as they ran near it.[16] The mechanism appeared to be a camera attached to some sort of barrel or turret, but identifying it was more difficult than one might imagine. Initially, it was speculated to be a remote-control gun capable of firing live ammunition. Indeed, such devices had already been developed for use in Gaza.[17] Upon further investigation, however, it was determined that the device in Bethlehem was not a gun but a water cannon, and a spokesperson for the Israel Defense Forces (IDF) later stated that the weapon is "part of our means for riot dispersal in Judea and Samaria [the West Bank]. The weapon is remote controlled and has the ability to fire water, tear gas grenades, etc."[18] This device thus displays many of the features unique to the Israeli regime of surveillance. It combines a high-tech and low-tech gaze; it involves riot control and brute force; and, as part of Israel's Apartheid Wall, it is part of the ongoing Zionist efforts to colonize Palestinian territory.

This is not to say that the Foucauldian notion of biopower is completely irrelevant in Palestine. While this particular device turned out not to be an automatic assault weapon, as had initially been reported, the confusion and anxiety its appearance caused is still very significant. Israel's surveillance regime is an intentionally elusive and contradictory enterprise. Facts on the ground are always changing, and it is difficult to get concrete information about the surveillance technologies being deployed. One never knows when one is being watched, but one is supposed to know that the authorities could be watching at any moment. Here, one may be reminded of the Allenby Bridge border crossing between Jordan and the West Bank. Israeli security officers sit hidden behind mirrors and are able watch over the Palestinian personnel at the passport control booths.[19]

By putting the technologies and practices of surveillance at the center of our study, however, we leave very little room for the agency of those who are being watched, and we therefore risk conceiving of surveilled populations as little more than passive bodies. Indeed, this is a broader problem within the field of surveillance studies—a technological determinism that reaches its apogee in the work of Virilio. "No more illusions about technology," he writes. "We do not control what we produce."[20] To counter this top-down view of surveillance, there has been a tendency in recent years to emphasize countersurveillance strategies. In Palestine, countersurveillance can take many different forms. They include the oppositional use of security footage, the documentation of Israeli practices with activists' own cameras, and the creation of media spectacles. The first of these countersurveillance practices often involve the participation of Israeli nongovernmental organizations and legal groups such as B'Tselem. By obtaining security footage or other media surveillance documentation, they are able to disprove the Israeli government's empirical claims. Here it is important to recognize that surveillance is not necessarily oppressive in and of itself.[21] Just because surveillance footage is taken to perpetuate oppression does not mean that it cannot be appropriated from below and used in other ways.[22]

A particularly compelling example of this first countersurveillance strat-egy involves the killing of two Palestinian teenagers—seventeen-year-old Nadeem Nawara and sixteen-year-old Mohammad Abu Daher—by IDF sol-diers in the town of Beitunia, near Ramallah, during Nakba Day activities in 2014. Initially the Israeli authorities denied any wrongdoing. On the one hand, IDF officials insisted that no live ammunition had been used and that the soldiers had fired only rubber bullets. On the other hand, Defense Min-ister Moshe Ya'alon claimed that the soldiers were being attacked by a mob armed with Molotov cocktails and that their very lives were at stake.[23] In the months following the two deaths, the London-based group Forensic Archi-tecture was able to obtain and synchronize camera footage from different sources, and by analyzing both the video and sound, they disproved Israel's claims. According to Forensic Architecture's report, the two Palestinian youths had been killed by live ammunition shot by IDF soldiers, and neither of them had been involved in any violent provocations, as Ya'alon had previ-ously claimed.[24] Another example of this countersurveillance strategy in-volves the death of fourteen-year-old Yousef al-Shawamreh, a Palestinian teenager who was shot in the back as he was attempting to cross from his village into another part of the West Bank. Although the Israeli military investigated the incident, the case was closed without any indictments. B'Tselem was later able to obtain the chat logs of WhatsApp, the messaging service used by the soldiers, to show that they knew they were about to am-bush children.[25]

While the first countersurveillance tactic involves the appropriation of the colonizer's cameras, a second technique entails turning the cameras back on the occupiers. In the past two decades a number of organized attempts have been made to use cameras to document the checkpoints, the conduct of Israeli soldiers, and the violence of Jewish settlers. These attempts have been led by both Israeli and Palestinian groups. In February 2001, for instance, a mixed group of Jewish and Palestinian women founded Machsom Watch, an organization that documents the treatment of Palestinians at the check-points.[26] Similarly, in 2007 B'Tselem launched a camera project in which video cameras are distributed to Palestinian families in the West Bank and Gaza to document life under occupation and the actions of Israeli security forces. One of the videos that was recorded as part of this project was later edited into a short documentary, *Smile and the World Will Smile Back* (dir. al-Haddad family, Yoav Gross, and Ehab Tarabieh, 2014) in which a family in Hebron filmed a group of soldiers who arrive for a night search of their home. Although the soldiers do not find anything incriminating, they are frustrated by the grin of the family's teenage son, Diaa, and refuse to leave until he stops smiling. Other examples of this second countersurveillance tactic include the Palestinian activists in the West Bank villages of Bil'in and Nabi Saleh who stage weekly demonstrations against the continued theft of their lands: Bil'in, since January 2005, and Nabi Saleh, since December 2009. These regular protests are always documented with still photography and video, and the footage is distributed online.

A third countersurveillance tactic lines up with another field of media studies: the discourse on tactical media interventions. This is the attempt by Palestinians to hijack the media narrative by turning their bodies into a spectacle for the cameras. That is, although the Palestinians do not have the same access to media production and distribution channels as their colonizers, they are attempting nevertheless to influence the global media narrative. In recent years, this has involved the staging of creative protests. Shortly after the release of the blockbuster *Avatar* (dir. James Cameron, 2009), demonstrators in Bil'in dressed themselves in the style of the film's fictional Na'vi. They put on blue makeup and donned loincloths and long-haired wigs. Like the Na'vi, the Palestinians claimed that they are an indigenous people being gradually displaced by the forces of colonialism. Other spectacles include the Freedom March in Hebron of March 2013, discussed in Chapter 1, and a protest in Bethlehem in December 2014 in which demonstrators carried signs calling for a "Christmas without occupation." Some of the Bethlehem protesters even dressed up as Santa Claus. These attempts to grab the attention of the global news media through spectacle recall the work of Dick Hebdige, who has argued that, faced with the seemingly omnipresent eye of the surveillance state, disaffected youths in the United Kingdom responded with "the only power at their disposal: the power to discomfit. The power, that is, to pose." For Hebdige, it is this subversive power that the developers of surveillance and security regimes overlook. In his words, "The fact of being under scrutiny [can translate] into the pleasure of being watched. It is a hiding in the light."[27]

While, as we have seen, the discourse of surveillance studies has traditionally failed to account for the agency of the person being watched, the discourse on countersurveillance has a rather different problem. By glorifying all of these various tactics as acts of counterhegemonic resistance, one is unable to distinguish among them. Indeed, as the Zionist project of settler-colonialism prepares to enter its fourteenth decade, the practice of posing for pictures in blueface makeup or in Santa Claus costumes might not seem like an effective strategy for combating Israel's ongoing ethnic cleansing nightmare. To use the words of Jean Genet, "Spectacle is only spectacle, and it may lead to mere figment, to no more than a colourful carnival."[28] Moreover, when one romanticizes these countersurveillance practices, one may fail to see how they can potentially serve to reinscribe and reproduce the very forms of hierarchy and domination they are intended to oppose. Just as Israeli surveillance footage can be appropriated from below, countersurveillance can be appropriated from above.[29]

This tendency for countersurveillance to actually reinforce regimes of oppression is particularly true in the case of violent media spectacles, including
terrorism. On the one hand, images of terrorism—from Leila Khaled and the
Popular Front for the Liberation of Palestine's notorious plane hijackings in
the late 1960s and early 1970s to the more recent phenomenon of suicide
bombing—are used by Israel to demonize the Palestinian opposition. On the
other hand, by enacting such forms of blind violence, the Palestinians risk
mimicking the violent tactics of the settler-colonialism regime they claim to
contest. As Said argued, "Very often 'terrorists' end up by reproducing the
very structures that have 'alienated' them."[30] Those few Palestinians who engage in terrorism undoubtedly believe they are striking a blow against Zionism. I would argue, however, that they are, in fact, perpetuating it. In a sense,
they are allowing Zionism to dictate their actions even in death, and if they
want to overcome Zionism, they must break out of this closed circle.[31]

III

Surveillance studies and the literature on media spectacle thus seem to stand
on opposite ends of the spectrum. While the former tends to emphasize the
agency of those who are doing the watching, the latter instead directs our
attention to the agency of those who are being watched. But these two positions may not be as different as they initially appear, and in both cases, the
discourse is rooted in a common epistemological concern with power and
resistance. While resistance can easily be romanticized as an effective antidote to oppression, such glorification is by no means warranted, and it fails
to recognize the degree to which resistance is bound to existing power structures. Thus, by uncritically championing resistance, one may actually be
inadvertently perpetuating the very institutions that one claims to contest.[32]

Over the years, there have been many attempts to articulate this interconnected relationship between power and resistance—from Herbert Marcuse's notion of repressive desublimation to Partha Chatterjee's writings on
anticolonialist movements.[33] Such works seek to show how resistance is generated from the matrix of power itself. Here it might be helpful to recall
Antonio Gramsci's notion of hegemony, the attempt by governing bodies to
rule by consent.[34] To be sure, some have questioned whether or not hegemony can be used to accurately describe the situation of the Palestinians
under Israeli occupation. Elia Zureik, for instance, argues that there have
been no significant attempts by the Israeli state to gain the Palestinians' consent—that is, no real effort to turn the Palestinians into good Zionists—and
for this reason, he proposes modifying the term in this context, calling it not
hegemony but "minimal hegemony."[35] Hegemony, however, does not necessarily entail the inculcation of a population with blind obedience and un-

critical support, and it is at its most insidious precisely when it involves attitudes of irony, cynicism, or even outright opposition. Indeed, *this is how hegemony works.*[36] In the context of Palestine, hegemony does not mean that ruling power structures are steadfastly trying to transform the Palestinians into good, flag-waving, Hebrew-speaking Zionists (although, as Shira Robinson has shown, such instances do exist).[37] Rather, hegemony means promoting the belief that Israel, in its contemporary ethnocratic form, is here to stay and that Arab-Jewish enmity is a natural and permanent condition; it means turning the Palestinians against one another or even into collaborators; it means convincing them that they are already beaten and that there is no other world beyond the horizon, no Palestinian future beyond the Zionist present. In short, for the Palestinians, Israeli hegemony means *politicide.*

Palestinian resistance thus cannot be understood as automatically posing an innate threat to Zionism, and sometimes it can actually work to perpetuate it. In his book *The Least of All Possible Evils*, Eyal Weizman draws our attention to this paradoxical potential. When the first legal challenge to the government's plans to build a separation wall reached the Israeli High Court in 2004, the Palestinian petitioners from the village of Beit Sourik were asked to provide a physical model of the wall. As a result, Weizman explains, "The first model of the wall to have ever been produced was not made by the party erecting the wall, but rather by those opposing it." As the court case continued, the Palestinians' lawyers found themselves in the position of suggesting alternative routes for the wall—routes that would be less intrusive to Palestinian neighborhoods and agricultural lands. In Weizman's words, they were put in a position to propose "the best of all possible walls." In this way, the Palestinians' attempts at resistance—their contestation of the wall at the level of the Israeli judiciary—ended up working against them and further solidified plans for the wall with their formal consent. As Weizman concludes, "If the wall does ever come to the designate the borders of a shrunken temporary Palestinian state, it will be the first such border to have been co-designed by humanitarian lawyers."[38]

But hegemony is not the only conceptual tool we can use to understand this intertwined relationship between power and resistance in the context of Israel and Palestine. While Gramsci's model of hegemony suggests that nonstate actors are somehow brainwashed or tricked into giving their consent to the governing authorities, others have attempted to show that, just as power generates resistance, resistance likewise generates power. The most influential source for this view remains Foucault, particularly the works of his middle period, *Discipline and Punish* and the first volume of *The History of Sexuality.*[39] In these books, Foucault argued that power is not something that one possesses. It is relational—maintained by both oppressor and oppressed. As he put it, "Power is not an institution, and not a structure; neither is it a certain strength we are endowed with; it is the name that one attributes to a complex strategical situation in a particular society."[40] For Foucault, nobody exists outside power, not even those who appear to be "out" of power. In his words, "There is no binary and all-encompassing opposition between rulers and ruled at the root of power relations."[41]

Accordingly, there is no privileged place that exists outside of or apart from power, no exterior position from which resistance can effectively be mounted. For Foucault, power inhabits a world of pure immanence and cannot be escaped. Quite simply, "Power is everywhere."[42] The popularity of Foucault's turn to immanence might be interpreted partially as a reaction to the failures of the twentieth century's many revolutionary projects. Indeed, the observation that utopian dreams can easily turn into dystopian nightmares led many post-1968 thinkers to abandon utopianism altogether—a feeling summed up in Hebdige's memorable comment that "all utopias come wrapped in barbed wire."[43] Importantly, Foucault's view of power should not be taken as suggesting that resistance is impossible. Rather, it simply suggests that resistance is always already part of power's positive universe. Foucault's famous formula—"where there is power, there is resistance"—can therefore be misleading.[44] His point was not simply that power generates resistance and predetermines it in advance but also that resistance generates power—or, even more accurately, that *resistance is a constitutive element of the field of power itself.* Lila Abu-Lughod made this same point by reversing Foucault's formula. In her words, "Where there is resistance, there is power."[45]

Thus, while Foucauldian analyses of power do not foreclose the possibility of resistance, they usually fail to provide an adequate theoretical basis for emancipation, and to the degree that Foucault's shadow looms over our understanding of Palestinian media visibility, I believe, we are unable to account adequately for the possibility of radical change. This problem was sensed by Said, and even though Foucault provided an important methodological model for *Orientalism,* Said nevertheless took umbrage with Foucault's notion of power. For Said, Foucault's thought fell victim to a "disturbing circularity" and a "theoretical overtotalization."[46] Although Foucault's work is often celebrated and used by writers concerned with social justice and political struggle, Said believed that Foucault's focus on domination was not "as contestatory or as oppositional as on the surface it seems to be."[47] As he argued, "Foucault's use of the term *pouvoir* [power] moves around too much, swallowing up every obstacle in its path (resistances to it, the class and economic bases that refresh and fuel it, the reserves it build up), obliterating change and mystifying its microphysical sovereignty."[48] Said believed that Foucault's view was a "profoundly pessimistic" one and that it did not make "even a nominal allowance for emergent movements, and none for revolutions, counterhegemony, or historical blocks."[49]

But Said's criticisms of Foucault never delved very far beneath the surface, sticking mostly to overtly political terms. For a more substantial challenge to Foucault's theoretical underpinnings, one must turn elsewhere.[50] Here I want to bring into the discussion the work of Jacques Rancière, whose subversive conceptualization of equality forms the groundless ground upon which I am basing the Palestinian Idea. In some respects, Rancière and Foucault appear to be quite similar in their methodological, theoretical, and political orientations. Indeed, Alain Badiou has even gone as far as to call Rancière "an heir to Foucault."[51] To be sure, Rancière does not contest Foucault's basic description of power relations, and while resistance has become something of a popular academic buzzword in recent years, it is not a very important concept in Rancière's oeuvre. Using language that Foucault himself undoubtedly would have endorsed, Rancière throws cold water on those more celebratory accounts of resistance, claiming that "resistance [. . .] often conceals submission to the order of things behind a heroic posture."[52]

However, there is nevertheless a crucial difference between the two figures—namely, the question of equality.[53] Rancière recognizes that Foucault backed himself into a corner and that he could not adequately theorize his own political position. As Rancière put it in an essay marking the twentieth anniversary of Foucault's death, "A philosopher's being in the street does not suffice for his philosophy to ground the movement, nor even his own presence there."[54] To escape this philosophical dead-end, Rancière, as we have already seen, opens up a dimension that Foucault left unexplored. What Foucault called power is roughly equivalent to what Rancière calls "the police," but while Foucault's vision did not extend beyond this closed world, Rancière has located another dimension hidden within power's cracks: the disavowed but ever present equality at the heart of inequality.[55]

On this point, it might be useful to draw an analogy with the discussion of politics and culture provided in the Introduction. While politics traditionally has been separated from culture, the feminist response to this view was to collapse politics into culture—a tendency perhaps best embodied by the famous feminist slogan "The Personal Is Political." In an analogous way, power and resistance have traditionally been conceived as separate, unconnected phenomena, and it is to Foucault's merit that he was able to penetrate this naïveté. For him, resistance was always already a co-constitutive element of power. In his words, "Resistance [. . .] always relies upon the situation against which it struggles."[56] Both of these assertions—both the second-wave feminist response to traditional politics and the Foucauldian response to power—have their flaws. If everything is political, then nothing is, and if power is everywhere, it ceases to function as a useful analytical concept. In both cases, Rancière's intervention is the same. On the one hand, Rancière redefines politics so that it is not a positive field but a disruption in that field, and on the other hand, he redefines equality so that it is not a future goal but a present presupposition that cuts through all hierarchical claims. Thus, Rancière suggests that, rather than chaining ourselves to an axis of power and resistance, we instead begin from an axis of equality and inequality.

By shifting our view in this fashion, we are able to avoid some of the problems encountered by those more Foucauldian-inspired analyses of power and resistance. Yes, power and resistance do generate each other, but these positive phenomena do not fully dominate the entire field. Power and resistance are more than just the sum of their parts, and there are other, hidden dimensions that contribute to their operations. Specifically, Israeli acts of oppression—including the development and deployment of surveillance technologies—are not only a response to Palestinian resistance. They are also an attempt to stamp out their own negation, the equality at the heart of inequality. We should therefore not completely reduce Palestinian resistance to the circumstances of the Israeli occupation. Palestinian resistance can also be fueled by another fire: the hidden subterranean fire of equality.

Ironically, then, Stuart Hall's critique of Foucauldian resistance as being "summoned up from no-where" turns out to be exactly right.[57] Insofar as resistance is radical and revolutionary, it *does* come from nowhere. It emanates from a nonplace, from the darkness that necessarily accompanies power like a shadow. Contrary to Foucault's claim that resistance is not "doomed to perpetual defeat," any resistance not located along this fault line exists in a parasitic relationship with oppression, thriving on the very power structures that it contests. Hence, it is by orienting oneself around equality that resistance has the potential to radically reconfigure the social order. When this disavowed equality begins seeping through the cracks, existing power structures begin to crumble, and the New begins to swallow the Old.

This change of perspective—from the positive to the negative, from the occupied to the unoccupied, and from inequality to equality—allows us to answer some of the enigmas encountered in discussions of Palestinian visibility. Whether Palestinians are visible, invisible, or hypervisible is not necessarily the most pressing issue. As I have shown, all of these forms of visibility can also be used against the Palestinians, whether through a surveillance camera or through the dissemination of a terrorist media spectacle. The question before us, then, is one not of visibility but of *visuality*.[58] That is, the problem is not *whether* the Palestinians are seen but *how* they are seen, and the Palestinians' task is not just to make their empirical bodies visible but to find a way to communicating the Palestinian Idea.

Furthermore, by shifting our focus from resistance to equality, we can also dodge the question of effectiveness. There is no guaranteed recipe for successful resistance, and while a certain act of rebellion may prove very effective in one particular context, the same act may turn out to be nothing more than a pathetic sideshow in another. One simply cannot predict what forms of resistance will work and what forms will not. Truly radical uprisings cannot be predicted by social science, and their occurrence always comes as a surprise.[59] By turning our gaze from resistance to equality, we can leave the crystal balls to the soothsayers and instead concern ourselves with identifying the disruptive egalitarian potential that is always bubbling just underneath the surface, preparing to erupt even when we least expect it.[60]

IV

In the concluding pages of this chapter, I turn to cinema and particularly to a film that explicitly deals with issues of Palestinian visibility and resistance, the director Hany Abu-Assad's feature *Paradise Now* (2005). This film and its critical reception provide an opportunity to test some of the ideas raised in the preceding pages, and insofar as both the positive and negative reviews of the film tend to reduce it to a story of power and resistance, another important dimension has often been sidelined.

Paradise Now follows two young Palestinian men—Said (Kais Nashif) and Khaled (Ali Suliman)—living in the West Bank city of Nablus. At the beginning of the film, they are working as mechanics when they meet Suha (Lubna Azabal), a Palestinian woman who has just returned from several years living abroad. The possibility of romance between Said and Suha is hinted at, but it is not meant to be. Jamal (Amer Hlehel), a representative of an unnamed Islamist militant group, approaches Said and informs him that he and Khaled have been selected to carry out a suicide bombing the next day in Tel Aviv. The rest of the film follows these two friends as they prepare to carry out their mission—filming martyr videos, eating their last meal, disguising themselves as wedding party attendees, and strapping bombs to their torsos.

The first attempt to cross into Israel goes awry. Said and Khaled are spotted almost immediately by Israeli military personnel, and they are split from each other. Khaled returns to the militant group's secret headquarters in Nablus, but Said spends the rest of the day as a ghost—visiting his old stomping grounds, his home, his workplace, and, finally, the grave of his father, who was executed for collaborating with Israel. Eventually, Said and Khaled reconnect and agree to try again, and the next day they make it to Tel Aviv. At the last minute, Khaled gets cold feet and begs Said to return home with him. Said, however, is determined to carry out the mission, and the last scene of the film shows Said sitting silently on a crowded Israeli bus. The camera gradually approaches Said and focuses on his eyes in an extreme close-up. Then, without a sound, the entire screen goes white.

The recipient of numerous honors and awards, including an Oscar nomination and a Golden Globe, *Paradise Now* remains one of the most successful and best-known Palestinian films to date. Despite its many achievements, however, the film was surrounded by controversy from its inception. Abu-Assad intended to shoot the film on location in Nablus, but it was viewed with great suspicion by rival Palestinian factions. At one point, the film's location manager was kidnapped, and Yasir Arafat himself had to personally intervene to negotiate his release.[61] Although *Paradise Now* was co-produced by an Israeli company, Lama Films, it was not received well in Israel. Abu-Assad's application for a grant from the Israeli Film Fund was denied, and one of the people behind the rejection later wrote a scathing review of the film with the inflammatory title "Anti-Semitism Now." In it, she described *Paradise Now* as "an exciting, quality Nazi film."[62] Moreover, although *Paradise Now* received wide distribution in Europe and even the United States, it was not picked up by any distribution companies in Israel.[63]

When *Paradise Now* was nominated for an Academy Award in early 2006, the families of three Israeli teenagers killed by suicide bombers organized an online petition demanding its immediate removal from the Oscar competition. It reportedly garnered more than thirty-two thousand signatures. Specifically, the petitioners accused the film of humanizing terrorists and naturalizing or even glorifying terrorism.[64] To be sure, grieving families were not the only ones to level these accusations, and others, such as the Israeli film scholar Raya Morag, have constructed similar arguments.[65] The first of these two criticisms can be dealt with briefly. In short, terrorists *are* human—as are the perpetrators of far more horrific crimes such as colonialism and genocide.[66] Recognizing this humanity is not an endorsement of their actions. Rather, it is precisely because they are human that they are capable of such horrendous crimes.

The second criticism, however, is the more substantial one. *Paradise Now* is accused of naturalizing suicide terrorism as the inevitable outcome of the Israeli occupation. As one of the Israeli petitioners argued, "Some of the dialogue manipulates the viewer into believing that the Palestinians have tried everything and have no choice. It was hard for me not to feel that I am to blame for the murder of my son."[67] Morag similarly asserts that the film creates a world in which the main character, Said, simply has no other options. Zionism is to be blamed for Palestinian terrorism, and the conditions of the occupation have left no room for Palestinian agency. In Morag's words, *Paradise Now* "succeeds in providing a 'complete' solution to the enigma of who is a suicide terrorist."[68] As in Foucauldian analyses of power, resistance is an outgrowth of the very practices it contests, and there is no way out of this closed circle. Notably, while some such as Morag criticize the film for explaining terrorism, others have praised it for precisely the same reason.[69]

This very deterministic view is shared by the film's main character, Said. He absolves himself of any responsibility for his actions, claiming that he has no other choice. As he tells Suha, "The occupation defines the resistance." Said's fatalism is memorably depicted in a scene in which he is drinking coffee with his mother. She takes his empty cup to read his fortune from the coffee grounds. However, there are no grounds to read. With a look of concern, she announces, "Your future is blank." Said raises a finger, indicating that he had wiped the cup clean himself. There are multiple ways to interpret this scene, and Said's blank future may initially seem to point to his imminent death. His future is blank because he is going to die. However, we should not necessarily interpret this blankness as finality, as it could also indicate openness. In my view, Said's future is blank because *it has not yet been written*, and as much as Said believes the Zionist occupation has predetermined the path of his resistance, the fact remains that he cleaned his coffee cup with his own fingers. That is, while Said may not believe it, he does indeed have a hand in shaping his own fate, and there are other possibilities that he is unable or unwilling to consider. Indeed, this openness is part and parcel of the Palestinian cause. To quote Fawaz Turki, "If the Palestinian revolution is armed with a philosophy at all, it is armed with the anti-determinist vision of the open-endedness of the future."[70] This dimension of the film—this open-endedness and the possibility of escaping power's grip—is lost when one approaches the text from the axis of power-resistance.

The emergency exit out of this fatalism appears only in hints and traces, and they come almost exclusively through the character of Suha. Although Suha is Palestinian, she has spent a significant number of years living abroad. Significantly, Suha is the only major character in the film to be played by a non-Palestinian actor: Lubna Azabal, who is of Morroccan and Spanish descent. This casting decision was presumably made to emphasize the character's foreignness, her insider-outsider status, even further. Suha appears in the opening frame of the film, walking through an Israeli checkpoint as she returns to Palestine from the wider world. This insider-outsider status does not go unnoticed by Said, who at one point tells her, "You come from a different world." But what if this other-worldliness also indicates something else? What if Suha represents not only another world *out there* but also another world *in here*—a world of equality hidden within the world of inequality, a world of the impossible buried within the world of the apparently possible? Indeed, this potential becomes evident during a debate between Suha and Khaled, and when Khaled explains his rationale for becoming a suicide bomber by claiming, "If we can't live as equals, at least we will die as equals," Suha responds, "If you can kill and die for equality you should be able to find a way to be equal in life." Whereas Khaled seems to understand equality as something that one has to achieve in the future, Suha sees equality as a starting point, as something that begins from within. For Khaled, equality is attained only in death, but for Suha, it begins with life. Indeed, perhaps this is also how we should understand the title of the film. If there is a Paradise, it is to be found *now* and not in some imagined hereafter.

The radical difference between Said's and Suha's worldviews appears in their conversation about movies. Whereas Suha is comfortable talking about different film genres and styles, Said's only memory of the cinema is of the one that he helped burn to the ground. Thus, for Suha the cinema represents a way out, a place where dreams become tangible and where the constraints of reality do not have the final say. For Said, by contrast, the cinema is just the cinema; it is just a physical place, a building that can be reduced to its empirical elements—four walls and a roof, a projector and a screen. Suha is therefore open to the imagination in a way that Said is not. She plays the role of prophet, able to simultaneously see both *the way the world is* and *the way it ought to be*. Said, however, lacks this ability, and he can see only the former. His vision cannot penetrate the Israeli occupation, and just as he mistakes the emptiness of his future for finality, he similarly mistakes the cinema for just another building rather than a site that gives us access to a dimension beyond Zionism's reach. In short, Said is unable to think beyond the horizon of the Zionist present. He is stuck in Nakba Time, and he cannot locate the cracks and crevices in which dreams of a better tomorrow are already alive today.

Contrary to the claims of many of the film's reviewers, then, *Paradise Now* is not simply a sociological analysis that attempts to completely explain the phenomenon of suicide bombing. Rather, *Paradise Now* is a movie about *failure*. While Morag and others read the film's final scene as a celebration of Palestinian martyrdom, it should instead be read as a tragedy. Indeed, this is how the director himself understands the film.[71] By becoming a terrorist, Said hopes to rectify the sins of his father who collaborated with Israel. What Said fails to realize is that, like his late father, he is actually playing into Zionism's hands. With his final act of blind violence, Said is mirroring the violence of the occupation, not transcending it. He is letting the occupation dominate him even in death. To recall Huey Newton's terms, he is committing not a revolutionary suicide but a reactionary one. Said has relinquished his own agency and become trapped in a closed circle, unable to find the way out. The impossible remains impossible. There is no unoccupied space and no Palestinian Idea. We can imagine that his terrorist act will achieve a certain media visibility—both through the martyr posters that will be circulated in the West Bank and the headlines that will appear in international news publications. However, this visibility will serve not to liberate the Palestinians but to perpetuate their oppression. The tragedy of *Paradise Now* is that *Said does not find Paradise*. He is concerned with visibility, not visuality.

He seeks to resist but is unable to do so in a way that escapes Zionism's terms. As Suha argues, "If you kill, there's no difference between victim and occupier." Or, to quote Rancière, "Servility and hatred are two characteristics of the very same world, two manifestations of the very same malady."[72] Power and resistance thereby generate each other in a closed loop, and the dimension of equality is neglected and forgotten.

6

Palestine in Black and White

There is an unmistakable coincidence between the
experiences of Arab Palestinians at the hands of Zionism and
the experience of those black, yellow, and brown people who
were described as inferior and subhuman by nineteenth-
century imperialists.
—EDWARD W. SAID, *The Question of Palestine*

To Israel's arrogant formula, "We are not a people like
others," the Palestinians have not stopped responding with
the cry [. . .] "we are a people like others."
—GILLES DELEUZE, "The Grandeur of Yasser Arafat"

Our struggles are particular, but we are not alone.
—AUDRE LORDE, *Sister Outsider*

There is a Gaza in all of us.
—SELMA DABBAGH, "Inventing Gaza"

I

For the already besieged and malnourished population of Gaza, the summer of 2014 was a summer of hell. For fifty-one days and nights, Israel
decimated the Strip, dropping some twenty thousand tons of explosives—
the rough equivalent of six nuclear bombs—on one of the world's dense-
ly populated territories: a piece of land smaller than Liechtenstein, about one-
tenth the size of Rhode Island, and inhabited by a captive population of
nearly two million people. Unable to escape the destruction, people took refuge wherever they could—in hospitals, schools, mosques, churches, and other
United Nations–designated shelters. However, even these buildings were not
spared.[1] By the end of the devastation, more than 2,200 Palestinians were
dead, more than ten thousand were wounded, and more than a quarter-mil-
lion were displaced. To use a metaphor frequently invoked by Israeli strate-
gists, this was just another instance of Israel "mowing the grass."[2]

While Israeli bombs were destroying Palestinian lives that summer in
Gaza, people in the United States were engaged in two social media cam-

paigns that had gone viral. The first was the Ice Bucket Challenge. Spread via YouTube, this campaign dared people to film themselves dumping a bucket of ice water over their heads as a way to raise funds to combat amyotrophic lateral sclerosis (ALS disease). Typically, these videos concluded with a challenge, and viewers were asked to either follow suit with their own bucket of ice or donate money to the ALS Association.

The second social media campaign making the rounds that summer began on August 9 when Michael Brown, an unarmed Black youth, was shot dead by a white police officer on the streets of Ferguson, Missouri. The unusual aspect of this event was not the shooting itself but the public response to it. In the days and weeks that followed, crowds of protesters converged on Ferguson, where they were met head-on by a hypermilitarized police force. Across the country, concerned citizens took to Twitter to share pictures of themselves holding their hands up and thereby imitating the slain teenager's final gesture of surrender. Thus, the Black-led Hands Up, Don't Shoot movement was born, and in this way, a large swathe of the U.S. public showed support for the Black community in Ferguson and called for an end to racist police brutality nationwide.[3]

Apart from the synchronous timing, these two social media campaigns could not have been more distinct. The Ice Bucket Challenge was an anodyne, celebrity-centered human interest story. Although it was billed as a *challenge*, there was absolutely nothing *challenging* about it—at least not in terms of mainstream U.S. ideology. Philanthropic charity is part of neoliberalism's bread and butter, and even technocratic and political elites such as Bill Gates and George W. Bush felt free to take part in the ostensibly humiliating—but in actuality brand-enhancing—ritual. Sadly, the image of Laura Bush drenching her husband with ice water is as close as we will ever come to seeing the tables turned on the president whose administration was responsible for instituting the practice of waterboarding.

The second campaign, however, was confrontational. To call out police brutality and entrenched forms of white supremacy in the U.S. criminal justice system is to stake out a radical position indeed, and while the politics of the first campaign were as cold as the ice in its buckets, the message of the second was as hot as Ferguson's fires. Whereas the first served merely to pour cold water on the idea of mass empowerment, the latter fanned the flames of collective mobilization and resistance. The simple act of holding up one's hands thereby became a disruptive gesture. It opened up a fissure in the body politic between those who supported the actions of an overwhelmingly white police force and those who instead identified with the Black victims of police brutality—a long and ever growing list of martyrs that includes such names as Tanisha Anderson, Sandra Bland, Khalif Browder, Philando Castile, John Crawford III, Sam DuBose, Ezell Ford, Eric Garner, Freddie Gray, Akai Gur-

Figure 6.1. Performing in whiteface for the Hamas versus Hummus Challenge. (YouTube.)

ley, Meagan Hockaday, Natasha McKenna, Kajieme Powell, Tony Robinson, Walter Scott, Alton Sterling, Nia Wilson, and twelve-year-old Tamir Rice.

Significantly, both campaigns eventually went global, even reaching the Middle East. Some Israeli politicians, such as Rabbi Dov Lipman—a U.S.-born Knesset representative for the secular Yesh Atid (There Is a Future) party—began taking part in the Ice Bucket Challenge and urged their colleagues to do the same. It is noteworthy that in the video of Lipman's public drenching, he chose to speak in both Hebrew and English. Clearly, his intention was to make a statement that would travel beyond the borders of the Israeli state.[4]

Soon, the Ice Bucket Challenge was being adapted to address distinctly regional concerns. Six weeks after the initiation of Israel's latest round of destruction in Gaza, three Israeli soldiers posted a video on YouTube to drum up even more support for the Israeli war machine. Appearing in military fatigues, the trio offered viewers what they called the Hamas versus Hummus Challenge. One of the soldiers addressed the camera in English and stated that "Hamas [. . .] is a terrorist organization that threatens the lives of both Palestinians and Israelis. Hummus, on the other hand, is delicious." As Figure 6.1 shows, the three soldiers then smeared hummus all over their faces and dared their friends to follow their example, saying, "You have twenty-four hours to complete the challenge or you must donate one hundred dollars to Friends of the IDF." While the Hamas versus Hummus Challenge was not nearly as successful as the ALS fundraiser, it did have a handful of imitators. Like the Ice Bucket Challenge, the Hamas versus Hummus Challenge was less a critique of the governing logic of de facto apartheid than an ostensibly innocent and playful extension of it.[5]

While certain Israelis were busy crowning each other with ice cubes and smearing hummus on one another's faces, a number of Palestinians partook in a very different social media activity and posted pictures of themselves on Facebook and Twitter holding up signs of solidarity with Black protesters in Ferguson. Using direct knowledge garnered from personal experience, some Palestinians even began tweeting instructions on how best to deal with the pepper spray and tear gas. On August 15, the online publication *Electronic Intifada* published a statement signed by numerous Palestinian activists, academics, and organizations in which they declared support for the people of Ferguson. It stated, in part:

> We recognize the disregard and disrespect for black bodies and black life endemic to the supremacist system that rules the land with wanton brutality. Your struggles through the ages have been an inspiration to us as we fight our own battles for basic human dignities. We continue to find inspiration and strength from your struggles through the ages and your revolutionary leaders, like Malcolm X, Huey Newton, Kwame Ture [previously known as Stokely Carmichael], Angela Davis, Fred Hampton, Bobby Seale and others. We honor the life of Michael Brown, cut short less than a week before he was due to begin university. And we honor the far too many more killed in similar circumstances, motivated by racism and contempt for black life.[6]

Unsurprisingly, the philanthropic Ice Bucket Challenge never seemed to catch on with the people of Gaza during this time of intensified crisis. However, some Palestinians did transform this fundraiser into something useful for the Palestinian cause. In a two-minute YouTube video posted on August 23, the Palestinian journalist Ayman al-Aloul stood in the midst of Gaza's ruins and emptied a bucket of dirt on his head.[7] Several other social media users responded to his call, dubbed the Rubble Bucket Challenge, including the singer Mohammed Assaf, a refugee from Gaza who had become famous after winning the *Arab Idol* contest the previous year.[8]

How are we to make sense of these two social media campaigns? How are we to understand their spread beyond the borders of the U.S. nation-state and their appearance in the Middle East at a time of heightened aggression and assault? It is my claim that the very different ways in which these media campaigns tended to be used by Israelis and Palestinians reflect two very different forms of transnationality. What we have here is nothing less than a tale of two solidarities. While certain Israelis were attracted to the Ice Bucket Challenge, some Palestinians and their supporters were instead drawn to the events in Ferguson. We might see both of these tendencies as *transnational assertions of political belonging*. On the one hand, we have Israelis who used social media to claim a connection to the whitewashed U.S. mainstream, and on the other hand, we have Palestinians who used social media to forge ties with protests against institutionalized racism in the policing of U.S. cities. Both communities, I contend, were constructing global racial imaginaries, and if the Israelis were making a *claim to whiteness*, then the Palestinians, as I argue, were instead making a *claim to blackness*.

Through decades of Israel-friendly journalism, political speeches, and Hollywood movies—everything from *Exodus* (dir. Otto Preminger, 1960), *Cast a Giant Shadow* (dir. Melville Shavelson, 1966), and *The Delta Force* (dir. Menahem Golan, 1986) to more recent Zionist extravaganzas such as *You Don't Mess with the Zohan* (dir. Dennis Dugan, 2008) and *World War Z* (dir. Marc Foster, 2013)—the U.S.-Israeli alliance is often treated as if it is a completely natural affair. Of course, this partnership is more than just rhetoric; it also entails massive U.S. economic and military aid to Israel (more than to any other country), mutual support at various international forums such as the United Nations, and the Israeli training of U.S. police forces, including two of the law enforcement agencies deployed in Ferguson in the wake of Michael Brown's murder.[9]

But if the hegemonic white settler-colonialist imaginaries of these two countries can envision each other as partners, is it also possible to imagine a parallel alignment arising from the shadows? Or, to frame the question another way, can media be used to counter *transnational white supremacy* with *transnational Black Power*? In this chapter, I conclude by tackling head-on the racial dimension to the Palestinian struggle that has been shadowing this entire book. Crucially, I contend that Black-Palestinian imaginaries should not be considered radical simply because they are Black or Palestinian. Rather, Black-Palestinian imaginaries should be considered radical precisely insofar as they escape the exclusive identitarianisms of the settler-colonialist projects they contest. That is, they should be considered radical precisely insofar as they embody the Palestinian Idea.

II

From a current-day perspective that encompasses both Ferguson's flames and Gaza's ashes, it may seem unsurprising that those surviving under the iron heel of the United States' and Israel's respective settler-colonialist projects would find common cause in each other's struggles. Such an imaginative constellation, however, is neither natural nor inevitable, and in fact, in decades past, many prominent Black leaders lavished praise on the Zionist movement and the nascent State of Israel. They included such figures as Marcus Garvey, Alain Locke, A. Philip Randolph, Paul Robeson, W. E. B. Du Bois, and Martin Luther King Jr., radicals who were otherwise scathing in their criticism of racism and imperialism globally. Indeed, a week before Israel declared its independence in 1948, Du Bois wrote a newspaper editorial in which he regurgitated several Zionist tropes about Palestine being an empty land that would benefit from the Jews' civilizing mission, and King once called Israel "one of the great outposts of democracy in the world."[10] This curious phenomenon of Black Zionism was driven by two major factors: a common religious

lexicon (e.g., the Exodus and Promised Land myths) and a common diasporic condition.[11] However, neither of these factors should be understood as automatically dictating support for settler-colonialism, and other Black intel-
lectuals, such as James Baldwin and George Schuyler, were able to discuss
Israel and the similarities between the Jewish and Black communities without
succumbing to Zionism.[12]

The de–Zionization/Palestinianization of Black consciousness can largely be traced to the mid-twentieth-century emergence of Elijah Muhammad's
Nation of Islam. Through its official publication, *Muhammad Speaks*, this
organization articulated support for Palestine on the basis of a perceived
common religious identity, and it criticized Israel as the Middle Eastern arm
of U.S. imperialism.[13] However, with the exception of its greatest spokesperson—Malcolm X, who publicly broke with Muhammad in 1964—the Nation
of Islam's influence on the broader Black community remained somewhat
limited. It was not until a few years later that support for Palestine would
begin to approach the secular Black mainstream.

Ironically, the watershed moment in the Black turn toward Palestine occurred at a time when pro-Israeli sentiments in the United States were at a
peak. Shortly after the Arab-Israeli War of June 1967, the Student Nonviolent
Coordinating Committee (SNCC)—then under Stokely Carmichael's leadership—printed a two-page spread in its official newsletter titled "Third World
Round-up: The Palestine Problem: Test Your Knowledge."[14] This piece, which
seems to have been largely lifted from a pamphlet published in 1966 by the
Palestine Research Center in Beirut, was composed of thirty-two damning
points about Zionism.[15] Its publication indicated a growing wedge between
SNCC and certain Jewish supporters of the Civil Rights Movement—a thaw
in relations that was mirrored forty years later, in 2016, when Black activists
published a policy platform that included strong support for Palestine, thus
bringing tensions to a head between the #BlackLivesMatter movement and
some U.S.-based Jewish groups.[16]

Significantly, the publication of "The Palestine Problem" came at an important moment in the history of the Black Freedom Movement—a time that
the tension between the competing nationalist and internationalist tendencies within SNCC and other activist groups could no longer be contained.
While advocates of the former were likely to see Palestinian liberation as a
matter unrelated to the goals of the Civil Rights Movement, those more internationally inclined activists endeavored to link the struggle for Black liberation with the cause of revolutionaries the world over, not only in Palestine but
also in places such as Algeria, Angola, Cuba, and Vietnam.[17] Indeed, Carmichael even turned Palestine into something of a litmus test for white activists,
and in a widely distributed speech in 1968, he echoed Max Horkheimer's famous quip about capitalism and fascism; whereas Horkheimer had argued

that "whoever is not willing to talk about capitalism should also keep quiet about fascism," Carmichael declared that "if white people who call themselves revolutionary or radical want our support, they have to condemn Zionism."[18] On this point, Black activists were following in the footsteps of Malcolm X, who argued that the struggles against colonialism abroad were intimately linked to the fight against racist injustice in America on both sides of the Mason-Dixon Line. "As long as we think [. . .] that we should get Mississippi straightened out before we worry about the Congo," he declared, "you'll never get Mississippi straightened out. Not until you start realizing your connection with the Congo."[19]

To be sure, SNCC was not the only Black organization calling for this radical paradigm shift, and that same summer, the newly established Black Panther Party (BPP) also began printing essays in defense of Palestine in its official newsletter, *Black Panther*. The essays even included translations of articles written by leading Palestinian figures such as Yasir Arafat and George Habash, leader of the Popular Front for the Liberation of Palestine. Indeed, Alex Lubin claims that this publication was, for its time, "one of the most reliable sources of news in the U.S. on the Israeli occupation of the West Bank."[20] While SNCC was undergoing something of an identity crisis in 1967, the BPP had even fewer qualms about making common cause with the Third World. Inspired by militant icons ranging from Frantz Fanon, Malcolm X, and Robert Williams to Che Guevara, Ho Chi Minh, and Mao Zedong, the Black Panthers saw themselves as another link in the chain of the global anticolonialist struggle. This is what the BPP's co-founder Huey Newton called "revolutionary intercommunalism," and it was in these terms that the BPP articulated support for Palestine.[21]

Within a decade, Black solidarity with Palestine was being expressed by more mainstream groups and figures. In late 1979, for instance, a delegation from the Southern Christian Leadership Conference (SCLC)—the Civil Rights organization previously associated with Martin Luther King Jr.—made a trip to Lebanon, where the delegation's members joined hands with Arafat for a singing of "We Shall Overcome." That same year, Andrew Young, a former SCLC member and personal aide to King, was stripped of his position as U.S. Ambassador to the United Nations after he broke official protocol by meeting with a representative of the Palestine Liberation Organization (PLO).[22] Such overtures toward the Palestinians from more established, less militant Black figures would have been inconceivable had it not been for the pioneering work of groups such as SNCC and the BPP. Of course, this is not to say that the legacy of Black Zionism was completely erased. The veteran organizer Bayard Rustin, for instance, reacted to such gestures of Black-Palestinian solidarity by publishing op-eds comparing the tactics of the PLO to the racist terrorism of the Ku Klux Klan (KKK), and after leading a fact-finding mission to the Middle East in 1981, he declared that the State of Israel was free of official racism.[23] Similarly, as acting U.S. president, Barack Obama justified his administration's support for Israel by appealing to the legacy of the Civil Rights Movement.[24] Despite the persistence of such Black overtures toward Israel, the groundwork for Black-Palestinian partnership had nevertheless been laid, and it continues to serve as a foundation for strategic alliance and coordination.

While in previous decades this global racial imaginary was forged through traditional media and the printed word, it is now being drawn through different communications technologies and platforms, including Facebook, Twitter, and YouTube, as well as film festivals, hip hop music, and staged news spectacles. In the hyperconnected, digital, wireless-enabled world in which we currently live, media is not incidental to the process of articulating links of global political belonging; it is fundamental. This point has long been argued in relation to national identities, from Marshall McLuhan's work on the Gutenberg press to Benedict Anderson's ruminations on print capital, and—more pointedly in this context—to the work of George Antonious whose tome *The Arab Awakening* (1938) traced the genesis of modern Arab nationalism to the introduction of the printing press to Beirut.[25] However, it is important to note that the identities forged through media and communications technologies can also transcend national borders. That is, just as media can work in the creation of imagined *national* communities, it can also assist in the formation of imagined *transnational* communities. Indeed, how else are people from different countries, different continents, different religions, and different ethnic and linguistic backgrounds to come together if not through media? Hence, if media are indeed some of the primary instruments being used to foster U.S.-Israeli amity, can they not also be used to stoke the flames of Black-Palestinian solidarity?

Such a possibility is not merely a theoretical prospect. It is already happening. Black support for Palestine can be found in the work of artists, activists, and academics ranging from Boots Riley and Lauryn Hill to Robin D. G. Kelley and Cornel West, all of whom appeared in a Black-Palestinian solidarity video uploaded to YouTube in October 2015 entitled "When I See Them, I See Us."[26] The filmmaker and actor Danny Glover has been involved in the making of several Palestinian films, serving as a producer for Elia Suleiman's *The Time That Remains* (2009) and Annemarie Jacir's *Salt of This Sea* (2008) and *When I Saw You* (2012), and Jacir was even awarded a Paul Robeson Fund for Independent Media Film Grant in 2007. Moreover, the Black comedian Dave Chappelle, a convert to Islam who is known for his biting political satire, regularly invites the Palestinian American comedian Mo Amer to open his live shows. Hip hop has also served as a musical medium linking Black radicalism to Palestine. In this regard, one of the more

outspoken artists is Lupe Fiasco. In October 2011, he appeared onstage at the
sixth annual Black Entertainment Television (BET) Hip Hop Awards holding a Palestinian flag as he performed his song "Words I Never Said."

Another significant example of Black-Palestinian solidarity presents itself in the work of the Pittsburgh-based emcee Jasiri X. After visiting Palestine in early 2014 with a delegation of other Black artists and activists, Jasiri
X produced "Checkpoint," a three-minute music video that he distributed on
YouTube.[27] In this short video, Jasiri X uses the term "checkpoint" more than
fifty times. It becomes redundant, expected, exasperating—just like the
physical space of the checkpoint itself.[28] But while Palestinian identity is
often constructed on the crucible of checkpoints, barriers, and borders, these
places can also play a role in the forging of transnational Black solidarity.
That is, such sites and practices of oppression can be transformed into places of liberation. This is true for the checkpoint just as it has historically been
true for other sites, such as the lynching tree and the prison.[29] While Jasiri
X's video emphasizes the oppressive role that media, technology, and architecture play in the lives of Palestinians—the fingerprint screens, the separation walls, the color-coded security levels—he also points out how media can
be used as a form of resistance, and the video is made up mostly of images
and footage that he took during the trip. The importance that the video places on Black-Palestinian unity is most evident in the lines that it repeats about
Martin Luther King and Malcolm X:

If Martin Luther King had a dream at the checkpoint
He'd wake up with loud screams from the scenes at the checkpoint
It's Malcolm X by any means at the checkpoint
Imagine if your daily routine was the checkpoint

Sometimes Black articulations of solidarity with the Palestinian struggle
appear in protests or as part of staged news spectacles. For instance, when
Israeli settlers kidnapped the sixteen-year-old Palestinian Mohammed Abu
Khdeir on a street near his home in Jerusalem in July 2014 and burned him
to death, some supporters in the United States created protest signs and Internet memes comparing him to Emmett Till, the fourteen-year-old Black
martyr whose gruesome murder in Mississippi in 1955 helped instigate the
Civil Rights Movement.[30] Moreover, in January 2015, some sixty to seventy
university students in California, including the prominent activist Kristian
Davis Bailey, celebrated Martin Luther King Day by disrupting traffic on the
heavily used San Mateo Bridge. Claiming that they wanted to take the federal holiday back, they planned to block traffic every twenty-eight minutes
to symbolize the statistic that every twenty-eight hours another Black person
is killed by a police officer or white vigilantes in the United States. Although

this was primarily a protest about Black lives, the protestors nevertheless unfurled a huge Palestinian flag on the bridge, thereby linking the two struggles. Footage of the protest taken from helicopters appeared on local television stations, and the image of the Palestinian flag was the most visible part of the protest.[31]

Importantly, Black-Palestinian solidarity is not a one-way street. It is also performed and enacted by Palestinians on the ground in Palestine and in the global diaspora. Just as some of the most radical Black articulators of Palestinian solidarity have been poets and performers, Palestinian spoken word artists and hip hop musicians have likewise contributed to this imaginative constellation. Here I am thinking specifically of Suheir Hammad and Remi Kanazi, two U.S.-based Palestinian poets. Hammad's first book is even titled *Born Palestinian, Born Black*, and both artists draw from a common pantheon of Black and Palestinian heroes: Amiri Baraka, Mahmoud Darwish, Martin Luther King, Audre Lorde, Malcolm X, Nelson Mandela, Rosa Parks, Edward Said, and Desmond Tutu.[32]

Hip hop music has been a major platform for the articulation of Black-Palestinian solidarity.[33] Tamer Nafar, a member of one of the best-known Palestinian hip hop groups, DAM, has explicitly linked his music to that of Black performers in the United States, such as Tupac Shakur. Quoting the hip hop legend Chuck D, Nafar claims that if hip hop can serve as a "Black CNN" to youth of color in the United States, then it can also serve as a "Palestinian Al Jazeera" and communicate the social and political realities of life under Israeli rule.[34] While the members of DAM usually get the most attention, especially since they were profiled in *Slingshot Hip Hop* (dir. Jackie Salloum, 2008), they are not the only Palestinian musicians constructing this global racial imaginary. Similar examples include Saz, the subject of the documentary *Saz: The Palestinian Rapper for Change* (dir. Gil Karni, 2005), and Shadia Mansour, a British-born Palestinian rapper who first performed in the United States at a benefit concert for the Black political prisoner Mumia Abu Jamal.[35] Her first single, "Al-Kufiya Arabiya" (The Keffiyah Is Arab), features vocals by M-1 from Dead Prez, and it was recorded in Chuck D's Terrordome Studio and mixed by the frequent Public Enemy collaborator Johnny "Juice" Rosado.[36]

Thanks both to the historical prominence of figures such as Elijah Muhammad and Malcolm X and the Muslim identity of some hip hop groups and musicians, Islam has sometimes been seen as a key ingredient in the forging of Black-Palestinian ties, but one should be careful not to overlook Christianity's potential as a conduit for camaraderie. The Greek Catholic theologian Joseph Raya, for instance, represents a direct link between the two struggles. Born in Lebanon, Raya spent fifteen years serving as a priest in Birmingham, Alabama, where he met Martin Luther King and participated in the Civil Rights Movement. When Raya welcomed members of Birmingham's Black community to his church's Sunday services, he was kidnapped and beaten by white vigilantes, including members of the KKK.[37] Following his time in Alabama, Raya was appointed as an archbishop in Israel, where he continued advocating for the dispossessed, specifically taking up the cause of Palestinian refugees. Just as Raya had previously participated in the March on Washington with Martin Luther King in 1963, he led a march on the Knesset that culminated in front of Prime Minister Golda Meir's office in 1972. There, Raya climbed on top of a jeep and quoted Bible verses against the government: "Jezebel, Jezebel, you took the vineyard from the poor. What is God going to do to you?"[38] But Raya is not the only direct Christian link between the two struggles. More recently, the Lutheran pastor Khader el-Yateem was involved in a successful campaign to remove a Confederate monument honoring Robert E. Lee from a cemetery in Brooklyn. El-Yateem, a Palestinian immigrant from Beit Jala who was previously tortured and subjected to long stints of solitary confinement in Israeli prisons, is committed to racial justice in both countries. "While we will never forget the history of slavery in America," he says, "we are ready to move forward and address racism at its root."[39]

While Black-Palestinian solidarity takes many forms, from rap to religious creed, some of the most powerful Palestinian appeals to Black radicalism have come in the form of media spectacles. Here, one may recall the Freedom March in Hebron discussed in Chapter 1, but this incident is hardly the only example of Palestinians formulating their egalitarian cause in the language of the Black Freedom Movement. Just sixteen months earlier, in November 2011, six Palestinians in the West Bank disrupted the governing logic of apartheid by simply boarding a bus. Imitating the historic Freedom Rides that took place across the U.S. South some fifty years earlier, these six Palestinians carried signs and wore T-shirts emblazoned with words such as "dignity," "freedom," and "justice." Included in this group of Freedom Riders were people such as Mazin Qumsiyeh, a Palestinian professor who writes and teaches about nonviolent resistance; Badia Dwaik, one of the activists who would go on to organize the Freedom March in Hebron in 2013; and Fadi Quran, a Palestinian activist who had previously studied at Stanford University with the playwright and Civil Rights Movement historian Clayborne Carson.

The Jerusalem-bound bus these Palestinian activists boarded was filled mostly with Jewish settlers, people who live in Israel's illegally constructed colonies in the West Bank. When the bus arrived at a checkpoint, several Israeli officers entered it and demanded to see the Palestinians' identity cards and permits. One of the Freedom Riders, Nadim Sharabati, asked a question of his own: "Do you demand permits from settlers who come to our area?"

When one of the officers explained that he was simply following the law, Sharabati replied, matter-of-factly, "Those are racist laws."[40] When they refused to get off the bus, all six of the Freedom Riders were physically dragged from it, handcuffed, and arrested. Some of the settler onlookers called them "terrorists," and one of them even told a reporter, "This is not a Martin Luther King bus."[41]

Media were a central component of the Freedom Riders' strategy. Speaking to a journalist, one of the activists—a pharmacist named Bassel al-A'raj, who was later killed by Israeli forces during a raid in March 2017—explained that the primary difference between this action and other acts of resistance was, in fact, the presence of media.[42] Before the Freedom Riders boarded the bus, they notified several journalists about their intent, and after their arrest, they released a statement to the press comparing their action to the original Freedom Rides. It read, in part, "Although the tactics and methodologies differ, both white supremacists and the Israeli occupiers commit the same crime: they strip a people of freedom, justice and dignity."[43] A number of journalists boarded the bus with them, and news of the event was picked up by a variety of established media outlets. The Brazilian-Lebanese cartoonist Carlos Latuff also helped memorialize the event by drawing a cartoon of Rosa Parks sitting on a bus dressed as a Palestinian.[44]

While the 2011 Freedom Ride was just a single occurrence, however, other activists in Palestine have turned it into a regular affair. Since 2012, members of the Jenin Freedom Theatre have organized an annual Freedom Bus that brings together international and local artists, academics, and activists for a one- to two-week trip through the West Bank. Sticking mostly to rural communities and villages, the Freedom Bus aims not only to connect internationals to locals but also to put members of different Palestinian communities in contact with one another, rural and urban, refugee and nonrefugee, diasporic and nondiasporic. Taking its name from the original Freedom Rides that crisscrossed the Jim Crow South, the Freedom Bus is not just a tour; it is a radical cultural event, and artists, bloggers, filmmakers, musicians (including DAM), photojournalists, and performers frequently participate. Those on the Freedom Bus take part in political demonstrations in places such as Bil'in and Nabi Saleh, where there are ongoing popular mobilization campaigns against settlements and land theft; they perform acts of community service, such as the planting of trees in the Jordan Valley and the escorting of Palestinian shepherds in the fields near at-Tuwani, where they are daily threatened by violent Jewish settlers; and they attend media and cultural events, including film screenings, musical concerts, and theatrical performances.

It is worth pointing out that several people involved with both the Jenin Freedom Theatre and the annual Freedom Bus are also intimately linked to Black radical movements in the United States. Constancia "Dinky" Romilly—

the onetime partner of the late SNCC leader James Forman—is the president of the New York–based Friends of the Jenin Freedom Theatre. Also on its board is Dorothy Zellner, another 1960s veteran who helped Stokely Carmichael draw the original panther logo later adopted by the BPP; she more recently embarked on a university speaking tour called "From Mississippi to Jerusalem" in which she discussed the connections between the Civil Rights Movement and Palestine. The Freedom Bus itself has a large list of endorsers, including Angela Davis, Desmond Tutu, Alice Walker, and, before her death in 2014, Maya Angelou, and organizational supporters of the Freedom Bus include the Bronx-based Peace Poets and the Highlander Research and Education Center, the late Myles Horton's folk school in rural Tennessee that once served as a training ground for such Civil Rights icons as Richard Abernathy, James Bevel, Septima Poinsette Clark, Martin Luther King Jr., John Lewis, and Rosa Parks.

In March 2014, I had the privilege of joining the Freedom Bus. While the connections between it and the Black Freedom Movement were not always explicit, they lurked beneath the surface and occasionally emerged into plain view. In the village of Nabi Saleh, for instance, we met with the longtime peace and justice activists Bassem and Nariman Tamimi. Bassem has been arrested more than a dozen times and spent more than three years in jail for his involvement in organizing protests against the Israeli theft of Palestinian land. He spoke to us about his advocacy of nonviolence and the inspiration provided by other global struggles, including the Civil Rights Movement. We joined him for one of Nabi Saleh's regular, weekly demonstrations against the gradual takeover of the village's lands and water spring by the Jewish settlers of Halamish. Armed with only our voices, we were nevertheless met with tear gas. Children from the village, including Bassem's daughter Ahed, often run to the front lines of these demonstrations, and while some people have criticized their participation at these potentially dangerous events, Bassem disagrees. Speaking to us afterward, he specifically pointed to the example of the Children's Crusade in Birmingham, Alabama, of 1963, in which Black children were met with Bull Connor's water cannons and police dogs.[45]

Bassem's daughter Ahed was quite young at the time of my visit in 2015, but she has since become something of a Palestinian icon. Just a few months after my trip to Nabi Saleh, her image went viral when she was photographed biting the hand of an Israeli soldier in an effort to rescue a boy that he was violently detaining. Even more significantly, in late 2017 a video of her slapping an Israeli soldier was widely distributed via social media, leading to her arrest on assault charges. For the next eight months, she remained behind bars.[46] Remarkably, the discourse surrounding Ahed quickly became a debate about race. Some in Israel had long viewed the Tamimis with suspicion, and it was revealed that the Knesset had once even instigated a classified investigation to determine whether they were a real family or a group of Palestinian actors.[47] According to this conspiracy theory, the Tamimis were all just playing parts, and Ahed was selected for her role because her fair skin and blond hair would elicit Western sympathy. Apparently for her Israeli critics, Ahed was simply too white.

While Knesset members were forming secret committees to solve the mystery of Ahed's whiteness, others were instead linking her to the Black struggle. In early 2017, Ahed was invited to take part in a U.S. speaking tour alongside Amanda Weatherspoon, a Black feminist liberation theologian. Ahed was forced to forgo the trip after the U.S. Consulate put her visa application under a prolonged "administrative review."[48] Moreover, shortly after Ahed was arrested, a Black journalist from Philadelphia used the occasion of Martin Luther King's birthday to compare her to Rosa Parks, and the U.S.-based Civil Rights organization Dream Defenders released a statement likening her to Trayvon Martin, the seventeen-year-old Black martyr from Florida: "From Trayvon Martin to Mohammed Abu Khdeir and Khalif Browder to Ahed Tamimi—racism, state violence and mass incarceration have robbed our people of their childhoods and their futures."[49] The statement was signed by many of the Black artists, academics, and activists mentioned in this chapter, including Michael Bennett, Angela Davis, Danny Glover, Jasiri X, Robin D. G. Kelley, Alice Walker, and Cornel West.[50]

But to return to the Freedom Bus trip of 2015, one of the strongest manifestations of Black radicalism I witnessed took place in al-Hadidiya, a small village in the Jordan Valley that sits just a few hundred yards from the fortified Jewish settlement of Ro'i. We gathered together under a makeshift tent with the longtime activist Abu Saqr and other village residents for a performance of improvisational "Playback Theater" in which the Palestinian actors listened to stories from the audience and interpreted them on the spot.[51] Most of that day's performances involved incidents of Israeli oppression—namely, confrontations with the Israel Defense Forces (IDF) and Jewish settlers. Toward the end of the performance, however, one of the Freedom Bus riders, a young African American woman, related the story of Eric Garner, the unarmed, Black New Yorker who broke up a fight in the summer of 2014, only to be approached by five police officers and tackled to the ground. As he collapsed underneath the force of a chokehold, Garner repeated the words "I can't breathe" eleven times before losing consciousness and dying (Figure 6.2). The entire event was recorded on video and widely shared on social media, but a grand jury refused to indict any of the officers who murdered him. There, in a tent in al-Hadidiya, amidst squawking chickens and bleating sheep, the Palestinian actor Motaz Malhees reenacted this saga, contorting his face to emulate Garner's final fatal moments (Figure 6.3). Most of the

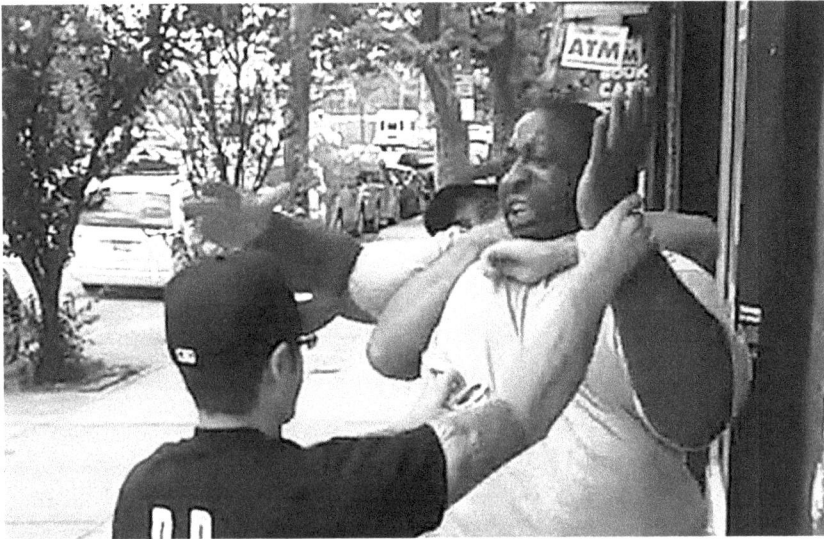

Figure 6.2. The murder of Eric Garner, July 2014. (YouTube.)

Figure 6.3. The Palestinian actor Motaz Malhees reenacting Garner's murder in March 2015. Paintings of fish by the artist Ala'a Albaba (see Chapter 5) are displayed in the background. (Photograph by the author.)

Palestinians in the audience had not heard the story of Garner, and seeing this tale of racist U.S. aggression reinterpreted in the context of Zionist settler-colonialism was powerful and moving. It was a moment in which the idea of tying together the oppressed communities of both countries became tangible, a moment in which transnational Black solidarity became more than mere specter.

III

But what about the other side of the coin? What about the hegemonic solidarity that Black and Palestinian activists are responding to, the global racial imaginary linking U.S. and Israeli power structures? Evidence of this underlying connection can sometimes appear in unexpected places. When executives at the History Channel produced a documentary in 1996 celebrating the establishment of the State of Israel, one can only wonder what possessed them to give it the same title as the first Hollywood blockbuster, D. W. Griffith's notoriously racist epic *The Birth of a Nation* (1915). Griffith's silent film was a reactionary reimagining of the U.S. Civil War and the Reconstruction Era that romanticized the KKK as a heroic band of champions guarding white civilization against the threat of Black disorder run amok. Based on Thomas Dixon's novel *The Clansman: An Historical Romance of the Ku Klux Klan* (1905), the film was even given a special White House screening by the U.S. president, Dixon's former university classmate Woodrow Wilson. "It is like writing history with lightning," Wilson allegedly commented after viewing the film, "and my only regret is that it is all so terribly true."[52]

Significantly, *The Birth of a Nation* appeared at a very particular time in U.S. history: the year 1915. As Cedric Robinson argued, 1915 marked a moment in which the racial constellations that would later come to characterize the twentieth-century American landscape were still in flux. This instability manifested itself in a number of phenomena. That same year, for instance, the second KKK was inaugurated on Stone Mountain, the Jewish factory superintendent Leo Frank was lynched by a mob of anti-Semites in Georgia, and the Black boxing champion Jack Johnson was defeated by Jess Willard, the latest incarnation of "the Great White Hope." Also of relevance here is the racialized discourse that accompanied the U.S. invasion and occupation of Haiti, which commenced that July.[53] Moreover, with the intra-European battles of World War I entering their second year, large immigrant communities in the United States remained deeply divided, and they still lacked a cohesive collective identity capable of bringing them together.[54]

Situated in the midst of this racial maelstrom, Robinson argued, *The Birth of a Nation* functioned as an important cinematic counterpart to a broader ideological project: *the whitening of America*. In his words, "What

Griffith consciously served as a midwife for was the birth of a new, virile American whiteness."[55] For Robinson, this whiteness—this unifying "myth of white solidarity" as he elsewhere put it—was not something that had existed from time immemorial.[56] Rather, it was a defensive reaction on the part of governing elites and their sympathizers to an underlying disorder, a restless discontent that included, among other things, *Black insurgency*.

While the decision to borrow the title of Griffith's film for a documentary about the founding of the State of Israel may have been accidental, a comparison of these two texts can nevertheless be quite revealing. Indeed, rewatching *Israel: Birth of a Nation* (dir. Herbert Krosney, 1996) today, one is struck by how much its basic ideological coordinates resemble those of its namesake. While Griffith's infamous film simultaneously whitewashed America's European immigrant groups and demonized Blacks, the History Channel's TV documentary homogenized Jews and scapegoated Palestinians; while the former film erased the history of slavery, the latter erased the ethnic cleansing of Palestine, and while the former glorified the KKK, the latter romanticized violent Zionist militia groups such as the Irgun. Moreover, both films present an upside-down, topsy-turvy view of their respective "nations," and the people at the top—the white and Ashkenazi elites—are reimagined as the victims, as an underdog David confronting a barbaric Goliath.[57]

Comparisons, of course, can easily be refuted, and a list of similarities between any two states, societies, or even cinematic texts can immediately be canceled by an even longer list of differences—facts negated by counterfacts; evidence, by counterevidence. Thus, if the births of these two nations are to be examined together, it behooves us to go beyond curious coincidences and happenstance analogies. Even more, we must discover how these distinct racial regimes interact with and influence each other. As David Theo Goldberg insists, our analysis not only must be comparative; it also must be *relational*.[58] In this regard, we should follow in the footsteps of scholars such as Nur Masalha, Gabriel Piterberg, Shira Robinson, Steven Salaita, and Patrick Wolfe, who understand the partnership between the U.S. and Israeli nation-states to be a result of an ideological bind—a common rootedness in *white settler-colonialism*.[59]

Importantly, if the critique of Zionism as a white settler-colonialist project applied to only a bygone era, it would just be another tale for the history books. However, in the case of Israel—as in the case of the United States—the practices and institutions of white settler-colonialism persist into the present. Significantly, Israel's power structures are not simply Jewish; they are Ashkenazi, and just as an attempt has been made to whiten certain groups within the U.S. body politic, a process of Europeanization has likewise been perpetuated against those Jews in Israel who do not completely match the Ashkenazi ideal. In Hebrew, there is even a word for this process: *lehishtaknez* (Ashkenazation).

Israel's whitening project has been aimed particularly at the state's single largest demographic bloc, the Mizrahim. Members of this community are either native to Palestine or from other parts of the Arab world. For many Mizrahim, such as those interviewed in the film *Forget Baghdad: Jews and Arabs—the Iraqi Connection* (dir. Samir, 2002), the initiation into Zionism was humiliating. When Jews from Iraq arrived in Israel in the 1950s, they were sprayed with DDT before they were allowed to disembark from the plane. Around the same time, laws were set up to keep Mizrahi Jews from swimming in the same public pools as the European Ashkenazim, just as Blacks under Jim Crow were not allowed to swim with whites.[60] Most notoriously, hundreds of Yemeni Jewish families alleged that when they came to Israel, their babies were taken from them and given to Ashkenazi couples, an incident that Shoshana Madmoni-Gerber has examined at length. Although this affair is commonly accepted as historical fact by Israel's Yemeni community, it is still firmly denied by mainstream (i.e., Ashkenazi) sources.[61]

It is not so surprising, then, that some of the first people to criticize Israel as a government and society shaped by a white power structure were Mizrahi. Significantly, many of them formulated their protests in the language of Black Power. In 1970, a group of young North African Jews living in Israel's impoverished slums created their own political organization. They called it the Israeli Black Panther Party.[62] Inspired by the image of revolutionary Black figures in the United States such as Angela Davis, they organized protests and tactical media interventions and even established contact with the PLO.[63] Their largest demonstration in Tel Aviv drew a crowd of more than seven thousand supporters. These efforts eventually culminated in an official meeting with Prime Minister Golda Meir, and she commented afterward, "They are not nice people."[64]

By aligning themselves with the politics of Black Power, these Mizrahi dissidents were appropriating the slurs that they had themselves experienced. Ashkenazi Israelis often referred to Mizrahi Jews as "blacks" (in Yiddish, *shvartze*), or even "black animals," and even David Ben-Gurion pejoratively likened them to the U.S. Black community.[65] Like the BPP of the United States, the Israeli Black Panthers were subjected to government surveillance, repression, and imprisonment, and the group soon fell apart. Some of its members followed in the footsteps of former Black Panther Eldridge Cleaver. Just as he had blazed a trail from the politics of revolution to the Republican Party, some of the Israeli Panthers likewise transformed themselves into right-wing patriots.[66] But others, such as Reuven Abergil, have stayed the course. In 1997, he came together with several other Mizrahi activists to form the Mizrahi Democratic Rainbow Coalition. This progressive political organization takes its name from the original Rainbow Coalition declared into existence in the 1960s by Fred Hampton, the Black Panther activist who was assassinated in his sleep at age twenty-one by a squad of Chicago police officers working in tandem with J. Edgar Hoover's Federal Bureau of Investigation.[67]

Israel's Ethiopian Jewish community has also faced practices of racist discrimination. In January 2013, the Israeli daily *Ha'aretz* confirmed long-standing accusations that Ethiopian women were being sterilized without their consent, a practice that has a long history in the United States.[68] Moreover, in April 2015 large protests took place in Jerusalem and Tel Aviv after a video emerged that showed two Israeli police officers assaulting an Ethiopian IDF soldier in uniform. Like the Mizrahi activists before them, many of these Ethiopian protesters drew inspiration from U.S. racial politics, and some of the demonstrators in Jerusalem reportedly chanted "Baltimore is here"—a reference to the urban rebellion that was simultaneously taking place in Maryland following the murder of Freddie Gray by police.[69]

Here it is worth pausing to also note the presence of African asylum seekers in Israel. In recent years, their arrival has triggered a spate of hate crimes and mob violence. Thousands of these immigrants have been rounded up and placed in prisons and detention camps. The Israeli government has even sent some of them back to the countries from which they were trying to escape. Asked about these asylum seekers in 2012, Miri Regev, a member of the Likud party and spokesperson for the IDF, called the Africans a "cancer." She later apologized for this comment—not to the asylum seekers but, rather, to Israeli cancer survivors; she expressed regret for comparing them to Africans. Three years later, she was appointed minister of culture. Around the same time of Regev's heartfelt apology to cancer victims, Interior Minister Eli Yishai of the Shas party was likewise incensed by the presence of Africans in Israel. He told a reporter, "This country belongs to us, to the white man." Continuing on, he stated that he would use "all the tools [necessary] to expel the foreigners, until not one infiltrator remains."[70]

To be sure, all of these communities of "Black Jews" exist in a strange, interstitial space within Israel's racial order. As Jews who are, as David Theo Goldberg puts it, "white but not quite," they represent a crack in Zionism's foundations.[71] However, this fact alone certainly does not guarantee a commitment to anticolonialist politics. Indeed, Eli Yishai is a Mizrahi Jew, born in Jerusalem to a family of Tunisian Jews. His claim to whiteness is thus a stark reminder that sociological categories do not necessarily correspond to political positions. As the case of Yishai demonstrates, even an Arab Jew can aspire to be lily white—just as a Black police officer in the United States can work to perpetuate the white power of a police force.[72] For the protests of such groups to truly be radical and point us beyond the Zionist present, they must *fully* reject Israel's white supremacist hierarchy. The question before the Mizrahim is therefore clear: do they aspire to join the colonizers or the colonized? That is, are they merely going to demand further inclusion in the existing oppressive order, or are they going to overturn that order by making common cause with the Palestinians?[73]

Analogies, of course, have their limits, and if Palestinians, Mizrahi Jews, and Ethiopian Israelis can all articulate their grievances in the terms of Black Power, then one might question the usefulness of this paradigm. Indeed, the objective structural differences among these various communities are substantial, and such transnational racial imaginaries should not be mistaken for declarations of sameness. Whatever similarities we may find are immediately canceled by a world of difference. To put it simply, Gaza is not Ferguson; the West Bank is not Watts; Baltimore is not Jerusalem. Here it is important to note that, strictly speaking, the position of Palestinians vis-à-vis Zionist settler-colonialism is more akin to that of the Native Americans vis-à-vis U.S. settler-colonialism, a point that has not been lost on Israeli leaders from David Ben-Gurion (who compared the challenges facing the Zionist project to the battles that U.S. colonists had fought against indigenous "redskins") to Miri Regev (who has pointed to the U.S. treatment of Native Americans as an example to be emulated).[74] Some Palestinians have made this same link. Elias Sanbar, for instance, declared, "We are [. . .] the American Indians of the Jewish settlers in Palestine."[75] However, our conception of Black-Palestinian solidarity need not exclude or erase the question of indigeneity, and if we focus on only empirical differences between the Black and Palestinian communities, we lose the point of the analogy. Declarations of solidarity and political belonging are rarely meant to be scientific comparisons. Those who participate in the imagining of Black-Palestinian ties are not simply describing the world as it already exists; they are creating something new. They are partaking in what Cedric Robinson calls a "specular imagining," giving flesh to a potential that had previously been hidden— *the prospect of transnational Black Power inhabiting the shadows of transnational white supremacy.*[76]

IV

These notions of transnational whiteness and blackness, of course, beg further explication, and there is perhaps no better place to start than with the writings of W. E. B. Du Bois. In his semiautobiographical work, *Darkwater*, Du Bois asked, "'But what on earth is whiteness that one should so desire it?' Then always, somehow, some way, silently but clearly, I am given to understand that whiteness is the ownership of the earth forever and ever, Amen!"[77] Du Bois thereby discussed whiteness simultaneously in concrete and theological terms, both as "the ownership of the earth" and as a desire—or, as he put it on the very next page of the text, as a "new religion."[78] It is imperative to grasp both of these dimensions—the physical and the metaphysical, the material and the ideal. This twofold nature of whiteness, the definite and the demonic, is also captured in the work of George Lipsitz, who understands whiteness as a possessive investment. Like any other property, one can both *possess* whiteness and *become possessed by* it. That is, whiteness is not an inherited biological trait but a subject position, and once a person has assumed this role, it informs his or her subsequent actions and behavior; he or she has become possessed by whiteness.[79]

Importantly, from this perspective, *anyone* can aspire to possess whiteness, even those who are otherwise not considered white. This apparent paradox is memorably discussed in Ghassan Hage's book *White Nation*. The first chapter begins with an anecdote about a Lebanese Muslim woman in Australia who was attacked by another shopper in a Sydney supermarket. Her headscarf was violently ripped from her head, and she was verbally assaulted. A number of similar incidents have been reported in the Australian press, and Hage managed to interview one of the assailants. She justified her actions, saying that "Muslims are dirty" and that "there's already too many of them here."[80] Sixty pages into the book, however, the other shoe drops. The perpetrator of this hateful action was not a white Aussie, as we are led to believe, but a Lebanese Christian immigrant. This incident therefore demonstrates the fact that whiteness can be claimed even by people who inhabit a lower position in society's pecking order. For Hage, whiteness is not an essence but a yearning for dominance. It is a desire for ownership and possession. Like Lacan's *objet petit a,* whiteness is an aspiration that will never be completely attained. This is what Hage calls the "White Nation fantasy."[81]

Such a view of whiteness opens up a Pandora's box. If whiteness is not ontologically grounded or passed down through one's DNA, then anyone can claim it—sociological categories be damned. Hence, recall Frantz Fanon's old quip, "Some blacks can be whiter than the whites."[82] The same also goes for the Palestinians. Indeed, Joseph Massad has made this very argument, and he criticizes certain Palestinian political leaders for appealing to the West in racialized terms. "Proving the 'whiteness' of Palestinians," he writes, "has been the underlying premise of the PLO's approach since the beginning of its outreach efforts to the West."[83]

A cinematic example of this tendency presents itself in *Miral* (dir. Julian Schnabel, 2010). Based on the life of the journalist Rula Jabreal, the film certainly has its merits—for instance, its inclusion of footage of a house demolition, a regular occurrence for Palestinians living under Israeli rule. However, the film nevertheless invites its audiences to sympathize with its Palestinian protagonist by racializing her as a good, clean, civilized, white Palestinian

who stands in stark contrast to the film's bad, Black, male Palestinian crimi-
nals and deviants who, as Omar el-Khairy points out, "spend their time rap-
ing, drooling over or marrying off their daughters."[84] Noncinematic examples
of "white Palestinians" include Anett Haskia, a Palestinian from the coastal
town of Acre who declared herself an "Arab Muslim Zionist" and attempted
to run for office as a member of the far-right religious party Habayit Haye-
hudi (Jewish Home), and Gabriel Naddaf, a Nazareth-based Greek Orthodox
priest who preaches not only integration into Israeli society but also a complete disavowal of Arab identity.[85] While other Christians, such as Joseph
Raya and Khader el-Yateem, practice a theology of liberation as a response to
Zionist oppression, Naddaf propagates the opposite view: a theology of defeat
and acquiescence—in short, a theology of whiteness.[86]

But what about blackness? Like whiteness, blackness is a slippery, elusive
concept; if whiteness involves making a possessive investment, then blackness can be conceived as the opposite—as a divestment or as a rejection of
the White Nation fantasy. In Du Bois's words, partaking in blackness means,
first of all, recognizing that "the title to the universe claimed by White Folk
is faulty."[87] This, in fact, is the view put forward by the late Black liberation
theologian James Cone. While his critics accused him of simplistically reversing white supremacy's terms and turning Jesus's skin from white to
black, Cone's view of race was actually much more complex. In his first book,
Black Theology and Black Power, Cone recognized that "being black [. . .] has
very little to do with skin color. To be black means that your heart, your soul,
your mind, and your body are where the dispossessed are."[88] For Cone,
blackness was not an inherited essence. Like whiteness, it was a subject position that one assumes; it was an aspiration or a consciousness. Thus, if whiteness involves possession, blackness involves dispossession. Whereas the former is an aspiration to dominate supremacist hierarchies, the latter is an
attempt to dismantle them.

While these notions of whiteness and blackness were developed in very
particular contexts (the United States in the case of Du Bois, Lipsitz, and
Cone; Australia in the case of Hage), I do not think their use can be confined
within the borders of those nation-states. Indeed, it is my claim that whiteness and blackness are alive and well in Palestine. In our increasingly globalized world, White Nation fantasies operate transnationally and serve as imaginary bridges linking the hegemonic ideologies of various settler-colonialist
societies, from the United States to Australia, and from Canada and to apartheid South Africa.[89] Indeed, this is exactly how I think we should understand
the adoption of the Ice Bucket Challenge by certain Israeli politicians. This
phenomenon was not merely an innocent attempt to combat a disease. It was
a claim to whiteness, an attempt to link Israel to a broader transnational
imaginary. Seen in this light, the spectacle of three Israeli soldiers smearing

their faces with hummus takes on new meaning. While in the past blackface minstrelsy was used by Irish, Italian, and Jewish performers as a way to disavow blackness (and thereby also as a way to claim whiteness), this trio was inverting the procedure for the same ends.[90] In their hands, hummus was transformed from a staple of Arab cuisine into makeup for whiteface performance. It was as if the soldiers were justifying Israel's ongoing bombing campaign in Gaza with a simple, racist assertion, and they might as well have stated it directly: "*We are white.*"[91]

But what about blackness? In using a term such as "transnational Black Power," my point is not to say that all of these groups share a culture or identity. We live in a world of infinite variety, and there are as many differences between the Black and Palestinian communities as there are within them. Instead, I am using blackness as an inherent disruption—a casting of shadows rather than a shining of lights. It is precisely here that blackness meets the Palestinian Idea, and if in Israel whiteness functions as a possessive investment in settler-colonialism, then blackness is its egalitarian negation. It is the anticolonialist antidote to Zionism's supremacist claims. This story, then, is not only a tale of two solidarities, as I previously indicated; it is also a tale of two worlds, a tale of two realities inhabiting the same reality—the reality of equality and the reality of inequality.

Like inequality, the white settler-colonialist ideologies of U.S. and Israeli politics do not have the final say. Their hegemony is never complete, and when the Freedom Marchers in Hebron or the Martin Luther King Day demonstrators on San Mateo Bridge staged protests and used the media to declare solidarity across the borders of space and time, not only were they communicating a fanciful dream for some far-flung future; they were also— in their very performative acts and gestures—bringing this future into being in the present. They were using media as a window into another world, an egalitarian world that already inhabits the shadows of the existing world. Thus, Black-Palestinian solidarity is not automatically radical just because it is Black or Palestinian. Rather, Black-Palestinian solidarity is radical insofar as it presupposes equality in the midst of inequality and thereby cuts through the hierarchical claims of white settler-colonialist discourse. By linking Black-Palestinian solidarity to the Palestinian Idea in this fashion, its political potential goes beyond empty rhetoric and takes on a new disruptive dimension.

This also goes for acts and statements of solidarity between Ferguson and Palestine during the summer of 2014. When demonstrators in Missouri were suddenly spotted carrying pro-Palestinian banners and when Palestinians in the West Bank began tweeting instructions about how to deal with the tear gas and pepper spray, these were not simply claims to empirical sameness. They were performative declarations, attempts not to replace one identitarian hierarchy with another but to bring an egalitarian possibility out from the shadows.

V

You do not have to be me in order for us to fight alongside each other. I do not have to be you to recognize that our wars are the same.
—AUDRE LORDE, *Sister Outsider*

For the intellectual the task, I believe, is explicitly universalize the crisis, to give greater human scope to what a particular race or nation suffered, to associate that experience with the suffering of others. [...] This does not at all mean a loss in historical specificity, but rather it guards against the possibility that a lesson learned about oppression in one place will be forgotten or violated in another place or time.
—EDWARD W. SAID, *Representations of the Intellectual*

Black Power Palestine—the very combination of these words is nothing if not provocative. It is an exhilarating possibility for some; a terrifying prospect for others. But in discussing this transnational constellation of protest, we should be careful not to assume that hostility to it stems from only the racist right. Indeed, stiff opposition has also emanated from certain quarters of the antiracist left. Thus, while some scholars, such as Angela Davis and Alex Lubin, favorably compared the American Studies Association's resolution in 2013 to boycott Israeli academic institutions to similar measures taken against Jim Crow during the Civil Rights era, others saw it through a drastically different lens, and one writer even denounced the resolution as something "aris[ing] from an anti-black calculus."[92] Similarly, when the Lebanese American journalist Rania Khalek took to social media in August 2014 to compare Israel's assault on Gaza to the hypermilitarized police force in Ferguson, she was aggressively attacked by other Twitter users, such as Imani Gandy (Twitter handle, AngryBlackLady), for appropriating the Black struggle. Moreover, in a widely distributed interview, the film theorist Frank Wilderson called statements of Black-Palestinian solidarity "bullshit." As he put it, "The Arabs and the Jews are as much a part of the Black slave trade [...] as anyone else. [... A]nti-Blackness is as important and necessary to the formation of Arab psychic life as it is to the formation of Jewish psychic life." Not one to mince words, Wilderson warned the Black community against "bonding with people who are really, primarily, using Black energy to catalyze and energize their [own] struggle."[93]

    If such skepticism were limited to just a handful of hostile tweets, it might not merit much attention. Wilderson's words, however, present us with a far more formidable challenge. Indeed, his work on Black ontology provides such antisolidarity sentiments with a complex theoretical backbone, and it would therefore be pertinent to engage his writings directly. For Wilderson, black- ness is a form of *social death*.[94] It was invented in the Middle Passage and retains no connection whatsoever to the African past. Like the Lacanian Real, blackness (slavery) functions as a structural absence with respect to the (white) symbolic order. Although blackness is necessary to that order, both materially and symbolically, it can never be part of it. Thus, for Wilderson, the Black is forever outside civil society, barred from membership in the ranks of humanity itself.

According to this view, blackness is incommensurable with other social identities. That is, even if other communities are in conflict with the ruling white hegemony, they nevertheless share an underlying grammar with it that the Black lacks. Indeed, he even argues that many groups—including the Native American community—are united with white society by an underly- ing "Negrophobia," and it is exactly on these grounds that he criticizes cer- tain Native American cultural products, such as Chris Eyre's film *Skins* (2002) and Leslie Marmon Silko's novel *Almanac of the Dead*.[95] Wilderson therefore bristles against the making of analogies and the forging of coali- tions between Blacks and any other groups. In his view, such comparisons and coalitions are not only incorrect; they are *anti-Black*. If we compare the relationship between the Black (slave) and the white (master) to the relation- ship between, say, the worker and capitalism, the woman and patriarchy, the homosexual and heteronormativity, or even the colonized and colonialism, we are effectively erasing the ontological violence that constitutes black- ness.[96] "One may call it environmentalism, multiculturalism, pacifism, or feminism," he writes, "but I call it anti-Black policing."[97] Wilderson even extends his list of forbidden comparisons to several historical examples, ar- guing that the structural antagonism that exists between Blacks and white society cannot be mapped onto the conflicts between Jews and Nazism, Na- tive Americans and white settler-colonialism, Iraqis and the U.S. military, or Palestinians and Israel. For him, these conflicts are better classified not as ontological antagonisms but as intrahuman skirmishes—as "little family quarrels," to use a rather unfortunate turn of phrase that Wilderson takes from Fanon.[98]

To Wilderson's credit, the ontology he constructs maintains a certain self- consistency, and it follows its own, tight inner logic. Once you plunge into this world, it can be difficult to find your way out. Nevertheless, if we are going to view Black-Palestinian solidarity as a radical project, our exit from this intel- lectual quagmire is essential. I therefore want to contest both Wilderson's totalizing vision of blackness as social death and his aversion to coalition politics. First, Wilderson uncritically adopts a mono-realist worldview in which oppression is everything. For Wilderson, the white social order—that is, humanity itself—seems to be the *only* social order. There are no cracks or crevices, and it has the final say in the creation of blackness. On this point, Wilderson and the white master seem to agree. Both assign ruling power structures an authority that seems impossible to challenge. Wilderson's radical posturing is thus not as radical as it pretends to be, and the militant, Fanonian language he uses serves only to cloak a mono-realist intellectual framework that is actually rather conservative.[99]

Contrary to Wilderson's claims, blackness is more than just oppression and defeat. To again quote Cone, "The beauty in black existence is as real as the brutality, and the beauty prevents the brutality from having the final word."[100] Simply put, *social death is not everything*. Hidden in the shadows, there is also *social life*—a real vibrancy and creativity, a love and a hope that emanate from the hidden places beyond (white) power's reach. The point here is not simply to reverse Wilderson's terms by saying that social death is a myth and that social life is real. Rather, my point is that social death and social life are *both* real. They constitute two different worlds inhabiting the same world. Like inequality and equality, like Zionism and the Palestinian Idea, like the dueling sounds of Israeli drones and chirping birds heard in *Growing Up in Gaza in the Dark* (dir. Matthew Cassel, 2017 [see Chapter 1]), they are two different realities that exist concurrently. By choosing to see only the former, Wilderson vanquishes not just the possibility of emancipation but its actuality—its objective existence.[101]

This replication of oppressive epistemological frameworks recalls the gesture of another would-be radical, Theodor Herzl, and lest we forget, Zionism emerged in the very specific context of nineteenth-century Europe, a time when the ideology of romantic nationalism was in the air. In his formulation of modern political Zionism, Herzl not only failed to question the ethno-essentialist nation-state framework he had internalized from his surroundings; he replicated it. In racial terms, he was imitating the white European colonialist paradigm—the very paradigm that he was claiming to reject. By calling for a flight from Europe geographically, he was hoping to join Europe culturally.[102] Herzl thus contested anti-Semitism by mirroring it—a tragic irony embodied by his love of the music of Richard Wagner, the anti-Semitic composer whose operas inspired Herzl during the writing of his landmark manifesto, *The Jewish State*.[103] With his view of blackness as social death, Wilderson risks repeating this same gesture, and the finality and totality he assigns oppressive discourses are shared by his white supremacist opponents. In this world, there are no cracks; there are no resources for rebellion; and there certainly is no place for sublime ideas such as the Black Radical Tradition or the Palestinian Idea. Wilderson's brand of Afropessimism, then, is not *too* radical; on the contrary, it is not radical enough.[104]

Another problem with Wilderson's work has to do with his deep aversion to coalition politics—an aversion that I believe is bound up more generally to his allergy to universality. Now, to be clear, Wilderson is surely correct that slavery cannot be casually mapped onto the landscapes of other struggles. To be a slave is indeed not the same as being a colonial subject, and it is to their credit that the six Palestinian activists who took part in the Freedom Ride of 2011 took great care to make this distinction.[105] But since when is the denial of universality in and of itself an inherently radical act? Indeed, racism works both ways, and, as Ghassan Hage reminds us, "Racism can often be experienced as a denial of particularity just as much as it can be a denial of universality."[106] If we so doggedly turn toward Black particularity, we lose sight of something else that is no less important: *Black universality*.

This is not a contradiction in terms. The gateway to the universal always goes through the particular, and by stripping blackness of its universal dimension, Wilderson neglects the fact that Black struggles have always exceeded the precise historical confines in which they emerge. In C. L. R. James's words, "The African bruises and breaks himself against his bars in the interest of freedoms wider than his own."[107] Indeed, if we pushed Wilderson's logic to its limits, we would find ourselves in the awkward position of having to accuse some of his heroes of being anti-Black. Lest we forget, it was Malcolm X who used the term "black" as a signifier for *all* struggling nonwhite people, "black, brown, red, or yellow," and it was also he who claimed that the Black community faced the same problems as oppressed peoples in places such as Latin America and Vietnam.[108] It was Fred Hampton, the Chicago-based Black Panther Party activist, who formed the original Rainbow Coalition as a way to bring Black radicals together in political solidarity with like-minded Chicanos, Native Americans, Puerto Ricans, and even poor Appalachian whites.[109] It was Assata Shakur, drawing from Huey P. Newton's notion of "revolutionary intercommunalism," who wrote that "the victory of oppressed people anywhere in the world is a victory for Black people."[110] And it was Aimé Césaire, another member of Wilderson's pantheon, who composed those beautiful, ecumenical lines that later inspired Edward Said as he contemplated the struggle of his own people:

> *no race possesses the monopoly of beauty,*
> *of intelligence, of force, and there*
> *is a place for all at the rendezvous*
> *of victory.*[111]

While all of these figures appear in Wilderson's work, this dimension of their thought—the *universal* dimension—remains conspicuously absent.

Again, none of this is meant to diminish or deny the specificity and uniqueness of slavery, Black positionality, or Black struggle. Balancing the particular and the universal in such a way as to take both dimensions into account without neglecting one or the other is admittedly a difficult task. While some observers, writers, and activists have too easily made Black-Palestinian analogies without sufficiently understanding the specificity of these two communities' situations, Wilderson makes the opposite error. His view of blackness leaves no room for claims of universality. As a result, coalitions are ontologically unjustifiable, and his work thereby falls into a kind of rigidly demarcated sectarianism.

Of course, Wilderson does not have a monopoly on blackness, and there are other versions of it that not only allow for Black-Palestinian racial imaginaries but even encourage them. Here I want to return to the work of Cedric Robinson. The gulf that separates Wilderson's brand of Afropessimism from Robinson's Black Radical Tradition could not be any wider. While Wilderson argues that Blacks are still slaves, Robinson maintained that they were never really slaves to begin with; while Wilderson sees Black freedom as a distant prospect, at best, Robinson understood it as a present reality; and while Wilderson defines blackness by its *fungibility*, Robinson celebrated its *fugitivity*.[112] Robinson's view of blackness—not as social death but as social life, not as a color but as a consciousness, not as the product of white oppression but as something that continuously eludes power's grasp—is thus one that actively celebrates Black universality.[113] As he put it in the final words of his book *Black Marxism,* "It is not the province of one people to be the solution or the problem. [. . .] But for now we must be as one."[114] To look in the face of difference—to peer through the seemingly impenetrable wall of cultural, religious, linguistic, historical, and, yes, even ontological difference—but to nevertheless claim a certain solidarity despite all: *that* is what social struggle is all about. While Wilderson contemptuously dismisses such romantic connections as nothing more than "bullshit," Robinson glimpsed in them something much more profound, something approaching the level of prophecy, or what he called a "specular imagining."[115]

Here we can juxtapose Wilderson's and Robinson's attitudes toward comparisons made between slavery and the Holocaust. Wilderson takes great pains to distinguish between the two. He even makes the perverse claim that "Jews went into Auschwitz and came out as Jews. Africans went into ships and came out as Blacks. The former is a Human holocaust; the latter is a Human *and* a metaphysical holocaust."[116] Robinson's take is both more grounded in history and more imaginative. The first Americans to arrive at the gates of the concentration camps of Dachau and Buchenwald were Black soldiers serving in the segregated U.S. Army. Looking at their accounts of this event, Robinson argues that these individuals interpreted the horrors before their eyes through their own history of oppression. They looked at the emaciated Jewish bodies in front of them and somehow saw themselves. Robinson writes, "This wasteland of broken humanity issuing from the camps was themselves and beyond themselves. It was history, both familiar and exteriorized, which they bore in their arms."[117] Or, as one of those Black soldiers, E. G. McConnell, commented, "This is the ultimate end of slavery."[118] While Wilderson's work warns against such comparisons, Robinson's theoretical framework embraces them. It allows us to see how difference is not always a hindrance or a blockage, and it is by meditating on difference and through difference that one's own history can sometimes be further illuminated.

Viewing Black-Palestinian solidarity in this way—as a specular imagining—opens up a number of doors, and I want to conclude this section by briefly discussing three consequences that stem from such a conception. First, Black-Palestinian global racial imaginaries are mutually beneficial. The point is not simply to apply lessons from one struggle to another in a direct copy-and-paste fashion but, rather, to let the two communities disrupt and perhaps even transform each other. The relationship between them should not be a hierarchical one, as if between a teacher and a pupil, but a relationship between equals. This point is demonstrated in the documentary *Al Helm: Martin Luther King in Palestine* (dir. Connie Field, 2012), which follows the members of a Black gospel choir as they travel to the West Bank for a series of joint performances with a Palestinian drama troupe. At the beginning of the film, the Black choir members seem to know very little about the Palestinians. In interviews to the camera, some of them seem more excited about the prospect of riding a camel than working with their new Palestinian colleagues, and they seem to have a very know-it-all approach to social struggle. They are coming to Palestine to teach the Palestinians the proper way to resist. As the film unfolds, however, their views change. Importantly, this awakening does not take place only as the result of encountering new empirical information about life under occupation. Instead, it is instigated by culture—specifically, by music. While in Jenin, several Black women share protest songs with a group of Palestinians, and the film is edited to suggest that this is the key moment in which the choir members begin to understand and identify with the Palestinians in a new way. Black-Palestinian solidarity did not come naturally to them. It had to be carefully forged, and the Palestinians can teach the Black choir members just as much as the Black choir members can teach the Palestinians.

It is important to emphasize here that support for the Palestinian struggle should not mean that one opposes Israel's oppressive policies, only to turn a blind eye when similar practices are perpetrated by one's own government, a point made in Jean-Luc Godard's film on Palestine, *Here and Elsewhere* (dir. Groupe Dziga Vertov, 1976).[119] Said made the same argument with respect to

Palestine's neighboring Arab governments, such as Egypt and Lebanon, and he pointed out that the "countries that make the loudest noises in support of Palestine treat Palestinians the worst."[120] For this reason, standing in solidarity with the Palestinian struggle can also mean fighting other struggles at home. For a person located in the United States today, showing support for Palestine might mean fighting white supremacist structures and institutions domestically, from Ferguson, Missouri, all the way to the White House. Indeed, to add yet another apparent paradox to this discussion, let me suggest that in the age of Obama, supporting Black Power Palestine even meant opposing an African American president.[121] This connection was clearly grasped by Lupe Fiasco. In his televised performance at the BET Hip Hop Awards in 2011, he sang the lyrics, "Gaza strip was getting bombed, Obama didn't say shit. That's why I ain't vote for him, next one either."

A second consequence involves space, and viewing Black-Palestinian solidarity as a specular imagining allows us to escape geographical limits. To be sure, the struggle in Palestine has always been global, ever since Zionist leaders first began approaching European governments with their colonialist plans in the late nineteenth and early twentieth centuries. This global dimension continues today, and it includes everything from Israel's strong presence in the world arms market to the ways that the U.S. government seems to be mimicking Israeli interpretations of international law in its ongoing "war on terror"—what Lisa Hajjar calls "the *Israelization* of international law."[122] Palestine is therefore *already* global, and our response to this globality should not be to retreat into parochial particularity (à la Wilderson) but to embrace it, to transform a wretched globality into an emancipatory one. Transnational oppression can be effectively fought only with transnational revolution.

Thus, to stand in solidarity with the Palestinians, one does not necessarily need to be physically located in Palestine itself. Partaking in the Palestinian cause can mean a variety of other things. For instance, one can support the Boycott, Divest, and Sanction (BDS) campaign against the Israeli settler-colonialist regime. To recall the advice Jasiri X gives in his music video, "Support BDS, don't give a dime to the checkpoint." Black radical academics and activists such as Angela Davis, Bill Fletcher, Robin D. G. Kelley, Barbara Ransby, Alice Walker, and Cornel West have endorsed BDS, and many Black artists and performers have respected the call for a cultural boycott by canceling their performances in Israel or at official Israeli functions. These artists and performers include Carl Craig, Lauryn Hill, Jason Moran, Gil Scott-Heron, Cassandra Wilson, and Stevie Wonder. Similarly, several Black football players from the National Football League caused a small scandal in February 2017 when they canceled their participation in an all-expense-paid public relations trip to Israel. Explaining the reasons behind his cancellation, the defensive lineman Michael Bennett said, "I want to be a voice for the voiceless, and I cannot do that by going on this kind of trip to Israel."[123]

Furthermore, in August 2016, a comprehensive policy paper was published by groups connected to the #BlackLivesMatter movement in which they endorsed BDS and accused Israel of being an "apartheid state" committing "genocide" against the Palestinian people.[124] Supporting the boycott was also one of the messages communicated by the six Palestinian Freedom Riders who were arrested for boarding a de facto segregated bus in November 2011. Their aim was more than simply a local one, and they called on the global community to assist them by boycotting Egged and Veolia, the two transportation companies running the Israeli bus system. Media have become an important battleground in the BDS campaign, and one can download a "buycott" application to one's smartphone for assistance in determining which products to avoid.[125]

Israeli responses to BDS have been strong. The Knesset has even made calling for a boycott a civil offense, a legislative strategy mimicked by several U.S. states. Many of the arguments advanced by Israel's apologists against BDS resemble the tired excuses used in the past by southern racists who were upset by the organized attempts to boycott Jim Crow—for instance, in Mississippi, where student activists successfully lobbied the cast of the popular television program *Bonanza* to cancel a public appearance in Jackson.[126] In both instances, reactions against efforts to organize a boycott give us an indication of these campaigns' effectiveness.

Third, and finally, conceiving Black-Palestinian solidarity not as an anti-Black delusion but as a specular imagining gives us an opportunity to reassess the way we conceptualize solidarity itself. This means moving beyond the tendency to see solidarity either as an acknowledgment of empirical sameness or as an unqualified celebration of difference. In contrast to such views, we should radicalize our notion of solidarity. Solidarity means transcending the plane of identities and engaging in the disruptive politics of equality. It means looking directly into the abyss, the *tohu wa-bohu*, and being forever changed. We are no longer the same people. Solidarity, properly conceived, thus involves destructive plasticity and the creation of new political subjects.[127]

Black-Palestinian racial imaginaries should therefore challenge the way we talk about solidarity. Today, in activist terms, it is common to talk about allies—for instance, male allies in the struggle against sexism, straight allies against homophobia, and so on. The academic version of such ally talk is perhaps Ernesto Laclau and Chantal Mouffe's notion of "chains of equivalence."[128] While such language is ostensibly meant to bring people together, it effectively does the opposite, erecting a barrier than can never be fully overcome. To call someone an ally is actually a form of distanciation. It is a way to hold one's nose and keep someone else at arm's length. An ally is a person who is perceived as always being *outside* the struggle, a person who lacks the necessary authenticity ever to be considered a true partner, a person who must always be watched with a degree of suspicion. Such a view is a remarkably cliquish and identitarian one, and, as I have been arguing throughout this book, there is absolutely no guaranteed link between an identity category and a political position. No one naturally "owns" any political struggle. Thus, when a person subjectively chooses to take part in a struggle, he or she is not merely an "ally." Rather, that person is, at least momentarily, a true part of that struggle. He or she is a comrade.[129] "For now," to again recall Robinson's words, "we must be as one."[130]

This is not simply a question of semantics but a deep-seated conceptual issue. By tying a struggle down to a particular people, one may, in fact, be killing that struggle. As Selma James puts it, "Once you treat a struggle as an exception you cut the throat of that struggle."[131] We should completely reject this way of thinking. Solidarity should not involve setting up new hierarchies to replace the old ones. Neither should it be about erecting new borders, tracing new perimeters, or drawing new lines of exclusion. That is the job of racists, white supremacists, and Zionists. They segregate; we desegregate. They separate; we unite. They build walls; we tear them down. They institute inequality; we presuppose and perform equality. Indeed, that is what the Palestinian Idea is all about

Coda

A spectre haunts European Zionism, the spectre that all its victims—Palestinians, Sephardim (as well as critical Ashkenazim, in and outside Israel, stigmatized as "self-hating" malcontents)—will perceive the linked analogies between their oppressions.
—ELLA SHOHAT, "Sephardim in Israel"

During a trip to the West Bank in 2014, I had the opportunity to visit Birzeit University and deliver a talk about some of my previous work on media and Black Power. Specifically, I addressed the image of the Black Panther Party's co-founder Bobby Seale as he sat bound, gagged, and chained to a chair at the Chicago Conspiracy Trial in 1969. Seale, along with his seven white co-defendants, had been accused of inciting a riot the previous year when thousands of demonstrators converged in Chicago during the Democratic National Convention to protest racism, poverty, and the war in Vietnam. At the trial, Seale invoked the right to represent himself, but the judge continuously denied it. When Seale continued trying to speak, the judge had him bound and gagged. Although this image was not captured by any cameras, it nevertheless resonated throughout popular culture. Coming at the tail end of that tumultuous decade, Seale's bound-and-gagged likeness appeared in multiple media forms—for instance, in the artist David Hammons's body print *Injustice Case*; in songs by Crosby, Stills, and Nash and Gil Scott-Heron; and in films such as Woody Allen's *Bananas* (1971), Peter Watkins's *Punishment Park* (1971), and Jean-Luc Godard and Jean-Pierre Gorin's *Vladimir et Rosa* (dir. Groupe Dziga Vertov, 1971). After Seale was gagged, demonstrators appeared outside the Chicago courthouse with white cloths wrapped around their mouths, mimicking the silencing of the sole Black defendant. Seale thus seemed to open up a gateway to the universal, and it was as if the protesters outside the court were declaring that they were all Bobby Seale and that they were all bound and gagged.[132]

During my brief time at Birzeit, I met a young Palestinian student who shared my interest in Black radical thought. We spoke for a few minutes, and it immediately became clear to me that she was completely immersed in the literature of Black and Third World radicalism. She told me that she was reading books by authors such as Angela Davis, Frantz Fanon, Albert Memmi, Huey Newton, and Assata Shakur. I was greatly impressed by both her knowledge and her enthusiasm, and I started to think that maybe I should have just sat down and let this remarkable undergraduate give the lecture in my place.

One week later, I was in Amman, Jordan, browsing news headlines at an Internet café when I came across a story about a couple of Palestinians who had been arrested at a protest near Ramallah. Three journalists had taken two locals to a protest site to act as translators. When they were leaving the area, they came to a checkpoint, where IDF soldiers accused the two Palestinians of throwing stones and arrested them. Three days later, one of these young translators appeared in court, shackled to her chair and dressed in the same clothes that she had been wearing when she was apprehended. To my great shock, I recognized her name. This was the same young woman I had spoken with at Birzeit, the same person who was reading books by Albert Memmi and Assata Shakur. Although she was threatened with three months in prison, she was soon released and was thus luckier than many of her fellow Palestinians, who are caught up for years in the Israeli detention system.

A few months later, during the summer of 2014—a time when Gaza was being razed by Israeli missiles, a time when Bill Gates and George Bush were dumping ice on their heads and young IDF soldiers were smearing hummus on one another's faces—I opened my Internet browser and looked at Twitter. There I noticed a number of Palestinians tweeting instructions to their virtual comrades in Ferguson about how best to deal with the tear gas and smoke grenades. As I browsed the comments, I could not help but notice a familiar name. One of the people using social media in this fashion was the same undergraduate I had met at Birzeit University; the same young woman who had been arrested by IDF soldiers; the same woman who had been shackled in front of an Israeli kangaroo court, just as Bobby Seale had in Chicago so many decades before. Like the other examples discussed in this chapter—like the Freedom Riders who boarded a segregated bus or the spoken word poets Suheir Hammad and Remi Kanazi, like the dreamers who disrupted traffic on San Mateo Bridge or Jasiri X's music video about checkpoints, like Danny Glover's involvement in Palestinian film production or Motaz Malhees's powerful reenactment of the murder of Eric Garner—this young woman was using media to forge a creative link of transnational solidarity between Black and Palestinian protesters. In so doing, she was elevating both causes and transforming the very nature of this global racial imaginary.

Notes

PREFACE AND ACKNOWLEDGMENTS

1. Ernst Bloch, *Traces*, translated by Anthony A. Nassar (1969; repr., Stanford, CA: Stanford University Press, 2006), p. 158.

2. Walter Benjamin, "In the Sun," in *Walter Benjamin: Selected Writings, 1927–1934*, vol. 2, translated by Rodney Livingstone, edited by Michael W. Jennings, Howard Eiland, and Gary Smith (Cambridge, MA: Harvard University Press, 1999), p. 664. Also quoted in Giorgio Agamben, *The Coming Community*, translated by Michael Hardt (1990; repr., Minneapolis: University of Minnesota Press, 1993), p. 53. Gershom Scholem later claimed to be the mysterious rabbi of the parable. See his letter in Walter Benjamin and Gershom Scholem, *The Correspondence of Walter Benjamin and Gershom Scholem, 1932–1940*, translated by Gary Smith and Andrea Lefevere, edited by Gershom Scholem (1980; repr., New York: Schocken, 1989), p. 123.

3. I use the term "Palestine" to refer to the whole of the land that is currently split among Israel, the West Bank, and the Gaza Strip.

4. This is the central thesis of Ariella Azoulay and Adi Ophir, *The One-State Condition: Occupation and Democracy in Israel/Palestine*, translated by Tal Haran (2008; repr., Stanford, CA: Stanford University Press, 2013). Saree Makdisi similarly contends, "The one-state solution is not [. . .] something that has to be worked out in advance, with a series of 'interim agreements' negotiated by armies of committees and subcommittees over a period of decades. *It is the present reality*": Saree Makdisi, *Palestine Inside Out: An Everyday Occupation* (2008; repr., New York: W. W. Norton, 2010), p. 294 (emphasis mine).

5. For instance, when Tony Judt published an essay pronouncing the two-state solution dead and arguing in favor of a single, democratic binationalist state, Yoel Esteron offered a stern rebuke, accusing him of advocating the annihilation of the Jews. Not so subtly linking Judt to the Holocaust, Esteron wrote, "Sixty years after the attempt to wipe

out the Jewish people in Europe, [. . .] along comes a historian who specializes in Europe and proposes that the Jews commit suicide": Tony Judt, "Israel: The Alternative," *New York Review of Books*, October 23, 2003, available at nybooks.com; Yoel Esteron, "Who's in Favor of Annihilating Israel?" *Ha'aretz*, November 28, 2003, available at haaretz.com.

6. In the words of the late Jewish Palestine Liberation Organization (PLO) member Ilan Halevi, "De-Zionization [. . .] does not, or at least not necessarily, imply the dismantling of the Israeli social formation, any more than the denial of the national rights of the Israeli people. It implies only the ending of apartheid and the establishment of a democracy for the two communities": Ilan Halevi, *A History of the Jews: Ancient and Modern*, translated by A. M. Barrett (1981; repr., London: Zed, 1988), p. 324.

7. Mahmood Mamdani argues that in Palestine "one could do away with settler privilege legally without having to do away with the person of the settler physically. Without a state that legally discriminated between settler and native, there would be no settler privilege and, thus, no settler[,] since all settlers would become as immigrants whose different historical origin would cease to have significance in law": Mahmood Mamdani, "Good Muslim, Bad Muslim: Post-apartheid Perspectives on America and Israel," *PoLAR: Political and Legal Anthropology Review* 27.1 (2004): 6. See also Mahmood Mamdani, *Good Muslim, Bad Muslim: America, the Cold War, and the Roots of Terror* (New York: Doubleday, 2004), p. 228.

8. Edward W. Said, "The Challenge of Palestine," *Journal of Refugee Studies* 2.1 (1989): 178.

9. W. E. B. Du Bois, *Black Reconstruction in America: 1860–1880* (1935; repr., New York: Touchstone, 1995); C. L. R. James, *The Black Jacobins: Toussaint L'Ouverture and the San Domingo Revolution*, 2d ed. (1938; repr., New York: Vintage, 1989); Cedric J. Robinson, *Black Marxism: The Making of the Black Radical Tradition* (1983; repr., Chapel Hill: University of North Carolina Press, 2000).

INTRODUCTION

1. Quoted in Emmanuel Sivan, "The Lights of Netzarim," *Ha'aretz*, November 7, 2003, available at haaretz.com. This incident is also discussed in Eyal Weizman, *The Least of All Possible Evils: Humanitarian Violence from Arendt to Gaza* (New York: Verso, 2011), p. 141; Gil Z. Hochberg, *Visual Occupations: Violence and Visibility in a Conflict Zone* (Durham, NC: Duke University Press, 2015), p. 27.

2. Neve Gordon, *Israel's Occupation* (Berkeley: University of California Press, 2008), p. 99; Ariella Azoulay and Adi Ophir, *The One-State Condition: Occupation and Democracy in Israel/Palestine*, translated by Tal Haran (2008; repr., Stanford, CA: Stanford University Press, 2013), p. 39.

3. For the history of Palestine's electrification, see Ronen Shamir, *Current Flow: The Electrification of Palestine* (Stanford, CA: Stanford University Press, 2013).

4. Weizman, *The Least of All Possible Evils*, p. 141. Explaining the decision to disengage from Gaza, Sharon's senior adviser Dov Weisglass told *Ha'aretz* that "the significance of the disengagement plan is the freezing of the peace process." In his words, "When you freeze that process, you prevent the establishment of a Palestinian state, and you prevent a discussion on the refugees, the borders and Jerusalem. Effectively, this whole package called the Palestinian state, with all that it entails, has been removed indefinitely from our agenda. And all this with authority and permission. All with a presidential blessing

and the ratification of both houses of Congress": quoted in Max Blumenthal, *The 51 Day War: Ruin and Resistance in Gaza* (New York: Nation, 2015), p. 4.

5. In April 2017, the Palestinian Authority (PA) reportedly asked Israel to stop supplying electricity to Gaza as part of an effort to undermine Hamas: "Israel Agrees to PA Request to Reduce Gaza Electricity," Al Jazeera, June 13, 2017, available at aljazeera.com.

6. Baruch Kimmerling, *Politicide: Ariel Sharon's War against the Palestinians* (New York: Verso, 2003).

7. In his diary entry for June 12, 1895, Herzl pondered ways to remove the Palestinians from their lands, writing, "We shall try to spirit the penniless population across the border by procuring employment for it in the transit countries, while denying it any employment in our country": Theodor Herzl, *The Complete Diaries of Theodor Herzl*, vol. 1, translated by Harry Zohn, edited by Raphael Patai (New York: Herzl Foundation, 1960), p. 88, quoted in Benny Morris, *The Birth of the Palestinian Refugee Problem, 1947–1949* (New York: Cambridge University Press, 1987), p. 41.

8. Quoted in Mairav Zonszein, "Binyamin Netanyahu: 'Arab Voters Are Heading to the Polling Stations in Droves,'" *The Guardian*, March 17, 2015, available at theguardian.com.

9. Cedric J. Robinson, *The Terms of Order: Political Science and the Myth of Leadership* (1980; repr., Chapel Hill: University of North Carolina Press, 2016).

10. Here I draw from the notion of "the unoccupied" developed in Ghassan Hage, *Alter-Politics: Critical Anthropology and the Radical Imagination* (Melbourne: Melbourne University Press, 2015), pp. 165–172. See also Ghassan Hage, "What Is a Public Intervention? Speaking Truth to the Oppressed," in *If Truth Be Told: The Politics of Public Ethnography*, edited by Didier Fassin (Durham, NC: Duke University Press, 2017), pp. 47–68.

11. See Carol Hanisch, "The Personal Is Political," in *Notes from the Second Year: Women's Liberation: Major Writings of the Radical Feminists*, edited by Shulie Firestone and Anne Koedt (New York: Radical Feminism, 1970), pp. 76–78. See also Shulamith Firestone, *The Dialectic of Sex: The Case for Feminist Revolution* (1972; repr., New York: Bantam, 1970), pp. 38–39.

12. Jacques Rancière, *Disagreement: Politics and Philosophy*, translated by Julie Rose (1995; repr., Minneapolis: University of Minnesota Press, 1999), p. 32.

13. For a concise critique of the culturalist position, see Hollis Griffin, "Lines in the Sand: Media Studies and the Neoliberal Academy," *Flow* 13.12 (2011), available at flowtv.org.

14. Jacques Rancière, *On the Shores of Politics*, translated by Liz Heron (1992; repr., New York: Verso, 2007); Rancière, *Disagreement*; Jacques Rancière, *Hatred of Democracy*, translated by Steve Corcoran (2005; repr., New York: Verso, 2009). See also his "Ten Theses on Politics," in Jacques Rancière, *Dissensus: On Politics and Aesthetics*, edited and translated by Steven Corcoran (New York: Continuum, 2010), pp. 27–44.

15. On "the police," see Rancière, *Disagreement*, pp. 21–42; Rancière, *Dissensus*, pp. 36–37. See also Samuel A. Chambers, "The Politics of the Police: From Neoliberalism to Anarchism, and Back to Democracy," in *Reading Rancière: Critical Dissensus*, edited by Paul Bowman and Richard Stamp (New York: Continuum, 2011), pp. 18–43.

16. Jacques Rancière, *Moments Politiques: Interventions 1977–2009*, translated by Mary Foster (2009; repr., New York: Seven Stories, 2014), p. 81. As Peter Hallward explains, "Politics is a matter of building a stage and sustaining a spectacle or 'show.' Politics is the contingent dramatization of a disruptive equality, the unauthorized and

impromptu improvisation of a democratic voice": Peter Hallward, "Staging Equality: Rancière's Theatrocracy," *New Left Review* 37 (2006): 111.

17. As Steven Salaita argues, "True liberation has never occurred through the legislative maneuvers of civilized men in designer suits": Steven Salaita, *Inter/Nationalism: Decolonizing Native America and Palestine* (Minneapolis: University of Minnesota Press, 2016), p. 69.

18. James H. Cone, *A Black Theology of Liberation*, 2d ed. (1970; repr., Maryknoll, NY: Orbis, 1986), p. 22.

19. Adi Kunstman and Rebecca L. Stein argue that recently in Israel, "The most banal of social media practices and gestures—'likes,' 'shares,' memes, and selfies—ha[ve] been harnessed as a means of supporting state violence": Adi Kuntsman and Rebecca L. Stein, *Digital Militarism: Israel's Occupation in the Social Media Age* (Stanford, CA: Stanford University Press, 2015), p. 37.

20. As Nurith Gertz and George Khleifi put it, *Ticket to Jerusalem* is about a man who "projects films to an audience that does not want to see them": Nurith Gertz and George Khleifi, *Palestinian Cinema: Landscape, Trauma, and Memory* (2005; repr., Bloomington: Indiana University Press, 2008), p. 109.

21. Hochberg, *Visual Occupations*, pp. 1–3.

22. For more on Masharawi, see Nurith Gertz, "The Stone at the Top of the Mountain: The Films of Rashid Masharawi," *Journal of Palestine Studies* 34.1 (2004): 23–36.

23. Rebecca L. Stein and Ted Swedenburg, "Introduction: Popular Culture, Transnationality, and Radical History," in *Palestine, Israel, and the Politics of Popular Culture*, edited by Rebecca L. Stein and Ted Swedenburg (Durham, NC: Duke University Press, 2005), p. 1. See also Helga Tawil-Souri, "Where Is the Political in Cultural Studies? In Palestine," *International Journal of Cultural Studies* 16.1 (2011): 467–482.

24. Some noteworthy recent entrees in the Palestinian cultural studies catalog include, for instance, Miriyam Aouragh, *Palestine Online: Transnationalism, the Internet and the Construction of Identity* (2011; repr., New York: I. B. Tauris, 2012); Terri Ginsberg, *Visualizing the Palestinian Struggle: Toward a Critical Analytic of Palestine Solidarity Films* (New York: Palgrave Macmillan, 2016); Hochberg, *Visual Occupations*; Sunaina Maira, *Jil Oslo: Palestinian Hip Hop, Youth Culture, and the Youth Movement* (Washington, DC: Tadween, 2013); David A. McDonald, *My Voice Is My Weapon: Music, Nationalism, and the Poetics of Palestinian Resistance* (Durham, NC: Duke University Press, 2013); Andrea L. Stanton, *"This Is Jerusalem Calling": State Radio in Mandatory Palestine* (Austin: University of Texas Press, 2013); Nadia Yaqub, *Palestinian Cinema in the Days of Revolution* (Austin: University of Texas Press, 2018). See also the relevant sections of Kay Dickinson, *Arab Cinema Travels: Transnational Syria, Palestine, Dubai, and Beyond* (London: BFI Palgrave, 2016); Laura U. Marks, *Hanan al-Cinema: Affections for the Moving Image* (Cambridge, MA: MIT Press, 2015); Kamran Rastegar, *Surviving Images: Cinema, War, and Cultural Memory in the Middle East* (New York: Oxford University Press, 2015). See also Tawil-Souri, "Where Is the Political in Cultural Studies?" pp. 467–482.

CHAPTER 1

1. Patricia Sellick, "The Old City of Hebron: Can It Be Saved?" *Journal of Palestine Studies* 23.4 (1994): 69–82. See also Baruch Kimmerling, *Zionism and Territory: The Socioterritorial Dimensions of Zionist Politics* (Berkeley: University of California Press, 1983),

pp. 156–157; Ian S. Lustick, *For the Land and the Lord: Jewish Fundamentalism in Israel* (New York: Council on Foreign Relations, 1988), pp. 42–43; Idith Zertal and Akiva Eldar, *Lords of the Land: The War over Israel's Settlements in the Occupied Territories, 1967–2007*, translated by Vivian Eden (2005; repr., New York: Nation, 2009), pp. 17–21.

2. Zertal and Eldar, *Lords of the Land*, pp. 119–121.

3. Jeff Klein, "A Visit to the Grave of Mass-Murderer Baruch Goldstein," *Mondoweiss*, July 4, 2013, available at mondoweiss.net.

4. Jeffrey Goldberg, "Among the Settlers," *New Yorker*, May 31, 2004, available at newyorker.com, quoted in Ben Ehrenreich, *The Way to the Spring: Life and Death in Palestine* (New York: Penguin, 2016), p. 148.

5. Ali Gharib, "'Obama, Come Here to Hebron,'" *Daily Beast*, March 20, 2013, available at thedailybeast.com; Alistair Dawber, "'Come Here, Obama, and Visit the Museum of Apartheid': Pro-Palestinian Protesters Clash with Army in West Bank as U.S. President Arrives in Tel Aviv," *Independent*, March 20, 2013, available at independent.co.uk.

6. Gaye Theresa Johnson, *Spaces of Conflict, Sounds of Solidarity: Music, Race, and Spatial Entitlement in Los Angeles* (Berkeley: University of California Press, 2013).

7. For Wilder, the demonstration did not reflect the attitudes of Hebron's Arab population. Instead, he claimed that it had been provoked by "foreign anarchists" who were meddling in local affairs—an ironic charge coming from a person who was born and raised in New Jersey: see David Wilder, "Fun and Games with Issa Amru in Hebron," *Arutz Sheva*, March 20, 2013, available at israelnationalnews.com.

8. Quoted in ibid.

9. Charlotte Silver, "Israel Indicts 'Palestinian Gandhi,'" *Electronic Intifada*, September 6, 2016, available at electronicintifada.net.

10. "Ahead of Obama Visit, PA Prohibits Reporting from Hebron," *Times of Israel*, March 19, 2013, available at timesofisrael.com.

11. David Shulman, "Hope in Hebron," *New York Review of Books* blog, March 22, 2013, available at nybooks.com.

12. Robin D. G. Kelley, *Freedom Dreams: The Black Radical Imagination* (Boston: Beacon, 2002), p. 9.

13. Edward W. Said, *Orientalism* (1978; repr., New York: Vintage, 2003). Even Aijaz Ahmad, a vehement critic of Said's Orientalism thesis, praises Said's work on Palestine. "The writings which deal directly with Palestine," Ahmad writes, "constitute not only the most enduring part of Said's work but also, by any standards, the most persuasive insertion of a national-liberation struggle into the American imagination, which is otherwise substantially formed by Zionist-colonial presumptions": Aijaz Ahmad, *In Theory: Classes, Nations, Literatures* (1992; repr., New York: Verso, 2008), p. 198.

14. Said uses "Palestinian answer" in his early essay "The Future of Palestine: A Palestinian Perspective," in *The Arab World: From Nationalism to Revolution*, edited by Abdeen Jabara and Janice Terry (Wilmette, IL: Medina University Press, 1971), p. 199. Alternatively, he uses "Palestinian vision" in Edward W. Said, *The Question of Palestine* (1979; repr., New York: Vintage, 1980), p. 164; Edward W. Said, *Peace and Its Discontents: Essays on Palestine in the Middle East Peace Process* (New York: Vintage, 1996), p. 182. Examples of "Palestinianism" include Edward W. Said, *After the Last Sky: Palestinian Lives* (New York: Pantheon, 1986), p. 112; Edward W. Said, *The Politics of Dispossession: The Struggle for Palestinian Self-Determination, 1969–1994* (1994; repr., New York: Vintage, 1995), pp. 3, 251.

15. Said, *The Question of Palestine*, pp. 220, 175.

16. Edward W. Said, "The Challenge of Palestine," *Journal of Refugee Studies* 2.1 (1989): 177.

17. Said, "The Future of Palestine," p. 200.

18. In some of the footage recovered from Palestine's militant cinema period that Mohanad Yaqubi used in his documentary *Off Frame: Revolution until Victory* (2015), a Palestinian youth says in voice-over, "We do not want to push the Jews into the sea or anything like that. We also do not want the Zionists to push us into the desert."

19. Said points out that Arthur Hertzberg's 1959 tome on Zionism, *The Zionist Idea*, contains fewer than a dozen pages that even refer to Arabs: Edward W. Said, "Arabs and Jews," *Journal of Palestine Studies* 3.2 (1974): 9. See also Arthur Hertzberg, ed., *The Zionist Idea: A Historical Analysis and Reader* (1959; repr., New York: Atheneum, 1984). More recently, Steven Salaita has pointed out this same contrast between Zionist exclusivity and Palestinian inclusivity, writing, "I would like to share both a nation and a national identity with my Jewish brothers and sisters. No Zionist I know shares that sentiment": Steven Salaita, *Uncivil Rites: Palestine and the Limits of Academic Freedom* (Chicago: Haymarket, 2015), p. 117.

20. Quoted in Edward W. Said, *Culture and Imperialism* (1993; repr., New York: Vintage, 1994), p. 280 (emphasis mine). Césaire's phrase *"rendez-vous de la conquête"* is usually translated from the French as "convocation of conquest." In choosing "rendezvous of victory," Said is following C. L. R. James's translation in *The Black Jacobins: Toussaint L'Ouverture and the San Domingo Revolution*, 2nd ed. (1938; repr., New York: Vintage, 1989), p. 401. James also chose this phrase as the title of an edited collection of his writings, *At the Rendezvous of Victory: Selected Writings* (London: Allison and Busby, 1984). See also Aimé Césaire, *Notebook of a Return to the Native Land*, edited and translated by Clayton Eshleman and Annette Smith (1947; repr., Middletown, CT: Wesleyan University Press, 2001), p. 44; Edward W. Said, *Representations of the Intellectual: The 1993 Reith Lectures* (1994; repr., New York: Vintage, 1996), p. 37.

21. See Musa Budeiri, *The Palestine Communist Party, 1919–1948: Arab and Jew in the Struggle for Internationalism* (1979; repr., Chicago: Haymarket, 2010). See also Ran Greenstein, *Zionism and Its Discontents: A Century of Radical Dissent in Israel/Palestine* (London: Pluto, 2014).

22. Gilles Deleuze and Elias Sanbar, "The Indians of Palestine," *Discourse* 20.3 (1998): 28. Regarding the PLO, Said went as far as to single out the organization's head, Yasir Arafat, as one of the primary articulators of the Palestinian Idea. Discussing Arafat, Said wrote that "[no] leader of any group in the Middle East so unambiguously sponsored so secular and genuinely liberating an idea: that Palestine might become the peacefully shared home of Arabs and Jews, and that no one group would have privileges over the other." As the years passed by, however, Said's feelings toward Arafat changed considerably, and after the signing of the Oslo Accords, he even called on Arafat and the rest of the PLO leadership to resign. In turn, by the late 1990s, the PLO reportedly banned Said's books: Said, *After the Last Sky*, p. 122; Serge Schmemann, "Palestinian Security Agents Ban Books by a Critic of Arafat," *New York Times Books*, August 25, 1996, available at nytimes.com. See also Joseph A. Massad, *The Persistence of the Palestinian Question: Essays on Zionism and the Palestinians* (New York: Routledge, 2006), pp. 112–113. For Said's later acerbic criticism of Arafat, see esp. his essays in Said, *Peace and Its Discontents*.

23. Suheir Hammad, *Born Palestinian, Born Black* (1996; repr., New York: UpSet,

2010), pp. 12–13. On Abu Thuraya, see Gideon Levy, "The Israeli Military First Took His Legs, Then His Life," *Ha'aretz*, December 19, 2017, available at haaretz.com. At the time of his death, Amira Hass opined that since he was unarmed it was perhaps his utter fearlessness that unnerved his Israeli assassin: Amira Hass, "The Shooting of a Legless Man," *Ha'aretz*, December 19, 2017, available at haaretz.com.

24. Shulman, "Hope in Hebron."

25. Joan Copjec, *Imagine There's No Woman: Ethics and Sublimation* (Cambridge, MA: MIT Press, 2002), p. 174.

26. Fredric Jameson, *The Political Unconscious: Narrative as a Socially Symbolic Act* (1981; repr., New York: Routledge, 2002), p. 88.

27. Said, *The Question of Palestine*, p. 170. Ernst Bloch similarly observes, "There is [. . .] in history a *socio-economic barrier to vision*, it cannot be scaled by even the most daring mind": Ernst Bloch, *The Principle of Hope*, vol. 1, translated by Neville Plaice, Stephen Plaice, and Paul Knight (1959; repr., Cambridge, MA: MIT Press, 1986), p. 130 (emphasis in original).

28. In Israel, Said argues, "realism dictated that any talk of seriously modifying the immigration laws and the completely Jewish institutions of the state was tantamount to being a fool or a knave or a traitor or all three. Realism, one was very often told by realists, was taking the country's mood into consideration, the fervent nationalism, the unchangeable characteristics of the state of Israel as it was presently constituted, and even Jewish racism. Those were realities with which one was not supposed to argue since they had the force of reality, of history, and—even though it wasn't always mentioned—the force of military power. Realism therefore was the uncrossable line": Said, "Arabs and Jews," p. 7.

29. Here, I am specifically thinking of Chomsky's positive citation of Huntington's line that "power remains strong when it remains in the dark; exposed to the sunlight it begins to evaporate." The only difference between the two thinkers is that whereas Huntington saw this as reason to keep the operations of power in the dark, Chomsky sees this as a reason to expose it: Samuel P. Huntington, *American Politics: The Promise of Disharmony* (Cambridge, MA: Harvard University Press, 1981), p. 75; Noam Chomsky, *Profit over People: Neoliberalism and the Global Order* (New York: Seven Stories, 1999), p. 140. For more on Chomsky's realism, see his dismissal of both the Boycott, Divestment, and Sanctions (BDS) campaign and the one-state solution on grounds of being unrealistic. Noam Chomsky, "On Israel-Palestine and BDS," *The Nation*, July 2, 2014, available at thenation.com.

30. Kelley, *Freedom Dreams*, p. 10.

31. As Jacques Rancière writes, "'The possible' [. . .] does not offer a great deal of possibilities": Jacques Rancière, *Chronicles of Consensual Times*, translated by Steven Corcoran (2005; repr., New York: Continuum, 2010), p. 9.

32. Alain Badiou, *Being and Event*, translated by Oliver Feltham (1988; repr., New York: Continuum, 2006). Since the late 1980s, there has been an attempt within film and cultural studies to reexamine Lacan, putting a particular emphasis on his register of the Real. Three of the most important voices leading the charge have been Joan Copjec, Todd McGowan, and Slavoj Žižek: see Joan Copjec, *Read My Desire: Lacan against the Historicists* (Cambridge, MA: MIT Press, 1994); Todd McGowan, *The Real Gaze: Film Theory after Lacan* (New York: State University of New York Press, 2007); Slavoj Žižek, *The Sublime Object of Ideology* (New York: Verso, 1989).

33. The phrase, *tohu wa-bohu*, occurs in Genesis 1:2, and it is commonly rendered into English as "formless and void" or "formless and empty." Although the term still exists in Modern Hebrew (*tohu va-vohu* in contemporary usage), it has lost its theological gravity. For more discussion on the theoretical importance of this concept, see Roland Boer, *Political Myth: On the Use and Abuse of Biblical Themes* (Durham, NC: Duke University Press, 2009), p. 77. On the *batin*, see Omnia El Shakry, *The Arabic Freud: Psychoanalysis and Islam in Modern Egypt* (Princeton, NJ: Princeton University Press, 2017), p. 48. For a helpful discussion of the Lacanian Real, see Tom Eyers, *Lacan and the Concept of the "Real"* (New York: Palgrave Macmillan, 2012). Bloch's concept of the "darkness of the lived moment" can be found in Bloch, *The Principle of Hope*, 1:287–316. For Lorde's "Black mother," see Audre Lorde, *Sister Outsider: Essays and Speeches* (1984; repr., Berkeley, CA: Crossing, 2007), pp. 38, 100.

34. As Ghassan Hage puts it, "We are continuously shadowed by realities in which we are dwelling, of which we are not fully aware, but which often induce in us a vague feeling, or a sense of their presence." In his words, "What we call 'reality' is merely a dominant reality, and [. . .] there are always minor realities in which we are equally enmeshed": Ghassan Hage, *Alter-Politics: Critical Anthropology and the Radical Imagination* (Melbourne: Melbourne University Press, 2015), pp. 70, 201.

35. Lorde, *Sister Outsider*, p. 162.

36. Catherine Malabou, *Ontology of the Accident: An Essay on Destructive Plasticity*, translated by Carolyn Shread (2009; repr., Malden, MA: Polity, 2012), p. 87.

37. Ibid., p. 85.

38. Said, *The Question of Palestine*, p. 56 (emphasis in original).

39. As Conor McCarthy reminds us, "Zionism took shape towards the end of the nineteenth century, at a time when the great European powers were engaged in the height of the imperial enterprise. Zionism emerged out of a context of virulent European antisemitism, but also out of a European intellectual milieu where the classification of overseas races and territories in hierarchical terms was considered canonical and natural. Accordingly, Zionism never spoke of itself unambiguously as a Jewish liberation movement, but rather as a Jewish project for colonial settlement in the Orient": Conor McCarthy, "The State, the Text and the Critic in a Globalized World: The Case of Edward Said," in *Thinking Palestine*, edited by Ronit Lentin (New York: Zed, 2008), p. 229.

40. Edward W. Said, *The Palestinian Question and the American Context* (Beirut: Institute for Palestine Studies, 1979), p. 28. Or, as Steven Salaita argues, "History has shown time and again that decolonial movements that open themselves to alternative influences are most successful." In his words, "Indigenous peoples transcend their immediate political conditions": Steven Salaita, *The Holy Land in Transit: Colonialism and the Quest for Canaan* (Syracuse, NY: Syracuse University Press, 2006), pp. 178, 181.

41. Jacques Rancière, *On the Shores of Politics*, translated by Liz Heron (1992; repr., New York: Verso, 2007), p. 84; Jacques Rancière, *The Ignorant Schoolmaster: Five Lessons in Intellectual Emancipation*, translated by Kristin Ross (1987; repr., Stanford, CA: Stanford University Press, 1991), p. 137 (emphasis in original).

42. See, e.g., the criticism of bourgeois equality in Karl Marx, *Capital: A Critique of Political Economy*, vol. 1, translated by Ben Fowkes (1867; repr., New York: Penguin, 1990), p. 280. For a more recent discussion, see Lisa Duggan, *The Twilight of Equality? Neoliberalism, Cultural Politics, and the Attack on Democracy* (Boston: Beacon, 2003).

43. Jonathan Cook, "'Visible Equality' as Confidence Trick," in *Israel and South Afri-*

ca: The Many Faces of Apartheid, edited by Ilan Pappé (London: Zed, 2015), pp. 123–159. Abu-Assad contrasts his treatment as an award-winning filmmaker in other countries with his treatment in Israel. "When I go to Park City, I am a filmmaker. A car waits to pick me up at the airport," he says. "But when I arrive in Israel, I need to stand in line for 3 or 4 hours in the sun just to arrive at my destination": quoted in Nurith Gertz and George Khleifi, *Palestinian Cinema: Landscape, Trauma, and Memory* (2005; repr., Bloomington: Indiana University Press, 2008), p. 48.

44. Although I am interested in teasing out the possible points of overlap between Rancière and Lacan, it should be noted that Rancière, by his own admission, does not consider himself a psychoanalytic thinker. In his words, "I have no particular competence regarding psychoanalytic theory": Jacques Rancière, *The Aesthetic Unconscious*, translated by Debra Keates and James Swenson (2001; repr., Malden, MA: Polity, 2009), p. 1. While Jodi Dean remains critical of Rancière's approach, she correctly perceives this overlap with Lacan, writing that, for Rancière, "equality is not only an aspect of the symbolic order but also a distorting of or gap within that order." In her words, "Rancière seems to be saying that something about equality is Real": Jodi Dean, "Politics without Politics," in *Reading Rancière: Critical Dissensus*, edited by Paul Bowman and Richard Stamp (New York: Continuum, 2011), p. 89.

45. See the discussion in Rancière, *On the Shores of Politics*, pp. 69–70, 82–86; Jacques Rancière, *Disagreement: Politics and Philosophy*, translated by Julie Rose (1995; repr., Minneapolis: University of Minnesota Press, 1999), pp. 23–28, 33.

46. Rancière, *On the Shores of Politics*, p. 69.

47. Jacques Rancière, *Hatred of Democracy*, translated by Steve Corcoran (2005; repr., New York: Verso, 2009), p. 48.

48. Rancière, *On the Shores of Politics*, p. 83.

49. bell hooks, "Lorde: The Imagination of Justice," in *I Am Your Sister: Collected and Unpublished Writings of Audre Lorde*, edited by Rudolph P. Byrd, Johnnetta Betsch Cole, and Beverly Guy-Sheftall (New York: Oxford University Press, 2009), p. 248; Wendy Brown, "Wounded Attachments," *Political Theory* 21.3 (1993): 390–410.

50. Regarding Rancière's dispute with Althusser, Peter Hallward explains, "Althusser had privileged scientific insight over popular delusion; Rancière has explored the consequences of the opposite presumption—that everyone is immediately and equally capable of thought": Peter Hallward, "Staging Equality: Rancière's Theatrocracy," *New Left Review* 37 (2006): 109. See also Rancière's discussion of Althusser and Bourdieu in Jacques Rancière, *Althusser's Lesson*, translated by Emiliano Battista (1974; repr., New York: Continuum, 2011); Jacques Rancière, *The Philosopher and His Poor*, edited by Andrew Parker, translated by John Drury, Corinne Oster, and Andrew Parker (1983; repr., Durham, NC: Duke University Press, 2004); Rancière, *On the Shores of Politics*.

51. Such a radical conception of equality is also advocated by several of Rancière's philosophical contemporaries. "Political equality," as Alain Badiou argues, "is not what we desire or plan; it is that which we declare to be." Joan Copjec likewise contends that "one must begin with an axiom of equality rather than foolishly trying to bring it into being": see Alain Badiou, *Metapolitics*, translated by Jason Barker (1998; repr., New York: Verso, 2005), p. 98; Copjec, *Imagine There's No Woman*, p. 175.

52. Jacques Rancière, *Dissensus: On Politics and Aesthetics*, edited and translated by Steven Corcoran (New York: Continuum, 2010), p. 50. Post-foundationalism should not be mistaken for anti-foundationalism. Between these two terms, there is an important

difference. As Oliver Marchart explains, "[Post-foundationalism] refers to a theoretical position which denies the existence of an ultimate foundation of the social without, and this makes it post- rather than anti-foundational, disputing the necessity of contingent groundings. For Rancière, social or political order cannot be instituted on a firm, quasi-natural ground, yet no nihilistic consequences follow from this, as the absence of ground is what makes politics possible in the first place": Oliver Marchart, "The Second Return of the Political: Democracy and the Syllogism of Equality," in *Reading Rancière: Critical Dissensus*, edited by Paul Bowman and Richard Stamp (New York: Continuum, 2011), p. 131.

53. Rancière, *The Ignorant Schoolmaster*.

54. Paulo Freire, *Pedagogy of the Oppressed*, translated by Myra Bergman Ramos (1970; repr., New York: Continuum, 2000). On Malas and Aljafari, see Nadia Yaqub, "Refracted Filmmaking in Muhammad Malas's *The Dream* and Kamal Aljafari's *The Roof*," *Middle East Journal of Culture and Communication* 7 (2014): 152–168. On Darwazah, see Chapter 4 in this volume.

55. Myles Horton's approach to equality can be summed up in a line from the opening pages of his autobiography. "People always ask, 'Can we wait till we have a society that's perfect to have equality?' Well, of course, we'll never achieve it unless we start where we are, so you begin incorporating principles of equality in everything you do": Myles Horton with Judith Kohl and Herbert Kohn, *The Long Haul: An Autobiography* (New York: Doubleday, 1990), p. 7. Recently, there have been several attempts to put these different pedagogies into conversation: see, e.g., Tyson E. Lewis, *The Aesthetics of Education: Theatre, Curiosity, and Politics in the Work of Jacques Rancière and Paulo Freire* (New York: Continuum, 2012); Barbara Thayer-Bacon, *Democracies Always in the Making: Historical and Current Philosophical Issues for Education* (Lanham, MD: Rowman and Littlefield, 2013). See also C. L. R. James, "Every Cook Can Govern," in *A New Notion: Two Works by C. L. R. James* (Oakland, CA: PM, 2010), pp. 129–155.

56. Angela Y. Davis, *Freedom Is a Constant Struggle: Ferguson, Palestine, and the Foundations of a Movement* (Chicago: Haymarket, 2016); Alex Kane, "'A Level of Racist Violence I Have Never Seen': UCLA Professor Robin D. G. Kelley on Palestine and the BDS Movement," *Mondoweiss*, February 16, 2012, available at mondoweiss.net; Robin D. G. Kelley, "Another Freedom Summer," *Journal of Palestine Studies* 44.1 (2014): 29–41; Robin D. G. Kelley, "Apartheid's Black Apologists," in *Apartheid Israel: The Politics of an Analogy*, edited by Jon Soske and Jean Jacobs (Chicago: Haymarket, 2015), pp. 125–141; Keith P. Feldman, *A Shadow over Palestine: The Imperial Life of Race in America* (Minneapolis: University of Minnesota Press, 2015); Alex Lubin, *Geographies of Liberation: The Making of an Afro-Arab Political Imaginary* (Chapel Hill: University of North Carolina Press, 2014); Alex Lubin, "Locating Palestine in Pre-1948 Black Internationalism," *Souls* 9.2 (2007): 95–108; and Alex Lubin, "'We Are All Israelis': The Politics of Colonial Comparisons," *South Atlantic Quarterly* 107.4 (2008): 671–690. See also Nadia Alahmed, "An Anthem for the Dream Land: The Legacy of Poetry for the Palestinian and African-American Nationalism in the 1960s and 1970s," *Human Architecture: Journal of the Sociology of Self-Knowledge* 7.5 (2009): 123–136; Melani McAlister, *Epic Encounters: Culture, Media, and U.S. Interests in the Middle East since 1945*, updated ed. (2001; repr., Berkeley: University of California Press, 2005), pp. 84–124; "Roundtable on Anti-Blackness and Black-Palestinian Solidarity," *Jadaliyya*, June 3, 2015, available at jadaliyya.com. For an earlier discussion of Black-Palestinian ties, see Lewis Young, "American Blacks

and the Arab-Israeli Conflict," *Journal of Palestine Studies* 2.1 (1972): 70–85. See also Chapter 6 in this volume.

57. C. L. R. James, *C. L. R. James and Revolutionary Marxism: Selected Writings of C. L. R. James, 1939–1949*, edited by Scott McLemee and Paul le Blanc (Atlantic Highlands, NJ: Humanities, 1994), p. 77.

58. Karl Marx and Friedrich Engels, *The Communist Manifesto*, translated by Samuel Moore (1848; repr., New York: Penguin, 1985), p. 94.

59. Cedric J. Robinson, *Black Marxism: The Making of the Black Radical Tradition* (1983; repr., Chapel Hill: University of North Carolina Press, 2000), pp. 121–122.

60. Ibid., p. 309.

61. The writings of the former slave Frederick Douglass contain the most famous discussion of the contested interpretations of slave spirituals. As he argued, the slaves sang "words which to many would seem unmeaning jargon, but which, nevertheless, were full of meaning to themselves": Frederick Douglass, *Narrative of the Life of Frederick Douglass, an American Slave, Written by Himself* (1845; repr., New York: Signet, 2005), p. 19. See also Jon Cruz, *Culture on the Margins: The Black Spiritual and the Rise of American Cultural Interpretation* (Princeton, NJ: Princeton University Press, 1999).

62. For more on this film, see Edward W. Said, "*Hanna K.*: Palestine with a Human Face," *Village Voice*, October 11, 1983. For a less positive take, see Richard Porton and Ella Shochat, "The Trouble with Hanna," *Film Quarterly* 38.2 (1984–1985): 50–55.

63. Quoted in Steven Osuna, "Class Suicide: The Black Radical Tradition, Radical Scholarship, and the Neoliberal Turn," in *Futures of Black Radicalism*, edited by Gaye Theresa Johnson and Alex Lubin (New York: Verso, 2017), p. 23.

64. Rancière also argues that within orders of inequality, equality operates as a kind of noise. "Political activity is whatever shifts a body from the place assigned to it or changes a place's designation. It makes visible what had no business being seen, and makes heard a discourse where once there was only place for noise; it makes understood as discourse what was once only heard as noise": Rancière, *Disagreement*, p. 30.

65. George Lipsitz, "What Is This Black in the Black Radical Tradition?" in *Futures of Black Radicalism*, edited by Gaye Theresa Johnson and Alex Lubin (New York: Verso, 2017), pp. 108–119.

66. Rosemary Sayigh, *The Palestinians: From Peasants to Revolutionaries* (1979; repr., New York: Zed, 2007), pp. 39–40.

67. The most glaring exception to this overall focus on blackness is Robinson's short book *An Anthropology of Marxism*, which includes a discussion of Medieval poverty movements as an example of pre-Marxist European socialism: see Cedric J. Robinson, *An Anthropology of Marxism* (Burlington, VT: Ashgate, 2001).

68. Cedric J. Robinson, *The Terms of Order: Political Science and the Myth of Leadership* (1980; repr., Chapel Hill: University of North Carolina Press, 2016), p. 73.

69. Ibid., p. 59.

70. Jacques Rancière, *Proletarian Nights: The Workers' Dream in Nineteenth-Century France*, translated by John Drury (1981; repr., New York: Verso, 2012). While I am identifying *Proletarian Nights* as Rancière's first major book to be published, it was preceded by the much slimmer monograph *Althusser's Lesson* in 1974.

71. Edward W. Said, "Between Worlds," *London Review of Books* 20.9 (1998): 3–7; Said, *Peace and Its Discontents*, p. 78.

72. See, e.g., Jacques Rancière, *The Emancipated Spectator*, translated by Gregory Elliott (2008; repr., New York: Verso, 2009), pp. 103–105; Rancière, *Chronicles of Consensual Times*, pp. 62–65. On Rancière's canceled lecture, see Ali Abunimah, "Noted French Theorist Jacques Rancière Cancels Israel Lecture, Heeding Boycott Call," *Electronic Intifada*, January 19, 2012, available at electronicintifada.net.

73. Edward W. Said, *The World, the Text, and the Critic* (Cambridge, MA: Harvard University Press, 1983), pp. 246–247, quoted in Cedric J. Robinson, *Forgeries of Memory and Meaning: Blacks and the Regimes of Race in American Theater and Film before World War II* (Chapel Hill: University of North Carolina Press, 2007), p. xii. For further discussion of the intersection between the Black Radical Tradition and the Palestinian Liberation Struggle, see my "Birth of a (Zionist) Nation: Black Radicalism and the Future of Palestine," in *Futures of Black Radicalism*, edited by Gaye Theresa Johnson and Alex Lubin (New York: Verso, 2017), pp. 120–132.

74. Nadera Shalhoub-Kevorkian, "Indigenizing Feminist Knowledge: Palestinian Feminist Thought between the Physics of International Power and the Theology of Racist 'Security,'" in *Arab Feminisms: Gender and Equality in the Middle East*, edited by Jean Said Makdisi, Noha Bayoumi, and Rafif Rida Sidawi (London: I. B. Tauris, 2014), p. 206.

75. Moreover, experience is never self-evident, and we should not assume that a focus on any particular experience will automatically lead to better theory. Experience, too, must always be interpreted and theorized, and to neglect this is to perpetuate what Lewis Gordon calls "experience-reductionism." Chandra Mohanty makes this same point, and she argues against "the tendency on the part of some women of color to assume the position of ultimate critic or judge on the basis of the authenticity of their personal experience of oppression": Lewis R. Gordon, "Through the Hellish Zone of Nonbeing: Thinking Through Fanon, Disaster, and the Damned of the Earth," *Human Architecture* 5 (2007): 6; Chandra Talpade Mohanty, *Feminism without Borders: Decolonizing Theory, Practicing Solidarity* (Durham, NC: Duke University Press, 2003), p. 93. For a helpful discussion of the contemporary debates and contradictions within the field of Arab feminism, see Layal Ftouni, "Rethinking Gender Studies: Towards an Arab Feminist Epistemology," in *Arab Cultural Studies: Mapping the Field*, edited by Tarik Sabry (New York: I. B. Tauris, 2012), pp. 162–185.

76. A similar contradictory soundscape opens *Wedding in Galilee* (dir. Michel Khleifi, 1987). The audience hears children's voices against the backdrop of Israeli jets.

77. Jonathan Cook, "Internet Users Paid to Spread Israeli Propaganda," *Electronic Intifada*, July 21, 2009, available at electronicintifada.net; Barak Ravid, "Prime Minister's Office Recruiting Students to Wage Online Hasbara Battles," *Ha'aretz*, August 13, 2013, available at haaretz.com.

78. A framed copy of this same poster briefly appears on a wall during an interview with Ilan Pappé in the documentary *The Great Book Robbery* (dir. Benny Brunner, 2012). For more on this poster, see Daniel Walsh, "*Visit Palestine*," *Liberation Graphics*, 2003, available at liberationgraphics.com.

79. Nurith Gertz, "The Early Israeli Cinema as Silencer of Memory," *Shofar* 24.1 (2005): 80.

80. Specifically, Gertz directs our attention to the absence of Holocaust narratives from these films. These traumatic memories of victimization were largely repressed in Israeli discourse until as late as the Adolf Eichmann trial of the early 1960s. Before this time, the survivors had been treated quite differently. David Ben-Gurion himself once

referred to them as a "people who would not have survived if they had not been what they were—hard, evil, and selfish people, and what they underwent there served to destroy what good qualities they had left": quoted in Massad, *The Persistence of the Palestinian Question*, p. 176. See also Hanna Yablonka, "The Development of Holocaust Consciousness in Israel: The Nuremberg, Kapos, Kastner, and Eichmann Trials," *Israel Studies* 8.3 (2003): 1–24; Idith Zertal, *From Catastrophe to Power: The Holocaust Survivors and the Emergence of Israel* (Berkeley: University of California Press, 1998).

81. As Judith Butler argues, "Israel has *never* been a Jewish state; it has always included, through subjugation, non-Jews, Christian and Muslim Palestinians, Druze, and Bedouins": Judith Butler, *Parting Ways: Jewishness and the Critique of Zionism* (New York: Columbia University Press, 2012), p. 211 (emphasis in original).

82. In her critique of Homi Bhabha, Rey Chow asks, "What kind of argument is it to say that the subaltern's 'voice' can be found in the *ambivalence* of the imperialist's speech? [. . .] All we would need to do would be to continue to study—to deconstruct— the rich and ambivalent language of the imperialist!": Rey Chow, "Where Have All the Natives Gone?" in *Displacements: Cultural Identities in Question*, edited by Angelika Bammer (Bloomington: Indiana University Press, 1994), p. 131 (emphasis in original).

83. Personal conversation with Annemarie Jacir, Amman, Jordan, April 13, 2014. For more information on the "CTRL+ALT+DELETE" graffiti, see the artist Filippo Minelli's website at filippominelli.com.

CHAPTER 2

1. Leela Jacinto, "No Room for Palestinian Film at the Oscars," ABC News, December 20, 2002, available at abcnews.go.com.

2. Ali Abunimah and Benjamin J. Doherty, "'Gaza Strip' Director to Return Student Academy Award to Protest Exclusion of Palestine," *Electronic Intifada*, December 20, 2002, available at electronicintifada.net.

3. Benjamin J. Doherty and Ali Abunimah, "Oscars' Double Standard Turns Palestinian Film into Refugee," *Electronic Intifada*, December 10, 2002, available at electronic intifada.net; Jacinto, "No Room for Palestinian Film at the Oscars."

4. Speaking to Reuters at the time, an anonymous Israeli diplomat justified this decision, saying, "No one, not even the Palestinians themselves, have declared the formal creation of Palestine yet, and thus the label would be inaccurate": quoted in "New Trouble for Paradise Now," Al Jazeera, February 12, 2006, available at aljazeera.com.

5. An AMPAS spokesperson claimed that the change of status was made possible as a result of the United Nations General Assembly's decision in 2012 to formally recognize Palestinian statehood: see Anna Newby, "Oscar Night for Palestine," *Slate*, March 3, 2014, available at slate.com; Ehab Zahriyeh, "'Omar' a Rare Palestinian Feature Film at the Oscars," Al Jazeera America, February 21, 2014, available at america.aljazeera.com.

6. Hamid Dabashi, "Getting Hollywood's Nod for Palestinian Film: What Will It Take for Hollywood to Recognize Palestinian Cinema?" Al Jazeera, November 1, 2014, available at aljazeera.com. See also the anthology Hamid Dabashi, ed., *Dreams of a Nation: On Palestinian Cinema* (New York: Verso, 2006).

7. Terri Ginsberg and Chris Lippard, eds., *Historical Dictionary of Middle Eastern Cinema* (Lanham, MD: Scarecrow, 2010), p. 319; Livia Alexander, "Is There a Palestinian Cinema? The National and Transnational in Palestinian Film Production," in *Palestine,*

Israel, and the Politics of Popular Culture, edited by Rebecca L. Stein and Ted Sweden-burg (Durham, NC: Duke University Press, 2005), pp. 150–172.

8. Nurith Gertz and George Khleifi, *Palestinian Cinema: Landscape, Trauma, and Memory* (2005; repr., Bloomington: Indiana University Press, 2008), pp. 13–14.

9. Ibid., pp. 19–20. See also Nadia Yaqub, *Palestinian Cinema in the Days of Revolution* (Austin: University of Texas Press, 2018), pp. 16–47.

10. Gertz and Khleifi, *Palestinian Cinema*, p. 22. See also Nurith Gertz and George Khleifi, "From Bleeding Memories to *Fertile Memories*: Palestinian Cinema in the 1970s," *Third Text* 20.3–4 (2006): 465–474.

11. Joseph Massad, "The Weapon of Culture: Cinema in the Palestinian Liberation Struggle," in Dabashi, *Dreams of a Nation*, p. 31.

12. On the background and work of these three filmmakers, see Yaqub, *Palestinian Cinema in the Days of Revolution*, pp. 48–83.

13. Gertz and Khleifi, *Palestinian Cinema*, pp. 20–30. See also the extensive discus-sion of this era of Palestinian filmmaking in Yaqub, *Palestinian Cinema in the Days of Revolution*. Over the years, some of the footage that had been sent to various interna-tional film festivals before the Israeli invasion of Beirut has been recovered. It forms the basis of Mohanad Yaqubi's montage film *Off Frame: Revolution until Victory* (2015): see Yaqub, *Palestinian Cinema in the Days of Revolution*, pp. 218–220.

14. Gertz and Khleifi, *Palestinian Cinema*, pp. 30–53.

15. One might compare this mixing of documentary and fictional film forms to what Joan Mellen identified as "the fictional documentary": see Joan Mellen, "Film and Style: The Fictional Documentary," *Antioch Review* 32.3 (1972): 403–425. See also Chap-ter 4 in this volume.

16. Annemarie Jacir, "'I Wanted That Story to Be Told' (Interview)," *Alif* 31 (2011): 245.

17. For a strong critique of this book's political and theoretical framework, see Terri Ginsberg, "Review of *Palestinian Cinema: Landscape, Trauma, and Memory*," *Middle East Journal of Culture and Communication* 2.2 (2009), pp. 315–321.

18. Alexander, "Is There a Palestinian Cinema?" p. 156.

19. In 2009, it was reported that a low-budget feature funded by Hamas had pre-miered at a cultural center in Gaza. Following the screening of it, Gaza's Interior Minister Fathi Hamad, who also produced the film, declared the dawn of a new age: "It's Hamas-wood instead of Hollywood." Although this quote was widely reported in the right-wing blogosphere, the film did not otherwise seem to attract much attention elsewhere: see Ben Child, "First Film Produced by Hamas Screens in Gaza," *The Guardian*, August 5, 2009, available at theguardian.com.

20. "Celebrity-Backed Cinema Jenin in Palestine Closes," *Al-Ahram Online*, Decem-ber 4, 2016, available at english.ahram.org.eg.

21. The theater that brought the two brothers, the Alamo Drafthouse, allowed them to select the first film they would see on the big screen. They chose *Cries and Whispers* (dir. Ingmar Bergman, 1972): see Harriet Sherwood, "Tarzan and Arab: The Gaza Art-ists Determined to Make It against All Odds," *The Guardian*, August 15, 2011, available at theguardian.com. On their trip to Texas, see Devin Faraci, "Escape from Gaza: How Palestinian Filmmakers Tarzan and Arab Made It to Austin," *Birth.Movies.Death*, Octo-ber 21, 2011, available at birthmoviesdeath.com.

22. Alia Arasoughly, "Film Education in Palestine Post-Oslo: The Experience of

Shashat," in *The Education of the Filmmaker in Africa, the Middle East, and the Americas*, edited by Mette Hjort (New York: Palgrave Macmillan, 2013), pp. 99–123.

23. Quoted in Lara Aburamadan, "In Photos: Red Carpet Film Festival Asserts Gaza's Pride and Talent," *Electronic Intifada*, May 19, 2015, available at electronicintifada.net.

24. Quoted in Asmaa al-Ghoul, "Film Festival Opens amid Gaza's Ruins," *Al-Monitor*, May 19, 2015, available at al-monitor.com.

25. Hamid Naficy, *An Accented Cinema: Exilic and Diasporic Filmmaking* (Princeton, NJ: Princeton University Press, 2001), pp. 59–60, 294.

26. Dabashi, "Getting Hollywood's Nod for Palestinian Film."

27. This financial difference is clear even from the opening credits, and both films clearly announce their main sources of funding. For *Salt*, this included support from organizations based in Belgium, France, the Netherlands, Spain, Switzerland, the United Kingdom, and the United States. For *When I Saw You*, the main sources included the Syrian-British businessman Ayman Asfari's foundation; Faliro House Productions, based in Greece; the Khalid Shoman Foundation, based in Jordan; and the Abu Dhabi Film Festival.

28. Alia Yunis, "The Pursuit of Heroes in Palestinian Cinema: An Interview with Annemarie Jacir," *Jadaliyya*, October 1, 2013, available at jadaliyya.com.

29. Quoted in Brooks, "We Have No Film Industry Because We Have No Country."

30. Quoted in ibid. For a discussion of the obstacles that confront Palestinians seeking Israeli funding, see Terri Ginsberg, *Visualizing the Palestinian Struggle: Toward a Critical Analytic of Palestine Solidarity Films* (New York: Palgrave Macmillan, 2016), pp. 54, 87–88.

31. Brooks, "We Have No Film Industry Because We Have No Country.". Accepting these funds did not come without its problems, even for a filmmaker as celebrated as Suleiman. As he explained in an interview, "When I had my legal battles with *Chronicles of a Disappearance*, one of the things the Israel Film Fund told me is that they hated my film because by making the Israelis into cartoon figures, I did not recognize their existence in this place": quoted in Nehad Khader, "Interview with Elia Suleiman: The Power of Ridicule," *Journal of Palestine Studies* 44.4 (2015): 24.

32. Although Israeli funds were used in producing *Paradise Now*, the film—which involves a Palestinian suicide bomber—was very controversial in that country, and it was not picked up by any Israeli distribution company: see Gertz and Khleifi, *Palestinian Cinema*, p. 193.

33. Hamoud justified her decision, arguing, "We are 20% of the population, we pay taxes. We are Palestinians and we are Israelis and people don't know what to make of this. People said, 'Don't take the Israeli money, get Arab funding.' This is an oxymoron. There were no Arab film funds, there was nothing I could get": quoted in Hannah Brown, "*In Between*: The Movie That Has Touched a Chord throughout the World and in Israel," *Jerusalem Post*, March 12, 2017, available at jpost.com.

34. Quoted in "'My Dream Is to Return'—Conversation with Saleh Bakri," *Le Mur a des Oreilles*, October 21, 2013, available at lemuradesoreilles.org. For a discussion of how Bakri has been treated as an object of Orientalist fantasy, see Belen Fernandez, "Those Exotic Arabs, and Other Orientalist Fetishes," Al Jazeera, August 24, 2013, available at aljazeera.com.

35. Bennett quoted in Gil Tanenbaum, "Bennett Insists Suha Arraf Give Israel Back $500K after Dubbing Her Film 'Palestinian,'" *Jewish Business News*, November 14, 2014,

available at jewishbusinessnews.com. See also Lahav Harkov, "Culture, Economy Ministries Withdraw Israeli Funds from 'Palestinian' Film," *Jerusalem Post*, August 27, 2014, available at jpost.com; Patrick O. Strickland, "Suha Arraf on Her 'Stateless' Palestinian Film," *Electronic Intifada*, October 9, 2014, available at electronicintifada.net.

36. Jonathan Freedland, "McCarthyism—Israeli Style," *Jewish Chronicle Online*, January 24, 2011, available at thejc.com.

37. Quoted in John Anderson, "The Hand That Feeds Bites Back: Israel and Suha Arraf Differ on Nationality of 'Villa Touma,'" *New York Times*, October 16, 2014, available at nytimes.com.

38. Quoted in "Golda Meir Scorns Soviets: Israeli Premier Explains Stand on Big-4 Talks, Security," *Washington Post* (June 16, 1969).

39. See the discussion of this film in Yaqub, *Palestinian Cinema in the Days of Revolution*, pp. 73–76.

40. Although he did not coin the phrase, the British Zionist Israel Zangwill is often credited with popularizing it in the early years of the twentieth century: see, e.g., Nur Masalha, *Expulsion of the Palestinians: The Concept of "Transfer" in Zionist Political Thought, 1882–1948* (Washington DC: Institute for Palestine Studies, 1992), pp. 5–8. Ghassan Hage points out that the settler-colonialist fantasy of the empty land did not originate with Zionism. Similar views were also deployed in relation to the British colonization of Australia: Ghassan Hage, *Against Paranoid Nationalism: Searching for Hope in a Shrinking Society* (London: Merlin, 2003), p. 80.

41. On the empty book, see "Empty Book on Palestinian History Becomes Instant Best-Seller on Amazon," *Ha'aretz*, June 22, 2017, available at haaretz.com. On the letter "P," see Matt Payton, "Israeli MP Claims the Palestine Nation Cannot Exist 'Because They Can't Pronounce the Letter P,'" *The Independent*, February 11, 2016, available at independent.co.uk. An earlier example is Joan Peters's notorious 1984 bestseller *From Time Immemorial* which relied on fabricated evidence in order to claim that most Palestinians are actually immigrants from neighboring Arab countries: see Joan Peters, *From Time Immemorial: The Origins of the Arab-Jewish Conflict over Palestine* (New York: Harper and Row, 1984). For a devastating critique of Peters's book, see Norman G. Finkelstein, "Disinformation and the Palestine Question: The Not-So-Strange Case of Joan Peters's *From Time Immemorial*," in *Blaming the Victims: Spurious Scholarship and the Palestinian Question*, edited by Edward W. Said and Christopher Hitchens (1988; repr., New York: Verso, 2001), pp. 33–69.

42. Quoted in Saree Makdisi, *Palestine Inside Out: An Everyday Occupation* (2008; repr., New York: W. W. Norton, 2010), p. 232. As Said likewise argued, "Every assertion of our nonexistence, every attempt to spirit us away, every new effort to prove that we were never really there, simply raises the question of why so much denial of, and such energy expended on, what was not there?": Edward W. Said, *After the Last Sky: Palestinian Lives* (New York: Pantheon, 1986), p. 42.

43. David Hirst, *The Gun and the Olive Branch: The Roots of Violence in the Middle East*, 3d ed. (1977; repr., New York: Thunder's Mouth, 2003), p. 369.

44. Quoted in Arthur Neslen, *Occupied Minds: A Journey through the Israeli Psyche* (Ann Arbor, MI: Pluto, 2006), p. 1 (emphasis mine). Ilan Halevi makes a similar argument when he claims, "It is not that the Zionists did not know that Palestine was inhabited, it is that they considered that the inhabitants of Palestine, being Arabs, did not exist as people": Ilan Halevi, "Zionism Today," *Arab Studies Quarterly* 7.2–3 (1985): 6.

45. More recently, the Israeli historian Shlomo Sand became the object of much scorn when he published *The Invention of the Jewish People*, a work that was controversial not for its theoretical underpinnings, which by now have become widely accepted in the academy, but simply because it applied these critical insights to the nationalist claims of Israel: see Ernest Gellner, *Nations and Nationalism* (Ithaca, NY: Cornell University Press, 1983); Eric J. Hobsbawm, *Nations and Nationalism since 1780: Programme, Myth, Reality*, 2d ed. (New York: Cambridge University Press, 1992); Shlomo Sand, *The Invention of the Jewish People*, translated by Yael Lotan (2008; repr., New York: Verso, 2009).

46. Joan Copjec, *Read My Desire: Lacan against the Historicists* (Cambridge, MA: MIT Press, 1994), p. 128.

47. Slavoj Žižek, *The Sublime Object of Ideology* (New York: Verso, 1989), p. 5.

48. For tales of DDT and other forms of mistreatment, see the fascinating interviews in the documentary *Forget Baghdad: Jews and Arabs—the Iraqi Connection* (dir. Samir, 2002).

49. It is worth noting that Weiss's essay was heavily promoted by the *Jerusalem Post*, and a link to it appeared on the main page of the periodical's website for more than two months after its publication in August 2014: Stewart Weiss, "In Plain Language: Man versus Morlock," *Jerusalem Post*, August 7, 2014, available at jpost.com. See also H. G. Wells, *The Time Machine* (1895; repr., New York: Penguin, 2005).

50. As David Theo Goldberg argues, "In the face of its own increasingly radically Jewish heterogeneity—radically Jewish and radically heterogeneous—and so in the face of its own internal implosion, Israel seeks its familial artifice by projecting a threat both internal and purged to its shifting and shifted boundaries, at once within and without": David Theo Goldberg, *The Threat of Race: Reflections on Racial Neoliberalism* (Malden, MA: Wiley-Blackwell, 2009), p. 113.

51. "If the Jew did not exist, the anti-Semite would invent him": Jean-Paul Sartre, *Anti-Semite and Jew: An Exploration of the Etiology of Hate*, translated by George J. Becker (1948; repr., New York: Schocken, 1995), p. 13.

52. Another example of omission presents itself in the guise of Christian apocalyptic literature—namely, the popular *Left Behind* series of novels and films. As Melani McAlister notes, "There are *no* Palestinian Arabs in a series where much of the action takes place in Jerusalem and the surrounding areas": Melani McAlister, "Prophecy, Politics, and the Popular: The *Left Behind* Series and Christian Evangelicalism's New World Order," in *Palestine, Israel, and the Politics of Popular Culture*, edited by Rebecca L. Stein and Ted Swedenburg (Durham, NC: Duke University Press, 2005), p. 305 (emphasis in original).

53. Ella Shohat, *Israeli Cinema: East/West and the Politics of Representation* (Austin: University of Texas Press, 1989), pp. 59–60. See also Dorit Naaman, "Orientalism as Alterity in Israeli Cinema," *Cinema Journal* 40.4 (2001): 36–54; Ilan Pappé, *The Idea of Israel: A History of Power and Knowledge* (New York: Verso, 2014), p. 58.

54. As Sunaina Maira and Magid Shihade assert, "The notion of the present absentee is not simply a metaphor that slides over from a juridical category of the Israeli state. The concept of the 'present absent' offers a profound analytic lens for understanding the fundamental contradictions of the social, political, and cultural conditions created by specific histories of settler colonialism for '48 Palestinians, who are simultaneously visible/invisible, internal/external, indigenous/inauthentic, and, always, absent/present": Sunaina Maira and Magid Shihade, "Hip Hop from '48 Palestine Youth, Music, and the Present/Absent," *Social Text* 30.3 (2012): 5. See also Makdisi, *Palestine Inside Out*, pp. 148, 231.

55. C. L. R. James, "Africans and Afro-Caribbeans: A Personal View (1984)," in *Writing Black Britain, 1948–1998: An Interdisciplinary Anthology*, edited by James Procter (New York: Manchester University Press, 2000), pp. 60–63. See also Stuart Hall, "'In but Not Of Europe': Europe and Its Myths," in *Figures d'Europe: Images and Myths of Europe*, edited by Luisa Passerini (New York: P. Lang, 2003), pp. 35–45.

56. Sigmund Freud, *Moses and Monotheism*, translated by Katherine Jones (1939; repr., New York: Vintage, 1967).

57. Judith Butler, *Parting Ways: Jewishness and the Critique of Zionism* (New York: Columbia University Press, 2012), pp. 15, 117.

58. Freud, *Moses and Monotheism*, p. 3.

59. Žižek, *The Sublime Object of Ideology*, pp. 47–49.

60. For further discussion of Freud's text, see Richard J. Bernstein, *Freud and the Legacy of Moses* (New York: Cambridge University Press, 1998); Edward W. Said, *Freud and the Non-European* (New York: Verso, 2003); Butler, *Parting Ways*, pp. 28–53. See also Slavoj Žižek, *Tarrying with the Negative: Kant, Hegel, and the Critique of Ideology* (Durham, NC: Duke University Press, 1993), pp. 220–221; Todd McGowan, "Hegel as Marxist: Žižek's Revision of German Idealism," in *Žižek Now: Current Perspectives in Žižek Studies*, edited by Jamil Khader and Molly Anne Rothenberg (Malden, MA: Polity, 2013), pp. 46–47.

61. On this point, the contemporary attempt to identify Jewish hereditary traits through genealogical science is particularly suspect: see Nadia Abu el-Haj, *The Genealogical Science: The Search for Jewish Origins and the Politics of Epistemology* (Chicago: University of Chicago Press, 2012).

62. Said, *Freud and the Non-European*, p. 44.

63. This is how Jacqueline Rose paraphrases Said's position: see Jacqueline Rose, "Response to Edward Said," in *Freud and the Non-European*, by Edward W. Said (New York: Verso, 2003), p. 66. See also the discussion in Jacqueline Rose, *The Last Resistance* (New York: Verso, 2007), pp. 75–88.

64. In an essay about Palestinian refugees in Lebanon, Julie Peteet reminds her readers that "it is important not to turn to an essentializing Palestinian experience or identity." Said likewise writes, "There are many different kinds of Palestinian experience, which cannot all be assembled into one." Gilbert Achcar makes a similar claim apropos "the Arabs." "It ought to be a truism," he writes, "that 'the Arabs' do not exist—at least not as a homogenous political or ideological subject. Yet such a use of a general category known as 'the Arabs' is common in both journalism and the specialist literature. 'The Arabs' are supposed to think and act or react in unison. Of course, like 'the Jews' or 'the Muslims,' 'the Arabs' as a politically and intellectually uniform group exist only in fantasy, engendered by the distorting prism of either ordinary racism or polemical fanaticism": see Julie M. Peteet, "Transforming Trust: Dispossession and Empowerment among Palestinian Refugees," in *Mistrusting Refugees*, edited by E. Valentine Daneil and John Chr. Knudsen (Berkeley: University of California Press, 1995), p. 176; Edward W. Said, *The Politics of Dispossession: The Struggle for Palestinian Self-Determination, 1969–1994* (1994; repr., New York: Vintage, 1995), p. 119; Gilbert Achcar, *The Arabs and the Holocaust: The Arab-Israeli War of Narratives*, translated by G. M. Goshgarian (2009; repr., New York: Metropolitan, 2010), p. 33. For an examination of Palestinian identity within different types of refugee camps, see Sari Hanafi, "Palestinian Refugee Camps in the Palestinian Territory: Territory of Exception and Locus of Resistance,"

in *The Power of Inclusive Exclusion: Anatomy of Israeli Rule in the Occupied Palestinian Territories*, edited by Adi Ophir, Michal Givoni, and Sari Hanafi (New York: Zone, 2009), pp. 495–517.

65. Quoted in Khaled Alashqar, "Gaza Cinema Struggles amid Post-war Ruins," Al Jazeera, December 13, 2014, available at aljazeera.com.

66. James Baldwin, *Notes of a Native Son* (1955; repr., New York: Bantam, 1968), p. 105 (emphasis in original).

67. S. Sayyid makes the same argument with respect to Islam. "To argue that Islam has no essence," he writes, "is not to suggest that it is a mere fabrication, nor is it remotely to threaten its dissolution, rather it is to open up investigations into its creative potential and demonstrate its significance." In Sayyid's words, "If Islam did indeed have an essence, a literal content that exhausted all it[s] meanings and permutations—this would not be the saving of Islam but its erasure": S. Sayyid, *A Fundamental Fear: Eurocentrism and the Emergence of Islamism* (2015; repr., London: Zed, 1997), p. xviii.

68. Thatcher quoted in Douglas Keay, "AIDS, Education and the Year 2000!" *Woman's Own*, October 31, 1987, p. 10; Ernesto Laclau and Chantal Mouffe, *Hegemony and Socialist Strategy: Towards a Radical Democratic Politics* (New York: Verso, 1985). For more on Thatcher's infamous statement, see the discussion in David Harvey, *A Brief History of Neoliberalism* (New York: Oxford University Press, 2005), pp. 22–23.

69. Jack G. Shaheen, *Reel Bad Arabs: How Hollywood Vilifies a People* (New York: Olive Branch, 2001); Jack G. Shaheen, *Guilty: Hollywood's Verdict on Arabs after 9/11* (Northampton, MA: Olive Branch, 2008). See also Karin Gwinn Wilkins, *Home/Land/Security: What We Learn about Arab Communities from Action-Adventure Films* (Lanham, MD: Lexington, 2009).

70. See Said, *The Question of Palestine*, p. 137; Said, *After the Last Sky*, pp. 113–114.

71. Here, it is important to point out my disagreement with those materialists who insist that identity categories are ontological insofar as they are produced by real, historical processes such as colonialism. I do not disagree that oppressive practices and institutions are intimately involved in the constitution of contemporary identities. However, it is a mistake to believe they have absolute authority. Identities are contingent, and recognizing this contingency is an important way to challenge those same processes. To deny the ontological fixity of identity constructions is not to ignore oppressive historical practices. Rather, in my view, this denial is the first crucial step in opposing them.

72. This is ultimately a major flaw in Louis Althusser's theory of interpellation. See his famous essay in Louis Althusser, *Lenin and Philosophy and Other Essays*, translated by Ben Brewster (1975; repr., New York: Verso, 2001), pp. 85–126. See also the critical discussion in Mladen Dolar, "Beyond Interpellation," *Qui Parle* 6.2 (1993): 75–96; Jacques Rancière, *Althusser's Lesson*, translated by Emiliano Battista (1974; repr., New York: Continuum, 2011). Also relevant here is the reversal of Althusser's formula in Jacques Rancière, *Dissensus: On Politics and Aesthetics*, edited and translated by Steven Corcoran (New York: Continuum, 2010), p. 37.

73. See Ernst Bloch, *The Principle of Hope*, vol. 1, translated by Neville Plaice, Stephen Plaice, and Paul Knight (1959; repr., Cambridge, MA: MIT Press, 1986), p. 195; Jacques Lacan, *The Seminar of Jacques Lacan, Book xx, On Feminine Sexuality: The Limits of Love and Knowledge: Encore 1972–1973*, edited by Jacques Alain-Miller, translated by Bruce Fink (1975; repr., New York: W. W. Norton, 1998), p. 7; Laclau and Mouffe, *Hegemony and Socialist Strategy*; Stuart Hall, "The Problem of Ideology: Marxism without Guar-

antees," in *Stuart Hall: Critical Dialogues in Cultural Studies*, edited by David Morley and Kuan-Hsing Chen (New York: Routledge, 1996), pp. 25–46; Huey P. Newton with J. Herman Blake, *Revolutionary Suicide* (1973; repr., New York: Penguin, 2009). Kanafani's line appears in his short story "Returning to Haifa," in *Palestine's Children: Returning to Haifa and Other Stories*, translated by Barbara Harlow and Karen E. Riley (Boulder, CO: Lynne Rienner, 2000), pp. 181–182.

74. Julie Peteet, "The Work of Comparison: Israel/Palestine and Apartheid," *Anthropological Quarterly* 89.1 (2016): 251.

75. Nirit Anderman and Noa Shpigel, "Israeli City Bars Screening of Film about Israeli-Arab Coexistence," *Ha'aretz*, November 2, 2016, available at haaretz.com.

76. In Said's words, "The relationship between Israelis and Arabs is not a fact of nature but the result of a specific, continuing process of dispossession, displacement, and colonial de facto apartheid": Said, *The Question of Palestine*, p. 37. Similarly, Alain Badiou argues that "the legitimate solution to the Middle East conflict is not the dreadful institution of two barbed-wire states. The solution is the creation of a secular and democratic Palestine, one subtracted from all predicates, and which [. . .] would show that it is perfectly possible to create a place in these lands where, from a political point of view and regardless of the apolitical continuity of customs, there is 'neither Arab nor Jew'": Alain Badiou, *Polemics*, translated by Steve Corcoran (2006; repr., New York: Verso, 2011), p. 164.

77. Frantz Fanon, *Black Skins, White Masks*, translated by Richard Philcox (1952; repr., New York: Grove, 2008), p. 163.

78. Elia Suleiman's oeuvre represents an example of antinationalist cinema, a fact that has won him his fair share of Palestinian critics. As he himself commented, "My approach is considered too critical for a time of national construction that is said to call for unity and even uniformity. They think that Palestinians should all speak with one voice": Elia Suleiman, "A Cinema of Nowhere," *Journal of Palestine Studies* 29.2 (2000): 100.

79. This is a key point for Hall, who writes, "Films are not necessarily good because black people make them. They are not necessarily 'right-on' by virtue of the fact that they deal with the black experience. Once you enter the politics of the end of the essential black subject you are plunged headlong into the maelstrom of a continuously contingent, unguaranteed, political argument and debate: a critical politics, a politics of criticism. You can no longer conduct black politics through the strategy of a simple set of reversals, putting in the place of the bad old essential white subject, the new essentially good black subject": Stuart Hall, "New Ethnicities (1988)," in *Writing Black Britain, 1948–1998: An Interdisciplinary Anthology*, edited by James Procter (New York: Manchester University Press, 2000), p. 268.

80. Much ink has been spilled searching for new ways to criticize those Black Americans who are perceived as perpetuating conservative or even white supremacist political views. Manning Marable, for instance, referred to Black capitalists as "Black Brahmins," and Robin Kelley goes as far as to call Black neocons "negrocons": Manning Marable, *How Capitalism Underdeveloped Black America: Problems in Race, Political Economy, and Society*, updated ed. (1983; repr., Cambridge, MA: South End, 2000), p. 180; Robin D. G. Kelley, *Yo' Mama's Disfunktional: Fighting the Cultural Wars in Urban America* (Boston: Beacon, 1997), p. 89. See also Robin D. G. Kelley, "House Negroes on the Loose: Malcolm X and the Black Bourgeoisie," *Callaloo* 21.2 (1998): 419–435.

81. The aforementioned couples "worker and proletarian," "woman and feminist,"

and "Black subject and Black radical" have been convincingly disentangled by Slavoj Žižek, bell hooks, and George Lipsitz, respectively: see, e.g., Slavoj Žižek, *The Ticklish Subject: The Absent Centre of Political Ontology* (1999; repr., New York: Verso, 2000), p. 227; bell hooks, *Feminism Is for Everybody: Passionate Politics* (Cambridge, MA: South End, 2000), p. 7; George Lipsitz, *The Possessive Investment in Whiteness: How White People Profit from Identity Politics*, 2nd ed. (1998; repr., Philadelphia: Temple University Press, 2006), p. viii. See also the helpful discussions in Patricia Hill Collins, *Black Feminist Thought: Knowledge, Consciousness, and the Politics of Empowerment* (1990; repr., New York: Routledge, 1991), pp. 19–40; Chandra Talpade Mohanty, *Feminism without Borders: Decolonizing Theory, Practicing Solidarity* (Durham, NC: Duke University Press, 2003), pp. 109, 112.

82. Homi Bhabha, "How Newness Enters the World: Postmodern Space, Postcolonial Times and the Trails of Cultural Translation," in *Writing Black Britain,, 1948–1998: An Interdisciplinary Anthology*, edited by James Procter (New York: Manchester University Press, 2000), p. 303.

83. As Marcuse had already argued, "Heresy by itself [. . .] is no token of truth": Herbert Marcuse, "Repressive Tolerance," in *A Critique of Pure Tolerance*, by Robert Paul Wolff, Barrington Moore Jr., and Herbert Marcuse (1965; repr., Boston: Beacon, 1969), p. 91.

84. Ella Shohat makes this same argument. "As a descriptive catch-all term," she writes, "'hybridity' per se fails to discriminate between the diverse modalities of hybridity, for example, forced assimilation, internalized self-rejection, political cooptation, social conformism, cultural mimicry, and creative transcendence": Ella Shohat, "Notes on the 'Post-Colonial,'" *Social Text* 31–32 (1992): 110.

85. Stuart Hall, "Subjects in History: Making Diasporic Identities," in *The House That Race Built: Black Americans, U.S. Terrain*, edited by Wahneema Lubiano (New York: Pantheon, 1997), p. 298. Or, as Mette Hjort argues with regard to the transnational turn in cinema studies, "quite against the intentions of those who use it, 'transnational' ends up playing a strangely homogenizing role": Mette Hjort, "On the Plurality of Cinematic Transnationalism," in *World Cinemas, Transnational Perspectives*, edited by Nataša Ďurovičová and Kathleen Newman (New York: Routledge, 2010), p. 15.

86. Edward W. Said, *Culture and Imperialism* (1993; repr., New York: Vintage, 1994), p. xxv. See also the discussion in Marwan M. Kraidy, *Hybridity, or the Cultural Logic of Globalization* (Philadelphia: Temple University Press, 2005).

87. On this point, one might also recall Cedric Robinson's humorous observation that "Western civilization is neither": quoted by Gerard Pigeon in "Radical Thought: Cedric J. Robinson," YouTube, video clip posted by University of California Television (UCTV)," November 6, 2008, available at https://www.youtube.com/watch?v=IK16BExR1KU.

88. Mosab Hassan Yousef with Ron Brackin, *Son of Hamas: A Gripping Account of Terror, Betrayal, Political Intrigue, and Unthinkable Choices* (Carol Stream, IL: Tyndale, 2010). *The Green Prince* received awards from the Israeli Film Academy, the Moscow International Film Festival, and the Sundance Film Festival, among others.

89. Ella Shohat and Robert Stam, *Unthinking Eurocentrism: Multiculturalism and the Media*, new ed. (1994; repr., New York: Routledge, 2014), p. 26.

90. Here, my argument closely resembles that of Chandra Mohanty who writes, "I [. . .] challenge the notion 'I am, therefore I resist!' That is, I challenge the idea that simply being a woman, or being poor or black or Latino, is sufficient ground to assume a

politicized oppositional identity. In other words, while questions of identity are crucially important, they can never be reduced to automatic self-referential, individualist ideas of the political (or feminist) subject": Mohanty, *Feminism without Borders*, p. 77.

91. Nadera Shalhoub-Kevorkian, for instance, sees the nakba as "the moral corner-stone of [Palestinian] feminist theorizing," and Amal Amireh claims that "the consensus among Palestinian historians is that *Al Nakba* [. . .] is the most important event in solidifying a Palestinian national identity": Nadera Shalhoub-Kevorkian, "Indigenizing Feminist Knowledge: Palestinian Feminist Thought between the Physics of International-al Power and the Theology of Racist 'Security,'" in *Arab Feminisms: Gender and Equality in the Middle East*, edited by Jean Said Makdisi, Noha Bayoumi, and Rafif Rida Sidawi (London: I. B. Tauris, 2014), p. 206; Amal Amireh, "Between Complicity and Subversion: Body Politics in Palestinian National Narrative," *South Atlantic Quarterly* 102.4 (2003): 751. On "ghettocentricity," see Robin D. G. Kelley, *Race Rebels: Culture, Politics, and the Black Working Class* (New York: Free Press, 1996), p. 209.

92. In the introduction to *Palestinian Identity*, Khalidi writes, "It is at [. . .] borders and barriers that six million Palestinians are singled out for 'special treatment,' and are forcefully reminded of their identity: of who they are, and of why they are different from others." As he argues, "Even those few Palestinians who by the chance of birth, marriage, or emigration have managed to acquire U.S., European, or other first world passports, find that barriers and borders remind them inexorably of who they are. This is especially true if they return to their homeland, which they have to do via points of entry controlled exclusively by Israel; or if they travel to virtually any Arab country": Rashid Khalidi, *Palestinian Identity: The Construction of Modern National Consciousness* (1997; repr., New York: Columbia University Press, 2010), pp. 1, 3–4.

93. Janet Walker is therefore justified in comparing incest stories to the Holocaust. Different as they might be, both of these painful injustices are indeed forms of collective, social trauma. Catherine Malabou has further expanded our view of trauma by bringing into the discussion the topic of brain injuries and neurological disorders. As she argues, "The behavior of subjects who are victims of trauma linked to mistreatment, war, terrorist attacks, captivity, or sexual abuse display striking resemblances with subjects who have suffered brain damage. It is possible to name these traumas 'sociopolitical traumas'": see Janet Walker, *Trauma Cinema: Documenting Incest and the Holocaust* (Berkeley: University of California Press, 2005); Catherine Malabou, *The New Wounded: From Neurosis to Brain Damage*, translated by Steven Miller (2007; repr., New York: Fordham University Press, 2012), p. 10.

94. Jean-Pierre Filiu raises the specter of the golem in his essay about the origins of Hamas: see Jean-Pierre Filiu, "The Origins of Hamas: Militant Legacy or Israeli Tool?" *Journal of Palestine Studies* 41.3 (2012): 54–70.

95. As Khalidi writes, "Although the Zionist challenge definitely helped to shape the specific form Palestinian national identification took, it is a serious mistake to suggest that Palestinian identity emerged mainly as a response to Zionism": Khalidi, *Palestinian Identity*, p. 20. See also Rosemary Sayigh, *The Palestinians: From Peasants to Revolutionaries* (1979; repr., New York: Zed, 2007); Baruch Kimmerling and Joel S. Migdal, *The Palestinian People: A History* (1994; repr., Cambridge, MA: Harvard University Press, 2003).

96. In Ann Kaplan's words, "How one reacts to a traumatic event depends on one's individual psychic history, on memories inevitably mixed with fantasies of prior catas-

trophes, and on the particular cultural and political context within which a catastrophe takes place, especially how it is 'managed' by institutions": E. Ann Kaplan, *Trauma Culture: The Politics of Terror and Loss in Media and Literature* (New Brunswick, NJ: Rutgers University Press, 2005), p. 1.

97. Constantine K. Zurayk, *The Meaning of the Disaster*, translated by R. Bayly Winder (1948; repr., Beirut: Khayat's, 1956), p. 48.

98. E. P. Thompson, *The Making of the English Working Class* (1963; repr., New York: Vintage, 1966), p. 194; Lisa Lowe, *Immigrant Acts: On Asian American Cultural Politics* (Durham, NC: Duke University Press, 1996), p. 66.

99. Jacques Rancière, *Moments Politiques: Interventions 1977–2009*, translated by Mary Foster (2009; repr., New York: Seven Stories, 2014), p. 45.

100. "A political subjectivation is the constitution of a collective statement and manifestation or demonstration. It can declare itself using the name of a subject—'we, citizens,' 'we, workers,' 'we, women'—but the political subjects thus defined only exist in relation between the pronoun and the noun, in the difference between them, and in the opposition that this difference brings out with regard to every form of identity assumed by a real group defined by a common social belonging." He continues, "A subjectivization is always a disidentification. 'We, citizens' separates itself from the collectivity of citizens defined simply by a national belonging; 'we, women' separates itself from the collectivity of women defined in terms of the distribution of identities and sexual functions. A foreigner should always be able to come among 'citizens,' a masculine individual among 'women,' the son of a wealthy family among 'workers'": Jacques Rancière, "A Politics of Aesthetic Indetermination: An Interview with Frank Ruda and Jan Voelker," in *Everything Is in Everything: Jacques Rancière between Intellectual Emancipation and Aesthetic Education*, edited by Jason E. Smith and Annette Weisser (New York: Art Center Graduate, 2011), p. 25. See also Jacques Rancière, *Disagreement: Politics and Philosophy*, translated by Julie Rose (1995; repr., Minneapolis: University of Minnesota Press, 1999), p. 59; Kristin Ross, *May '68 and Its Afterlives* (Chicago: University of Chicago Press, 2002), 57–58.

101. On Khaled Said, see Marwan M. Kraidy, *The Naked Blogger of Cairo: Creative Insurgency in the Arab World* (Cambridge, MA: Harvard University Press, 2016), pp. 65–68. On hip hop, see Rayya El Zein, "Call and Response, Radical Belonging, and Arabic Hip-Hop in 'the West,'" in *American Studies Encounters the Middle East*, edited by Alex Lubin and Marwan M. Kraidy (Chapel Hill: University of North Carolina Press, 2016), pp. 106–135.

102. Of course, the "we are all" formulation is not necessarily emancipatory, and it can also be used to reassert existing hierarchies. When Parisians in 1968 said, "We are all German Jews," they meant something very different from what their grandchildren suggested in early 2015 with the words "We are all Charlie Hebdo." Whereas the former slogan served to disrupt the hegemonic order, the latter served to perpetuate it. Similarly, "We are all Palestinians" is easily countered by the opposite claim, "We are all Israelis": see the discussion in Slavoj Žižek, "In the Grey Zone," *London Review of Books Online*, February 5, 2015, available at lrb.co.uk. See also Alex Lubin, "'We Are All Israelis': The Politics of Colonial Comparisons," *South Atlantic Quarterly* 107.4 (2008): 671–690.

103. Newton with Blake, *Revolutionary Suicide*, p. 5.

104. "Revolutionary suicide does not mean that I and my comrades have a death wish; it means just the opposite. We have such a strong desire to live with hope and

human dignity that existence without them is impossible. When reactionary forces crush us, we must move against these forces, even at the risk of death. We will have to be driven out with a stick. [. . .] When scholars call our actions suicidal, they should be logically consistent and describe all historical revolutionary movements in the same way. Thus the American colonists, the French of the late eighteenth century, the Russians of 1917, the Jews of Warsaw, the Cubans, the NLF [National Liberation Front of South Vietnam, also known as the Viet Cong], the North Vietnamese—any people who struggle against a brutal and powerful force—are suicidal. [. . .] The concept of revolutionary suicide is not defeatist or fatalistic. On the contrary, it conveys an awareness of reality in combination with the possibility of hope—reality because the revolutionary must always be prepared to face death, and hope because it symbolizes a resolute determination to bring about change": ibid., pp. 3, 5–6. One might compare this notion to Marx's idea that the duty of the last proletarian was to abolish himself—that is, to commit *class suicide.* "When the proletariat wins victory, it by no means becomes the absolute side of society, for it wins victory only by abolishing itself and its opposite. Both the proletariat itself and its conditioning opposite—private property—disappear with the victory of the proletariat": Karl Marx, "Alienation and Social Classes," in *The Marx-Engels Reader*, 2d ed., edited by Robert C. Tucker (1972; repr., New York: W. W. Norton, 1978), p. 134. See also Steven Osuna, "Class Suicide: The Black Radical Tradition, Radical Scholarship, and the Neoliberal Turn," in *Futures of Black Radicalism*, edited by Gaye Theresa Johnson and Alex Lubin (New York: Verso, 2017), pp. 21–38.

105. Assata Shakur, *Assata: An Autobiography* (Westport, CT: Lawrence Hill, 1987), p. 203.

106. Here, I think Shlomo Sand is completely mistaken in his renunciation of Jewish identity. Although Sand repeatedly claims to reject all forms of ethnic or racial essentialism, he nevertheless seems to advance a very essentialist understanding of Jewishness when he fails to see how it can be articulated in non-Zionist terms. See his strange, short book *How I Stopped Being a Jew*, translated by David Fernbach (2004; repr., New York: Verso, 2013).

107. Leila Khaled, *My People Shall Live: The Autobiography of a Revolutionary*, edited by George Hajjar (London: Hodder and Stoughton, 1973), pp. 51, 41.

108. See, e.g., Amal Amireh, "Liberation Struggles: Reflections on the Palestinian Women's Movement," in *Arab Feminisms: Gender and Equality in the Middle East*, edited by Jean Said Makdisi, Noha Bayoumi, and Rafif Rida Sidawi (London: I. B. Tauris, 2014), pp. 195–204; Islah Jad, "Patterns of Relations within the Palestinian Family during the Intifada," in *Palestinian Women of Gaza and the West Bank*, translated by Magida Abu Hassabo, edited by Suha Sabbagh (Bloomington: Indiana University Press, 1998), pp. 53–62; Islah Jad, "The Demobilization of a Palestinian Women's Movement: From Empowered Active Militants to Powerless and Stateless 'Citizens,'" in *Women's Movements in the Global Era: The Power of Local Feminisms*, edited by Amrita Basu (Boulder, CO: Westview, 2010), pp. 343–375; Eileen S. Kuttab, "Palestinian Women in the *Intifada*: Fighting on Two Fronts," *Arab Studies Quarterly* 15.2 (1993): 69–85. See also Sahar Khalifeh, "Comments by Five Women Activists: Siham Abdullah, Amal Kharisha Barghouthi, Rita Giacaman, May Mistakmel Nassar, Amal Wahdan," in *Palestinian Women of Gaza and the West Bank*, translated by Nagla el-Bassiouni, edited by Suha Sabbagh (Bloomington: Indiana University Press, 1998), pp. 192–215; Julie Peteet, "Icons and Militants: Mothering in the Danger Zone," *Signs* 23.1 (1997): 103–129; Nadera Shal-

houb-Kevorkian, "Reexamining Femicide: Breaking the Silence and Crossing 'Scientific' Borders," *Signs* 28.2 (2003): 581–608.

109. Emma Jones, "The Female Director Who Was Issued a Fatwa for Her First Film," BBC, September 3, 2017, available at bbc.com; Nosheen Iqbal, "How Sex, Drugs and Politics Earned *In Between*'s Director a Fatwa," *The Guardian*, September 28, 2017, available at theguardian.com.

110. See, e.g., Catherine Malabou, *The Future of Hegel: Plasticity, Temporality and Dialectic*, translated by Lisabeth During (1996; repr., New York: Routledge, 2005); Catherine Malabou, *What Should We Do with Our Brain?* translated by Sebastian Rand (2004; repr., New York: Fordham University Press, 2008); Malabou, *The New Wounded*.

111. Malabou, *The New Wounded*, p. 17.

112. Catherine Malabou, *Plasticity at the Dusk of Writing: Dialectic, Destruction, Deconstruction*, translated by Carolyn Shread (2005; repr., New York: Columbia University Press, 2010), p. 66.

CHAPTER 3

1. Joseph A. Massad, "The Weapon of Culture: Cinema in the Palestinian Liberation Struggle," in *Dreams of a Nation: On Palestinian Cinema*, edited by Hamid Dabashi (New York: Verso, 2006), p. 32.

2. Ibid., p. 41.

3. Bhaskar Sarkar, *Mourning the Nation: Indian Cinema in the Wake of Partition* (Durham, NC: Duke University Press, 2009); Kyung Hyun Kim, *The Remasculinization of Korean Cinema* (Durham, NC: Duke University Press, 2004); Kim Soyoung, "Gendered Trauma in Korean Cinema: *Peppermint Candy* and *My Own Breathing*," *New Cinemas* 8.3 (2011): 179–187. See also Bhaskar Sarkar, "Beyond Partition: The Political Horizons of Contemporary Indian and Korean War Films," *Journal of the Moving Image* 7 (2008), available at jmionline.org.

4. Rosemary Sayigh points out that the Palestinian Nakba remains largely absent from the field of trauma studies: Rosemary Sayigh, "On the Exclusion of the Palestinian Nakba from the 'Trauma Genre,'" *Journal of Palestine Studies* 43.1 (2013): 51–60.

5. Quoted in Miriam Bratu Hansen, "*Schindler's List* Is Not *Shoah*: The Second Commandment, Popular Modernism, and Public Memory," *Critical Inquiry* 22.2 (1996): 301. Lanzmann is one of the targets of Alain Badiou and Eric Hazan's polemics. Mocking him, they write that if "anyone chances to write or utter the word 'Auschwitz,' Claude Lanzmann considers whether this was in a permissible context, and if he decides that the author transgressed this, he takes up his trumpet and sends *Le Monde* an article that is always published in a good position": Alain Badiou, Eric Hazan, and Ivan Segré, *Reflections on Anti-Semitism*, translated by David Fernbach (2011; repr., New York: Verso, 2013) p. 35.

6. Theodor W. Adorno, *Prisms*, translated by Samuel and Shierry Weber (1967; repr., Cambridge, MA: MIT Press, 1981), p. 34.

7. This is one of the key points of Herbert Marcuse, and he writes that "art as a political force is art only insofar as it preserves the images of liberation; in a society which is in its totality the negation of these images, art can preserve them only by total refusal, that is, by not succumbing to the standards of the unfree reality, either in style, or in form, or in substance. The more totalitarian these standards become, the more reality controls

all language and all communication, the more irrealistic and surrealistic will art tend to be, the more will it be driven from the concrete to the abstract, from harmony to dissonance, from content to form. *Art is thus the refusal of everything that has been made part and parcel of reality*": Herbert Marcuse, *Soviet Marxism: A Critical Analysis* (1958; repr., New York: Vintage, 1961), pp. 117–118 (emphasis mine). See also Herbert Marcuse, *The Aesthetic Dimension: Toward a Critique of Marxist Aesthetics*, translated by Herbert Marcuse and Erica Sherover (1977; repr., Boston: Beacon, 1978).

8. Adorno's moving passage is worth quoting in full. He writes, "Perennial suffering has as much right to expression as a tortured man has to scream; hence it may have been wrong to say that after Auschwitz you could no longer write poems. But it is not wrong to raise the less cultural question whether after Auschwitz you can go on living—especially whether one who escaped by accident, one who by rights should have been killed, may go on living. His mere survival calls for the coldness, the basic principle of bourgeois subjectivity, without which there could have been no Auschwitz; this is the drastic guilt of him who was spared. By way of atonement he will be plagued by dreams such as that he is no longer living at all, that he was sent to the ovens in 1944 and his whole existence since has been imaginary, an emanation of the insane wish of a man killed twenty years earlier": Theodor W. Adorno, *Negative Dialectics*, translated by E. B. Ashton (1966; repr., New York: Continuum, 2005), pp. 362–363.

9. Jacques Rancière, *Figures of History*, translated by Julie Rose (2012; repr., Malden, MA: Polity, 2014), p. 49. See also the discussion in Sarkar, *Mourning the Nation*; Janet Walker, *Trauma Cinema: Documenting Incest and the Holocaust* (Berkeley: University of California Press, 2005).

10. Ghassan Kanafani, *Men in the Sun and Other Palestinian Stories*, translated by Hilary Kilpatrick (1978; repr., Boulder, CO: Lynne Rienner, 1997); Ghassan Kanafani, *Palestine's Children: Returning to Haifa and Other Stories*, translated by Barbara Harlow and Karen E. Riley (Boulder, CO: Lynne Rienner, 2000), pp. 149–196.

11. For more on *The Dupes*, see Nadia Yaqub, "*The Dupes* (Tawfik Saleh): Three Generations Uprooted from Palestine and Betrayed," in *Film in the Middle East and North Africa: Creative Dissidence*, edited by Josef Gugler (Austin: University of Texas Press, 2011), pp. 113–124. See also Nouri Bouzid, "New Realism in Arab Cinema: The Defeat-Conscious Cinema," *Alif* 15 (1995): 242–250.

12. As curator of the Dreams of a Nation traveling Palestinian film festival, Annemarie Jacir managed to locate a print of this film and screen it in Jerusalem in 2003. See her description of the film and the Jerusalem screening in Annemarie Jacir, "Coming Home: Palestinian Cinema," *Electronic Intifada*, February 27, 2007, available at electronicintifada.net. See also Nadia Yaqub, *Palestinian Cinema in the Days of Revolution* (Austin: University of Texas Press, 2018), pp. 157–161; Kamran Rastegar, *Surviving Images: Cinema, War, and Cultural Memory in the Middle East* (New York: Oxford University Press, 2015), pp. 100–102.

13. It is worth pointing out that the Nakba has also occasionally been treated in Israeli cinema, including Lia Tarachansky's investigation into Nakba denial, *On the Side of the Road* (2012). Moreover, in 2013, Zochrot, an Israeli organization dedicated to commemorating the Nakba, organized its first film festival dedicated exclusively to films about 1948, and more installments of this festival have taken place in subsequent years.

14. Janet Walker uses the term "demon memories" in her book on films dealing with the traumas of incest and the Holocaust: Walker, *Trauma Cinema*, p. xvi. For a more

robust discussion of *The Milky Way*, see Nurith Gertz and George Khleifi, *Palestinian Cinema: Landscape, Trauma, and Memory* (2005; repr., Bloomington: Indiana University Press, 2008), pp. 119–130.

15. For further discussion of the relationship between the Nakba and cinema, see Haim Bresheeth, "The Continuity of Trauma and Struggle: Recent Cinematic Representations of the Nakba," in *Nakba: Palestine, 1948, and the Claims of Memory*, edited by Ahmad H. Sa'di and Lila Abu-Lughod (New York: Columbia University Press, 2007), pp. 161–187. Depictions of the Nakba also appear in the Egyptian film *Gate of the Sun* (dir. Yousry Nasrallah, 2003). See the discussion in Terri Ginsberg, *Visualizing the Palestinian Struggle: Toward a Critical Analytic of Palestine Solidarity Films* (New York: Palgrave Macmillan, 2016), pp. 99–108.

16. Benny Morris, *1948 and After: Israel and the Palestinians*, rev. ed. (1990; repr., New York: Oxford University Press, 1994), pp. 42–43 (emphasis in original). For a critical discussion of Morris, see Joel Beinin, "No More Tears: Benny Morris and the Road Back from Liberal Zionism," *Middle East Report* 230 (2004): 38–45.

17. Gish Amit, "Salvage or Plunder? Israel's 'Collection' of Private Palestinian Libraries in West Jerusalem," *Journal of Palestine Studies* 40.4 (2011): 7.

18. As Sherene Seikaly argues, "The Palestinian archive is expansive and flexible. It is not the historian alone who conducts the labor of compiling and reading it": Sherene Seikaly, "Gaza as Archive," in *Gaza as Metaphor*, edited by Helga Tawil-Souri and Dina Matar (London: Hurst, 2016), p. 231.

19. George Lipsitz, *Time Passages: Collective Memory and American Popular Culture* (Minneapolis: University of Minnesota Press, 1990), p. 223.

20. Commenting on *Waltz with Bashir*, Raya Morag notes that the film's hybrid use of animation and newsreel footage "has its origins in the 'old' logic of cinema aesthetics—the alleged disparity between the icon (animation) and the index (live footage)—and moves between the two. This transformation endows the archive with a truth value that animation apparently lacks": Raya Morag, *Waltzing with Bashir: Perpetrator Trauma and Cinema* (New York: I. B. Tauris, 2013), p. 137. See also the critical discussions in Rastegar, *Surviving Images*, pp. 185–204; Raz Yosef, *The Politics of Loss and Trauma in Contemporary Israeli Cinema* (New York: Routledge, 2011), pp. 149–154.

21. The presence of Ben-Gurion's gaze over the humiliating procedures can be likened to the framed portrait of Hosni Mubarak during the subjugation of Egyptian activists to virginity tests in 2011: see Marwan M. Kraidy, *The Naked Blogger of Cairo: Creative Insurgency in the Arab World* (Cambridge, MA: Harvard University Press, 2016), pp. 172–174.

22. Annemarie Jacir, "'I Wanted That Story to Be Told' (Interview)," *Alif* 31 (2011): 246, 249–250, 252.

23. "Post-memory" is a term used by Marianne Hirsch in her discussion of intergenerational memory and the Holocaust: see Marianne Hirsch, "Family Pictures: *Maus*, Mourning, and Post-memory," *Discourse* 15.2 (1992): 3–29. See also the helpful discussion in Walker, *Trauma Cinema*, pp. 160–168; Yosef, *The Politics of Loss and Trauma in Contemporary Israeli Cinema*, pp. 14–18.

24. Eyal Weizman, *The Least of All Possible Evils: Humanitarian Violence from Arendt to Gaza* (New York: Verso, 2011), p. 145.

25. Quoted in Baruch Kimmerling, *Politicide: Ariel Sharon's War against the Palestinians* (New York: Verso, 2003), p. 150.

26. Jacir, "'I Wanted That Story to Be Told,'" p. 250. The hip hop artist Chuck D makes this same point vis-à-vis U.S. white supremacy and the legacy of slavery. "You have people saying, 'But the problems of the past are over, let's not even think about it,'" he says. "But the problems growing out of hundreds of years of slavery remain for millions of black people": quoted in Lipsitz, *Time Passages*, p. 103.

27. See Saleh Abdel Jawad, "Zionist Massacres: The Creation of the Palestinian Refugee Problem in the 1948 War," in *Israel and the Palestinian Refugees*, edited by Eyal Benvenisti, Chaim Gans, and Sari Hanafi (New York: Springer, 2007), pp. 90–92; Benny Morris, *The Birth of the Palestinian Refugee Problem, 1947–1949* (New York: Cambridge University Press, 1987), pp. 222–223; Ilan Pappé, *The Ethnic Cleansing of Palestine* (Oxford: Oneworld, 2006), pp. 195–197.

28. In their negative review of the film, Naira Antoun and Mohanad Yaqubi claim that Jacir privileged the story of an American-born Palestinian over that of a West Bank Palestinian and, in so doing, peddled recycled, romantic clichés about Palestine. As they say in the very title of their essay, "Yaffa [Jaffa] Is Not an Orange." While I think these authors are correct to criticize the use of archetypes in the film (although they grossly overstate their case), their argument about clichés is entirely misguided. The film serves not to reinforce these romantic notions but to explode them. Jacir herself understands her film in these terms. As she put it in an interview, "[Soraya] finds out that those Jaffa oranges are nothing but empty. I wanted to slap her in the face with that, and, in the film, mock the idea that 'You think Palestine is oranges?' My response (via Emad) is 'Fuck your oranges.'" This mocking of the romanticized notions of Palestine often held by Palestinians in the diaspora has become a common theme in Jacir's work. In her third feature, *Wajib* (2017), there is a scene in which one of the protagonists, an older Palestinian man from Nazareth named Shadi (Mohammad Bakri), is speaking on the phone to a PLO member living in Italy. When the PLO member asks what Shadi is currently looking at, he lies and tells him that he is looking at beautiful orange trees when in fact he is looking at a flea market selling cheap Christmas paraphernalia. (Here one may similarly recall the credo of one of the characters from Elias Khoury's novel *Gate of the Sun*: "The homeland isn't oranges. The homeland is us.") But to return to the hostile review of Jacir's film, I believe that Antoun and Yaqubi's criticism amounts to a crude claim of authenticity in which a West Bank Palestinian is considered more legitimate than a Palestinian who is part of the global diaspora. As I have already argued, this form of identity politics is actually very reactionary. There are many Palestinian stories, and it is wrong to suggest that some are more authentic than others. I also think it is very telling that Antoun and Yaqubi praise Jacir's earlier short *like twenty impossibles* (2003). Despite the title, everything in *like twenty impossibles* is entirely possible. *Salt*, by contrast, is less realist in its approach to fiction, and I suspect that this may be a major reason behind their harsh rejection of the film: see Naira Antoun and Mohanad Yaqubi, "Yaffa Is Not an Orange: The Limits of Archetypes," *Jadaliyya*, July 25, 2011, available at jadaliyya. com; Jacir, "'I Wanted That Story to Be Told,'" p. 250. See also Elias Khoury, *Gate of the Sun*, translated by Humphrey Davies (1998; repr., New York: Archipelago, 2005), p. 26.

29. Of course, like Nakba, the term "Intifada" refers to precise historical events. However, just as it would be a mistake to limit the Nakba to 1948, so, too, should we refrain from strictly historicizing the Intifada. In this I am again following in the footsteps of Edward Said, who argued that "[the Intifada] did not just happen on a certain day—in this case December 8, 1987—but [. . .] has been long in the making, and deep in

its intensity and force": Edward W. Said, "The Challenge of Palestine," *Journal of Refugee Studies* 2.1 (1989): 172.

30. The bank robbery scene has a number of cinematic precedents, most famously the scene in *The Battle of Algiers* (dir. Gillo Pontecorvo, 1966) in which three Algerian women disguise themselves as secular French girls to smuggle bombs past the checkpoints. But perhaps an even better comparison can be made with the less well-known *Black Sister's Revenge* (dir. Jamaa Fanaka, 1976), in which a Black woman robs a bank to get the funds to pay her boyfriend's bail. Notably, her decision to commit this crime follows a discussion in which it is argued that the money filling white, capitalist banks is expropriated from the impoverished, Black ghetto. Soraya similarly sees her crime as a form of justice, and she resorts to theft only after all other avenues have reached a deadend. Her crime, then, was simply not letting the Nakba have the final say.

31. In 2004, Mer-Khamis co-directed *Arna's Children* (dir. Danniel Danniel and Juliano Mer-Khamis, 2004), a documentary about his mother and her work with children in the Jenin refugee camp. ·

32. Kanafani, *Palestine's Children*, pp. 149–196.

33. Pappé, *The Ethnic Cleansing of Palestine*, pp. 166–170.

34. Mike Wayne makes this point about Third Cinema. Writing specifically about the tragic ending of *The Last Supper* (dir. Tomás Gutiérrez Alea, 1976), he argues that a conclusion of defeat can also serve to anticipate "the later struggles that *will succeed* but which can only come at the expense of preceding generations sacrificing their lives": Mike Wayne, *Political Film: The Dialectics of Third Cinema* (London: Pluto, 2001), p. 68 (emphasis in original).

35. Suzy Salamy, "Palestine Is Still Waiting," *Warscapes*, September 6, 2012, available at warscapes.com.

36. Jacir, "'I Wanted That Story to Be Told,'" pp. 253–254.

37. Importantly, Jacir insisted that *When I Saw You* play at the Jaffa Theater, even though the rest of the festival took place at the Tel-Aviv Cinematheque. This appears to have been a symbolic decision, and it put the film in a majority Arab neighborhood instead of a cosmopolitan Tel Aviv cineplex.

38. Alex Shams, "Tel Aviv 'Nakba' Film Festival Keeps Alive Memories of 1948 in Israel," Ma'an News Agency, December 1, 2013, available at maannews.net.

39. In using the term "Living Dead," I am, of course, indebted to the metaphor developed in George A. Romero's zombie films beginning with *Night of the Living Dead* (1968). I am also drawing from Giorgio Agamben and Slavoj Žižek's discussion of how the Nazis treated their starving prisoners—in the Nazis' derogatory terms, the *Muselmänner*—as a kind of Living Dead: see Robin Wood, "Apocalypse Now: Notes on the Living Dead," in *The American Nightmare: Essays on the Horror Film*, edited by Robin Wood and Richard Lippe (Toronto, Festival of Festivals, 1979), pp. 91–97; Slavoj Žižek, *The Parallax View* (Cambridge, MA: MIT Press, 2006), p. 112; Slavoj Žižek, *Welcome to the Desert of the Real! Five Essays on September 11 and Related Dates* (New York: Verso, 2002), pp. 138–140; Giorgio Agamben, *Homo Sacer: Sovereign Power and Bare Life*, translated by Daniel Heller-Roazen (1995; repr., Stanford, CA: Stanford University Press, 1998), p. 185.

40. It should, of course, be noted that some forms of oppression usually categorized as traditional or indigenous have been exaggerated or even instigated by the occupation. As Julie Peteet's work shows, one of the results of the exile was an increased prominence

of patrilineal descent in Palestinian family relations: Julie Peteet, "Icons and Militants: Mothering in the Danger Zone," *Signs* 23.1 (1997): 112.

41. David A. McDonald, *My Voice Is My Weapon: Music, Nationalism, and the Poetics of Palestinian Resistance* (Durham, NC: Duke University Press, 2013), pp. 52–56; Annemarie Jacir, "(Re)searching When I Saw You (*Lamma Shoftak*)," *The River Has Two Banks*, n.d., available at theriverhastwobanks.net.

42. In depicting the fedayeen, Jacir drew extensively on footage from the militant cinema period that she discovered while working as the curator of the Dreams of a Nation traveling Palestinian film festival: see Nadia Yaqub, *Palestinian Cinema in the Days of Revolution* (Austin: University of Texas Press, 2018), pp. 208–209.

43. In an interview, Jacir gives an interesting response to the charge of romanticization: "Of course I have romanticized them. Why do people accept being romantic about Che Guevara or *Braveheart* [dir. Mel Gibson, 1995] but not about Palestinians? Isn't there something racist in that? They were romantic, young people . . . and so am I." Nevertheless, she goes on to argue that she meant not only to romanticize the fighters from this period but also to critique them. "In the end, one has to read the film on a deeper level. On the surface the film is a romantic homage to that generation, but more than that, it is also a deep criticism and poses a serious question to them. The inner fighting, the rising egos, the boyish behavior. . . . So finally in the end our hero Tarek sees them as only rhetoric. The film is about Tarek moving beyond the fedayeen. They are left behind": Alia Yunis, "The Pursuit of Heroes in Palestinian Cinema: An Interview with Annemarie Jacir," *Jadaliyya*, October 1, 2013, available at jadaliyya.com. For an intriguing perspective on this piece of Palestinian history, see the remarkable account of the two years the French novelist and playwright Jean Genet spent with Palestinians in Jordan: Jean Genet, *Prisoner of Love*, translated by Barbara Bray (1986; repr., London: Picador, 1990).

44. Todd May makes this very point in his anarchist-Rancièrian discussion of the First and Second Intifadas: Todd May, *Contemporary Political Movements and the Thought of Jacques Rancière: Equality in Action* (Edinburgh: Edinburgh University Press, 2010), pp. 46–71. See also the critique of May's conflation of Rancière with anarchism in Samuel A. Chambers, "The Politics of the Police: From Neoliberalism to Anarchism, and Back to Democracy," in *Reading Rancière: Critical Dissensus*, edited by Paul Bowman and Richard Stamp (New York: Continuum, 2011), pp. 18–43.

45. This same footage appears in Mohanad Yaqubi's *Off Frame: Revolution until Victory* (2015).

46. To be clear, despite his personal political failings Arafat remains important particularly in the way his image has been deployed by the Palestinians themselves. The director Elia Suleiman plays with this aspect of Arafat's image in *Divine Intervention*: in the film, we see his face on a balloon that floats over the Israeli checkpoints. Or, as a student at Birzeit University reportedly put it in the early 1980s, "Arafat is the stone we throw at the world": quoted in Thomas L. Friedman, *From Beirut to Jerusalem*, updated ed. (1989; repr., New York: Anchor, 1995).

47. Jean Genet, Layla Shahid Barrada, and Rudiger Wischenbart, "Jean Genet: Affirmation of Existence through Rebellion," *Journal of Palestine Studies* 16.2 (1987): 77.

48. Gabriel Piterberg, *The Returns of Zionism: Myths, Politics and Scholarship in Israel* (New York: Verso, 2008), pp. 96–101. Piterberg points out a distinction between the Hebrew words *galut* and *golah*. Even though they are derived from the same root,

and even though they are both translated into English as "exile" or "diaspora," there is an important difference. While *galut* means exile as a state of consciousness, *golah* signifies the actual circumstance of living outside the land of Israel. See ibid., pp. 95–96.

49. Quoted in ibid., pp. 97–98.

50. Quoted in Barak Ravid, "Netanyahu on UN Settlement Vote: Israel Will Not Turn the Other Cheek," *Ha'aretz*, December 26, 2016, available at haaretz.com.

51. It is with this understanding of Jewishness in mind that we can make sense of Edward Said's audacious declaration that he was "the last Jewish intellectual": Edward W. Said, *Power, Politics, and Culture: Interviews with Edward W. Said*, edited by Gauri Viswanathan (New York: Pantheon, 2001), p. 458.

52. On *shatat*, see May Telmissany, "Displacement and Memory: Visual Narratives of *al-Shatat* in Michel Khleifi's Films," *Comparative Studies of South Asia, Africa and the Middle East* 30.1 (2010): 69–84.

53. C. L. R. James, "Africans and Afro-Caribbeans: A Personal View (1984)," in *Writing Black Britain, 1948–1998: An Interdisciplinary Anthology*, edited by James Procter (New York: Manchester University Press, 2000), pp. 60–63.

54. Robert Allen Warrior, "A Native American Perspective: Canaanites, Cowboys, and Indians," in *Voices from the Margin: Interpreting the Bible in the Third World*, 3d ed., edited by R. S. Sugirtharajah (1991; repr., Maryknoll, NY: Orbis, 2006), pp. 235–241.

55. Warrior's reversal of the biblical myth has its cinematic counterpart in Avi Mograbi's polemical documentary *Avenge but One of My Two Eyes* (2005). Mograbi's film is remarkable in that it does not merely dismiss the myths of Exodus, Samson, or Masada as illusionary hocus-pocus. Instead, the film reverses them to show how in the present day, the position of the Jews in these myths is now inhabited by the oppressed Palestinians.

56. See Žižek, *The Parallax View*, pp. 3–13.

57. Jacir, "(Re)searching When I Saw You."

58. Quoted in Barbara Harlow, "Narrative in Prison: Stories from the Palestinian *Intifada*," *Modern Fiction Studies* 35.1 (1989): 39.

59. Kanafani, *Men in the Sun and Other Palestinian Stories*.

60. Yaqub, "*The Dupes* (Tawfik Saleh)," pp. 116–117.

61. As Hilary Kilpatrick, the English translator of Kanafani's text, notes, there is a significant difference between the original story and the film version. Whereas the three men go to their death silently in Kanafani's text, the film version has them banging against the vehicle for their very lives. Kilpatrick interprets this shift as an indication of the political changes that had taken place in the decades separating the publication of Kanfani's novella and the production of the film. The question of whether or not the Palestinians knocked has frequently made its way into Palestinian political discourse. In a speech in 1998, Yasir Arafat declared, "We are not mere refugees asking for handouts; we are a deeply rooted people, part of an ancient nation, banging on the walls of the dark tank." Similarly, the Lebanese novelist Elias Khoury writes that today "the Palestinians are knocking, not just with their fists, but with their lives and bullet-riddled bodies and the uprooted trees of their lands. Who would dare to claim that 'the Palestinians are not 'knocking'? Wouldn't it be more accurate to ask, 'Why do you not hear?' Or rather, 'Why do you pretend to be deaf when you hear the knocking?'": Hilary Kilpatrick, "Introduction," in *Men in the Sun and Other Palestinian Stories*, by Ghassan Kanafani, translated by Hilary Kilpatrick (1978; repr., Boulder, CO: Lynne Rienner, 1997), pp. 3–4; Arafat,

quoted in Amal Amireh, "Between Complicity and Subversion: Body Politics in Palestinian National Narrative," *South Atlantic Quarterly* 102.4 (2003): 754; Elias Khoury,
"Remembering Ghassan Kanafani, or How a Nation Was Born of Story Telling," *Journal
of Palestine Studies* 42.3 (2013): 90.

62. "Plasticity," as Malabou argues, "refers precisely to *the indestructible*, to something that can be damaged or destroyed, but which never disappears entirely": Catherine Malabou, *Ontology of the Accident: An Essay on Destructive Plasticity*, translated
by Carolyn Shread (2009; repr., Malden, MA: Polity, 2012), p. 48 (emphasis mine).

CHAPTER 4

1. Ernst Bloch, *The Principle of Hope*, vol. 3, translated by Neville Plaice, Stephen
Plaice, and Paul Knight (1959; repr., Cambridge, MA: MIT Press, 1986), p. 1374.

2. Rancière writes, "Disagreement is not the conflict between one who says white
and another who says black. It is the conflict between one who says white and another
who also says white but does not understand the same thing by it": Jacques Rancière,
Disagreement: Politics and Philosophy, translated by Julie Rose (1995; repr., Minneapolis:
University of Minnesota Press, 1999), p. x.

3. Sari Hanafi, "Spacio-cide: Colonial Politics, Invisibility, and Rezoning in Palestinian Territory," *Contemporary Arab Affairs* 2.1 (2009): 106–121.

4. Notably, these two companies rely on Israeli infrastructure to function: see Helga
Tawil-Souri, "Occupation Apps," *Jacobin* 17 (2015), available at jacobinmag.com.

5. Eyal Weizman, *Hollow Land: Israel's Architecture of Occupation* (2007; repr., New
York: Verso, 2012), p. 15. Haim Bresheeth similarly argues that "there are two virtual
countries within the same space, two parallel universes disregarding and disparag-
ing each other, and yet, totally bound to each other": Haim Bresheeth, "A Symphony
of Absence: Borders and Liminality in Elia Suleiman's 'Chronicle of a Disappearance,'"
Framework 43.2 (2002): 71. For an earlier discussion of Zionism and space, see Baruch
Kimmerling, *Zionism and Territory: The Socio-territorial Dimensions of Zionist Politics*
(Berkeley: University of California Press, 1983).

6. Gabriel Piterberg, *The Returns of Zionism: Myths, Politics and Scholarship in Israel*
(New York: Verso, 2008), p. 95. See also Gabriel Piterberg, "Erasures," *New Left Review*
10 (2001): 31–46.

7. Theodor Herzl, *The Jewish State* (1896; repr., New York: American Zionist Emergency Council, 1946), p. 145. In his notorious book *The Arab Mind*, Raphael Patai even
claimed that Arabic as a language was not fit for modern civilization. "Before Arabic can
become a medium adequate for the requirements of modern life [. . . it must] transform
its perfect and imperfect verb forms into semantic equivalents of the past and future
tenses respectively of Standard Average European": Raphael Patai, *The Arab Mind*, rev.
ed. (1973; repr., New York: Charles Scribner's Sons, 1983), p. 72.

8. As Elia Zureik puts it, "The Zionist narrative depicts time in the Jewish experience as dynamic and eternal; in the Palestinian one as empty, static, and discontinu-
ous": Elia Zureik, "Colonialism, Surveillance, and Population Control: Israel/Palestine,"
in *Surveillance and Control in Israel/Palestine: Population, Territory, and Power*, edited
by Elia Zureik, David Lyon, and Yasmeen Abu-Laban (New York: Routledge, 2011), p.
18. Yonatan Mendel has shown how this temporal dynamic operates with respect to
the Zionist treatment of Judaism and Islam. "The idea that Jewish religious concepts

evolve and change with time, and have been interpreted and re-interpreted, is taken to be natural and obvious within Israeli-Jewish discourse," Mendel writes. "However, the Islamic texts, and the related concepts, are perceived as frozen in time, kept unchanged through the generations, incapable of any development whatsoever": Yonatan Mendel, "The Politics of Non-translation: On Israeli Translations of *Intifada*, *Shahid*, *Hudna* and Islamic Movements," *Cambridge Literary Review* 1.3 (2010): 202.

9. Quoted in Nur Masalha, *Expulsion of the Palestinians: The Concept of "Transfer" in Zionist Political Thought, 1882-1948* (Washington DC: Institute for Palestine Studies, 1992), p. 17.

10. Talal Asad, "Anthropological Texts and Ideological Problems: An Analysis of Cohen on Arab Villages in Israel," *Economy and Society* 4.3 (1975): 251–282. See also Dan Rabinowitz, "Oriental Othering and National Identity: A Review of Early Israeli Anthropological Studies of Palestinians," *Global Studies in Culture and Power* 9 (2002): 305–324.

11. Johannes Fabian, *Time and the Other: How Anthropology Makes Its Object* (New York: Columbia University Press, 1983), pp. 17–18, 30. See also Edward W. Said, *Orientalism* (1978; repr., New York: Vintage, 2003), pp. 233–234.

12. Julie Peteet, "Stealing Time," *Middle East Research and Information Project* 248 (2008): 14–15. See also Zureik, "Colonialism, Surveillance, and Population Control," pp. 17–18.

13. Quoted in Nur Masalha, *The Palestine Nakba: Decolonising History, Narrating the Subaltern, Reclaiming Memory* (New York: Zed, 2012), p. 43. Nur Masalha similarly argues that "for the millions of Palestinian refugees the past is still present and the sense of displacement remains heightened. The processes of ethnic cleansing and transfer in Palestine continue": ibid., p. 251.

14. Elias Sanbar, "Out of Place, Out of Time," translated by Ruth Morris, *Mediterranean Historical Review* 16.1 (2001): 90.

15. See the concept of "trauma time" developed in Jenny Edkins, *Trauma and the Memory of Politics* (New York: Cambridge University Press, 2003).

16. Frank B. Wilderson III, *Red, White, and Black: Cinema and the Structure of U.S. Antagonisms* (Durham, NC: Duke University Press, 2010), p. 315. Wilderson, of course, would bristle at the comparison I am making here. See my critique of his work in Chapter 6 in this volume.

17. Ella Shohat, *Israeli Cinema: East/West and the Politics of Representation* (Austin: University of Texas Press, 1989), pp. 57–114.

18. Nurith Gertz and George Khleifi, *Palestinian Cinema: Landscape, Trauma, and Memory* (2005; repr., Bloomington: Indiana University Press, 2008), pp. 134–170.

19. Ella Shohat also recognizes this temporal contradiction in the film. "Although subordination to martial law was abolished for Israeli-Palestinians in 1966—only to be installed a year later in the newly occupied territories—*Wedding in Galilee* tells the story of a Palestinian village under military control in the Galilee, within Israel, in the present. [. . .] This confounding implies that although Palestinians within pre-1967 Israel can legally take part in the Israeli 'democratic processes,' they nevertheless experience a national oppression that is inseparable from that of the Palestinians on the West Bank and in Gaza": Ella Shohat, "*Wedding in Galilee*," *Middle East Report* 154 (1988): 45–46. See also Ella Shohat and Robert Stam, *Unthinking Eurocentrism: Multiculturalism and the Media*, new ed. (1994; repr., New York: Routledge, 2014), p. 278.

20. As Arraf explains in an interview, "When I wrote *Villa Touma*, I decided in the first act that I wanted to cheat you as a viewer. I wanted you to believe that you are in a period film set in the 1960s. I didn't want you to discover that it's set in 2000 [. . .] until later": quoted in Kaleem Aftab, "Suha Arraf's *Villa Touma* Offers a World View That's Uniquely Palestinian Yet Very European," *The National*, September 2, 2014, available at thenational.ae.

21. Kamran Rastegar, *Surviving Images: Cinema, War, and Cultural Memory in the Middle East* (New York: Oxford University Press, 2015), pp. 93–98.

22. Ibid., pp. 110–111.

23. Ernst Bloch, *The Principle of Hope*, vol. 1, translated by Neville Plaice, Stephen Plaice, and Paul Knight (1959; repr., Cambridge, MA: MIT Press, 1986), p. 145.

24. In addition to the other literature cited in this chapter, notable attempts to ground utopia in reality include Terry Eagleton, "Utopia and Its Opposites," in *Necessary and Unnecessary Utopias*, edited by Leo Panitch and Colin Leys (New York: Monthly Review, 1999), pp. 31–40; Tom Moylan, *Demand the Impossible: Science Fiction and the Utopian Imagination*, edited by Raffaella Baccolini (1986; repr., Bern, Germany: Peter Lang, 2014).

25. James chose this phrase as the title of one of the edited collections of his work: C. L. R. James, *The Future in the Present: Selected Writings* (Westport, CT: Lawrence Hill, 1977). See also C. L. R. James, *Spheres of Existence: Selected Writings* (Westport, CT: Lawrence Hill, 1980), p. 79.

26. C. L. R. James and Grace C. Lee with Cornelius Castoriadis, *Facing Reality: The New Society: Where to Look for It and How to Bring It Closer* (1958; repr., Chicago: Charles H. Kerr, 2006), p. 118.

27. Ibid., p. 110.

28. Stefano Harney and Fred Moten, *The Undercommons: Fugitive Planning and Black Study* (New York: Minor Compositions, 2013), p. 131 (emphasis mine).

29. Cedric J. Robinson, *An Anthropology of Marxism* (Burlington, VT: Ashgate, 2001), pp. 138–139; Cedric J. Robinson, *Black Movements in America* (New York: Routledge, 1997), p. 153.

30. On Robinson and the future, see my "Birth of a (Zionist) Nation: Black Radicalism and the Future of Palestine," in *Futures of Black Radicalism*, edited by Gaye Theresa Johnson and Alex Lubin (New York: Verso, 2017), pp. 120–132. Other thinkers working in and around the Black Radical Tradition have identified this temporal aspect of Black struggle to include Achille Mbembe, who uses the term "Black Time." Damien Sojoyner similarly calls it "Black radical time": see Achille Mbembe, *Critique of Black Reason*, translated by Laurent Dubois (2013; repr., Durham, NC: Duke University Press, 2017), pp. 120–125; Damien M. Sojoyner, "Dissonance in Time: (Un)Making and (Re)Mapping of Blackness," in *Futures of Black Radicalism*, edited by Gaye Theresa Johnson and Alex Lubin (New York: Verso, 2017), p. 60.

31. One could also add Herbert Marcuse to this list, and he similarly argued that dialectical materialism contained an idealistic core: see Herbert Marcuse, *Counterrevolution and Revolt* (Boston: Beacon, 1972), p. 70. See also Avery F. Gordon, *Keeping Good Time: Reflections on Knowledge, Power, and People* (Boulder, CO: Paradigm, 2004), pp. 113–132. For further discussion of Bloch and similar thinkers in their historical context, see Michael Löwy, *Redemption and Utopia: Jewish Libertarian Thought in Central Europe: A Study in Elective Affinity*, translated by Hope Heaney (1988; repr., Stanford,

CA: Stanford University Press, 1992). Also of relevance here is the discussion of James and Bloch in José Esteban Muñoz, *Cruising Utopia: The Then and There of Queer Futurity* (New York: New York University Press, 2009).

32. In Ernst Bloch, *The Utopian Function of Art and Literature: Selected Essays*, translated by Jack Zipes and Frank Mecklenburg (1988; repr., Cambridge, MA: MIT Press, 1996), p. 1.

33. Bloch, *The Principle of Hope*, p. 1:56 (emphasis in original). For Bloch, "Psychoanalysis [. . .] judges all dreams only as roads to what has been repressed, and only knows reality as that of bourgeois society and its existing world": ibid., p. 1:87.

34. Ibid., p. 1:297 (emphasis in original). See also Ernst Bloch, *A Philosophy of the Future*, translated by John Cumming (1963; repr., New York: Herder and Herder, 1970); Ernst Bloch, "Man as Possibility," *Cross Currents* 18.3 (1968): 273–283.

35. Bloch, *The Principle of Hope*, p. 1:223.

36. Walter Benjamin, *Illuminations*, edited by Hannah Arendt, translated by Harry Zohn (1968; repr., New York: Schocken, 1969), p. 264.

37. Quoted in Mohammad Malas, *The Dream: A Diary of the Film*, translated by Samirah Alkassim (1991; repr., Cairo: American University of Cairo Press, 2016), p. 30. Upon learning that Malas's film would be about dreams, a Palestinian writer expressed disappointment, saying, "I thought the film would be an attempt to study the effect of the Revolution on the sociological aspects of the Palestinian camps, with respect to changing values and ideologies. Haven't you read Frantz Fanon's book about society and the sociology of revolution?": quoted in ibid., p. 20.

38. Hamid Dabashi, "Introduction," in *Dreams of a Nation: On Palestinian Cinema*, edited by Hamid Dabashi (New York: Verso, 2006), p. 18.

39. Helga Tawil-Souri argues that "with the rise of these video games, the few spaces of nonviolence available to Palestinian youth are all but disappearing": Helga Tawil-Souri, "The Political Battlefield of Pro-Arab Video Games on Palestinian Screens," *Comparative Studies of South Asia, Africa and the Middle East* 27.3 (2007): 550. See also Ghassan Hage's essay "The Unoccupied," in Ghassan Hage, *Alter-Politics: Critical Anthropology and the Radical Imagination* (Melbourne: Melbourne University Press, 2015), pp. 165–172.

40. Hage, *Alter-Politic*, p. 167.

41. Joan Mellen, "Film and Style: The Fictional Documentary," *Antioch Review* 32.3 (1972): 421. See also Michael Renov, *The Subject of Documentary* (Minneapolis: University of Minnesota Press, 2004), pp. 21–42.

42. Of course, one can always find exceptions, and being raised as a settler does not automatically foreclose participation in the Palestinian struggle. Here I am thinking specifically of Lia Tarachansky, the director of a film about Israeli Nakba denial, *On the Side of the Road* (2012). Although Tarachansky spent her childhood in a settlement, she has since become a notable journalist and filmmaker who espouses anti-Zionist views.

43. Another example of this cognitive dissonance presents itself in the figure of Ariel Sharon. Baruch Kimmerling points out how during his tenure as prime minister, most of Sharon's constituency knew very little about his past actions—particularly, his involvement with the Sabra and Shatila massacres of 1982. However, Kimmerling argued that "even those who happen to know about his past actions do not regard them as sins. On the contrary, Sharon is considered a hero": Baruch Kimmerling, *Politicide: Ariel Sharon's War against the Palestinians* (New York: Verso, 2003), pp. 152–153.

44. For Ilan Pappé, this is the problem with purely positivist historical research. "From a purely factual standpoint," he writes, "the neo-Zionist version of 1948 did not differ significantly from that of the post-Zionists or the new historians. The difference lay in the response or interpretation of the facts. What the new historians saw as human and civil rights abuses or even as atrocities and war crimes are treated in the new research as normal and sometimes even commendable actions by the Israeli military. What the post-Zionists interpreted as shameful chapters in Israeli history are, in the new research, justified": Ilan Pappé, *The Idea of Israel: A History of Power and Knowledge* (New York: Verso, 2014), p. 277. While Benny Morris's work in the Hebrew archives validated many long-standing Palestinian grievances, he himself retreated into reactionary politics, claiming that the ethnic cleansing was in fact justified and that such actions may even need to be repeated in the future. Referring to the minority of Palestinians who hold Israeli citizenship as "a time bomb" and "a potential fifth column," Morris made a grim proposal: "If Israel again finds itself in a situation of existential threat, as in 1948, it may be forced to act as it did then. [. . .] If the threat to Israel is existential, *expulsion will be justified*": Benny Morris, "On Ethnic Cleansing: Introduction and Interview by Ari Shavit," *New Left Review* 26 (2004): 45 (emphasis mine). Also published as Ari Shavit, "Survival of the Fittest? An Interview with Benny Morris," *CounterPunch*, January 16, 2004, available at counterpunch.org. See also Ari Shavit, *My Promised Land: The Triumph and Tragedy of Israel* (New York: Spiegel and Grau, 2013). On settler activists, see Ian S. Lustick, "Making Sense of the Nakba," *Journal of Palestine Studies* 44.2 (2015): 7–27. On social media, see Adi Kuntsman and Rebecca L. Stein, *Digital Militarism: Israel's Occupation in the Social Media Age* (Stanford, CA: Stanford University Press, 2015).

45. Herbert Marcuse, *One-Dimensional Man: Studies in the Ideology of Advanced Industrial Society* (1964; repr., New York: Routledge, 2002), p. 16.

46. Darwazah's first film, *Take Me Home* (2008), is a look at her own dispersed Palestinian family. She was also one of four contributors to the omnibus film *Mawsem Hisad* (dir. Nassim Amaouche, Mais Darwazah, Erige Sehiri, and Sameh Zoabi, 2012).

47. See Malas, *The Dream*; Nadia Yaqub, "Refracted Filmmaking in Muhammad Malas's *The Dream* and Kamal Aljafari's *The Roof*," *Middle East Journal of Culture and Communication* 7 (2014): 152–168. I have Hatim el-Hibri to thank for initially drawing my attention to this film.

48. "The dream is thought of mostly as night dream. However, we dream not only at night; the day is also interwoven with dreams": Bloch, "Man as Possibility," p. 273.

49. This ghostly nature of the future is noted by Avery Gordon, who argues that "from a certain vantage point the ghost also simultaneously represents a future possibility, a hope": Avery F. Gordon, *Ghostly Matters: Haunting and the Sociological Imagination* (1997; repr., Minneapolis: University of Minnesota Press, 2008), p. 64.

50. Christina Sharpe, *In the Wake: On Blackness and Being* (Durham, NC: Duke University Press, 2016).

51. See Linda Paganelli, "Painting in a Refugee Camp, Dreaming of the Sea," *Electronic Intifada*, June 13, 2016, available at electronicintifada.net; Daniel Monterescu, "The Palestinian Trail of Fish: Artist's Graffiti Dives into Heart of Refugee Struggle," *Ha'aretz*, November 30, 2017, available at haaretz.com.

52. This pastime by Acre's youth is also treated in the documentary *It's Better to Jump* (dir. Gina Angelone, Mouna Stewart, and Patrick Alexander Stewart, 2013).

53. Another documentary that shows the fragility of the Apartheid Wall is Raed

Andoni's *Fix ME*. While the film is rather realist, there is one strangely surreal scene with computer-generated effects in which an entire of the panel of the wall is made to suddenly collapse and fall over.

54. In the post-screening discussion that followed the showing of her film at the London Palestine Film Festival in 2014, Darwazah recounted her efforts to make sure that her shots of the Mediterranean did not include any images of this Israeli flag. As she argued, she did not want to give Israel that victory.

55. Fred Hampton, "The People Have to Have the Power," in *Let Nobody Turn Us Around: Voices of Resistance, Reform, and Renewal: An African American Anthology*, edited by Manning Marable and Leith Mullings (Lanham, MD: Rowman and Littlefield, 2000), p. 481.

CHAPTER 5

1. Edward W. Said, "Preface," in *Dreams of a Nation: On Palestinian Cinema*, edited by Hamid Dabashi (New York: Verso, 2006), p. 2.

2. Joseph Schechla, "The Invisible People Come to Light: Israel's 'Internally Displaced' and the 'Unrecognized Villages.'" *Journal of Palestine Studies* 31.1 (2001): 23–24. One such village—Ayn Hawd—is featured in Rachel Leah Jones's documentary *500 Dunam on the Moon* (2002).

3. Investigating the use of media by Palestinians in the refugee camps of Lebanon, Laleh Khalili argues that "virtual images of Palestinian places and landscapes have been crucial in *reterritorializing* Palestinians and reinforcing their ties to concrete locales and spaces": Laleh Khalili, "Virtual Nation: Palestinian Cyberculture in Lebanese Camps," in *Palestine, Israel, and the Politics of Popular Culture*, edited by Rebecca L. Stein and Ted Swedenburg (Durham, NC: Duke University Press, 2005), p. 135 (emphasis in original).

4. Paul Virilio, *Popular Defense and Ecological Struggles*, translated by Mark Polizzotti (1978; repr., New York: Semiotext(e), 1990), p. 57.

5. "The MESA Debate: The Scholars, the Media, and the Middle East," *Journal of Palestine Studies* 16.2 (1987): 93.

6. John Collins makes this point with regard to Palestinian hypervisibility. "In the case of the Palestinians," he writes, "to be in the media [. . .] has often meant being subject to a global regime of compulsory discursive hyper-visibility that makes Palestinians seem and (to a lesser extent) heard—but only in forms that are constructed and tightly controlled by others. Within such a regime, one's identity is routinely transmogrified into a question, a source of fear, a call to arms, a nagging 'problem' that will not go away. It means constantly having to defend oneself against broad-brush and often racist charges of 'terrorism' even as one is defending oneself against the theft of one's land": John Collins, *Global Palestine* (New York: Columbia University Press, 2011), p. 6.

7. George Orwell, *Nineteen Eighty-Four* (1949; repr., New York: Plum, 2003); Michel Foucault, *Discipline and Punish: The Birth of the Prison*, translated by Alan Sheridan (1975; repr., New York: Vintage, 1977), pp. 200–209.

8. Franz Kafka, *The Castle*, translated by Anthea Bell (1926; repr., New York: Oxford University Press, 2009); Loren Thompson, "Air Force's Secret 'Gorgon Stare' Program Leaves Terrorists Nowhere to Hide," *Forbes*, April 10, 2015, available at forbes.com.

9. Michel Foucault, *The History of Sexuality, Volume 1: An Introduction*, translated by Robert Hurley (1976; repr., New York: Vintage, 1990), pp. 140–145.

10. Andrea Smith argues that "the manner in which Foucauldian analyses of the state tend to temporarily situate bio-power during the era of the modern state disappears the biopolitics of settler colonialism and transatlantic slavery." In her words, "Surveillance studies's focus on the modern state [. . .] hides an analysis of the settler colonialist and white supremacist logics of surveillance that precede the ascendancy of the modern state": Andrea Smith, "Not-Seeing: State Surveillance, Settler Colonialism, and Gender Violence," in *Feminist Surveillance Studies*, edited by Rachel E. Dubrofsky and Shoshana Amielle Magnet (Durham, NC: Duke University Press, 2015), p. 23.

11. Simone Browne, *Dark Matters: On the Surveillance of Blackness* (Durham, NC: Duke University Press, 2015), pp. 31–33.

12. See, e.g., Chandak Sengoopta, *Imprint of the Raj: How Fingerprinting Was Born in Colonial India* (London: Macmillan, 2003); Armand Mattelart, *The Globalization of Surveillance: The Origin of the Securitarian Order*, translated by Susan Gruenheck Taponier and James A. Cohen (Malden, MA: Polity, 2010).

13. Helga Tawil-Souri, "Colored Identity: The Politics and Materiality of ID Cards in Palestine/Israel," *Social Text* 29.2 (2011): 71.

14. To quote Julie Peteet, "A prominent mode of embedding the power of the dominant group is to beat, daily and publicly, Palestinian male bodies": Julie Peteet, "Male Gender and the Rituals of Resistance in the Palestinian *Intifada*: A Cultural Politics of Violence," *American Ethnologist* 21.1 (1994): 33.

15. Jesse Rosenfeld, "The Palestinian Authority Is Using a New Cybercrimes Law to Crack Down on Dissent," *Intercept* (December 18, 2017), available at theintercept .com. For more background on the Israeli outsourcing of surveillance to the PA, see Nigel Parsons, "The Palestinian Authority Security Apparatus: Biopolitics, Surveillance, and Resistance in the Occupied Palestinian Territories," in *Surveillance and Control in Israel/ Palestine: Population, Territory, and Power*, edited by Elia Zureik, David Lyon, and Yasmeen Abu-Laban (New York: Routledge, 2011), pp. 355–370.

16. Haggai Matar, "Israeli Army Installs New, Remote-Controlled Weapon atop Separation Wall," *+972 Magazine*, April 19, 2014, available at 972mag.com.

17. Noah Shachtman, "Robo-Snipers, 'Auto Kill Zones' to Protect Israeli Borders," *Wired*, June 4, 2007, available at wired.com.

18. Quoted in Matar, "Israeli Army Installs New, Remote-Controlled Weapon atop Separation Wall."

19. Eyal Weizman, *Hollow Land: Israel's Architecture of Occupation* (New York: Verso, 2007), p. 141.

20. Paul Virilio and Sylvère Lotringer, *Pure War: Twenty-Five Years Later*, translated by Mark Polizzotti (1983; repr., New York: Semiotext(e), 2008), p. 76.

21. "Surveillance often shows two faces," as David Lyon argues. In his words, "The electronic eye may blink benignly": David Lyon, *The Electronic Eye: The Rise of Surveillance Society* (Minneapolis: University of Minnesota Press, 1994), p. ix.

22. As Douglas Kellner argues, "It is [. . .] a genetic fallacy simply to denounce something because of its origins, especially in the case of technology that can be used to criticise the interests of its creators and can be reconfigured to meet individual and oppositional group needs and purposes": Douglas Kellner, "Globalisation from Below? Toward a Radical Democratic Technopolitics," *Angelaki* 4.2 (1999): 106.

23. Khaled Abu Toameh and Yaakov Lappin, "2 Palestinians Killed by Israeli Secu-

rity Forces in Violent Clash near Ramallah," *Jerusalem Post*, May 15, 2014, available at jpost.com.

24. Eyal Weizman, Nick Axel, Steffen Kraemer, Lawrence Abu Hamdan, and Jacob Burns, "The Nakba Day Denial," *Mondoweiss*, March 10, 2015, available at mondoweiss. net; Ali Abunimah, "Video Analysis Pinpoints Israeli Killer of Palestinian Teen," *Electronic Intifada*, November 21, 2014, available at electronicintifada.net. The full report is available at the Forensic Architecture website, beitunia.forensic-architecture.org.

25. Patrick Strickland, "WhatsApp Messages Show Israeli Soldiers Knew They Were about to Kill a Child," *Electronic Intifada*, June 21, 2015, available at electronicintifada.net.

26. On Machsom Watch, see Dorit Naaman, "The Silenced Outcry: A Feminist Perspective from the Israeli Checkpoints in Palestine," *NWSA Journal* 18.3 (2006): 168–180; Maia Carter Hallward, "Negotiating Boundaries, Narrating Checkpoints: The Case of Machsom Watch," *Critique: Critical Middle Eastern Studies* 17.1 (2008): 21–40.

27. Dick Hebdige, *Hiding in the Light: On Images and Things* (New York: Routledge, 1988), pp. 18, 35. See also Dick Hebdige, "Posing . . . Threats, Striking . . . Poses: Youth, Surveillance, and Display," *SubStance* 11–12.37–38 (1982): 68–88.

28. Genet, *Prisoner of Love*, p. 85.

29. As Torin Monahan notes, "Resistance to surveillance can also function within and therefore unintentionally reinforce [. . .] security cultures if it does not also challenge the rules that govern possibilities for resistance": Torin Monahan, *Surveillance in the Time of Insecurity* (New Brunswick, NJ: Rutgers University Press, 2010), p. 128. Alastair Bonnett makes a similar observation with regard to the Situationists, and he writes that the practice of "*détournement* has been incorporated as a standard practice within the advertising industry": Alastair Bonnett, "Situationist Strategies and Mutant Technologies," *Angelaki* 4.2 (1999): 27.

30. Edward W. Said, *The Politics of Dispossession: The Struggle for Palestinian Self-Determination, 1969–1994* (1994; repr., New York: Vintage, 1995), p. 351.

31. Douglas Kellner, Alain Badiou, and Jacques Rancière have all made this same argument vis-à-vis the attacks of September 11, 2001. For them, the terrorists believed they were fighting the U.S. empire, but they were really doing nothing more than replicating it. In Kellner's words, "Terrorists have used spectacles of terror to promote their agenda in a media-saturated era and [. . .] two Bush administrations have also deployed terror spectacle to promote their geo-political ends." Badiou similarly claims that "both Bin Laden (or whoever financed the crime), on one side, and the foundations of the American superpower, on the other, belong to the same world": see Douglas Kellner, "September 11: Spectacles of Terror and Media Manipulation: A Critique of Jihadist and Bush Media Politics," *Logos* 2.1 (2003): 86; Alain Badiou, *Polemics*, translated by Steve Corcoran (2006; repr., New York: Verso, 2011), p. 31; Jacques Rancière, *Dissensus: On Politics and Aesthetics*, edited and translated by Steven Corcoran (New York: Continuum, 2010), pp. 97–104.

32. Lila Abu-Lughod warns against this uncritical glorification. As she writes, "There is [. . .] a tendency to romanticize resistance, to read all forms of resistance as signs of the ineffectiveness of systems of power and of the resilience and creativity of the human spirit in its refusal to be dominated. By reading resistance in this way, we collapse distinctions between forms of resistance and foreclose certain questions about the workings of power": Lila Abu-Lughod, "The Romance of Resistance: Tracing Transformations of Power through Bedouin Women," *American Ethnologist* 17.1 (1990): 41–42.

33. For Herbert Marcuse, repressive desublimation referred to the process in which an empirical action loses its sublime dimension—for instance, the moment when the sexual revolution became simply sex. The act itself remains exactly the same, but it no longer functions in a radical way. Partha Chatterjee's writings on anticolonialism emphasize the degree to which such movements are shaped by the colonialist regimes they are fighting: see Herbert Marcuse, *One-Dimensional Man: Studies in the Ideology of Advanced Industrial Society* (1964; repr., New York: Routledge, 2002); Partha Chatterjee, *Nationalist Thought and the Colonial World: A Derivative Discourse* (1986; repr., London: Zed, 1993).

34. While Gramsci did not invent the term, he greatly developed it, and most discussions of hegemony today are directly indebted to his formulation. In *Prison Notebooks*, Gramsci provided a deceptively straightforward definition of hegemony as "the 'spontaneous' consent given by the great masses of the population to the general direction imposed on social life by the dominant fundamental group": Antonio Gramsci, *Selections from the Prison Notebooks*, edited and translated by Quintin Hoare and Geoffrey Nowell Smith (1971; repr., New York: International, 2008), p. 12. Paul Bowman suggests that Rancière's notion of the police be viewed as a theory of hegemony: Paul Bowman, "Rancière and the Disciplines: An Introduction to Rancière before Film Studies," in *Rancière and Film*, edited by Paul Bowman (Edinburgh: Edinburgh University Press, 2013), p. 9.

35. Elia Zureik, "Colonialism, Surveillance, and Population Control: Israel/Palestine," in *Surveillance and Control in Israel/Palestine: Population, Territory, and Power*, edited by Elia Zureik, David Lyon, and Yasmeen Abu-Laban (New York: Routledge, 2011), p. 21.

36. To quote George Lipsitz, "This is the way hegemony works. Those who rule choose not only *their* leaders but *our* leaders. They not only articulate their own politics but circumscribe the range of allowable responses to those politics. They make us think that we need to be like them: that is *they* have heroic leaders, *we* need heroic leaders, that if *they* succeed by promoting hate, hurt, and fear, *we* need to promote counterhate, counterhurt, and counterfear": George Lipsitz, "Breaking the Chains and Steering the Ship: How Activism Can Help Change Teaching and Scholarship," in *Engaging Contradictions: Theory, Politics, and Methods of Activist Scholarship*, edited by Charles R. Hale (Berkeley: University of California Press, 2008), p. 98 (emphasis in original).

37. See Shira Robinson, *Citizen Strangers: Palestinians and the Birth of Israel's Liberal Settler State* (Stanford, CA: Stanford University Press, 2013), pp. 113–152. See also Hillel Cohen, *Good Arabs: The Israeli Security Agencies and the Israeli Arabs, 1948–1967*, translated by Haim Watzman (2009; repr., Berkeley: University of California Press, 2010).

38. Eyal Weizman, *The Least of All Possible Evils: Humanitarian Violence from Arendt to Gaza* (New York: Verso, 2011), pp. 68, 76, 78.

39. Foucault, *Discipline and Punish*; Foucault, *The History of Sexuality*.

40. Foucault, *The History of Sexuality*, p. 93.

41. Ibid., p. 94.

42. Ibid., p. 93.

43. Hebdige, *Hiding in the Light*, p. 196.

44. Foucault, *A History of Sexuality*, p. 95.

45. Abu-Lughod , "The Romance of Resistance," p. 42.

46. Edward W. Said, *The World, the Text, and the Critic* (Cambridge, MA: Harvard University Press, 1983), p. 246.

47. Edward W. Said, *Reflections on Exile and Other Essays* (Cambridge, MA: Harvard University Press, 2000), p. 242.

48. Said, *The World, the Text, and the Critic*, p. 245.

49. Said, *Reflections on Exile and Other Essays*, p. 241; Said, *The World, the Text, and the Critic*, p. 246. One of the only moments I have found in which Said directly criticizes Foucauldian theory in relation to Middle Eastern politics occurred in an interview in 1989. Said argued that "Foucault ultimately becomes the scribe of domination. In other words, the imagination of Arab people is really an account of the victories of the power dominating them. The site of resistance is eliminated": quoted in Jennifer Wicke and Michael Sprinker, "Interview with Edward Said," in *Edward Said: A Critical Reader*, edited by Michael Sprinker (Cambridge, MA: Blackwell, 1992), p. 240.

50. One of the more formidable critiques of Foucault has come from the pens of Lacanian theorists such as Joan Copjec, Todd McGowan, and Slavoj Žižek. According to them, Foucault's immanent view of power effectively eradicates the possibility of radical change or the introduction of the New, and they argue that Foucault's universe is a closed and limited one and that his abandonment of Hegelian philosophy and Freudian psychoanalysis consequently resulted in a loss of the possibility of negation. In Lacanian terms, Foucault operated at the level of the Symbolic without taking into account the register of the Real: see Joan Copjec, *Read My Desire: Lacan against the Historicists* (Cambridge, MA: MIT Press, 1994); Todd McGowan, *Enjoying What We Don't Have: The Political Project of Psychoanalysis* (Lincoln: University of Nebraska Press, 2013), pp. 124–125, 152–153, 167–168; Slavoj Žižek, *Less than Nothing: Hegel and the Shadow of Dialectical Materialism* (New York: Verso, 2012), pp. 328–333, 990–994; Slavoj Žižek, *The Ticklish Subject: The Absent Centre of Political Ontology* (1999; repr., New York: Verso, 2000), pp. 247–264. Judith Butler similarly discusses Žižek's challenge to Foucault in *Bodies That Matter: On the Discursive Limits of Sex* (New York: Routledge, 1993), pp. 141–148.

51. Alain Badiou, *Metapolitics*, translated by Jason Barker (1998; repr., New York: Verso, 2005), p. 107.

52. Jacques Rancière, *Moments Politiques: Interventions 1977–2009*, translated by Mary Foster (2009; repr., New York: Seven Stories, 2014), p. 144.

53. In Rancière's words, "It's the question of equality—which for Foucault had no *theoretical* pertinence—that makes the difference between us": quoted in Solange Guénoun and James H. Kavanagh, "Jacques Rancière: Literature, Politics, Aesthetics: Approaches to Democratic Disagreement," *SubStance* 29.2 (2000): 13 (emphasis in original). In 1977, Rancière was part of an editorial collective that interviewed Foucault. While at this time Rancière's notion of equality had not yet fully crystallized, one can already sense this future trajectory in the questions the collective posed to Foucault about power: see Michel Foucault, *Power/Knowledge: Selected Interviews and Other Writings, 1972–1977*, edited by Colin Gordon, translated by Colin Gordon, Leo Marshall, John Mepham, and Kate Soper (New York: Pantheon, 1980), pp.141–142.

54. Jacques Rancière, *Chronicles of Consensual Times*, translated by Steven Corcoran (2005; repr., New York: Continuum, 2010), p. 126.

55. Rancière is careful to point out his differences with Foucault. As he puts it in *Disagreement*, "While it is important to show, as Michel Foucault has done magnificently, that the police order extends well beyond its specialized institutions and techniques, it is equally important to say that nothing is political in itself merely because power

relationships are at work in it. For a thing to be political, it must give rise to a meeting of police logic and egalitarian logic that is never set up in advance." Or, as he puts it elsewhere, "Everything Foucault is focusing on is situated in the space of what I call the police": Jacques Rancière, *Disagreement: Politics and Philosophy*, translated by Julie Rose (1995; repr., Minneapolis: University of Minnesota Press, 1999), p. 32; Rancière, quoted in Simons Maarten and Jan Masschelein, "Governmental, Political and Pedagogic Subjectivation: Foucault with Rancière," *Educational Philosophy and Theory* 42.5–6 (2010): 591. For further comparisons between Foucault and Rancière, see Samuel A. Chambers, *The Lessons of Rancière* (New York: Oxford University Press, 2013); Todd May, "Anarchism from Foucault to Rancière," in *Contemporary Anarchist Studies: An Introductory Anthology of Anarchy in the Academy*, edited by Randall Amster, Abraham DeLeon, Luis A. Fernandez, Anthony J. Nocella II, and Deric Shannon (New York: Routledge, 2009), pp. 11–17.

56. Michel Foucault, *Foucault Live (Interviews, 1961–1984)*, edited by Sylvère Lotringer, translated by Lysa Hochroth and John Johnston (1989; repr., New York: Semiotext(e), 1996), p. 387.

57. Quoted in Lawrence Grossberg, "On Postmodernism and Articulation: An Interview with Stuart Hall," *Journal of Communication Inquiry* 10.2 (1986): 48.

58. For a fuller discussion of visuality, see Nicholas Mirzoeff, *The Right to Look: A Counterhistory of Visuality* (Durham, NC: Duke University Press, 2011).

59. It is for this reason that I do not think Said was not completely fair to his opponents when he attacked them for failing to foresee the Iranian Revolution of 1979 or the outbreak of the first Palestinian Intifada in 1987: see Edward W. Said, *Covering Islam: How the Media and the Experts Determine How We See the Rest of the World*, rev. ed. (1981; repr., New York: Vintage, 1997), pp. 22–23.

60. This unexpected nature of politics is fundamental to the work of Rancière. As Samuel Chambers explains, "For Rancière, politics is always a surprise. [. . .] Democratic revolutions are not something one can predict in advance; a mere transition of power may be subject to the social scientific calculus of putative prediction, but *a real revolution is always unexpected*": Chambers, *The Lessons of Rancière*, pp. 5, 7.

61. Dan Georgakas and Barbara Saltz, "This Is a Film You Should See Twice: An Interview with Hany Abu-Assad," *Cinéaste* 31.1 (2005): 16.

62. Irit Linor, "Anti-Semitism Now," *Ynet*, February 7, 2006, available at ynetnews. com. See also Nurith Gertz and George Khleifi, *Palestinian Cinema: Landscape, Trauma, and Memory* (2005; repr., Bloomington: Indiana University Press, 2008), p. 193.

63. Gertz and Khleifi, *Palestinian Cinema*, p. 193.

64. Chris McGreal, "Bomb Victims' Parents Petition Academy to Reject Movie," *The Guardian*, March 1, 2006, available at theguardian.com.

65. In her discussion of the film, Raya Morag proposes a new term: the "detonatorg," a combination of detonator and organism. This jargon does little to advance our critical analyses of the phenomenon, but it does work to dehumanize the suicide bombers. They are no longer humans but dystopian cyborgs: Raya Morag, "The Living Body and the Corpse—Israeli Documentary Cinema and the Intifadah," *Journal of Film and Video* 60.3–4 (2008): 11. This essay was later republished in her book *Waltzing with Bashir: Perpetrator Trauma and Cinema* (New York: I. B. Tauris, 2013). For a more convincing analysis of the film, see Nadia Yaqub's essay in which she argues that we should read the film as an anti-wedding movie: Nadia G. Yaqub, "*Paradise Now* (Hany Abu-

Assad): Narrating a Failed Politics," in *Film in the Middle East and North Africa: Creative Dissidence*, edited by Josef Gugler (Austin: University of Texas Press, 2011), pp. 219–227.

66. This is a point made by Ghassan Hage, who writes, "Terrorism is not the worst kind of violence that humans are capable of. [. . .] The fact that we approach suicide bombing with such trepidation, in contrast to how we approach the violence of colonial domination, for example, indicates the symbolic violence that shapes our understanding of what constitutes ethically and politically illegitimate violence": Ghassan Hage, "'Comes a Time We Are All Enthusiasm': Understanding Palestinian Suicide Bombers in Times of Exighophobia," *Public Culture* 15.1 (2003): 72. Mahmood Mamdani similarly argues that "to take seriously the point of view of the suicide bomber is not to imply that suicide bombing (or neck-lacing) was necessary or justified under certain conditions. The point is to understand both responses to particular conditions, i.e., apartheid or settler domination, as a first step to forging alternative ways of changing those conditions." For Mamdani, "Suicide bombing needs to be understood as a feature of modern political violence rather than stigmatized as a mark of barbarism": Mahmood Mamdani, "A Rejoinder to Critics," *PoLAR: Political and Legal Anthropology Review* 27.1 (2004): 20; Mahmood Mamdani, "Good Muslim, Bad Muslim: Post-apartheid Perspectives on America and Israel," *PoLAR: Political and Legal Anthropology Review* 27.1 (2004): 3.

67. Quoted in McGreal, "Bomb Victims' Parents Petition Academy to Reject Movie."

68. Morag, "The Living Body and the Corpse," p. 15.

69. One reviewer of the film writes that "suicidal resistance proceeds logically, like any other forms of violence against any colonial power, from the ethnocidal and politicidal practices of the occupation inflicted against the Palestinians and their resistance movements": Nouri Gana, "Reel Violence: *Paradise Now* and the Collapse of the Spectacle," *Comparative Studies of South Asia, Africa and the Middle East* 28.1 (2008): 30.

70. Fawaz Turki, "Meaning in Palestinian History: Text and Context," *Arab Studies Quarterly* 3.4 (1981): 381.

71. See Georgakas and Saltz, "This Is a Film You Should See Twice," p. 17.

72. Jacques Rancière, *Proletarian Nights: The Workers' Dream in Nineteenth-Century France*, translated by John Drury (1981; repr., New York: Verso, 2012), p. 83.

CHAPTER 6

1. In one instance, a school administered by the United Nations in the Jabalya refugee camp where three thousand Palestinians had taken shelter was targeted by Israeli artillery even after UN officials provided the Israeli authorities with precise GPS coordinates no fewer than seventeen times: see Sudarsan Raghavan, William Booth, and Ruth Eglas, "U.N. Says Israel Violated International Law, after Shells Hit School in Gaza," *Washington Post*, July 30, 2014, available at washingtonpost.com. See also Max Blumenthal, *The 51 Day War: Ruin and Resistance in Gaza* (New York: Nation, 2015); Pierre Krähenbühl, "Gaza as Metaphor for Unsustainability," in *Gaza as Metaphor*, edited by Helga Tawil-Souri and Dina Matar (London: Hurst, 2016), pp. 53–59.

2. See, e.g., Yaakov Katz, "Analysis: Easy to Start, Hard to End," *Jerusalem Post*, March 10, 2012, available at jpost.com; Efraim Inbar and Eitan Shamir, "Mowing the Grass in Gaza," *Jerusalem Post*, July 22, 2014, available at jpost.com.

3. For more on the murder of Michael Brown and its aftermath, see Nicholas Mir-

zoeff, *The Appearance of Black Lives Matter* (Miami: [NAME], 2017); Keeanga-Yamahtta Taylor, *From #BlackLivesMatter to Black Liberation* (Chicago: Haymarket, 2016).

4. "ALS Ice Bucket Challenge—MK Dov Lipman," YouTube, video posted by "Dov Lipman," August 18, 2014, available at https://www.youtube.com/watch?v=PXCeMgHH5w8.

5. "Hamas versus Hummus," YouTube, video posted by "Corey Feldman," August 18, 2014, available at https://www.youtube.com/watch?v=vIoiUQ0RMNI.

6. Quoted in Rana Baker, "Palestinians Express 'Solidarity with the People of Ferguson' in Mike Brown Statement," *Electronic Intifada*, August 15, 2015, available at electronicintifada.net.

7. "Rubble Bucket Challenge in Gaza. Ice Bucket Challenge in #Gaza," YouTube, video posted by "Team Palestina," August 23, 2014, available at https://www.youtube.com/watch?v=2Zqnxme3GSc.

8. "Palestine Unbound," *Journal of Palestine Studies* 44.2 (2015): 108–115. Assaf's journey to fame became the subject of Hany Abu-Assad's film *The Idol* (2015).

9. Rania Khalek, "Israel-Trained Police 'Occupy' Missouri after Killing of Black Youth," *Electronic Intifada*, August 15, 2014, available at electronicintifada.net. Kristian Davis Bailey gives a number of specific instances in which the police officers and departments involved in cases of brutality were connected to Israel. "In 2006, 92-year-old Kathryn Johnson was shot and killed by Atlanta police, who had participated in an exchange program with Israeli soldiers on counterterrorism and drug enforcement. The Oakland police who used tear gas and rubber bullets against Occupy Oakland protesters in 2010 were fresh off a joint training exercise with Israeli and Bahraini police forces. An NYPD official reported that the department's now-disbanded 'Demographics Unit,' which spied on Muslim and Arab citizens, was modeled on Israel's practices in the West Bank": Kristian Davis Bailey, "The Ferguson/Palestine Connection," *Ebony*, August 19, 2014, available at ebony.com.

10. W. E. B. Du Bois, "The Case for the Jews," *Chicago Star*, May 8, 1948. To be fair to Du Bois, his position already seemed to have shifted following the Suez Crisis in 1956: see Robin D. G. Kelley, "Apartheid's Black Apologists," in *Apartheid Israel: The Politics of an Analogy*, edited by Jon Soske and Sean Jacobs (Chicago: Haymarket, 2015), pp. 129–130; Alex Lubin, *Geographies of Liberation: The Making of an Afro-Arab Political Imaginary* (Chapel Hill: University of North Carolina Press, 2014), pp. 105–106; Vaughn Rasberry, *Race and the Totalitarian Century: Geopolitics in the Black Literary Imagination* (Cambridge, MA: Harvard University Press, 2016), pp. 280–284. King, quoted in Kelley, "Apartheid's Black Apologists," p. 136.

11. This identification of shared circumstances sometimes went both ways. Hannah Arendt, for instance, began an essay in 1959 on the Civil Rights Movement with the declaration, "As a Jew I take my sympathy for the cause of the Negroes": Hannah Arendt, "Reflections on Little Rock," *Dissent* 6.1 (1959): 46.

12. Keith P. Feldman, *A Shadow over Palestine: The Imperial Life of Race in America* (Minneapolis: University of Minnesota Press, 2015), pp. vii–xi; Kelley, "Apartheid's Black Apologists," pp. 131–132. See also Alex Lubin, "Locating Palestine in Pre-1948 Black Internationalism," *Souls* 9.2 (2007): 95–108.

13. Lewis Young, "American Blacks and the Arab-Israeli Conflict," *Journal of Palestine Studies* 2.1 (1972): 75–77. See also Melani McAlister, *Epic Encounters: Culture, Media, and U.S. Interests in the Middle East since 1945*, updated ed. (2001; repr., Berkeley: University of California Press, 2005), pp. 84–124.

14. "Third World Round-up: The Palestine Problem: Test Your Knowledge," *SNCC Newsletter* 1.4 (1967): 4–5. See also Feldman, *A Shadow over Palestine*, p. 74; Clayborne Carson, *In Struggle: SNCC and the Black Awakening of the 1960s* (Cambridge, MA: Harvard University Press, 1981), pp. 267–269; Kelley, "Apartheid's Black Apologists," pp. 136–137. While Carmichael usually gets all the credit, Keith Feldman suggests that the person most responsible for encouraging SNCC's pro-Palestine position was probably Ethel Minor, an activist who had previously been a member of the Nation of Islam and a follower of Malcolm X: Keith P. Feldman, "Representing Permanent War: Black Power's Palestine and the End(s) of Civil Rights," *CR: The New Centennial Review* 8.2 (2008): 213; Feldman, *A Shadow over Palestine*, pp. 74–75, 78.

15. Feldman, *A Shadow over Palestine*, p. 75; Carson, *In Struggle*, p. 268.

16. Mazin Sidahmed, "Critics Denounce Black Lives Matter Platform Accusing Israel of 'Genocide,'" *The Guardian*, August 11, 2016, available at theguardian.com.

17. See Young, "American Blacks and the Arab-Israeli Conflict," pp. 70–85.

18. Max Horkheimer, "The Jews and Europe," in *Critical Theory and Society: A Reader*, edited by Stephen Eric-Bronner and Douglas MacKay Kellner (New York: Routledge, 1989), p. 78; Stokely Carmichael [Kwame Ture], *Stokely Speaks: From Black Power to Pan-Africanism*, edited by Ethel N. Minor (1971; repr., Chicago: Lawrence Hill, 2007), p. 140.

19. Malcolm X, *Malcolm X Speaks: Selected Speeches and Statements*, edited by George Breitman (1965; repr., New York: Grove, 1990), p. 90. It should be noted that the history of Black internationalism long predates the interventions of the Nation of Islam and Malcolm X. Forms of internationalism had already been developed and advocated by prominent men such as W. E. B. Du Bois and Marcus Garvey but also by nineteenth-century Black feminists such as Anna Julia Cooper and Pauline Hopkins: see Hazel V. Carby, "'On the Threshold of Woman's Era': Lynching, Empire, and Sexuality in Black Feminist Theory," *Critical Inquiry* 12.1 (1985): 262–277.

20. Lubin, *Geographies of Liberation*, p. 122.

21. Huey P. Newton, *To Die for the People: The Writings of Huey P. Newton*, edited by Toni Morrison (1972; repr., San Francisco: City Lights, 2009), pp. 31–32.

22. "Foreign Policy, Black America and the Andy Young Affair," *Ebony* 35.3 (January 1980): 116–118, 120, 122. See also Jake C. Miller, "Black Viewpoints on the Mid-East Conflict," *Journal of Palestine Studies* 10.2 (1981): 44; Feldman, *A Shadow over Palestine*, pp. 99–101.

23. As Rustin put it in the *Chicago Tribune*, "The PLO is a terrorist movement whose tactics are little different from those of America's Ku Klux Klan": Bayard Rustin, "Do Blacks Have Anything to Gain from Ties to PLO?" *Chicago Tribune*, October 14, 1979, pp. A1–2. See also John L. Jackson Jr., *Thin Description: Ethnography and the African Hebrew Israelites of Jerusalem* (Cambridge, MA: Harvard University Press, 2013), pp. 202–203.

24. See Obama's interview in Jeffrey Goldberg, "'Look . . . It's My Name on This': Obama Defends the Iran Nuclear Deal," *The Atlantic*, May 21, 2015, available at theatlantic.com.

25. Marshall McLuhan, *The Gutenberg Galaxy: The Making of Typographic Man* (London: Routledge, 1962); Benedict Anderson, *Imagined Communities: Reflections on the Origin and Spread of Nationalism*, rev. ed. (1983; repr., New York: Verso, 1991); George Antonius, *The Arab Awakening: The Story of the Arab National Movement* (New York: G. P. Putnam's Sons, 1946).

26. "WHEN I SEE THEM I SEE US," YouTube, video posted by "Black-Palestinian Solidarity," October 14, 2015, available at https://www.youtube.com/watch?v=xsdpg-9cmSw.

27. "Checkpoint—Jasiri X," YouTube, video posted by "jasirix," January 28, 2014, available at https://www.youtube.com/watch?v=Dq6Y6LSjulU.

28. For an ethnographic study of the checkpoint, see Helga Tawil-Souri, "New Palestinian Centers: An Ethnography of the Checkpoint Economy," *International Journal of Cultural Studies* 12.3 (2009): 217–235. See also Helga Tawil-Souri, "Qalandia Checkpoint as Space and Nonplace," *Space and Culture* 14.1 (2011): 4–26.

29. On the emancipatory possibilities of lynching tree imagery, see James H. Cone, *The Cross and the Lynching Tree* (Maryknoll, NY: Orbis, 2011).

30. On Till, see Christine Harold and Kevin Michael DeLuca, "Behold the Corpse: Violent Images and the Case of Emmett Till," *Rhetoric and Public Affairs* 8.2 (2005): 263–286.

31. Caleb Smith and Catherine Zaw, "Students Shut Down San Mateo-Hayward Bridge; 68 People Arrested, 11 Jailed," *Stanford Daily*, January 19, 2015, available at stanforddaily.com.

32. Suheir Hammad, *Born Palestinian, Born Black* (1996; repr., New York: UpSet, 2010); Remi Kanazi, *Poetic Injustice: Writings on Resistance and Palestine* (New York: RoR, 2011).

33. Sunaina Maira, "'We Ain't Missing': Palestinian Hip Hop—a Transnational Youth Movement," *CR: The New Centennial Review* 8.2 (2008): 161–192; Sunaina Maira and Magid Shihade, "Hip Hop from '48 Palestine Youth, Music, and the Present/Absent," *Social Text* 30.3 (2012): 1–26.

34. Maira and Shihade, "Hip Hop from '48 Palestine," p. 9.

35. On Saz, see Sunaina Maira, *Jil Oslo: Palestinian Hip Hop, Youth Culture, and the Youth Movement* (Washington, DC: Tadween, 2013), pp. 54–57.

36. "The First Lady of Arabic Hip Hop," *Mondomix*, May 10, 2010, available at mondomix.com. For more on Palestinian hip hop and international solidarity, see Rayya El Zein, "Call and Response, Radical Belonging, and Arabic Hip-Hop in 'the West,'" in *American Studies Encounters the Middle East*, edited by Alex Lubin and Marwan M. Kraidy (Chapel Hill: University of North Carolina Press, 2016), pp. 106–135. See also Maira, *Jil Oslo*.

37. Lesya Michalina Sabada, "Religious Peacebuilding: The Life and Work of Archbishop Raya as a Model for Religious Peacebuilding" (Ph.D. diss., Saint Paul University, Faculty of Theology, Ottawa, 2017), pp. 87–88. See also Naim Stifan Ateek, *Justice and Only Justice: A Palestinian Theology of Liberation* (Maryknoll, NY: Orbis, 1989), p. 57.

38. Sabada, "Religious Peacebuilding," pp. 127–128. The quoted words are loosely taken from 1 Kings 21.

39. Notably, el-Yateem was previously a student of the Palestinian liberation theologian Naim Stifan Ateek: see Aviva Stahl, "Khader El-Yateem Could Be the First Socialist Palestinian Pastor on the City Council," *Village Voice*, September 5, 2017, available at villagevoice.com.

40. Quoted in Joel Greenberg, "Palestinian 'Freedom Riders' Arrested on Bus to Jerusalem," *Washington Post*, November 15, 2011, available at washingtonpost.com.

41. Quoted in Tovah Lazaroff, "Six Activists Arrested after 'Freedom Ride,'" *Jerusalem Post*, November 15, 2011, available at jpost.com, and in Greenberg, "Palestinian 'Freedom Riders' Arrested on Bus to Jerusalem."

42. Khaled Diab, "Arrests Greet Palestinian Freedom Riders," Salon.com, November 16, 2011, available at salon.com. On the March 2017 raid, see Maureen Clare Murphy, "Prominent Palestinian Activist Killed in Israeli Raid," *Electronic Intifada*, March 6, 2017, available at electronicintifada.net.

43. Quoted in Adam Horowitz, "Six Palestinian Freedom Riders Arrested Traveling on Israeli-Only Bus," *Mondoweiss*, November 15, 2011, available at mondoweiss.net.

44. For more on this event, see Maryam S. Griffin, "Freedom Rides in Palestine: Racial Segregation and Grassroots Politics on the Bus," *Race and Class* 56.4 (2015): 73–84.

45. The Tamimis are the main protagonists in Ben Ehrenreich, *The Way to the Spring: Life and Death in Palestine* (New York: Penguin, 2016).

46. Gili Cohen, "Palestinian Women, Children Stop IDF Soldier Detaining a Minor," *Ha'aretz*, August 28, 2015, available at haaretz.com; Bassem Tamimi, "My Daughter, These Are Tears of Struggle," *Ha'aretz*, December 31, 2017, available at haaretz.com.

47. Yotam Berger and Jonathan Lis, "Israel Secretly Probed Whether Family Members of Palestinian Teen Ahed Tamimi Are Non-related 'Light-Skinned' Actors," *Ha'aretz*, January 25, 2018, available at haaretz.com.

48. Nora Barrows-Friedman, "Resisting Youth Incarceration from US to Palestine," *Electronic Intifada*, January 27, 2017, available at electronicintifada.net.

49. David A. Love, "Ahed Tamimi Is the Palestinian Rosa Parks," Al Jazeera, January 15, 2018, available at aljazeera.com. Relatedly, an Israeli songwriter provoked the wrath of Defense Minister Avigdor Lieberman after he posted a poem on Instagram comparing Ahed Tamimi to Anne Frank: see Allison Kaplan Sommer, "After Comparing Palestinian Teen Tamimi to Anne Frank, Israeli Songwriter Faces Wrath of Defense Minister," *Ha'aretz*, January 23, 2018, available at haaretz.com.

50. Taly Krupkin, "Rosario Dawson, Angela Davis among 27 U.S. Figures Calling for Release of Jailed Palestinian Teen Ahed Tamimi," *Ha'aretz*, February 12, 2018, available at haaretz.com.

51. Abu Saqr is one of the Palestinians featured in the documentary *Last Shepherds of the Valley* (dir. Mariam Shahin and George Azar, 2012).

52. Quoted in Michael Rogin, "'The Sword Became a Flashing Vision': D. W. Griffith's *The Birth of a Nation*," *Representations* 9 (1985): 151.

53. Cedric J. Robinson, "In the Year 1915: D.W. Griffith and the Rewhitening of America," in *Forgeries of Memory and Meaning: Blacks and the Regimes of Race in American Theater and Film before World War II* (Chapel Hill: University of North Carolina Press, 2007), pp. 82–126. An earlier version of this chapter appeared as Cedric J. Robinson, "In the Year 1915: D.W. Griffith and the Whitening of America," *Social Identities* 3.2 (1997): 161–192.

54. As Robinson writes, "From the 1890s to World War I the country had no national political consciousness, no hegemonic cultural core, no dominant historical identity, no definite social solidarity": Robinson, *Forgeries of Memory and Meaning*, p. 181.

55. Ibid., p. 108.

56. Cedric J. Robinson, *Black Marxism: The Making of the Black Radical Tradition* (1983; repr., Chapel Hill: University of North Carolina Press, 2000), p. 80.

57. In 1906, Thomas Dixon, author of the book on which *The Birth of a Nation* is based, explained his hope that the book would serve as a testament to white victimhood. "My object is to teach the north, the young north, what it has never known—the awful suffering of the white man during the dreadful reconstruction period," he said. "I believe

that Almighty God anointed the white men of the south by their suffering during that time. . . . To demonstrate to the world that the white man must and shall be supreme": quoted in Thomas Cripps, *Slow Fade to Black: The Negro in American Film, 1900–1942* (New York: Oxford University Press, 1993), p. 44.

58. David Theo Goldberg, "Racial Comparisons, Relational Racisms: Some Thoughts on Method," *Ethnic and Racial Studies* 32.7 (2009): 1271–1282.

59. See, e.g., Nur Masalha, *Expulsion of the Palestinians: The Concept of "Transfer" in Zionist Political Thought, 1882–1948* (Washington DC: Institute for Palestine Studies, 1992); Nur Masalha, *The Palestine Nakba: Decolonising History, Narrating the Subaltern, Reclaiming Memory* (New York: Zed, 2012); Gabriel Piterberg, *The Returns of Zionism: Myths, Politics and Scholarship in Israel* (New York: Verso, 2008); Shira Robinson, *Citizen Strangers: Palestinians and the Birth of Israel's Liberal Settler State* (Stanford, CA: Stanford University Press, 2013); Steven Salaita, *The Holy Land in Transit: Colonialism and the Quest for Canaan* (Syracuse, NY: Syracuse University Press, 2006); Steven Salaita, *Inter/Nationalism: Decolonizing Native America and Palestine* (Minneapolis: University of Minnesota Press, 2016); Patrick Wolfe, "Settler Colonialism and the Elimination of the Native," *Journal of Genocide Research* 8.4 (2006): 387–409; Patrick Wolfe, *Settler Colonialism and the Transformation of Anthropology: The Politics and Poetics of an Ethnographic Event* (New York: Cassell, 1999). See also Maxime Rodinson's pathbreaking *Israel: A Colonial-Settler State?*, translated by David Thorstad (New York: Pathfinder, 1973).

60. Joseph A. Massad, *The Persistence of the Palestinian Question: Essays on Zionism and the Palestinians* (New York: Routledge, 2006), pp. 60, 69.

61. Shoshana Madmoni-Gerber, *Israeli Media and the Framing of Internal Conflict: The Yemenite Babies Affair* (New York: Palgrave Macmillan, 2009). For more on the Mizrahim's struggle against Ashkenazation, see Bryan K. Roby, *The Mizrahi Era of Rebellion: Israel's Forgotten Civil Rights Struggle, 1948–1966* (Syracuse, NY : Syracuse University Press, 2015).

62. Oz Frankel points out that "the [Israeli] Black Panthers['] most defiant move was to assume the name of an organization that the Israeli establishment had denounced as staunchly anti-Zionist and anti-Semitic": Oz Frankel, "The Black Panthers of Israel and the Politics of the Radical Analogy," in *Black Power beyond Borders: The Global Dimensions of the Black Power Movement*, edited by Nico Slate (New York: Palgrave Macmillan, 2012), p. 82.

63. The Israeli Black Panther Reuven Abergil claims that he had a meeting with a PLO representative in Europe in 1974: Madmoni-Gerber, *Israeli Media and the Framing of Internal Conflict*, p. 164.

64. Quoted in Oz Frankel, "What's in a Name? The Black Panthers in Israel," *The Sixties* 1.1 (2008): 9. Golda Meir also accused the Israeli Black Panthers of taking their name from "a group of Black Anti-Semites": quoted in Madmoni-Gerber, *Israeli Media and the Framing of Internal Conflict*, p. 164.

65. Ella Shohat, "Sephardim in Israel: Zionism from the Standpoint of Its Jewish Victims," *Social Text* 19–20 (1988): 5–6; Madmoni-Gerber, *Israeli Media and the Framing of Internal Conflict*, p. 95.

66. Cleaver's downward spiral is marked by the publication of two books one decade apart: Eldridge Cleaver, *Soul on Ice* (New York: Delta, 1968); Eldridge Cleaver, *Soul on Fire* (Waco, TX: Word, 1978). On the demise of the Israeli Black Panthers, see

Erik Cohen, "The Black Panthers and Israeli Society," in *Migration, Ethnicity and Community*, vol. 1, *Studies of Israeli Society*, edited by Ernest Krausz (New Brunswick, NJ: Transaction, 1980), pp. 147–163.

67. On the Mizrahi organization, see Sami Shalom Chetrit, "Mizrahi Politics in Israel: Between Integration and Alternative," *Journal of Palestine Studies* 29.4 (2000): 51–65. On the original Rainbow Coalition, see Amy Sonnie and James Tracy, *Hillbilly Nationalists, Urban Race Rebels, and Black Power: Community Organizing in Radical Times* (New York: Melville House, 2011); Jakobi Williams, *From the Bullet to the Ballot: The Illinois Chapter of the Black Panther Party and Racial Coalition Politics in Chicago* (Chapel Hill: University of North Carolina Press, 2013). On the assassination of Fred Hampton, see Jeffrey Haas, *The Assassination of Fred Hampton: How the FBI and the Chicago Police Murdered a Black Panther* (Chicago: Lawrence Hill, 2010). See also the film *The Murder of Fred Hampton* (dir. Howard Alk, 1971).

68. Talila Nesher, "Israel Admits Ethiopian Women Were Given Birth Control Shots," *Ha'aretz*, January 27, 2013, available at haaretz.com. On U.S. sterilization practices, see, e.g., Angela Y. Davis, *Women, Race, and Class* (1981; repr., New York: Vintage, 1983), pp. 202–221.

69. Jonathan Beck, "Police Chief: Cop Filmed Beating Soldier to Be Fired," *Times of Israel*, April 29, 2015, available at timesofisrael.com; Ben Norton, "'Baltimore Is Here': Ethiopian Israelis Protest Police Brutality in Jerusalem," *Mondoweiss*, May 1, 2015, available at mondoweiss.net.

70. Regev quoted in Ali Abunimah, "Israeli Lawmaker Miri Regev: 'Heaven Forbid' We Compare Africans to Human Beings," *Electronic Intifada*, May 31, 2012, available at electronicintifada.net; Yishai, quoted in Dana Weiler-Polak, "Israel Enacts Law Allowing Authorities to Detain Illegal Migrants for Up to 3 Years," *Ha'aretz*, June 3, 2012, available at haaretz.com.

71. David Theo Goldberg, "Racial Palestinianization," in *Thinking Palestine*, edited by Ronit Lentin (New York: Zed, 2008), p. 33.

72. As James Baldwin put it, "We feared black cops even more than white cops, because the black cop had to work so much harder—on *your* head—to prove to himself and his colleagues that he was not like all the other niggers": James Baldwin, "Negroes Are Anti-Semitic Because They're Anti-White," *New York Times*, April 9, 1967, available at nytimes.com (emphasis in original). See also James Baldwin, *The Devil Finds Work* (1976; repr., New York: Vintage, 2011), p. 63; Nikhil Pal Singh, "The Whiteness of Police," *American Quarterly* 66.4 (2014): 1091–1099.

73. Notably, some of the Arabic-speaking Mizrahim were forging links with the Palestinians even before the establishment of the State of Israel: see Shohat, "Sephardim in Israel," pp. 10–11; Madmoni-Gerber, *Israeli Media and the Framing of Internal Conflict*, p. 23.

74. Salaita, *The Holy Land in Transit*, p. 56; Salaita, *Inter/Nationalism*, p. 63.

75. Gilles Deleuze and Elias Sanbar, "The Indians of Palestine," *Discourse* 20.3 (1998): 27. Ella Shohat similarly argues, "One might reflect on a useful structural analogy in which Palestinians have replayed the historical role of the dispossessed and occupied Native Americans for Zionism while Arab Jews were cast as its displaced and exploited blacks": Ella Shohat, "Rupture and Return: Zionist Discourse and the Study of Arab Jews," *Social Text* 21.2 (2003): 71.

76. Cedric J. Robinson, "Manichaeism and Multiculturalism," in *Mapping Multicul-*

turalism, edited by Avery F. Gordon and Christopher Newfield (Minneapolis: University of Minnesota Press, 1996), p. 117.

77. W. E. B. Du Bois, *Darkwater: Voices from within the Veil* (1920; repr., New York: Schocken, 1969), p. 30.

78. Ibid., p. 31.

79. George Lipsitz, *The Possessive Investment in Whiteness: How White People Profit from Identity Politics*, 2nd ed. (1998; repr., Philadelphia: Temple University Press, 2006). See also Cheryl I. Harris, "Whiteness as Property," *Harvard Law Review* 106.8 (1993): 1707–1791.

80. Ghassan Hage, *White Nation: Fantasies of White Supremacy in a Multicultural Society* (New York: Routledge, 2000), pp. 27–28, 36–37.

81. Ibid., p. 18.

82. Frantz Fanon, *The Wretched of the Earth*, translated by Richard Philcox (1961; repr., New York: Grove, 2004), p. 93.

83. Massad, *The Persistence of the Palestinian Question*, p. 111.

84. In his blistering review, el-Khairy calls *Miral* "a film that reeks of liberal morality" and accuses its producers of "kowtow[ing] to commercial imperatives and the assumed tastes of mainstream Western audiences": Omar el-Khairy, "Film Review: Palestine as Hollywood Fantasy in 'Miral,'" *Electronic Intifada*, November 23, 2010, available at electronicintifada.net.

85. Gabriel Naddaf appears to be the butt of a joke in Annemarie Jacir's *Wajib* (2017). At one point in the film, the father and son protagonists (played by the real-life father and son Mohammad and Saleh Bakri) have a conversation about the Angel Gabriel as they are driving down a road in Nazareth. A few minutes later, they pass a priest on the side of the road. The father explains that this priest has sold out to the Zionists, and the son yells a curse at him for betraying the Palestinian cause.

86. On Haskia, see Roy Arad, "When a 'Good Arab' Woos Israeli Right-Wingers," *Ha'aretz*, December 29, 2014, available at haaretz.com. On Naddaf, see Mitch Ginsburg, "The Unorthodox Priest Who Stands with the Jews," *Times of Israel*, May 19, 2014, available at timesofisrael.com; Mark Tooley, "An Israeli Priest Defends Israel: The Case for Jewish-Christian Collaboration," *Weekly Standard*, December 1, 2014, available at weeklystandard.com.

87. Du Bois, *Darkwater*, p. 31.

88. James H. Cone, *Black Theology and Black Power* (New York: Seabury, 1969), p. 151. In Cone's view, "The coming of Christ means a denial of what we thought we were. It means destroying the white devil in us. Reconciliation to God means that white people are prepared to deny themselves (whiteness), to take up the cross (blackness) and follow Christ (black ghetto)." As he puts it, "God's Word of reconciliation means that we can only be justified by becoming black. Reconciliation makes us all black": ibid., pp. 150–151.

89. As Hage himself argues, "Israel is, as much as Australia, Canada or Britain, a multicultural society. But it is also a white society in the sense I have used whiteness to denote the dominance of a white colonial fantasy in *White Nation*, involving a spatially empowered white modern First World self facing a Third World–looking other": Ghassan Hage, *Alter-Politics: Critical Anthropology and the Radical Imagination* (Melbourne: Melbourne University Press, 2015), p. 8. For more on transnational whiteness and race, see Nadine Suleiman Nader, "Imperial Whiteness and the Diasporas of Empire," *Ameri-*

can Quarterly 66.4 (2014): 1107–1115; David Theo Goldberg, *The Threat of Race: Reflections on Racial Neoliberalism* (Malden, MA: Wiley-Blackwell, 2009).

90. As Ghassan Hage argues, "Blackness [. . .] allows various non-Blacks an access to Whiteness. All the cappuccinos, macchiatos and caffe lattes of the world that are neither black nor white, skin-colour wise, can use the Blackness of the Aboriginal people to emphasise their non-Blackness and their capacity to enter the field of Whiteness": Hage, *White Nation*, p. 57. On blackface performance and its relationship to whiteness, see Michael Rogin, *Blackface, White Noise: Jewish Immigrants in the Hollywood Melting Pot* (1996; repr., Berkeley: University of California Press, 1998).

91. Alex Lubin gives this interpretation to the claim "We are all Israelis." As he argues, "The slogan 'We are all Israelis' is a heuristic of imperial rule, but it is possible to disrupt its logic by reading it as an invitation to compare settler colonial technologies in the United States and Israel. In doing so, I view the slogan as an attempt to universalize ('we are all') the norms of colonialism; yet, I also see it as a critical framework for viewing the technologies of settler colonialism as they animate ongoing military projects and as they haunt the (post)colonial present": Alex Lubin, "'We Are All Israelis': The Politics of Colonial Comparisons," *South Atlantic Quarterly* 107.4 (2008): 673.

92. Alex Lubin, "Breaking 'America's Last Taboo,'" *Middle East Research and Information Project* (November 27, 2013); Alex Lubin, "Why I'm Voting to Boycott Israel," *The Nation*, December 13, 2013, available at thenation.com; Nicholas Brady, "The Void Speaks Back: Black Suffering as the Unthought of the American Studies Association's Academic Boycott of Israel," *Out of Nowhere*, December 23, 2013, available at outofno whereblog.wordpress.com.

93. For Wilderson's original interview, see Frank B. Wilderson III, "Irreconcilable Anti-Blackness and Police Violence," *i MiX WHAT i LiKE*, October 1, 2014, available at imixwhatilike.org. For the transcript, see "'We're Trying to Destroy the World': Anti-Blackness and Police Violence after Ferguson: An Interview with Frank B. Wilderson, III," *Ill Will Editions*, 2014, available at ill-will-editions.tumblr.com.

94. Frank B. Wilderson III, *Red, White, and Black: Cinema and the Structure of U.S. Antagonisms* (Durham, NC: Duke University Press, 2010); Frank B. Wilderson III, "Gramsci's Black Marx: Whither the Slave in Civil Society?" *Social Identities* 9.2 (2003): 225–240; Frank B. Wilderson, "Grammar and Ghosts: The Performative Limits of African Freedom," *Theatre Survey* 50.1 (2009): 119–125; Frank B. Wilderson, "The Prison Slave as Hegemony's (Silent) Scandal," *Social Justice* 30.2 (2003): 18–27. Wilderson borrows the term "social death" from Orlando Patterson, *Slavery and Social Death: A Comparative Study* (Cambridge, MA: Harvard University Press, 1982).

95. In Wilderson's words, "A refusal to be authorized by the Slave is an effect of the Negrophobia that the 'Savage' [Native American] shares with the Settler/Master": Wilderson, *Red, White, and Black*, p. 241. See also Leslie Marmon Silko, *Almanac of the Dead* (1991; repr., New York: Penguin, 1992).

96. See Wilderson, *Red, White, and Black*, pp. 3, 37, 45, 66, 122, 141, 149–150, 215, 247.

97. Ibid., p. 138.

98. Ibid., p. 138. Although Fanon is one of the most important theoretical sources for Wilderson and other Afropessimists, their particular interpretation of Fanon's voice is, in some respects, unrecognizable. As George Ciccariello-Maher quips, "Despite Fanon's recent influence on what has come to be known as 'Afro-Pessimism,' he was

never a very good pessimist": George Ciccariello-Maher, *Decolonizing Dialectics* (Durham, NC: Duke University Press, 2017), p. 78.

99. In some respects, this problem exists within the work of Fanon himself, and Ghassan Hage argues that in *Black Skin, White Masks*, Fanon, too, imitates the European constructs that he claims to contest: see Hage, *Alter-Politics*, pp. 120–41.

100. Cone, *The Cross and the Lynching Tree*, p. 95.

101. Drawing from Hannah Arendt, Fred Moten makes a similar claim in his critique of Afropessimism: Fred Moten, "Blackness and Nothingness (Mysticism in the Flesh)," *South Atlantic Quarterly* 112.4 (2013): 739–740.

102. As Amnon Raz-Krakotzkin argues, "Paradoxically, the exit from Europe and the wish to establish a distinct Jewish entity in the East was a way of being integrated into the Christian West on the basis of complete identification with the European self-image": quoted in Piterberg, *The Returns of Zionism*, p. 246.

103. Theodor Herzl, *The Jewish State* (1896; repr., New York: American Zionist Emergency Council, 1946). Commenting on the writing of this book, Herzl wrote, "I worked on it every day to the point of utter exhaustion. My only recreation was listening to Wagner's music in the evening, particularly to *Tannhäuser*, an opera which I attended as often as it was produced. Only on the evenings when there was no opera did I have any doubts as to the truth of my ideas": Theodor Herzl, *Zionist Writings: Essays and Addresses, Volume 1: January, 1896–June, 1898*, translated by Harry Zohn (New York: Herzl, 1973), pp. 17–18, quoted in Piterberg, *The Returns of Zionism*, p. 31. Ilan Halevi similarly argues that "the early Zionist leaders had absolutely no pangs of conscience in admitting that the anti-Semites were their best allies": Ilan Halevi, "Zionism Today," *Arab Studies Quarterly* 7.2–3 (1985): 5.

104. Here I am reminded of Robinson's critique of the Black nationalism advocated by figures such as Stokely Carmichael and Louis Farrakhan, which he saw as nothing more than an inversion of the oppressive racial order. He thereby deemed it a "fictive radicalism": quoted in Chuck Morse, "Capitalism, Marxism, and the Black Radical Tradition: An Interview with Cedric Robinson," *Perspectives on Anarchist Theory* 3.1 (1999): 1.

105. "In the 1960s U.S. South, black people had to sit in the back of the bus; in occupied Palestine, Palestinians are not even allowed ON the bus": quoted in Griffin, "Freedom Rides in Palestine," pp. 79–80.

106. Hage, *Alter-Politics*, p. 125.

107. C. L. R. James, *A History of Pan-African Revolt* (1939; repr., Chicago: Charles H. Kerr, 2005), p. 116.

108. Malcolm X, *Malcolm X Speaks*, pp. 50, 218.

109. Sonnie and Tracy, *Hillbilly Nationalists, Urban Race Rebels, and Black Power*; Williams, *From the Bullet to the Ballot*.

110. Assata Shakur, *Assata: An Autobiography* (Westport, CT: Lawrence Hill, 1987), p. 267.

111. Quoted in Edward W. Said, *Culture and Imperialism* (1993; repr., New York: Vintage, 1994), p. 280.

112. This divergence can even be seen in the opposing ways these two thinkers use Fanon. Wilderson and Robinson agree that the Fanon who wrote *Black Skin, White Masks* is quite different from the Fanon who wrote *The Wretched of the Earth*, but whereas Wilderson emphasizes the earlier Fanon, Robinson preferred the latter. Wilderson argues, "There is no analogy between the postcolonials' guarantee of restoration

predicated on their need to put the Settler out of the picture—the Fanon of *The Wretched of the Earth*—and Slaves' guarantee of restoration predicated on their need to put the Human out of the picture—the Fanon of *Black Skin, White Masks*": Wilderson, *Red, White, and Black*, p. 122. See also Cedric J. Robinson, "The Appropriation of Frantz Fanon," *Race and Class* 35.1 (1993): 79–90.

113. As Robinson put it in an interview, "According to some scholars, the slaves . . . [had] no ambitions, except to perhaps live or perhaps to die. They had experienced social death. Well that's nonsense. Because they were something more than was what was expected of them, they could invent, manufacture, conspire, and organize way beyond the possibilities." Quoted in Robin D. G. Kelley, "Cedric J. Robinson: The Making of a Black Radical Intellectual," *CounterPunch*, June 17, 2016, available at counterpunch .org.

114. Robinson, *Black Marxism*, p. 318.

115. Robinson, "Manichaeism and Multiculturalism," p. 117.

116. Wilderson, *Red, White, and Black*, p. 38.

117. Robinson, "Manichaeism and Multiculturalism," p. 117.

118. Quoted in ibid., p. 117.

119. In Elliot Colla's view, "Godard argues that solidarity with others elsewhere may be a slogan raised by militants unable (or unwilling) to engage in meaningful revolutionary action in their own local contexts": Elliot Colla, "Sentimentality and Redemption: The Rhetoric of Egyptian Pop Culture Intifada Solidarity," in *Palestine, Israel, and the Politics of Popular Culture*, edited by Rebecca L. Stein and Ted Swedenburg (Durham, NC: Duke University Press, 2005), p. 359.

120. Edward W. Said, *The Politics of Dispossession: The Struggle for Palestinian Self-Determination, 1969–1994* (1994; repr., New York: Vintage, 1995), p. 290.

121. Keeanga-Yamahtta Taylor points out these apparent contradictions of race struggle in the context of Ferguson, Missouri. "When a Black mayor, governing a largely Black city, aids in the mobilization of a military unit led by a Black woman to suppress a Black rebellion, we are in a new period of the Black freedom struggle": Taylor, *From #BlackLivesMatter to Black Liberation*, p. 80.

122. Lisa Hajjar, "Toward a Sociology of Human Rights: Critical Globalization Studies, International Law, and the Future of War," in *Critical Globalization Studies*, edited by Richard P. Appelbaum and William I. Robinson (New York: Routledge, 2005), p. 213 (emphasis in original). See also John Collins, *Global Palestine* (New York: Columbia University Press, 2011); Jeff Halper, *War against the People: Israel, the Palestinians and Global Pacification* (London: Pluto, 2015).

123. "More than Half of NFL Players Booked for Israel PR Trip Withdraw," *The Guardian*, February 15, 2017, available at theguardian.com.

124. Mazin Sidahmed, "Critics Denounce Black Lives Matter Platform Accusing Israel of 'Genocide,'" *The Guardian*, August 11, 2016, available at theguardian.com

125. Robin D. G. Kelley, "Another Freedom Summer," *Journal of Palestine Studies* 44.1 (2014): 32.

126. Steven D. Classen, *Watching Jim Crow: The Struggles over Mississippi TV, 1955–1969* (Durham, NC: Duke University Press, 2004), pp. 94–104.

127. The creation of new political subjects should not be mistaken for the creation of new, essentialized identities such as the Israeli Sabra or the New Palestinian Man, as I have already argued. See also the discussion of solidarity in Chandra Talpade Mohanty,

Feminism without Borders: Decolonizing Theory, Practicing Solidarity (Durham, NC: Duke University Press, 2003).

128. Ernesto Laclau and Chantal Mouffe, *Hegemony and Socialist Strategy: Towards a Radical Democratic Politics* (New York: Verso, 1985).

129. David Roediger, a scholar who is very attentive to the use of words, suggests that the term "accomplice" is preferable to "ally": David R. Roediger, *Class, Race, and Marxism* (New York: Verso, 2017), p. 158.

130. Robinson, *Black Marxism*, p. 318.

131. Selma James, *Sex, Race, and Class: The Perspective of Winning: A Selection of Writings, 1952-2011* (Oakland, CA: PM, 2012), p. 524.

132. See my "Prometheus in Chicago: The Chaining and Gagging of Bobby Seale and the 'Real-ization' of Resistance," *Cinema Journal* 54.4 (2015): 26–49.

Filmography

Ajami (dir. Scandar Copti and Yaron Shani, 2009)
Al Helm: Martin Luther King in Palestine (dir. Connie Field, 2012)
Arna's Children (dir. Danniel Danniel and Juliano Mer-Khamis, 2004)
Avatar (dir. James Cameron, 2009)
Avenge but One of My Two Eyes (dir. Avi Mograbi, 2005)
Bananas (dir. Woody Allen, 1971)
The Band's Visit (dir. Eran Kolirin, 2007)
The Battle of Algiers (dir. Gillo Pontecorvo, 1966)
Bethlehem (dir. Yuval Adler, 2013)
The Birth of a Nation (dir. D. W. Griffith, 1915)
Black Sister's Revenge (dir. Jamaa Fanaka, 1976)
Bonboné (dir. Rakan Mayasi, 2017)
Braveheart (dir. Mel Gibson, 1995)
Canticle of the Stones (dir. Michel Khleifi, 1989)
Cast a Giant Shadow (dir. Melville Shavelson, 1966)
Chic Point (dir. Sharif Waked, 2003)
Chronicle of a Disappearance (dir. Elia Suleiman, 1996)
Cinema Palestine (dir. Tim Schwab, 2013)
Colorful Journey (dir. Arab and Tarzan Nasser, 2010)
Cries and Whispers (dir. Ingmar Bergman, 1972)
Crossing Kalandia (dir. Sobi al-Zobaidi, 2003)
The Delta Force (dir. Menahem Golan, 1986)
Divine Intervention (dir. Elia Suleiman, 2002)
Dog Days (dir. Eyas Salman, 2009)
The Dream (dir. Mohammad Malas, 1987)

The Dupes (dir. Tawfik Saleh, 1972)
Encounter Point (dir. Ronit Avni and Julia Bacha, 2006)
Exodus (dir. Otto Preminger, 1960)
Eyes of a Thief (dir. Najwa Najjar, 2014)
Fertile Memory (dir. Michel Khleifi, 1980)
5 Broken Cameras (dir. Emad Burnat and Guy Davidi, 2011)
500 Dunam on the Moon (dir. Rachel Leah Jones, 2002)
Fix ME (dir. Raed Andoni, 2010)
A Force More Powerful (dir. Steve York, 1999)
Ford Transit (dir. Hany Abu-Assad, 2003)
Forget Baghdad: Jews and Arabs—the Iraqi Connection (dir. Samir, 2002)
Gate of the Sun (dir. Yousry Nasrallah, 2003)
Gaza Strip (dir. James Longley, 2002)
Gett: The Trial of Viviane Amsalem (dir. Ronit Elkabetz and Shlomi Elkabetz, 2014)
Ghost Hunting (dir. Raed Andoni, 2017)
The Great Book Robbery (dir. Benny Brunner, 2012)
The Green Prince (dir. Nadav Schirman, 2014)
Growing Up in Gaza in the Dark (dir. Matthew Cassel, 2017)
Hanna K. (dir. Costa-Gavras, 1983)
Here and Elsewhere (dir. Groupe Dziga Vertov, 1976)
Hill 24 Doesn't Answer (dir. Thorold Dickinson, 1955)
The Human Resources Manager (dir. Eran Riklis, 2010)
The Idol (dir. Hany Abu-Assad, 2015)
In Between (dir. Maysaloun Hamoud, 2016)
In Search of Palestine (dir. Charles Bruce, 1998)
Israel: Birth of a Nation (dir. Herbert Krosney, 1996)
It's Better to Jump (dir. Gina Angelone, Mouna Stewart, and Patrick Alexander Stewart, 2013)
Jenin, Jenin (dir. Mohammad Bakri, 2003)
Junction 48 (dir. Udi Aloni, 2016)
Kings and Extras (dir. Azza el-Hassan, 2004)
Laila's Birthday (dir. Rashid Masharawi, 2008)
Last Shepherds of the Valley (dir. Mariam Shahin and George Azar, 2012)
The Last Supper (dir. Tomás Gutiérrez Alea, 1976)
Leila Khaled: Hijacker (dir. Lina Makboul, 2006)
like twenty impossibles (dir. Annemarie Jacir, 2003)
Ma'loul Celebrates Its Destruction (dir. Michel Khleifi, 1985)
Mawsem Hisad (dir. Nassim Amaouche, Mais Darwazah, Erige Sehiri, and Sameh Zoabi, 2012)
The Milky Way (dir. Ali Nasser, 1997)
Minority Report (dir. Steven Spielberg, 2002)
Miral (dir. Julian Schnabel, 2010)
The Murder of Fred Hampton (dir. Howard Alk, 1971)
My Love Awaits Me by the Sea (dir. Mais Darwazah, 2013)
Nazareth 2000 (dir. Hany Abu-Assad, 2001)
Night of the Living Dead (dir. George A. Romero, 1968)
1948 (dir. Mohammad Bakri, 1998)

Occupation 101 (dir. Abdallah Omeish and Sufyan Omeish, 2006)
Off Frame: Revolution until Victory (dir. Mohanad Yaqubi, 2015)
Omar (dir. Hany Abu-Assad, 2013)
On the Side of the Road (dir. Lia Tarachansky, 2012)
Paradise Now (dir. Hany Abu-Assad, 2005)
Pillar of Fire (dir. Larry Frisch, 1959)
Planet of the Arabs (dir. Jackie Salloum, 2005)
Punishment Park (dir. Peter Watkins, 1971)
Rana's Wedding (dir. Hany Abu-Assad, 2002)
Return to Haifa (dir. Kassem Hawal, 1981)
Route 181: Fragments of a Journey in Palestine-Israel (dir. Michel Khleifi and Eyal Sivan, 2004)
Salt of This Sea (dir. Annemarie Jacir, 2008)
Sand Storm (dir. Elite Zexer, 2016)
Saz: The Palestinian Rapper for Change (dir. Gil Karni, 2005)
Schindler's List (dir. Steven Spielberg, 1993)
The Shadow of the West (dir. Geoff Dunlop, 1986)
Shoah (dir. Claude Lanzmann, 1985)
Skins (dir. Chris Eyre, 2002)
Slingshot Hip Hop (dir. Jackie Salloum, 2008)
Smile and the World Will Smile Back (dir. al-Haddad family, Yoav Gross, and Ehab Tarabieh, 2014)
Take Me Home (dir. Mais Darwazah, 2008)
Thank God It's Friday (dir. Jan Beddegenoodts, 2013)
They Do Not Exist (dir. Mustafa Abu Ali, 1974)
Ticket to Jerusalem (dir. Rashid Masharawi, 2002)
The Time That Remains (dir. Elia Suleiman, 2009)
To Be Continued (dir. Sharif Waked, 2009)
Villa Touma (dir. Suha Arraf, 2014)
Vladimir et Rosa (dir. Groupe Dziga Vertov, 1971)
Wajib (dir. Annemarie Jacir, 2017)
Waltz with Bashir (dir. Ari Folman, 2008)
Wedding in Galilee (dir. Michel Khleifi, 1987)
When I Saw You (dir. Annemarie Jacir, 2012)
World War Z (dir. Marc Foster, 2013)
You Don't Mess with the Zohan (dir. Dennis Dugan, 2008)
Z (dir. Costa-Gavras, 1979)

Bibliography

Abu el-Haj, Nadia. *The Genealogical Science: The Search for Jewish Origins and the Politics of Epistemology* (Chicago: University of Chicago Press, 2012).

Abu-Lughod, Lila. "The Romance of Resistance: Tracing Transformations of Power through Bedouin Women." *American Ethnologist* 17.1 (1990): 41–55.

Abunimah, Ali. "Israeli Lawmaker Miri Regev: 'Heaven Forbid' We Compare Africans to Human Beings." *Electronic Intifada*, May 31, 2012. Available at electronicintifada.net.

———. "Noted French Theorist Jacques Rancière Cancels Israel Lecture, Heeding Boycott Call." *Electronic Intifada*, January 19, 2012. Available at electronicintifada.net.

———. "Video Analysis Pinpoints Israeli Killer of Palestinian Teen." *Electronic Intifada*, November 21, 2014. Available at electronicintifada.net.

Abunimah, Ali, and Benjamin J. Doherty. "'Gaza Strip' Director to Return Student Academy Award to Protest Exclusion of Palestine." *Electronic Intifada*, December 20, 2002. Available at electronicintifada.net.

Aburamadan, Lara. "In Photos: Red Carpet Film Festival Asserts Gaza's Pride and Talent." *Electronic Intifada*, May 19, 2015. Available at electronicintifada.net.

Abu Toameh, Khaled, and Yaakov Lappin. "2 Palestinians Killed by Israeli Security Forces in Violent Clash near Ramallah." *Jerusalem Post*, May 15, 2014. Available at jpost.com.

Achcar, Gilbert. *The Arabs and the Holocaust: The Arab-Israeli War of Narratives*, translated by G. M. Goshgarian (2009; repr., New York: Metropolitan, 2010).

Adorno, Theodor W. *Negative Dialectics*, translated by E. B. Ashton (1966; repr., New York: Continuum, 2005).

———. *Prisms*, translated by Samuel and Shierry Weber (1967; repr., Cambridge, MA: MIT Press, 1981).

Aftab, Kaleem. "Suha Arraf's Villa Touma Offers a World View That's Uniquely Palestinian Yet Very European." *The National*, September 2, 2014. Available at thenational.ae.

Agamben, Giorgio. *The Coming Community*, translated by Michael Hardt (1990; repr.,
Minneapolis: University of Minnesota Press, 1993).

———. *Homo Sacer: Sovereign Power and Bare Life*, translated by Daniel Heller-Roazen
(1995; repr., Stanford, CA: Stanford University Press, 1998).

"Ahead of Obama Visit, PA Prohibits Reporting from Hebron." *Times of Israel*, March
19, 2013. Available at timesofisrael.com.

Ahmad, Aijaz. *In Theory: Classes, Nations, Literatures* (1992; repr., New York: Verso,
2008).

Alahmed, Nadia. "An Anthem for the Dream Land: The Legacy of Poetry for the Palestinian and African-American Nationalism in the 1960s and 1970s." *Human Architecture: Journal of the Sociology of Self-Knowledge* 7.5 (2009): 123–136.

Alashqar, Khaled. "Gaza Cinema Struggles amid Post-war Ruins," Al Jazeera, December
13, 2014. Available at aljazeera.com.

Alexander, Livia. "Is There a Palestinian Cinema? The National and Transnational in
Palestinian Film Production." In *Palestine, Israel, and the Politics of Popular Culture*, edited by Rebecca L. Stein and Ted Swedenburg (Durham, NC: Duke University Press, 2005), pp. 150–172.

Althusser, Louis. *Lenin and Philosophy and Other Essays*, translated by Ben Brewster
(1975; repr., New York: Verso, 2001).

Amireh, Amal. "Activists, Lobbyists, and Suicide Bombers: Lessons from the Palestinian Women's Movement." *Comparative Studies of South Asia, Africa and the Middle
East* 32.2 (2012): 437–446.

———. "Between Complicity and Subversion: Body Politics in Palestinian National Narrative." *South Atlantic Quarterly* 102.4 (2003): 747–772.

———. "Liberation Struggles: Reflections on the Palestinian Women's Movement."
In *Arab Feminisms: Gender and Equality in the Middle East*, edited by Jean Said
Makdisi, Noha Bayoumi, and Rafif Rida Sidawi (London: I. B. Tauris, 2014), pp.
195–204.

Amit, Gish. "Salvage or Plunder? Israel's 'Collection' of Private Palestinian Libraries in
West Jerusalem." *Journal of Palestine Studies* 40.4 (2011): 6–23.

Anderman, Nirit, and Noa Shpigel. "Israeli City Bars Screening of Film about Israeli-
Arab Coexistence." *Ha'aretz*, November 2, 2016. Available at haaretz.com.

Anderson, Benedict. *Imagined Communities: Reflections on the Origin and Spread of
Nationalism*, rev. ed. (1983; repr., New York: Verso, 1991).

Anderson, John. "The Hand That Feeds Bites Back: Israel and Suha Arraf Differ on Nationality of 'Villa Touma.'" *New York Times*, October 16, 2014. Available at nytimes.com.

Antonius, George. *The Arab Awakening: The Story of the Arab National Movement* (1938;
repr., New York: G. P. Putnam's Sons, 1946).

Antoun, Naira, and Mohanad Yaqubi. "Yaffa Is Not an Orange: The Limits of Archetypes." *Jadaliyya*, July 25, 2011. Available at jadaliyya.com.

Aouragh, Miriyam. *Palestine Online: Transnationalism, the Internet and the Construction of Identity* (2011; repr., New York: I. B. Tauris, 2012).

Arad, Roy. "When a 'Good Arab' Woos Israeli Right-Wingers." *Ha'aretz*, December 29,
2014. Available at haaretz.com.

Arasoughly, Alia. "Film Education in Palestine Post-Oslo: The Experience of Shashat." In *The Education of the Filmmaker in Africa, the Middle East, and the Americas,* edited by Mette Hjort (New York: Palgrave Macmillan, 2013), pp. 99–123.

Arendt, Hannah. "Reflections on Little Rock." *Dissent* 6.1 (1959): 45–56.

Asad, Talal. "Anthropological Texts and Ideological Problems: An Analysis of Cohen on Arab Villages in Israel." *Economy and Society* 4.3 (1975): 251–282.

Ateek, Naim Stifan. *Justice and Only Justice: A Palestinian Theology of Liberation* (Maryknoll, NY: Orbis, 1989).

Azoulay, Ariella, and Adi Ophir. *The One-State Condition: Occupation and Democracy in Israel/Palestine,* translated by Tal Haran (2008; repr., Stanford, CA: Stanford University Press, 2013).

Badiou, Alain. *Being and Event,* translated by Oliver Feltham (1988; repr., New York: Continuum, 2006).

———. *Metapolitics,* translated by Jason Barker (1998; repr., New York: Verso, 2005).

———. *Polemics,* translated by Steve Corcoran (2006; repr., New York: Verso, 2011).

Badiou, Alain, Eric Hazan, and Ivan Segré. *Reflections on Anti-Semitism,* translated by David Fernbach (2011; repr., New York: Verso, 2013).

Bailey, Kristian Davis. "The Ferguson/Palestine Connection." *Ebony,* August 19, 2014. Available at ebony.com.

Baker, Rana. "Palestinians Express 'Solidarity with the People of Ferguson' in Mike Brown Statement." *Electronic Intifada,* August 15, 2015. Available at electronicintifada.net.

Baldwin, James. *The Devil Finds Work* (1976; repr., New York: Vintage, 2011), p. 63.

———. "Negroes Are Anti-Semitic Because They're Anti-White." *New York Times,* April 9, 1967. Available at nytimes.com.

———. *Notes of a Native Son* (1955; repr., New York: Bantam, 1968).

Barrows-Friedman, Nora. "Resisting Youth Incarceration from US to Palestine." *Electronic Intifada,* January 27, 2017. Available at electronicintifada.net.

Beck, Jonathan. "Police Chief: Cop Filmed Beating Soldier to Be Fired." *Times of Israel,* April 29, 2015. Available at timesofisrael.com.

Beinin, Joel. "No More Tears: Benny Morris and the Road Back from Liberal Zionism." *Middle East Report* 230 (2004): 38–45.

Benjamin, Walter. *Illuminations,* edited by Hannah Arendt, translated by Harry Zohn (1968; repr., New York: Schocken, 1969).

———. "In the Sun." In *Walter Benjamin: Selected Writings, 1927–1934,* vol. 2, translated by Rodney Livingstone, edited by Michael W. Jennings, Howard Eiland, and Gary Smith (Cambridge, MA: Harvard University Press, 1999), pp. 662–665.

Benjamin, Walter, and Gershom Scholem. *The Correspondence of Walter Benjamin and Gershom Scholem, 1932–1940,* translated by Gary Smith and Andrea Lefevere, edited by Gershom Scholem (1980; repr., New York: Schocken, 1989).

Berger, Yotam, and Jonathan Lis. "Israel Secretly Probed Whether Family Members of Palestinian Teen Ahed Tamimi Are Non-related 'Light-Skinned' Actors." *Ha'aretz,* January 25, 2018. Available at haaretz.com.

Bernstein, Richard J. *Freud and the Legacy of Moses* (New York: Cambridge University Press, 1998).

Bhabha, Homi. "How Newness Enters the World: Postmodern Space, Postcolonial Times and the Trails of Cultural Translation." In *Writing Black Britain, 1948–1998: An In-*

terdisciplinary Anthology, edited by James Procter (New York: Manchester University Press, 2000), pp. 300–307.

Bloch, Ernst. "Man as Possibility." *Cross Currents* 18.3 (1968): 273–283.

———. *A Philosophy of the Future*, translated by John Cumming (1963; repr., New York: Herder and Herder, 1970).

———. *The Principle of Hope*, vol. 1, translated by Neville Plaice, Stephen Plaice, and Paul Knight (1959; repr., Cambridge, MA: MIT Press, 1986).

———. *The Principle of Hope*, vol. 3, translated by Neville Plaice, Stephen Plaice, and Paul Knight (1959; repr., Cambridge, MA: MIT Press, 1986).

———. *Traces*, translated by Anthony A. Nassar (1969; repr., Stanford, CA: Stanford University Press, 2006).

———. *The Utopian Function of Art and Literature: Selected Essays*, translated by Jack Zipes and Frank Mecklenburg (1988; repr., Cambridge, MA: MIT, 1996).

Blumenthal, Max. *The 51 Day War: Ruin and Resistance in Gaza* (New York: Nation, 2015).

Boer, Roland. *Political Myth: On the Use and Abuse of Biblical Themes* (Durham, NC: Duke University Press, 2009).

Bonnett, Alastair. "Situationist Strategies and Mutant Technologies." *Angelaki* 4.2 (1999): 25–32.

Bouzid, Nouri. "New Realism in Arab Cinema: The Defeat-Conscious Cinema." *Alif* 15 (1995): 242–250.

Bowman, Paul. "Rancière and the Disciplines: An Introduction to Rancière before Film Studies." In *Rancière and Film*, edited by Paul Bowman (Edinburgh: Edinburgh University Press, 2013), pp. 1–19.

Brady, Nicholas. "The Void Speaks Back: Black Suffering as the Unthought of the American Studies Association's Academic Boycott of Israel." *Out of Nowhere*, December 23, 2013. Available at outofnowhereblog.wordpress.com.

Bresheeth, Haim. "The Continuity of Trauma and Struggle: Recent Cinematic Representations of the Nakba." In *Nakba: Palestine, 1948, and the Claims of Memory*, edited by Ahmad H. Sa'di and Lila Abu-Lughod (New York: Columbia University Press, 2007), pp. 161–187.

———. "A Symphony of Absence: Borders and Liminality in Elia Suleiman's 'Chronicle of a Disappearance.'" *Framework* 43.2 (2002): 71–84.

Brooks, Xan. "We Have No Film Industry Because We Have No Country." *The Guardian*, April 12, 2006. Available at theguardian.com.

Brown, Hannah. "*In Between*: The Movie That Has Touched a Chord throughout the World and in Israel." *Jerusalem Post*, March 12, 2017. Available at jpost.com/.

Brown, Wendy. "Wounded Attachments." *Political Theory* 21.3 (1993): 390–410.

Browne, Simone. *Dark Matters: On the Surveillance of Blackness* (Durham, NC: Duke University Press, 2015).

Budeiri, Musa. *The Palestine Communist Party, 1919–1948: Arab and Jew in the Struggle for Internationalism* (1979; repr., Chicago: Haymarket, 2010).

Burris, Greg. "Birth of a (Zionist) Nation: Black Radicalism and the Future of Palestine." In *Futures of Black Radicalism*, edited by Gaye Theresa Johnson and Alex Lubin (New York: Verso, 2017), pp. 120–132.

———. "Prometheus in Chicago: The Chaining and Gagging of Bobby Seale and the 'Real-ization' of Resistance." *Cinema Journal* 54.4 (2015): 26–49.

Butler, Judith. *Bodies That Matter: On the Discursive Limits of Sex* (New York: Routledge, 1993).

———. *Parting Ways: Jewishness and the Critique of Zionism* (New York: Columbia University Press, 2012).

Carby, Hazel V. "'On the Threshold of Woman's Era': Lynching, Empire, and Sexuality in Black Feminist Theory." *Critical Inquiry* 12.1 (1985): 262–277.

Carmichael, Stokely [Kwame Ture]. *Stokely Speaks: From Black Power to Pan-Africanism*, edited by Ethel N. Minor (1971; repr., Chicago: Lawrence Hill, 2007).

Carson, Clayborne. *In Struggle: SNCC and the Black Awakening of the 1960s* (Cambridge, MA: Harvard University Press, 1981).

"Celebrity-Backed Cinema Jenin in Palestine Closes." *Al-Ahram Online*, December 4, 2016. Available at english.ahram.org.eg.

Césaire, Aimé. *Notebook of a Return to the Native Land*, edited and translated by Clayton Eshleman and Annette Smith (1947; repr., Middletown, CT: Wesleyan University Press, 2001).

Chambers, Samuel A. *The Lessons of Rancière* (New York: Oxford University Press, 2013).

———. "The Politics of the Police: From Neoliberalism to Anarchism, and Back to Democracy." In *Reading Rancière: Critical Dissensus*, edited by Paul Bowman and Richard Stamp (New York: Continuum, 2011), pp. 18–43.

Chatterjee, Partha. *Nationalist Thought and the Colonial World: A Derivative Discourse* (1986; repr., London: Zed, 1993).

Chetrit, Sami Shalom. "Mizrahi Politics in Israel: Between Integration and Alternative." *Journal of Palestine Studies* 29.4 (2000): 51–65.

Child, Ben. "First Film Produced by Hamas Screens in Gaza." *The Guardian*, August 5, 2009. Available at theguardian.com.

Chomsky, Noam. "On Israel-Palestine and BDS." *The Nation*, July 2, 2014. Available at thenation.com.

———. *Profit over People: Neoliberalism and the Global Order* (New York: Seven Stories, 1999).

Chow, Rey. "Where Have All the Natives Gone?" In *Displacements: Cultural Identities in Question*, edited by Angelika Bammer (Bloomington: Indiana University Press, 1994), pp. 125–151.

Ciccariello-Maher, George. *Decolonizing Dialectics* (Durham, NC: Duke University Press, 2017).

Classen, Steven D. *Watching Jim Crow: The Struggles over Mississippi TV, 1955–1969* (Durham, NC: Duke University Press, 2004).

Cleaver, Eldridge. *Soul on Fire* (Waco, TX: Word, 1978).

———. *Soul on Ice* (New York: Delta, 1968).

Cohen, Erik. "The Black Panthers and Israeli Society." In *Migration, Ethnicity and Community, Volume 1: Studies of Israeli Society*, edited by Ernest Krausz (New Brunswick, NJ: Transaction, 1980), pp. 147–163.

Cohen, Gili. "Palestinian Women, Children Stop IDF Soldier Detaining a Minor." *Ha'aretz*, August 28, 2015. Available at haaretz.com.

Cohen, Hillel. *Good Arabs: The Israeli Security Agencies and the Israeli Arabs, 1948–1967*, translated by Haim Watzman (2009; repr., Berkeley: University of California Press, 2010).

Colla, Elliot. "Sentimentality and Redemption: The Rhetoric of Egyptian Pop Culture Intifada Solidarity." In *Palestine, Israel, and the Politics of Popular Culture*, edited by Rebecca L. Stein and Ted Swedenburg (Durham, NC: Duke University Press, 2005), pp. 338–364.

Collins, John. *Global Palestine* (New York: Columbia University Press, 2011).

Collins, Patricia Hill. *Black Feminist Thought: Knowledge, Consciousness, and the Politics of Empowerment* (1990; repr., New York: Routledge, 1991).

Cone, James H. *Black Theology and Black Power* (New York: Seabury, 1969).

———. *A Black Theology of Liberation*, 2d ed. (1970; repr., Maryknoll, NY: Orbis, 1986).

———. *The Cross and the Lynching Tree* (Maryknoll, NY: Orbis, 2011).

Cook, Jonathan. "Internet Users Paid to Spread Israeli Propaganda." *Electronic Intifada*, July 21, 2009. Available at electronicintifada.net.

———. "'Visible Equality' as Confidence Trick." In *Israel and South Africa: The Many Faces of Apartheid*, edited by Ilan Pappé (London: Zed, 2015), pp. 123–159.

Copjec, Joan. *Imagine There's No Woman: Ethics and Sublimation* (Cambridge, MA: MIT Press, 2002).

———. *Read My Desire: Lacan against the Historicists* (Cambridge, MA: MIT Press, 1994).

Cripps, Thomas. *Slow Fade to Black: The Negro in American Film, 1900–1942* (New York: Oxford University Press, 1993).

Cruz, Jon. *Culture on the Margins: The Black Spiritual and the Rise of American Cultural Interpretation* (Princeton, NJ: Princeton University Press, 1999).

Dabashi, Hamid, ed. *Dreams of a Nation: On Palestinian Cinema* (New York: Verso, 2006).

———. "Getting Hollywood's Nod for Palestinian Film: What Will It Take for Hollywood to Recognize Palestinian Cinema?" Al Jazeera, November 1, 2014. Available at aljazeera.com

———. "Introduction." In *Dreams of a Nation: On Palestinian Cinema*, edited by Hamid Dabashi (New York: Verso, 2006), pp. 7–22.

Dabbagh, Selma. "Inventing Gaza." In *Gaza as Metaphor*, edited by Helga Tawil-Souri and Dina Matar (London: Hurst, 2016), pp. 127–133.

Davis, Angela Y. *Freedom Is a Constant Struggle: Ferguson, Palestine, and the Foundations of a Movement* (Chicago: Haymarket, 2016).

———. *Women, Race, and Class* (1981; repr., New York: Vintage, 1983).

Dawber, Alistair. "'Come Here, Obama, and Visit the Museum of Apartheid': Pro-Palestinian Protesters Clash with Army in West Bank as U.S. President Arrives in Tel Aviv." *Independent*, March 20, 2013. Available at independent.co.uk.

Dean, Jodi. "Politics without Politics." In *Reading Rancière: Critical Dissensus*, edited by Paul Bowman and Richard Stamp (New York: Continuum, 2011), pp. 73–94.

Deleuze, Gilles. "The Grandeur of Yasser Arafat," translated by Timothy S. Murphy. *Discourse* 20.3 (1998): 30–33.

Deleuze, Gilles, and Elias Sanbar. "The Indians of Palestine." *Discourse* 20.3 (1998): 25–29.

Diab, Khaled. "Arrests Greet Palestinian Freedom Riders." Salon.com, November 16, 2011. Available at salon.com.

Dickinson, Kay, *Arab Cinema Travels: Transnational Syria, Palestine, Dubai, and Beyond* (London: BFI Palgrave, 2016).

Doherty, Benjamin J., and Ali Abunimah. "Oscars' Double Standard Turns Palestinian

Film into Refugee." *Electronic Intifada*, December 10, 2002. Available at electronic intifada.net.

Dolar, Mladen. "Beyond Interpellation." *Qui Parle* 6.2 (1993): 75–96.

Douglass, Frederick. *Narrative of the Life of Frederick Douglass, an American Slave, Written by Himself* (1845; repr., New York: Signet, 2005).

Du Bois, W. E. B. *Black Reconstruction in America: 1860–1880* (1935; repr., New York: Touchstone, 1995).

———. "The Case for the Jews." *Chicago Star*, May 8, 1948.

———. *Darkwater: Voices from within the Veil* (1920; repr., New York: Schocken, 1969).

———. "Where Do We Go from Here? (1933): (A Lecture on Negroes' Economic Plight)." In *A. W. E. B. Du Bois Reader*, edited by Andrew Paschal (New York: Macmillan, 1971), pp. 146–162.

Duggan, Lisa. *The Twilight of Equality? Neoliberalism, Cultural Politics, and the Attack on Democracy* (Boston: Beacon, 2003).

Eagleton, Terry. "Utopia and Its Opposites." In *Necessary and Unnecessary Utopias*, edited by Leo Panitch and Colin Leys (New York: Monthly Review, 1999), pp. 31–40.

Edkins, Jenny. *Trauma and the Memory of Politics* (New York: Cambridge University Press, 2003).

Ehrenreich, Ben. *The Way to the Spring: Life and Death in Palestine* (New York: Penguin, 2016).

"Empty Book on Palestinian History Becomes Instant Best-Seller on Amazon." *Ha'aretz*, June 22, 2017. Available at haaretz.com.

Esteron, Yoel. "Who's in Favor of Annihilating Israel?" *Ha'aretz*, November 28, 2003. Available at haaretz.com.

"'The Ethnic Cleansing of Palestine Never Stopped'—Conversation with Annemarie Jacir." *Le Mur a des Oreilles*, December 12, 2013. Available at lemuradesoreilles.org.

Eyers, Tom. *Lacan and the Concept of the "Real"* (New York: Palgrave Macmillan, 2012).

Fabian, Johannes. *Time and the Other: How Anthropology Makes Its Object* (New York: Columbia University Press, 1983).

Fanon, Frantz. *Black Skins, White Masks*, translated by Richard Philcox (1952; repr., New York: Grove, 2008).

———. *The Wretched of the Earth*, translated by Richard Philcox (1961; repr., New York: Grove, 2004).

Faraci, Devin. "Escape from Gaza: How Palestinian Filmmakers Tarzan and Arab Made It to Austin." *Birth.Movies.Death*, October 21, 2011. Available at birthmoviesdeath .com.

Feldman, Keith P. "Representing Permanent War: Black Power's Palestine and the End(s) of Civil Rights." *CR: The New Centennial Review* 8.2 (2008): 193–231.

———. *A Shadow over Palestine: The Imperial Life of Race in America* (Minneapolis: University of Minnesota Press, 2015).

Fernandez, Belen. "Those Exotic Arabs, and Other Orientalist Fetishes." Al Jazeera, August 24, 2013. Available at aljazeera.com.

Filiu Jean-Pierre. "The Origins of Hamas: Militant Legacy or Israeli Tool?" *Journal of Palestine Studies* 41.3 (2012): 54–70.

Finkelstein, Norman G. "Disinformation and the Palestine Question: The Not-So-Strange Case of Joan Peters's *From Time Immemorial*." In *Blaming the Victims: Spurious*

Scholarship and the Palestinian Question, edited by Edward W. Said and Christopher Hitchens (1988; repr., New York: Verso, 2001), pp. 33–69.

Firestone, Shulamith. *The Dialectic of Sex: The Case for Feminist Revolution* (1970; repr., New York: Bantam, 1972).

"The First Lady of Arabic Hip Hop." *Mondomix*, May 10, 2010. Available at mondomix .com.

"Foreign Policy, Black America and the Andy Young Affair." *Ebony* 35.3 (January 1980): 116–118, 120, 122.

Foucault, Michel. *Discipline and Punish: The Birth of the Prison*, translated by Alan Sheridan (1975; repr., New York: Vintage, 1977).

———. *Foucault Live (Interviews, 1961–1984)*, edited by Sylvère Lotringer, translated by Lysa Hochroth and John Johnston (1989; repr., New York: Semiotext(e), 1996).

———. *The History of Sexuality, Volume 1: An Introduction*, translated by Robert Hurley (1976; repr., New York: Vintage, 1990).

———. *Power/Knowledge: Selected Interviews and Other Writings, 1972–1977*, edited by Colin Gordon, translated by Colin Gordon, Leo Marshall, John Mepham, and Kate Soper (New York: Pantheon, 1980).

Frankel, Oz. "The Black Panthers of Israel and the Politics of the Radical Analogy." In *Black Power beyond Borders: The Global Dimensions of the Black Power Movement*, edited by Nico Slate (New York: Palgrave Macmillan, 2012), pp. 81–106.

———. "What's in a Name? The Black Panthers in Israel." *The Sixties* 1.1 (2008): 9–26.

Freedland, Jonathan. "McCarthyism—Israeli Style." *Jewish Chronicle Online*, January 24, 2011. Available at thejc.com.

Freire, Paulo. *Pedagogy of the Oppressed*, translated by Myra Bergman Ramos (1970; repr., New York: Continuum, 2000).

Freud, Sigmund. *Moses and Monotheism*, translated by Katherine Jones (1939; repr., New York: Vintage, 1967).

Friedman, Thomas L. *From Beirut to Jerusalem*, updated ed. (1989; repr., New York: Anchor, 1995).

Ftouni, Layal. "Rethinking Gender Studies: Towards an Arab Feminist Epistemology." In *Arab Cultural Studies: Mapping the Field*, edited by Tarik Sabry (New York: I. B. Tauris, 2012), pp. 162–185.

Gana, Nouri. "Reel Violence: Paradise Now and the Collapse of the Spectacle." *Comparative Studies of South Asia, Africa and the Middle East* 28.1 (2008): 20–37.

Gellner, Ernest. *Nations and Nationalism* (Ithaca, NY: Cornell University Press, 1983).

Genet, Jean. *Prisoner of Love*, translated by Barbara Bray (1986; repr., London: Picador, 1990).

Genet, Jean, Layla Shahid Barrada, and Rudiger Wischenbart. "Jean Genet: Affirmation of Existence through Rebellion." *Journal of Palestine Studies* 16.2 (1987): 64–84.

Georgakas, Dan, and Barbara Saltz. "This Is a Film You Should See Twice: An Interview with Hany Abu-Assad." *Cinéaste* 31.1 (2005): 16–19.

Gertz, Nurith. "The Early Israeli Cinema as Silencer of Memory." *Shofar* 24.1 (2005): 67–80.

———. "The Stone at the Top of the Mountain: The Films of Rashid Masharawi." *Journal of Palestine Studies* 34.1 (2004): 23–36.

Gertz, Nurith, and George Khleifi. "From Bleeding Memories to Fertile Memories: Palestinian Cinema in the 1970s." *Third Text* 20.3–4 (2006): 465–474.

———. *Palestinian Cinema: Landscape, Trauma, and Memory* (2005; repr., Bloomington: Indiana University Press, 2008).

Gharib, Ali. "'Obama, Come Here to Hebron.'" *Daily Beast*, March 20, 2013. Available at thedailybeast.com.

Ghoul, Asmaa al-. "Film Festival Opens amid Gaza's Ruins." *Al-Monitor*, May 19, 2015. Available at al-monitor.com.

Ginsberg, Terri. "Review of *Palestinian Cinema: Landscape, Trauma, and Memory*." *Middle East Journal of Culture and Communication* 2.2 (2009): 315–321.

———. *Visualizing the Palestinian Struggle: Toward a Critical Analytic of Palestine Solidarity Films* (New York: Palgrave Macmillan, 2016).

Ginsberg, Terri, and Chris Lippard, eds. *Historical Dictionary of Middle Eastern Cinema* (Lanham, MD: Scarecrow, 2010).

Ginsburg, Mitch. "The Unorthodox Priest Who Stands with the Jews." *Times of Israel*, May 19, 2014. Available at timesofisrael.com.

"Golda Meir Scorns Soviets: Israeli Premier Explains Stand on Big-4 Talks, Security." *Washington Post*, June 16, 1969.

Goldberg, David Theo. "Racial Comparisons, Relational Racisms: Some Thoughts on Method." *Ethnic and Racial Studies* 32.7 (2009): 1271–1282.

———. "Racial Palestinianization." In *Thinking Palestine*, edited by Ronit Lentin (New York: Zed, 2008), pp. 25–45.

———. *The Threat of Race: Reflections on Racial Neoliberalism* (Malden, MA: Wiley-Blackwell, 2009).

Goldberg, Jeffrey. "Among the Settlers." *New Yorker*, May 31, 2004. Available at newyorker.com.

———. "'Look . . . It's My Name on This': Obama Defends the Iran Nuclear Deal." *The Atlantic*, May 21, 2015. Available at theatlantic.com.

Gordon, Avery F. *Ghostly Matters: Haunting and the Sociological Imagination* (1997; repr., Minneapolis: University of Minnesota Press, 2008).

———. *Keeping Good Time: Reflections on Knowledge, Power, and People* (Boulder, CO: Paradigm, 2004).

Gordon, Lewis R. "Through the Hellish Zone of Nonbeing: Thinking Through Fanon, Disaster, and the Damned of the Earth." *Human Architecture* 5 (2007): 5–11.

Gordon, Neve. *Israel's Occupation* (Berkeley: University of California Press, 2008).

Gramsci, Antonio. *Selections from the Prison Notebooks*, edited and translated by Quintin Hoare and Geoffrey Nowell Smith (1971; repr., New York: International, 2008).

Greenberg, Joel. "Palestinian 'Freedom Riders' Arrested on Bus to Jerusalem." *Washington Post*, November 15, 2011. Available at washingtonpost.com.

Greenstein, Ran. *Zionism and Its Discontents: A Century of Radical Dissent in Israel/Palestine* (London: Pluto, 2014).

Griffin, Hollis. "Lines in the Sand: Media Studies and the Neoliberal Academy." *Flow* 13.12 (2011). Available at flowtv.org.

Griffin, Maryam S. "Freedom Rides in Palestine: Racial Segregation and Grassroots Politics on the Bus." *Race and Class* 56.4 (2015): 73–84.

Grossberg, Lawrence. "On Postmodernism and Articulation: An Interview with Stuart Hall." *Journal of Communication Inquiry* 10.2 (1986): 45–60.

Guénoun, Solange, and James H. Kavanagh. "Jacques Rancière: Literature, Politics, Aesthetics: Approaches to Democratic Disagreement." *SubStance* 29.2 (2000): 3–24.

Haas, Jeffrey. *The Assassination of Fred Hampton: How the FBI and the Chicago Police Murdered a Black Panther* (Chicago: Lawrence Hill, 2010).

Hage, Ghassan. *Against Paranoid Nationalism: Searching for Hope in a Shrinking Society* (London: Merlin, 2003).

———. *Alter-Politics: Critical Anthropology and the Radical Imagination* (Melbourne: Melbourne University Press, 2015).

———. "'Comes a Time We Are All Enthusiasm': Understanding Palestinian Suicide Bombers in Times of Exighophobia." *Public Culture* 15.1 (2003): 65–89.

———. "What Is a Public Intervention? Speaking Truth to the Oppressed." In *If Truth Be Told: The Politics of Public Ethnography*, edited by Didier Fassin (Durham, NC: Duke University Press, 2017), pp. 47–68.

———. *White Nation: Fantasies of White Supremacy in a Multicultural Society* (New York: Routledge, 2000).

Hajjar, Lisa. "Toward a Sociology of Human Rights: Critical Globalization Studies, International Law, and the Future of War." In *Critical Globalization Studies*, edited by Richard P. Appelbaum and William I. Robinson (New York: Routledge, 2005), pp. 207–216.

Halevi, Ilan. *A History of the Jews: Ancient and Modern*, translated by A. M. Barrett (1981; repr., London: Zed, 1988).

———. "Zionism Today." *Arab Studies Quarterly* 7.2–3 (1985): 3–10.

Hall, Stuart. "'In but Not Of Europe': Europe and Its Myths." In *Figures d'Europe: Images and Myths of Europe*, edited by Luisa Passerini (New York: P. Lang, 2003), pp. 35–45.

———. "New Ethnicities (1988)." In *Writing Black Britain, 1948–1998: An Interdisciplinary Anthology*, edited by James Procter (New York: Manchester University Press, 2000), pp. 265–275.

———. "Old and New Identities." In *Culture, Globalization, and the World-System: Contemporary Conditions for the Representation of Identity*, edited by Anthony D. King (Minneapolis: University of Minnesota Press, 1997), pp. 41–68.

———. "The Problem of Ideology: Marxism without Guarantees." In *Stuart Hall: Critical Dialogues in Cultural Studies*, edited by David Morley and Kuan-Hsing Chen (New York: Routledge, 1996), pp. 25–46.

———. "Subjects in History: Making Diasporic Identities." In *The House That Race Built: Black Americans, U.S. Terrain*, edited by Wahneema Lubiano (New York: Pantheon, 1997), pp. 289–299.

Hallward, Maia Carter. "Negotiating Boundaries, Narrating Checkpoints: The Case of Machsom Watch." *Critique: Critical Middle Eastern Studies* 17.1 (2008): 21–40.

Hallward, Peter. "Staging Equality: Rancière's Theatrocracy." *New Left Review* 37 (2006): 109–129.

Halper, Jeff. *War against the People: Israel, the Palestinians and Global Pacification* (London: Pluto, 2015).

Hammad, Suheir. *Born Palestinian, Born Black* (1996; repr., New York: UpSet, 2010).

Hampton, Fred. "The People Have to Have the Power." In *Let Nobody Turn Us Around: Voices of Resistance, Reform, and Renewal: An African American Anthology*, edited by Manning Marable and Leith Mullings (Lanham, MD: Rowman and Littlefield, 2000), pp. 478–482.

Hanafi, Sari. "Palestinian Refugee Camps in the Palestinian Territory: Territory of Exception and Locus of Resistance." In *The Power of Inclusive Exclusion: Anatomy of Israeli Rule in the Occupied Palestinian Territories*, edited by Adi Ophir, Michal Givoni, and Sari Hanafi (New York: Zone, 2009), pp. 495–517.

———. "Spacio-cide: Colonial Politics, Invisibility, and Rezoning in Palestinian Territory." *Contemporary Arab Affairs* 2.1 (2009): 106–121.

Hanisch, Carol. "The Personal Is Political" In *Notes from the Second Year: Women's Liberation: Major Writings of the Radical Feminists*, edited by Shulie Firestone and Anne Koedt (New York: Radical Feminism, 1970), pp. 76–78.

Hansen, Miriam Bratu. "*Schindler's List* Is Not *Shoah*: The Second Commandment, Popular Modernism, and Public Memory." *Critical Inquiry* 22.2 (1996): 292–312.

Harkov, Lahav. "Culture, Economy Ministries Withdraw Israeli Funds from 'Palestinian' Film." *Jerusalem Post*, August 27, 2014. Available at jpost.com.

Harlow, Barbara. "Narrative in Prison: Stories from the Palestinian Intifada." *Modern Fiction Studies* 35.1 (1989): 29–46.

Harney, Stefano, and Fred Moten. *The Undercommons: Fugitive Planning and Black Study* (New York: Minor Compositions, 2013).

Harold, Christine, and Kevin Michael DeLuca. "Behold the Corpse: Violent Images and the Case of Emmett Till." *Rhetoric and Public Affairs* 8.2 (2005): 263–286.

Harris, Cheryl I. "Whiteness as Property." *Harvard Law Review* 106.8 (1993): 1707–1791.

Harvey, David. *A Brief History of Neoliberalism* (New York: Oxford University Press, 2005).

Hass, Amira. "The Shooting of a Legless Man." *Ha'aretz*, December 19, 2017. Available at haaretz.com.

Hebdige, Dick. *Hiding in the Light: On Images and Things* (New York: Routledge, 1988).

———. "Posing . . . Threats, Striking . . . Poses: Youth, Surveillance, and Display." *Sub-Stance* 11–12.37–38 (1982): 68–88.

Hertzberg, Arthur, ed. *The Zionist Idea: A Historical Analysis and Reader* (1959; repr., New York: Atheneum, 1984).

Herzl, Theodor. *The Complete Diaries of Theodor Herzl*, vol. 1, translated by Harry Zohn, edited by Raphael Patai (New York: Herzl Foundation, 1960).

———. *The Jewish State* (1946; repr., New York: American Zionist Emergency Council, 1986).

———. *Zionist Writings: Essays and Addresses, Volume 1: January 1896–June 1898*, translated by Harry Zohn (New York: Herzl, 1973).

Hirsch, Marianne. "Family Pictures: *Maus*, Mourning, and Post-Memory." *Discourse* 15.2 (1992): 3–29.

Hirst, David. *The Gun and the Olive Branch: The Roots of Violence in the Middle East*, 3d ed. (1977; repr., New York: Thunder's Mouth, 2003).

Hjort, Mette. "On the Plurality of Cinematic Transnationalism." In *World Cinemas, Transnational Perspectives*, edited by Nataša Ďurovičová and Kathleen Newman (New York: Routledge, 2010), pp. 12–33.

Hobsbawm, Eric J. *Nations and Nationalism since 1780: Programme, Myth, Reality*, 2d ed. (New York: Cambridge University Press, 1992).

Hochberg, Gil Z. *Visual Occupations: Violence and Visibility in a Conflict Zone* (Durham, NC: Duke University Press, 2015).

hooks, bell. *Feminism Is for Everybody: Passionate Politics* (Cambridge, MA: South End, 2000).

———. "Lorde: The Imagination of Justice." In *I Am Your Sister: Collected and Unpublished Writings of Audre Lorde*, edited by Rudolph P. Byrd, Johnnetta Betsch Cole, and Beverly Guy-Sheftall (New York: Oxford University Press, 2009), pp. 242–248.

Horkheimer, Max. "The Jews and Europe." In *Critical Theory and Society: A Reader*, edited by Stephen Eric-Bronner and Douglas MacKay Kellner (New York: Routledge, 1989), pp. 77–94.

Horowitz, Adam. "Six Palestinian Freedom Riders Arrested Traveling on Israeli-Only Bus." *Mondoweiss*, November 15, 2011. Available at mondoweiss.net.

Horton, Myles, with Judith Kohl and Herbert Kohn. *The Long Haul: An Autobiography* (New York: Doubleday, 1990).

Huntington, Samuel P. *American Politics: The Promise of Disharmony* (Cambridge, MA: Harvard University Press, 1981).

Inbar, Efraim, and Eitan Shamir. "Mowing the Grass in Gaza." *Jerusalem Post*, July 22, 2014. Available at jpost.com.

Indiana, Gary. "Minority Report." *Film Comment* 39.1 (2003): 28–31.

Iqbal, Nosheen. "How Sex, Drugs and Politics Earned *In Between*'s Director a Fatwa." *The Guardian*, September 28, 2017. Available at theguardian.com.

"Israel Agrees to PA Request to Reduce Gaza Electricity." Al Jazeera, June 13, 2017. Available at aljazeera.com.

Jacinto, Leela. "No Room for Palestinian Film at the Oscars." ABC News, December 20, 2002. Available at abcnews.go.com.

Jacir, Annemarie. "Coming Home: Palestinian Cinema." *Electronic Intifada*, February 27, 2007. Available at electronicintifada.net.

———. "'I Wanted That Story to Be Told' (Interview)." *Alif* 31 (2011): 241–254.

———. "(Re)searching When I Saw You (*Lamma Shoftak*)." *The River Has Two Banks*, n.d. Available at theriverhastwobanks.net.

Jackson, John L., Jr. *Thin Description: Ethnography and the African Hebrew Israelites of Jerusalem* (Cambridge, MA: Harvard University Press, 2013).

Jad, Islah. "The Demobilization of a Palestinian Women's Movement: From Empowered Active Militants to Powerless and Stateless 'Citizens.'" In *Women's Movements in the Global Era: The Power of Local Feminisms*, edited by Amrita Basu (Boulder, CO: Westview, 2010), pp. 343–375.

———. "Patterns of Relations within the Palestinian Family during the Intifada." In *Palestinian Women of Gaza and the West Bank*, translated by Magida Abu Hassabo, edited by Suha Sabbagh (Bloomington: Indiana University Press, 1998), pp. 53–62.

James, C. L. R. "Africans and Afro-Caribbeans: A Personal View (1984)." In *Writing Black Britain, 1948–1998: An Interdisciplinary Anthology*, edited by James Procter (New York: Manchester University Press, 2000), pp. 60–63.

———. *At the Rendezvous of Victory: Selected Writings* (London: Allison and Busby, 1984).

———. *The Black Jacobins: Toussaint L'Ouverture and the San Domingo Revolution*, 2d ed. (1938; repr., New York: Vintage, 1989).

———. *C. L. R. James and Revolutionary Marxism: Selected Writings of C. L. R. James, 1939–1949*, edited by Scott McLemee and Paul le Blanc (Atlantic Highlands, NJ: Humanities, 1994).

———. "Every Cook Can Govern." In *A New Notion: Two Works by C. L. R. James* (Oakland, CA: PM, 2010), pp. 129–155.

————. *The Future in the Present: Selected Writings* (Westport, CT: Lawrence Hill, 1977).

————. *A History of Pan-African Revolt* (1939; repr., Chicago: Charles H. Kerr, 2005).

————. *Spheres of Existence: Selected Writings* (Westport, CT: Lawrence Hill, 1980).

James, C. L. R., and Grace C. Lee, with Cornelius Castoriadis. *Facing Reality: The New Society: Where to Look for It and How to Bring It Closer* (1958; repr., Chicago: Charles H. Kerr, 2006).

James, Selma. *Sex, Race, and Class: The Perspective of Winning: A Selection of Writings, 1952–2011* (Oakland, CA: PM, 2012).

Jameson, Fredric. *The Political Unconscious: Narrative as a Socially Symbolic Act* (1981; repr., New York: Routledge, 2002).

Jawad, Saleh Abdel. "Zionist Massacres: The Creation of the Palestinian Refugee Problem in the 1948 War." In *Israel and the Palestinian Refugees*, edited by Eyal Benvenisti, Chaim Gans, and Sari Hanafi (New York: Springer, 2007), pp. 59–128.

Johnson, Gaye Theresa. *Spaces of Conflict, Sounds of Solidarity: Music, Race, and Spatial Entitlement in Los Angeles* (Berkeley: University of California Press, 2013).

Jones, Emma. "The Female Director Who Was Issued a Fatwa for Her First Film." BBC, September 3, 2017. Available at bbc.com.

Judt, Tony. "Israel: The Alternative." *New York Review of Books*, October 23, 2003. Available at nybooks.com.

Kafka, Franz. *The Castle*, translated by Anthea Bell (1926; repr., New York: Oxford University Press, 2009).

Kanafani, Ghassan. *Men in the Sun and Other Palestinian Stories*, translated by Hilary Kilpatrick (1978; repr., Boulder, CO: Lynne Rienner, 1997).

————. *Palestine's Children: Returning to Haifa and Other Stories*, translated by Barbara Harlow and Karen E. Riley (Boulder, CO: Lynne Rienner, 2000).

Kanazi, Remi. *Poetic Injustice: Writings on Resistance and Palestine* (New York: RoR, 2011).

Kane, Alex. "'A Level of Racist Violence I Have Never Seen': UCLA Professor Robin D. G. Kelley on Palestine and the BDS Movement." *Mondoweiss*, February 16, 2012. Available at mondoweiss.net.

Kaplan, E. Ann. *Trauma Culture: The Politics of Terror and Loss in Media and Literature* (New Brunswick, NJ: Rutgers University Press, 2005).

Katz, Yaakov. "Analysis: Easy to Start, Hard to End." *Jerusalem Post*, March 10, 2012. Available at jpost.com.

Keay, Douglas. "AIDS, Education and the Year 2000!" *Woman's Own*, October 31, 1987, pp. 8–10

Kelley, Robin D. G. "Another Freedom Summer." *Journal of Palestine Studies* 44.1 (2014): 29–41.

————. "Apartheid's Black Apologists." In *Apartheid Israel: The Politics of an Analogy*, edited by Jon Soske and Jean Jacobs (Chicago: Haymarket, 2015), pp. 125–141.

————. "Cedric J. Robinson: The Making of a Black Radical Intellectual." *CounterPunch*, June 17, 2016. Available at counterpunch.org.

————. *Freedom Dreams: The Black Radical Imagination* (Boston: Beacon, 2002).

————. "House Negroes on the Loose: Malcolm X and the Black Bourgeoisie." *Callaloo* 21.2 (1998): 419–435.

————. *Race Rebels: Culture, Politics, and the Black Working Class* (New York: Free Press, 1996).

———. *Yo' Mama's Disfunktional: Fighting the Cultural Wars in Urban America* (Boston: Beacon, 1997).

Kellner, Douglas. "Globalisation from Below? Toward a Radical Democratic Techno-politics." *Angelaki* 4.2 (1999): 101–113.

———. "September 11: Spectacles of Terror and Media Manipulation: A Critique of Ji-hadist and Bush Media Politics." *Logos* 2.1 (2003): 86–102.

Khader, Nehad. "Interview with Elia Suleiman: The Power of Ridicule." *Journal of Palestine Studies* 44.4 (2015): 21–31.

Khairy, Omar, el-. "Film Review: Palestine as Hollywood Fantasy in 'Miral.'" *Electronic Intifada*, November 23, 2010. Available at electronicintifada.net.

Khaled, Leila. *My People Shall Live: The Autobiography of a Revolutionary*, edited by George Hajjar (London: Hodder and Stoughton, 1973).

Khalek, Rania. "Israel-Trained Police 'Occupy' Missouri after Killing of Black Youth." *Electronic Intifada*, August 15, 2014. Available at electronicintifada.net.

Khalidi, Rashid. *Palestinian Identity: The Construction of Modern National Consciousness* (1997; repr., New York: Columbia University Press, 2010).

Khalifeh, Sahar. "Comments by Five Women Activists: Siham Abdullah, Amal Kharisha Barghouthi, Rita Giacaman, May Mistakmel Nassar, Amal Wahdan." In *Palestinian Women of Gaza and the West Bank*, translated by Nagla el-Bassiouni, edited by Suha Sabbagh (Bloomington: Indiana University Press, 1998), pp. 192–215.

Khalili, Laleh. "Virtual Nation: Palestinian Cyberculture in Lebanese Camps." In *Palestine, Israel, and the Politics of Popular Culture*, edited by Rebecca L. Stein and Ted Swedenburg (Durham, NC: Duke University Press, 2005), pp. 126–149.

Khoury, Elias. *Gate of the Sun*, translated by Humphrey Davies (1998; repr., New York: Archipelago, 2005).

———. "Remembering Ghassan Kanafani, or How a Nation Was Born of Story Telling." *Journal of Palestine Studies* 42.3 (2013): 85–91.

Kilpatrick, Hilary. "Introduction." In *Men in the Sun and Other Palestinian Stories*, by Ghassan Kanafani, translated by Hilary Kilpatrick (1978; repr., Boulder, CO: Lynne Rienner, 1997), pp. 1–7.

Kim, Kyung Hyun. *The Remasculinization of Korean Cinema* (Durham, NC: Duke University Press, 2004).

Kimmerling, Baruch. *Politicide: Ariel Sharon's War against the Palestinians* (New York: Verso, 2003).

———. *Zionism and Territory: The Socio-territorial Dimensions of Zionist Politics* (Berkeley: University of California Press, 1983).

Kimmerling, Baruch, and Joel S. Migdal. *The Palestinian People: A History* (1994; repr., Cambridge, MA: Harvard University Press, 2003).

Klein, Jeff. "A Visit to the Grave of Mass-Murderer Baruch Goldstein." *Mondoweiss*, July 4, 2013. Available at mondoweiss.net.

Krähenbühl, Pierre. "Gaza as Metaphor for Unsustainability." In *Gaza as Metaphor*, edited by Helga Tawil-Souri and Dina Matar (London: Hurst, 2016), pp. 53–59.

Kraidy, Marwan M. *Hybridity, or the Cultural Logic of Globalization* (Philadelphia: Temple University Press, 2005).

———. *The Naked Blogger of Cairo: Creative Insurgency in the Arab World* (Cambridge, MA: Harvard University Press, 2016).

Krupkin, Taly. "Rosario Dawson, Angela Davis among 27 U.S. Figures Calling for Release of Jailed Palestinian Teen Ahed Tamimi." *Ha'aretz*, February 12, 2018. Available at haaretz.com.

Kuntsman, Adi, and Rebecca L. Stein. *Digital Militarism: Israel's Occupation in the Social Media Age* (Stanford, CA: Stanford University Press, 2015).

Kuttab, Eileen S. "Palestinian Women in the Intifada: Fighting on Two Fronts." *Arab Studies Quarterly* 15.2 (1993): 69–85.

Lacan, Jacques. *The Seminar of Jacques Lacan, Book 20: Encore—On Feminine Sexuality, the Limits of Love and Knowledge*, edited by Jacques Alain-Miller, translated by Bruce Fink (1975; repr., New York: W. W. Norton, 1998).

Laclau, Ernesto, and Chantal Mouffe. *Hegemony and Socialist Strategy: Towards a Radical Democratic Politics* (New York: Verso, 1985).

Lazaroff, Tovah. "Six Activists Arrested after 'Freedom Ride.'" *Jerusalem Post*, November 15, 2011. Available at jpost.com.

Levy, Gideon. "The Israeli Military First Took His Legs, Then His Life." *Ha'aretz*, December 19, 2017. Available at haaretz.com.

Lewis, Tyson E. *The Aesthetics of Education: Theatre, Curiosity, and Politics in the Work of Jacques Rancière and Paulo Freire* (New York: Continuum, 2012).

Linor, Irit. "Anti-Semitism Now." *Ynet*, February 7, 2006. Available at ynetnews.com.

Lipsitz, George. "Breaking the Chains and Steering the Ship: How Activism Can Help Change Teaching and Scholarship." In *Engaging Contradictions: Theory, Politics, and Methods of Activist Scholarship*, edited by Charles R. Hale (Berkeley: University of California Press, 2008), pp. 88–111.

———. *The Possessive Investment in Whiteness: How White People Profit from Identity Politics*, 2d ed. (1998; repr., Philadelphia: Temple University Press, 2006).

———. *Time Passages: Collective Memory and American Popular Culture* (Minneapolis: University of Minnesota Press, 1990).

———. "What Is This Black in the Black Radical Tradition?" In *Futures of Black Radicalism*, edited by Gaye Theresa Johnson and Alex Lubin (New York: Verso, 2017), pp. 108–119.

Lorde, Audre. *Sister Outsider: Essays and Speeches* (1984; repr., Berkeley, CA: Crossing, 2007).

Love, David A. "Ahed Tamimi Is the Palestinian Rosa Parks." Al Jazeera, January 15, 2018. Available at aljazeera.com.

Lowe, Lisa. *Immigrant Acts: On Asian American Cultural Politics* (Durham, NC: Duke University Press, 1996).

Löwy, Michael. *Redemption and Utopia: Jewish Libertarian Thought in Central Europe: A Study in Elective Affinity*, translated by Hope Heaney (1988; repr., Stanford, CA: Stanford University Press, 1992).

Lubin, Alex. "Breaking 'America's Last Taboo.'" *Middle East Research and Information Project* (November 27, 2013).

———. *Geographies of Liberation: The Making of an Afro-Arab Political Imaginary* (Chapel Hill: University of North Carolina Press, 2014).

———. "Locating Palestine in Pre-1948 Black Internationalism." *Souls* 9.2 (2007): 95–108.

———. "'We Are All Israelis': The Politics of Colonial Comparisons." *South Atlantic Quarterly* 107.4 (2008): 671–690.

———. "Why I'm Voting to Boycott Israel." *The Nation*, December 13, 2013. Available at thenation.com.

Lustick, Ian S. *For the Land and the Lord: Jewish Fundamentalism in Israel* (New York: Council on Foreign Relations, 1988).

———. "Making Sense of the Nakba." *Journal of Palestine Studies* 44.2 (2015): 7–27.

Lyon, David. *The Electronic Eye: The Rise of Surveillance Society* (Minneapolis: University of Minnesota Press, 1994).

Maarten, Simons, and Jan Masschelein. "Governmental, Political and Pedagogic Subjectivation: Foucault with Rancière." *Educational Philosophy and Theory* 42.5–6 (2010): 588–600.

Madmoni-Gerber, Shoshana. *Israeli Media and the Framing of Internal Conflict: The Yemenite Babies Affair* (New York: Palgrave Macmillan, 2009).

Maira, Sunaina. *Jil Oslo: Palestinian Hip Hop, Youth Culture, and the Youth Movement* (Washington, DC: Tadween, 2013).

———. "'We Ain't Missing': Palestinian Hip Hop—a Transnational Youth Movement." *CR: The New Centennial Review* 8.2 (2008): 161–192.

Maira, Sunaina, and Magid Shihade. "Hip Hop from '48 Palestine Youth, Music, and the Present/Absent." *Social Text* 30.3 (2012): 1–26.

Makdisi, Saree. *Palestine Inside Out: An Everyday Occupation* (2008; repr., New York: W. W. Norton, 2010).

Malabou, Catherine. *The Future of Hegel: Plasticity, Temporality and Dialectic*, translated by Lisabeth During (1996; repr., New York: Routledge, 2005).

———. *The New Wounded: From Neurosis to Brain Damage*, translated by Steven Miller (2007; repr., New York: Fordham University Press, 2012).

———. *Ontology of the Accident: An Essay on Destructive Plasticity*, translated by Carolyn Shread (2009; repr., Malden, MA: Polity, 2012).

———. *Plasticity at the Dusk of Writing: Dialectic, Destruction, Deconstruction*, translated by Carolyn Shread (2005; repr., New York: Columbia University Press, 2010).

———. *What Should We Do with Our Brain?* translated by Sebastian Rand (2004; repr., New York: Fordham University Press, 2008).

Malas, Mohammad. *The Dream: A Diary of the Film*, translated by Samirah Alkassim (1991; repr., Cairo: American University of Cairo Press, 2016).

Malcolm X. *Malcolm X Speaks: Selected Speeches and Statements*, edited by George Breitman (1965; repr., New York: Grove, 1990).

Mamdani, Mahmood. *Good Muslim, Bad Muslim: America, the Cold War, and the Roots of Terror* (New York: Doubleday, 2004).

———. "Good Muslim, Bad Muslim: Post-apartheid Perspectives on America and Israel." *PoLAR: Political and Legal Anthropology Review* 27.1 (2004): 1–15.

———. "A Rejoinder to Critics." *PoLAR: Political and Legal Anthropology Review* 27.1 (2004): 20–23.

Marable, Manning. *How Capitalism Underdeveloped Black America: Problems in Race, Political Economy, and Society*, updated ed. (1983; repr., Cambridge, MA: South End, 2000).

Marchart, Oliver. "The Second Return of the Political: Democracy and the Syllogism of Equality." In *Reading Rancière: Critical Dissensus*, edited by Paul Bowman and Richard Stamp (New York: Continuum, 2011), pp. 129–147.

Marcuse, Herbert. *The Aesthetic Dimension: Toward a Critique of Marxist Aesthetics*, translated by Herbert Marcuse and Erica Sherover (1977; repr., Boston: Beacon, 1978).

——. *Counterrevolution and Revolt* (Boston: Beacon, 1972).

——. *An Essay on Liberation* (Boston: Beacon, 1969).

——. *One-Dimensional Man: Studies in the Ideology of Advanced Industrial Society* (1964; repr., New York: Routledge, 2002).

——. "Repressive Tolerance." In *A Critique of Pure Tolerance*, by Robert Paul Wolff, Barrington Moore Jr., and Herbert Marcuse (1965; repr., Boston: Beacon, 1969), pp. 81–123.

——. *Soviet Marxism: A Critical Analysis* (1958; repr., New York: Vintage, 1961).

Marks, Laura U. *Hanan al-Cinema: Affections for the Moving Image* (Cambridge, MA: MIT Press, 2015).

Marx, Karl. "Alienation and Social Classes." In *The Marx-Engels Reader*, 2d ed., edited by Robert C. Tucker (1972; repr., New York: W. W. Norton, 1978), pp. 133–135.

——. *Capital: A Critique of Political Economy*, vol. 1, translated by Ben Fowkes (1867; repr., New York: Penguin, 1990).

Marx, Karl, and Friedrich Engels. *The Communist Manifesto*, translated by Samuel Moore (1848; repr., New York: Penguin, 1985).

Masalha, Nur. *Expulsion of the Palestinians: The Concept of "Transfer" in Zionist Political Thought, 1882–1948* (Washington DC: Institute for Palestine Studies, 1992).

——. *The Palestine Nakba: Decolonising History, Narrating the Subaltern, Reclaiming Memory* (New York: Zed, 2012).

Massad, Joseph A. *The Persistence of the Palestinian Question: Essays on Zionism and the Palestinians* (New York: Routledge, 2006).

——. "The Weapon of Culture: Cinema in the Palestinian Liberation Struggle." In *Dreams of a Nation: On Palestinian Cinema*, edited by Hamid Dabashi (New York: Verso, 2006), pp. 30–42.

Matar, Haggai. "Israeli Army Installs New, Remote-Controlled Weapon atop Separation Wall." *+972 Magazine*, April 19, 2014. Available at 972mag.com.

Mattelart, Armand. *The Globalization of Surveillance: The Origin of the Securitarian Order*, translated by Susan Gruenheck Taponier and James A. Cohen (Malden, MA: Polity, 2010).

May, Todd. "Anarchism from Foucault to Rancière." In *Contemporary Anarchist Studies: An Introductory Anthology of Anarchy in the Academy*, edited by Randall Amster, Abraham DeLeon, Luis A. Fernandez, Anthony J. Nocella II, and Deric Shannon (New York: Routledge, 2009), pp. 11–17.

——. *Contemporary Political Movements and the Thought of Jacques Rancière: Equality in Action* (Edinburgh: Edinburgh University Press, 2010).

Mbembe, Achille. *Critique of Black Reason*, translated by Laurent Dubois (2013; repr., Durham, NC: Duke University Press, 2017).

McAlister, Melani. *Epic Encounters: Culture, Media, and U.S. Interests in the Middle East since 1945*, updated ed. (2001; repr., Berkeley: University of California Press, 2005).

——. "Prophecy, Politics, and the Popular: The *Left Behind* Series and Christian Evangelicalism's New World Order." In *Palestine, Israel, and the Politics of Popular Culture*, edited by Rebecca L. Stein and Ted Swedenburg (Durham, NC: Duke University Press, 2005), pp. 288–312.

McCarthy, Conor. "The State, the Text and the Critic in a Globalized World: The Case of Edward Said." In *Thinking Palestine*, edited by Ronit Lentin (New York: Zed, 2008), pp. 221–235.

McDonald, David A. *My Voice Is My Weapon: Music, Nationalism, and the Poetics of Palestinian Resistance* (Durham, NC: Duke University Press, 2013).

McGowan, Todd. *Enjoying What We Don't Have: The Political Project of Psychoanalysis* (Lincoln: University of Nebraska Press, 2013).

———. "Hegel as Marxist: Žižek's Revision of German Idealism." In *Žižek Now: Current Perspectives in Žižek Studies*, edited by Jamil Khader and Molly Anne Rothenberg (Malden, MA: Polity, 2013), pp. 31–53.

———. *The Real Gaze: Film Theory after Lacan* (New York: State University of New York Press, 2007).

McGreal, Chris. "Bomb Victims' Parents Petition Academy to Reject Movie." *The Guardian*, March 1, 2006. Available at theguardian.com.

McLuhan, Marshall. *The Gutenberg Galaxy: The Making of Typographic Man* (London: Routledge, 1962).

Mellen, Joan. "Film and Style: The Fictional Documentary." *Antioch Review* 32.3 (1972): 403–425.

Mendel, Yonatan. "The Politics of Non-translation: On Israeli Translations of Intifada, Shahid, Hudna and Islamic Movements." *Cambridge Literary Review* 1.3 (2010): 179–206.

"The MESA Debate: The Scholars, the Media, and the Middle East." *Journal of Palestine Studies* 16.2 (1987): 85–104.

Miller, Jake C. "Black Viewpoints on the Mid-East Conflict." *Journal of Palestine Studies* 10.2 (1981): 37–49.

Mirzoeff, Nicholas. *The Appearance of Black Lives Matter* (Miami: [NAME], 2017).

———. *The Right to Look: A Counterhistory of Visuality* (Durham, NC: Duke University Press, 2011).

Mohanty, Chandra Talpade. *Feminism without Borders: Decolonizing Theory, Practicing Solidarity* (Durham, NC: Duke University Press, 2003).

Monahan, Torin. *Surveillance in the Time of Insecurity* (New Brunswick, NJ: Rutgers University Press, 2010).

Monterescu, Daniel. "The Palestinian Trail of Fish: Artist's Graffiti Dives into Heart of Refugee Struggle." *Ha'aretz*, November 30, 2017. Available at haaretz.com.

Morag, Raya. "The Living Body and the Corpse—Israeli Documentary Cinema and the Intifadah." *Journal of Film and Video* 60.3–4 (2008): 3–24.

———. *Waltzing with Bashir: Perpetrator Trauma and Cinema* (New York: I. B. Tauris, 2013).

"More than Half of NFL Players Booked for Israel PR Trip Withdraw." *The Guardian*, February 15, 2017. Available at theguardian.com.

Morris, Benny. *The Birth of the Palestinian Refugee Problem, 1947–1949* (New York: Cambridge University Press, 1987).

———. *1948 and After: Israel and the Palestinians*, rev. ed. (1990; repr., New York: Oxford University Press, 1994).

———. "On Ethnic Cleansing: Introduction and Interview by Ari Shavit." *New Left Review* 26 (2004): 35–51.

Morse, Chuck. "Capitalism, Marxism, and the Black Radical Tradition: An Interview with Cedric Robinson." *Perspectives on Anarchist Theory* 3.1 (1999): 1, 6–8.

Moten, Fred. "Blackness and Nothingness (Mysticism in the Flesh)." *South Atlantic Quarterly* 112.4 (2013): 739–740.

Moylan, Tom. *Demand the Impossible: Science Fiction and the Utopian Imagination*, edited by Raffaella Baccolini (1986; repr., Bern, Germany: Peter Lang, 2014).

Mullenneaux, Lisa. "A Bitter Sea." *Z Magazine* 23.11 (2010). Available at zcomm.org.

Muñoz, José Esteban. *Cruising Utopia: The Then and There of Queer Futurity* (New York: New York University Press, 2009).

Murphy, Maureen Clare. "Prominent Palestinian Activist Killed in Israeli Raid." *Electronic Intifada*, March 6, 2017. Available at electronicintifada.net.

"'My Dream Is to Return'—Conversation with Saleh Bakri." *Le Mur a des Oreilles*, October 21, 2013. Available at lemuradesoreilles.org.

Naaman, Dorit. "Orientalism as Alterity in Israeli Cinema." *Cinema Journal* 40.4 (2001): 36–54.

———. "The Silenced Outcry: A Feminist Perspective from the Israeli Checkpoints in Palestine." *NWSA Journal* 18.3 (2006): 168–180.

Nader, Nadine Suleiman. "Imperial Whiteness and the Diasporas of Empire." *American Quarterly* 66.4 (2014): 1107–1115.

Naficy, Hamid. *An Accented Cinema: Exilic and Diasporic Filmmaking* (Princeton, NJ: Princeton University Press, 2001).

Nesher, Talila. "Israel Admits Ethiopian Women Were Given Birth Control Shots." *Ha'aretz*, January 27, 2013. Available at haaretz.com.

Neslen, Arthur. *Occupied Minds: A Journey through the Israeli Psyche* (Ann Arbor, MI: Pluto, 2006).

Newby, Anna. "Oscar Night for Palestine." *Slate*, March 3, 2014. Available at slate.com.

Newton, Huey P. *To Die for the People: The Writings of Huey P. Newton*, edited by Toni Morrison (1972; repr., San Francisco: City Lights, 2009).

Newton, Huey P., with J. Herman Blake. *Revolutionary Suicide* (1973; repr., Penguin: New York, 2009).

"New Trouble for Paradise Now." Al Jazeera, February 12, 2006. Available at aljazeera.com.

Norton, Ben. "'Baltimore Is Here': Ethiopian Israelis Protest Police Brutality in Jerusalem." *Mondoweiss*, May 1, 2015. Available at mondoweiss.net.

Orwell, George. *Nineteen Eighty-Four* (1949; repr., New York: Plum, 2003).

Osuna, Steven. "Class Suicide: The Black Radical Tradition, Radical Scholarship, and the Neoliberal Turn." In *Futures of Black Radicalism*, edited by Gaye Theresa Johnson and Alex Lubin (New York: Verso, 2017), pp. 21–38.

Paganelli, Linda. "Painting in a Refugee Camp, Dreaming of the Sea." *Electronic Intifada*, June 13, 2016. Available at electronicintifada.net.

"Palestine Unbound." *Journal of Palestine Studies* 44.2 (2015): 108–115.

Pappé, Ilan. *The Ethnic Cleansing of Palestine* (Oxford: Oneworld, 2006).

———. *The Idea of Israel: A History of Power and Knowledge* (New York: Verso, 2014).

Parsons, Nigel. "The Palestinian Authority Security Apparatus: Biopolitics, Surveillance, and Resistance in the Occupied Palestinian Territories." In *Surveillance and Control in Israel/Palestine: Population, Territory, and Power*, edited by Elia Zureik, David Lyon, and Yasmeen Abu-Laban (New York: Routledge, 2011), pp. 355–370.

Patai, Raphael. *The Arab Mind*, rev. ed. (1973; repr., New York: Charles Scribner's Sons, 1983).

Patterson, Orlando. *Slavery and Social Death: A Comparative Study* (Cambridge, MA: Harvard University Press, 1982).

Payton, Matt. "Israeli MP Claims the Palestine Nation Cannot Exist 'Because They Can't Pronounce the Letter P.'" *Independent*, February 11, 2016. Available at independent. co.uk.

Peteet, Julie M. "Icons and Militants: Mothering in the Danger Zone." *Signs* 23.1 (1997): 103–129.

———. "Male Gender and the Rituals of Resistance in the Palestinian Intifada: A Cultural Politics of Violence." *American Ethnologist* 21.1 (1994): 31–49.

———. "Stealing Time." *Middle East Research and Information Project* 248 (2008): 14–15.

———. "Transforming Trust: Dispossession and Empowerment among Palestinian Refugees." In *Mistrusting Refugees*, edited by E. Valentine Daneil and John Chr. Knudsen (Berkeley: University of California Press, 1995), pp. 168–186.

———. "The Work of Comparison: Israel/Palestine and Apartheid." *Anthropological Quarterly* 89.1 (2016): 247–282.

Peters, Joan. *From Time Immemorial: The Origins of the Arab-Jewish Conflict over Palestine* (New York: Harper and Row, 1984).

Piterberg, Gabriel. "Erasures." *New Left Review* 10 (2001): 31–46.

———. *The Returns of Zionism: Myths, Politics and Scholarship in Israel* (New York: Verso, 2008).

Porton, Richard, and Ella Shochat. "The Trouble with Hanna." *Film Quarterly* 38.2 (1984–1985): 50–55.

Rabinowitz, Dan. "Oriental Othering and National Identity: A Review of Early Israeli Anthropological Studies of Palestinians." *Global Studies in Culture and Power* 9 (2002): 305–324.

Raghavan, Sudarsan, William Booth, and Ruth Eglas. "U.N. Says Israel Violated International Law, after Shells Hit School in Gaza." *Washington Post*, July 30, 2014. Available at washingtonpost.com.

Rancière, Jacques. *The Aesthetic Unconscious*, translated by Debra Keates and James Swenson (2001; repr., Malden, MA: Polity, 2009).

———. *Althusser's Lesson*, translated by Emiliano Battista (1974; repr., New York: Continuum, 2011).

———. *Chronicles of Consensual Times*, translated by Steven Corcoran (2005; repr., New York: Continuum, 2010).

———. *Disagreement: Politics and Philosophy*, translated by Julie Rose (1995; repr., Minneapolis: University of Minnesota Press, 1999).

———. *Dissensus: On Politics and Aesthetics*, edited and translated by Steven Corcoran (New York: Continuum, 2010).

———. *The Emancipated Spectator*, translated by Gregory Elliott (2008; repr., New York: Verso, 2009).

———. *Figures of History*, translated by Julie Rose (2012; repr., Malden, MA: Polity, 2014).

———. *Hatred of Democracy*, translated by Steve Corcoran (2005; repr., New York: Verso, 2009), p. 48.

———. *The Ignorant Schoolmaster: Five Lessons in Intellectual Emancipation*, translated by Kristin Ross (1987; repr., Stanford, CA: Stanford University Press, 1991).

———. *Moments Politiques: Interventions 1977–2009*, translated by Mary Foster (2009; repr., New York: Seven Stories, 2014).

———. *On the Shores of Politics*, translated by Liz Heron (1992; repr., New York: Verso, 2007).

———. *The Philosopher and His Poor*, edited by Andrew Parker, translated by John Drury, Corinne Oster, and Andrew Parker (1983; repr., Durham, NC: Duke University Press, 2004).

———. "A Politics of Aesthetic Indetermination: An Interview with Frank Ruda and Jan Voelker." In *Everything Is in Everything: Jacques Rancière between Intellectual Emancipation and Aesthetic Education*, edited by Jason E. Smith and Annette Weisser (New York: Art Center Graduate, 2011), pp. 10–33.

———. *Proletarian Nights: The Workers' Dream in Nineteenth-Century France*, translated by John Drury (1981; repr., New York: Verso, 2012).

Rasberry, Vaughn. *Race and the Totalitarian Century: Geopolitics in the Black Literary Imagination* (Cambridge, MA: Harvard University Press, 2016).

Rastegar, Kamran. *Surviving Images: Cinema, War, and Cultural Memory in the Middle East* (New York: Oxford University Press, 2015).

Ravid, Barak. "Netanyahu on UN Settlement Vote: Israel Will Not Turn the Other Cheek." *Ha'aretz*, December 26, 2016. Available at haaretz.com.

———. "Prime Minister's Office Recruiting Students to Wage Online Hasbara Battles." *Ha'aretz*, August 13, 2013. Available at haaretz.com.

Renov, Michael. *The Subject of Documentary* (Minneapolis: University of Minnesota Press, 2004).

Robinson, Cedric J. *An Anthropology of Marxism* (Burlington, VT: Ashgate, 2001).

———. "The Appropriation of Frantz Fanon." *Race and Class* 35.1 (1993): 79–90.

———. *Black Marxism: The Making of the Black Radical Tradition* (1983; repr., Chapel Hill: University of North Carolina Press, 2000).

———. *Black Movements in America* (New York: Routledge, 1997).

———. *Forgeries of Memory and Meaning: Blacks and the Regimes of Race in American Theater and Film before World War II* (Chapel Hill: University of North Carolina Press, 2007).

———. "In the Year 1915: D. W. Griffith and the Whitening of America." *Social Identities* 3.2 (1997): 161–192.

———. "Manichaeism and Multiculturalism." In *Mapping Multiculturalism*, edited by Avery F. Gordon and Christopher Newfield (Minneapolis: University of Minnesota Press, 1996), pp. 116–124.

———. *The Terms of Order: Political Science and the Myth of Leadership* (1980; repr., Chapel Hill: University of North Carolina Press, 2016).

Robinson, Shira. *Citizen Strangers: Palestinians and the Birth of Israel's Liberal Settler State* (Stanford, CA: Stanford University Press, 2013).

Roby, Bryan K. *The Mizrahi Era of Rebellion: Israel's Forgotten Civil Rights Struggle, 1948–1966* (Syracuse, NY: Syracuse University Press, 2015).

Rodinson, Maxime. *Israel: A Colonial-Settler State?*, translated by David Thorstad (New York: Pathfinder, 1973).

Roediger, David R. *Class, Race, and Marxism* (New York: Verso, 2017).

Rogin, Michael. *Blackface, White Noise: Jewish Immigrants in the Hollywood Melting Pot* (1996; repr., Berkeley: University of California Press, 1998).

———. "'The Sword Became a Flashing Vision': D. W. Griffith's *The Birth of a Nation*." *Representations* 9 (1985): 150–195.

Rose, Jacqueline. *The Last Resistance* (New York: Verso, 2007).

——. "Response to Edward Said." In *Freud and the Non-European*, by Edward W. Said (New York: Verso, 2003), pp. 63–79.

Rosenfeld, Jesse. "The Palestinian Authority Is Using a New Cybercrimes Law to Crack Down on Dissent." *Intercept*, December 18, 2017. Available at theintercept.com.

Ross, Kristin. *May '68 and Its Afterlives* (Chicago: University of Chicago Press, 2002).

"Roundtable on Anti-Blackness and Black-Palestinian Solidarity." *Jadaliyya*, June 3, 2015. Available at jadaliyya.com.

Rustin, Bayard. "Do Blacks Have Anything to Gain from Ties to PLO?" *Chicago Tribune*, October 14, 1979, pp. A1–2.

Sabada, Lesya Michalina. "Religious Peacebuilding: The Life and Work of Archbishop Raya as a Model for Religious Peacebuilding" (Ph.D. diss., Saint Paul University, Faculty of Theology, Ottawa, 2017).

Said, Edward W. *After the Last Sky: Palestinian Lives* (New York: Pantheon, 1986).

——. "Arabs and Jews." *Journal of Palestine Studies* 3.2 (1974): 3–14.

——. "Between Worlds." *London Review of Books* 20.9 (1998): 3–7.

——. "The Challenge of Palestine." *Journal of Refugee Studies* 2.1 (1989): 170–178.

——. *Covering Islam: How the Media and the Experts Determine How We See the Rest of the World*, rev. ed. (1981; repr., New York: Vintage, 1997).

——. *Culture and Imperialism* (1993; repr., New York: Vintage, 1994).

——. *Freud and the Non-European* (New York: Verso, 2003).

——. "The Future of Palestine: A Palestinian Perspective." In *The Arab World: From Nationalism to Revolution*, edited by Abdeen Jabara and Janice Terry (Wilmette, IL: Medina University Press, 1971), pp. 192–200.

——. "*Hanna K.*: Palestine with a Human Face." *Village Voice*, October 11, 1983.

——. *Orientalism* (1978; repr., New York: Vintage, 2003).

——. *The Palestinian Question and the American Context* (Beirut: Institute for Palestine Studies, 1979).

——. *Peace and Its Discontents: Essays on Palestine in the Middle East Peace Process* (New York: Vintage, 1996).

——. *The Politics of Dispossession: The Struggle for Palestinian Self-Determination, 1969–1994* (1994; repr., New York: Vintage, 1995).

——. *Power, Politics, and Culture: Interviews with Edward W. Said*, edited by Gauri Viswanathan (New York: Pantheon, 2001).

——. "Preface." In *Dreams of a Nation: On Palestinian Cinema*, edited by Hamid Dabashi (New York: Verso, 2006), pp. 1–5.

——. *The Question of Palestine* (1979; repr., New York: Vintage, 1980).

——. *Reflections on Exile and Other Essays* (Cambridge, MA: Harvard University Press, 2000).

——. *Representations of the Intellectual: The 1993 Reith Lectures* (1994; repr., New York: Vintage, 1996).

——. *The World, the Text, and the Critic* (Cambridge, MA: Harvard University Press, 1983).

Salaita, Steven. *The Holy Land in Transit: Colonialism and the Quest for Canaan* (Syracuse, NY: Syracuse University Press, 2006).

——. *Inter/Nationalism: Decolonizing Native America and Palestine* (Minneapolis: University of Minnesota Press, 2016).

——. *Uncivil Rites: Palestine and the Limits of Academic Freedom* (Chicago: Haymarket, 2015).

Salamy, Suzy. "Palestine Is Still Waiting." *Warscapes*, September 6, 2012. Available at warscapes.com.

Sanbar, Elias. "Out of Place, Out of Time," translated by Ruth Morris. *Mediterranean Historical Review* 16.1 (2001): 87–94.

Sand, Shlomo. *How I Stopped Being a Jew*, translated by David Fernbach (2004; repr., New York: Verso, 2013).

———. *The Invention of the Jewish People*, translated by Yael Lotan (2008; repr., New York: Verso, 2009).

Sarkar, Bhaskar. "Beyond Partition: The Political Horizons of Contemporary Indian and Korean War Films." *Journal of the Moving Image* 7 (2008). Available at jmionline.org.

———. *Mourning the Nation: Indian Cinema in the Wake of Partition* (Durham, NC: Duke University Press, 2009).

Sartre, Jean-Paul. *Anti-Semite and Jew: An Exploration of the Etiology of Hate*, translated by George J. Becker (1948; repr., New York: Schocken, 1995).

Sayigh, Rosemary. "On the Exclusion of the Palestinian Nakba from the 'Trauma Genre.'" *Journal of Palestine Studies* 43.1 (2013): 51–60.

———. *The Palestinians: From Peasants to Revolutionaries* (1979; repr., New York: Zed, 2007).

Sayyid, S. *A Fundamental Fear: Eurocentrism and the Emergence of Islamism* (1997; repr., London: Zed, 2015).

Schechla, Joseph. "The Invisible People Come to Light: Israel's 'Internally Displaced' and the 'Unrecognized Villages.'" *Journal of Palestine Studies* 31.1 (2001): 20–31.

Schmemann, Serge. "Palestinian Security Agents Ban Books by a Critic of Arafat." *New York Times Books*, August 25, 1996. Available at nytimes.com.

Seikaly, Sherene. "Gaza as Archive." In *Gaza as Metaphor*, edited by Helga Tawil-Souri and Dina Matar (London: Hurst, 2016), pp. 225–231.

Sellick, Patricia. "The Old City of Hebron: Can It Be Saved?" *Journal of Palestine Studies* 23.4 (1994): 69–82.

Sengoopta, Chandak. *Imprint of the Raj: How Fingerprinting Was Born in Colonial India* (London: Macmillan, 2003).

Shachtman, Noah. "Robo-Snipers, 'Auto Kill Zones' to Protect Israeli Borders." *Wired*, June 4, 2007. Available at wired.com.

Shaheen, Jack G. *Guilty: Hollywood's Verdict on Arabs after 9/11* (Northampton, MA: Olive Branch, 2008).

———. *Reel Bad Arabs: How Hollywood Vilifies a People* (New York: Olive Branch, 2001).

Shakry, Omnia El. *The Arabic Freud: Psychoanalysis and Islam in Modern Egypt* (Princeton, NJ: Princeton University Press, 2017).

Shakur, Assata. *Assata: An Autobiography* (Westport, CT: Lawrence Hill, 1987).

Shalhoub-Kevorkian, Nadera. "Indigenizing Feminist Knowledge: Palestinian Feminist Thought between the Physics of International Power and the Theology of Racist 'Security.'" In *Arab Feminisms: Gender and Equality in the Middle East*, edited by Jean Said Makdisi, Noha Bayoumi, and Rafif Rida Sidawi (London: I. B. Tauris, 2014), pp. 205–216.

———. "Reexamining Femicide: Breaking the Silence and Crossing 'Scientific' Borders." *Signs* 28.2 (2003): 581–608.

Shamir, Ronen. *Current Flow: The Electrification of Palestine* (Stanford, CA: Stanford University Press, 2013).

Shams, Alex. "Tel Aviv 'Nakba' Film Festival Keeps Alive Memories of 1948 in Israel." Ma'an News Agency, December 1, 2013. Available at maannews.net.

Sharpe, Christina. *In the Wake: On Blackness and Being* (Durham, NC: Duke University Press, 2016).

Shavit, Ari. *My Promised Land: The Triumph and Tragedy of Israel* (New York: Spiegel and Grau, 2013).

———. "Survival of the Fittest? An Interview with Benny Morris." *CounterPunch*, January 16, 2004. Available at counterpunch.org.

Sherwood, Harriet, "Tarzan and Arab: The Gaza Artists Determined to Make It against All Odds." *The Guardian*, August 15, 2011. Available at theguardian.com.

Shohat, Ella. *Israeli Cinema: East/West and the Politics of Representation* (Austin: University of Texas Press, 1989).

———. "Notes on the 'Post-Colonial.'" *Social Text* 31–32 (1992): 99–113.

———. "Rupture and Return: Zionist Discourse and the Study of Arab Jews." *Social Text* 21.2 (2003): 49–74.

———. "Sephardim in Israel: Zionism from the Standpoint of Its Jewish Victims." *Social Text* 19–20 (1988): 1–35.

———. "*Wedding in Galilee.*" *Middle East Report* 154 (1988): 45–46.

Shohat, Ella, and Robert Stam. *Unthinking Eurocentrism: Multiculturalism and the Media*, new ed. (1994; repr., New York: Routledge, 2014).

Shulman, David. "Hope in Hebron." *New York Review of Books* blog, March 22, 2013. Available at nybooks.com.

Sidahmed, Mazin. "Critics Denounce Black Lives Matter Platform Accusing Israel of 'Genocide.'" *The Guardian*, August 11, 2016. Available at theguardian.com.

Silko, Leslie Marmon. *Almanac of the Dead* (1991; repr., New York: Penguin, 1992).

Silver, Charlotte. "Israel Indicts 'Palestinian Gandhi.'" *Electronic Intifada*, September 6, 2016. Available at electronicintifada.net.

Singh, Nikhil Pal. "The Whiteness of Police." *American Quarterly* 66.4 (2014): 1091–1099.

Sivan, Emmanuel. "The Lights of Netzarim." *Ha'aretz*, November 7, 2003. Available at haaretz.com.

Smith, Andrea. "Not-Seeing: State Surveillance, Settler Colonialism, and Gender Violence." In *Feminist Surveillance Studies*, edited by Rachel E. Dubrofsky and Shoshana Amielle Magnet (Durham, NC: Duke University Press, 2015), pp. 21–38.

Smith, Caleb, and Catherine Zaw. "Students Shut Down San Mateo-Hayward Bridge; 68 People Arrested, 11 Jailed." *Stanford Daily*, January 19, 2015. Available at stanford daily.com.

Sojoyner, Damien M. "Dissonance in Time: (Un)Making and (Re)Mapping of Blackness." In *Futures of Black Radicalism*, edited by Gaye Theresa Johnson and Alex Lubin (New York: Verso, 2017), pp. 59–71.

Sommer, Allison Kaplan. "After Comparing Palestinian Teen Tamimi to Anne Frank, Israeli Songwriter Faces Wrath of Defense Minister." *Ha'aretz*, January 23, 2018. Available at haaretz.com.

Sonnie, Amy, and James Tracy. *Hillbilly Nationalists, Urban Race Rebels, and Black Power: Community Organizing in Radical Times* (New York: Melville House, 2011).

Soyoung, Kim. "Gendered Trauma in Korean Cinema: *Peppermint Candy* and *My Own Breathing.*" *New Cinemas* 8.3 (2011): 179–187.

Stahl, Aviva. "Khader El-Yateem Could Be the First Socialist Palestinian Pastor on the City Council." *Village Voice*, September 5, 2017. Available at villagevoice.com.

Stanton, Andrea L. *"This Is Jerusalem Calling": State Radio in Mandatory Palestine* (Austin: University of Texas Press, 2013).

Stein, Rebecca L., and Ted Swedenburg. "Introduction: Popular Culture, Transnationality, and Radical History." In *Palestine, Israel, and the Politics of Popular Culture*, edited by Rebecca L. Stein and Ted Swedenburg (Durham, NC: Duke University Press, 2005), pp. 1–26.

Strickland, Patrick O. "Suha Arraf on Her 'Stateless' Palestinian Film." *Electronic Intifada*, October 9, 2014. Available at electronicintifada.net.

———. "WhatsApp Messages Show Israeli Soldiers Knew They Were about to Kill a Child." *Electronic Intifada*, June 21, 2015. Available at electronicintifada.net.

Suleiman, Elia. "A Cinema of Nowhere." *Journal of Palestine Studies* 29.2 (2000): 95–101.

Tamimi, Bassem. "My Daughter, These Are Tears of Struggle." *Ha'aretz*, December 31, 2017. Available at haaretz.com.

Tanenbaum, Gil. "Bennett Insists Suha Arraf Give Israel Back $500K after Dubbing Her Film 'Palestinian.'" *Jewish Business News*, November 14, 2014. Available at jewishbusinessnews.com.

Tawil-Souri, Helga. "Colored Identity: The Politics and Materiality of ID Cards in Palestine/Israel." *Social Text* 29.2 (2011): 67–97.

———. "New Palestinian Centers: An Ethnography of the Checkpoint Economy." *International Journal of Cultural Studies* 12.3 (2009): 217–235.

———. "Occupation Apps." *Jacobin* 17 (2015). Available at jacobinmag.com.

———. "The Political Battlefield of Pro-Arab Video Games on Palestinian Screens." *Comparative Studies of South Asia, Africa and the Middle East* 27.3 (2007): 536–551.

———. "Qalandia Checkpoint as Space and Nonplace." *Space and Culture* 14.1 (2011): 4–26.

———. "Where Is the Political in Cultural Studies? In Palestine." *International Journal of Cultural Studies* 16.1 (2011): 467–482.

Taylor, Keeanga-Yamahtta. *From #BlackLivesMatter to Black Liberation* (Chicago: Haymarket, 2016).

Telmissany, May. "Displacement and Memory: Visual Narratives of al-Shatat in Michel Khleifi's Films." *Comparative Studies of South Asia, Africa and the Middle East* 30.1 (2010): 69–84.

Thayer-Bacon, Barbara. *Democracies Always in the Making: Historical and Current Philosophical Issues for Education* (Lanham, MD: Rowman and Littlefield, 2013).

"Third World Round-up: The Palestine Problem: Test Your Knowledge." *SNCC Newsletter* 1.4 (1967): 4–5.

Thompson, E. P. *The Making of the English Working Class* (1963; repr., New York: Vintage, 1966).

Thompson, Loren. "Air Force's Secret 'Gorgon Stare' Program Leaves Terrorists Nowhere to Hide." *Forbes*, April 10, 2015. Available at forbes.com.

Tooley, Mark. "An Israeli Priest Defends Israel: The Case for Jewish-Christian Collaboration." *Weekly Standard*, December 1, 2014. Available at weeklystandard.com.

Turki, Fawaz. "Meaning in Palestinian History: Text and Context." *Arab Studies Quarterly* 3.4 (1981): 371–383.

———. *Soul in Exile: Lives of a Palestinian Revolutionary* (New York: Monthly Review, 1988).

Virilio, Paul. *Popular Defense and Ecological Struggles*, translated by Mark Polizzotti (1978; repr., New York: Semiotext(e), 1990).

Virilio, Paul, and Sylvère Lotringer. *Pure War: Twenty-Five Years Later*, translated by Mark Polizzotti (1983; repr., New York: Semiotext(e), 2008).

Walker, Janet. *Trauma Cinema: Documenting Incest and the Holocaust* (Berkeley: University of California Press, 2005).

Walsh, Daniel. "*Visit Palestine.*" *Liberation Graphics*, 2003. Available at liberationgraphics.com.

Warrior, Robert Allen. "A Native American Perspective: Canaanites, Cowboys, and Indians." In *Voices from the Margin: Interpreting the Bible in the Third World*, 3d ed., edited by R. S. Sugirtharajah (1991; repr., Maryknoll, NY: Orbis, 2006), pp. 235–241.

Wayne, Mike. *Political Film: The Dialectics of Third Cinema* (London: Pluto, 2001).

Weiler-Polak, Dana. "Israel Enacts Law Allowing Authorities to Detain Illegal Migrants for Up to 3 Years." *Ha'aretz*, June 3, 2012. Available at haaretz.com.

Weiss, Stewart. "In Plain Language: Man versus Morlock." *Jerusalem Post*, August 7, 2014. Available at jpost.com.

Weizman, Eyal. *Hollow Land: Israel's Architecture of Occupation* (2007; repr., New York: Verso, 2012).

———. *The Least of All Possible Evils: Humanitarian Violence from Arendt to Gaza* (New York: Verso, 2011).

Weizman, Eyal, Nick Axel, Steffen Kraemer, Lawrence Abu Hamdan, and Jacob Burns. "The Nakba Day Denial." *Mondoweiss*, March 10, 2015. Available at mondoweiss.net.

Wells, H. G. *The Time Machine* (1895; repr., New York: Penguin, 2005).

"'We're Trying to Destroy the World': Anti-Blackness and Police Violence after Ferguson: An Interview with Frank B. Wilderson, III." *Ill Will Editions*, 2014. Available at ill-will-editions.tumblr.com.

Wicke, Jennifer, and Michael Sprinker. "Interview with Edward Said." In *Edward Said: A Critical Reader*, edited by Michael Sprinker (Cambridge, MA: Blackwell, 1992), pp. 221–264.

Wilder, David. "Fun and Games with Issa Amru in Hebron." *Arutz Sheva*, March 20, 2013. Available at israelnationalnews.com.

Wilderson, Frank B., III. "Grammar and Ghosts: The Performative Limits of African Freedom." *Theatre Survey* 50.1 (2009): 119–125.

———. "Gramsci's Black Marx: Whither the Slave in Civil Society?" *Social Identities* 9.2 (2003): 225–240.

———. "Irreconcilable Anti-Blackness and Police Violence." *i MiX WHAT i LiKE*, October 1, 2014. Available at imixwhatilike.org.

———. "The Prison Slave as Hegemony's (Silent) Scandal." *Social Justice* 30.2 (2003): 18–27.

———. *Red, White, and Black: Cinema and the Structure of U.S. Antagonisms* (Durham, NC: Duke University Press, 2010).

Wilkins, Karin Gwinn. *Home/Land/Security: What We Learn about Arab Communities from Action-Adventure Films* (Lanham, MD: Lexington, 2009).

Williams, Jakobi. *From the Bullet to the Ballot: The Illinois Chapter of the Black Panther Party and Racial Coalition Politics in Chicago* (Chapel Hill: University of North Carolina Press, 2013).

Wolfe, Patrick. "Settler Colonialism and the Elimination of the Native." *Journal of Genocide Research* 8.4 (2006): 387–409.

———. *Settler Colonialism and the Transformation of Anthropology: The Politics and Poetics of an Ethnographic Event* (New York: Cassell, 1999).

Wood, Robin. "Apocalypse Now: Notes on the Living Dead." In *The American Nightmare: Essays on the Horror Film*, edited by Robin Wood and Richard Lippe (Toronto: Festival of Festivals, 1979), pp. 91–97.

Yablonka, Hanna. "The Development of Holocaust Consciousness in Israel: The Nuremberg, Kapos, Kastner, and Eichmann Trials." *Israel Studies* 8.3 (2003): 1–24.

Yaqub, Nadia G. "*The Dupes* (Tawfik Saleh): Three Generations Uprooted from Palestine and Betrayed." In *Film in the Middle East and North Africa: Creative Dissidence*, edited by Josef Gugler (Austin: University of Texas Press, 2011), pp. 113–124.

———. *Palestinian Cinema in the Days of Revolution* (Austin: University of Texas Press, 2018).

———. "*Paradise Now* (Hany Abu-Assad): Narrating a Failed Politics." In *Film in the Middle East and North Africa: Creative Dissidence*, edited by Josef Gugler (Austin: University of Texas Press, 2011), pp. 219–227.

———. "Refracted Filmmaking in Muhammad Malas's *The Dream* and Kamal Aljafari's *The Roof*." *Middle East Journal of Culture and Communication* 7 (2014): 152–168.

Yosef, Raz. *The Politics of Loss and Trauma in Contemporary Israeli Cinema* (New York: Routledge, 2011).

Young, Lewis. "American Blacks and the Arab-Israeli Conflict." *Journal of Palestine Studies* 2.1 (1972): 70–85.

Yousef, Mosab Hassan, with Ron Brackin. *Son of Hamas: A Gripping Account of Terror, Betrayal, Political Intrigue, and Unthinkable Choices* (Carol Stream, IL: Tyndale, 2010).

Yunis, Alia. "The Pursuit of Heroes in Palestinian Cinema: An Interview with Annemarie Jacir." *Jadaliyya*, October 1, 2013. Available at jadaliyya.com.

Zahriyeh, Ehab. "'Omar' a Rare Palestinian Feature Film at the Oscars." Al Jazeera America, February 21, 2014. Available at america.aljazeera.com.

Zein, Rayya El. "Call and Response, Radical Belonging, and Arabic Hip-Hop in 'the West.'" In *American Studies Encounters the Middle East*, edited by Alex Lubin and Marwan M. Kraidy (Chapel Hill: University of North Carolina Press, 2016), pp. 106–135.

Zertal, Idith. *From Catastrophe to Power: The Holocaust Survivors and the Emergence of Israel* (Berkeley: University of California Press, 1998).

Zertal, Idith, and Akiva Eldar. *Lords of the Land: The War over Israel's Settlements in the Occupied Territories, 1967–2007*, translated by Vivian Eden (2005; repr., New York: Nation, 2009).

Žižek, Slavoj. "In the Grey Zone." *London Review of Books Online*, February 5, 2015. Available at lrb.co.uk.

———. *Less than Nothing: Hegel and the Shadow of Dialectical Materialism* (New York: Verso, 2012).

———. *The Parallax View* (Cambridge, MA: MIT Press, 2006).

————. *The Sublime Object of Ideology* (New York: Verso, 1989).

————. *Tarrying with the Negative: Kant, Hegel, and the Critique of Ideology* (Durham, NC: Duke University Press, 1993).

————. *The Ticklish Subject: The Absent Centre of Political Ontology* (1999; repr., New York: Verso, 2000).

————. *Welcome to the Desert of the Real! Five Essays on September 11 and Related Dates* (New York: Verso, 2002).

Zonszein, Mairav. "Binyamin Netanyahu: 'Arab Voters Are Heading to the Polling Stations in Droves.'" *The Guardian*, March 17, 2015. Available at theguardian.com.

Zurayk, Constantine K. *The Meaning of the Disaster*, translated by R. Bayly Winder (1948; repr., Beirut: Khayat's, 1956).

Zureik, Elia. "Colonialism, Surveillance, and Population Control: Israel/Palestine." In *Surveillance and Control in Israel/Palestine: Population, Territory, and Power*, edited by Elia Zureik, David Lyon, and Yasmeen Abu-Laban (New York: Routledge, 2011), pp. 3–46.

Index

GREG BURRIS is an Assistant Professor of Media Studies in the Department of Sociology, Anthropology, and Media Studies at the American University of Beirut in Lebanon. His writings on race, film, and cultural theory have appeared in such publications as *CineAction*, *Cinema Journal*, *Electronic Intifada*, *Jadaliyya*, and *Quarterly Review of Film and Video* and in the edited collections *Futures of Black Radicalism* and *Global Raciality: Empire, Post-Coloniality, DeColoniality*.

www.ingramcontent.com/pod-product-compliance
Lightning Source LLC
Chambersburg PA
CBHW050808270326
41926CB00026B/4622